THE INDUSTRIOUS CITY

THE INDUSTRIOUS CITY

URBAN INDUSTRY IN THE DIGITAL AGE

Edited by
Hiromi Hosoya and
Markus Schaefer

Lars Müller Publishers

Photo Essays | Coversations | Essays

Photo Essays | Coversations | Essays | Swiss Cases and Scenarios

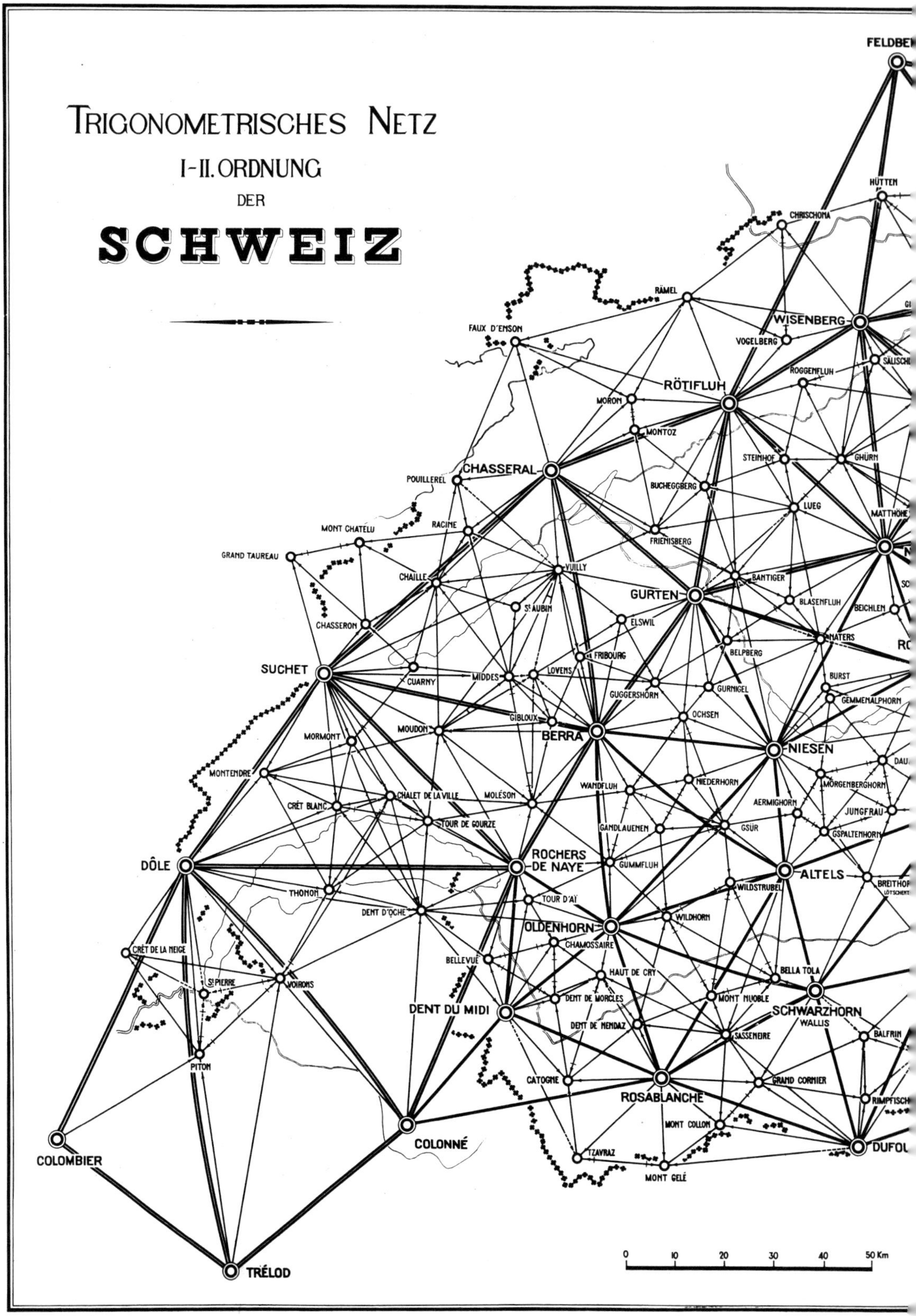

Topographical survey as basis for infrastructure and industry

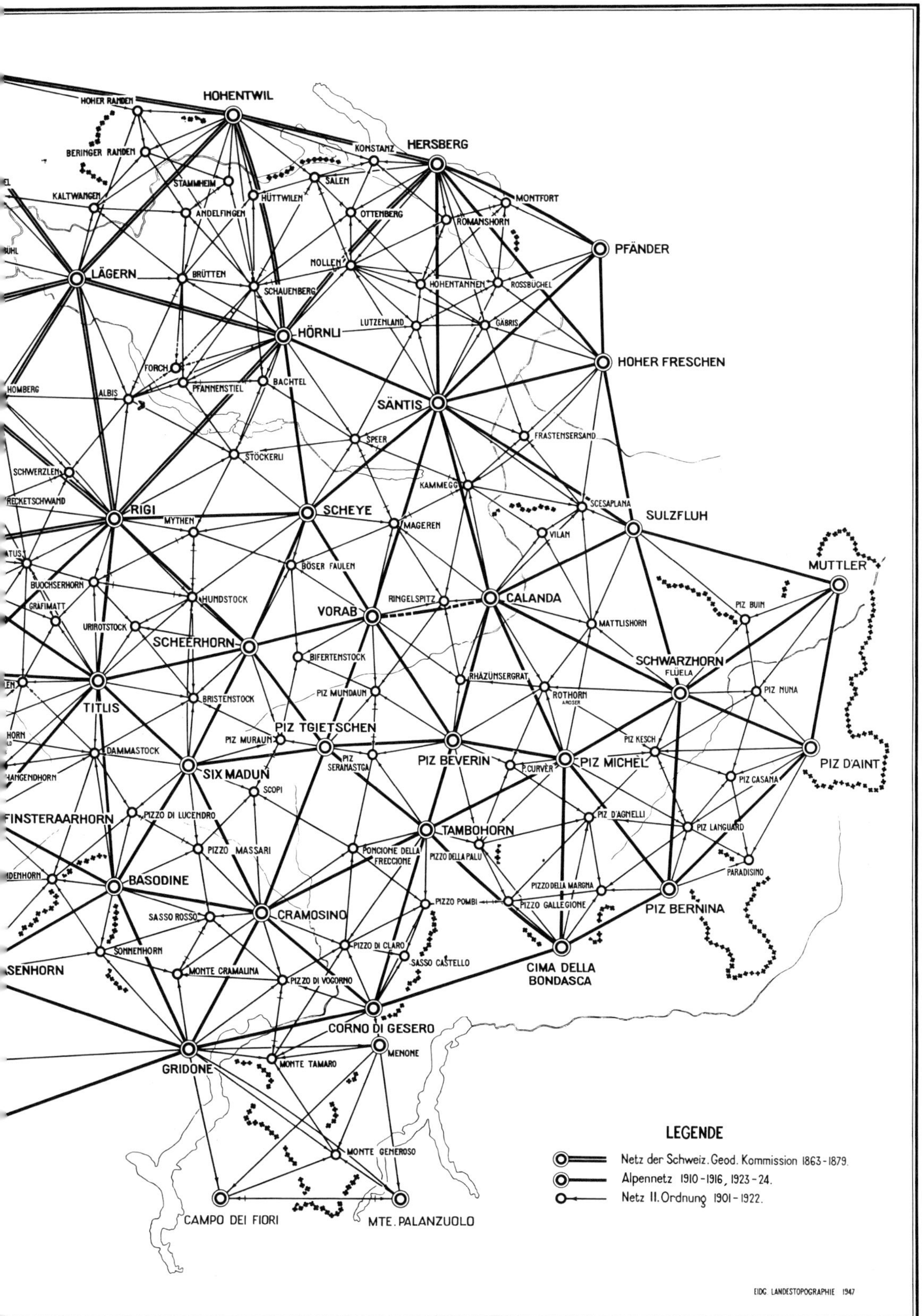
HOHENTWIL
HOHER RANDEN
BERINGER RANDEN
KONSTANZ
HERSBERG
STAMMHEIM
SALEN
MONTFORT
KALTWANGEN
HÜTTWILEN
ANDELFINGEN
OTTENBERG
ROMANSHORN
PFÄNDER
LÄGERN
BRÜTTEN
NOLLEN
SCHAUENBERG
HOHENTANNEN
ROSSBÜCHEL
LUTZENLAND
GÄBRIS
HÖRNLI
HOHER FRESCHEN
FORCH
PFANNENSTIEL
BACHTEL
HOMBERG
ALBIS
SÄNTIS
FRASTENSERSAND
SPEER
STÖCKERLI
SCHWERZLEN
KAMMEGG
SCESAPLANA
RIGI
MYTHEN
SCHEYE
MAGEREN
SULZFLUH
VILAN
BÖSER FAULEN
BUCHSERHORN
GRÄFIMATT
HUNDSTOCK
RINGELSPITZ
CALANDA
MUTTLER
VORAB
PIZ BUIN
URIROTSTOCK
SCHEERHORN
MATTLISHORN
BIFERTENSTOCK
SCHWARZHORN
FLÜELA
RHÄZÜNSERGRAT
TITLIS
BRISTENSTOCK
PIZ MUNDAUN
ROTHORN
AROSER
PIZ NUNA
PIZ TGIETSCHEN
PIZ KESCH
PIZ MURAUN
DAMMASTOCK
PIZ SERANASTGA
PIZ BEVERIN
P. CURVÈR
PIZ MICHEL
PIZ D'AINT
SIX MADUN
PIZ CASANA
SCOPI
FINSTERAARHORN
PIZZO DI LUCENDRO
PIZ D'AGNELLI
TAMBOHORN
PIZ LANGUARD
PIZZO MASSARI
PONCIONE DELLA FRECCIONE
PIZZO DELLA PALU
PARADISINO
BASODINE
PIZZO DELLA MARGNA
PIZ BERNINA
PIZZO POMBI
PIZZO GALLEGIONE
SASSO ROSSO
CRAMOSINO
PIZZO DI CLARO
SONNENHORN
SASSO CASTELLO
CIMA DELLA BONDASCA
MONTE CRAMALINA
PIZZO DI VOGORNO
CORNO DI GESERO
GRIDONE
MENONE
MONTE TAMARO
MONTE GENEROSO
CAMPO DEI FIORI
MTE. PALANZUOLO
LEGENDE
Netz der Schweiz. Geod. Kommission 1863-1879.
Alpennetz 1910-1916, 1923-24.
Netz II. Ordnung 1901-1922.
EIDG. LANDESTOPOGRAPHIE 1947

Pieter Bruegel the Elder, *Children's Games*, 1560

PROLOGUE

Imagine a medieval town, bustling with activity on a busy market day. People of all walks of life shoving past each other, admiring the products of the local technological elite working in shops adjacent to their stands. Materials and produce sourced from the region, diligently recycled, as they are scarce and only the most precious traded over long distance. Some pilfered from Roman ruins in an early form of urban mining. The latest ideas, however, open source and shared from as far as the Middle East, or even further, traveling via the Silk Road, the internet of the day. New work added to old in a process of constant reinvention. The monastery adjacent to the market preserving a shadow of the splendor and cultural complexity of the Roman Empire, compressed and transformed into new rituals and customs, information storage and service protocols, almost like the genetic code in a seed awaiting spring.

And now, project this image to the future somewhen beyond today.

The peak of globalization has passed. Diplomatic ties, markets and global culture are still intact. But the degree of connectedness has been recalibrated. The overall fragility of the global system became too painfully obvious in the climate crisis, the spread of diseases and the political unrest following the mounting inequality in a global economy.

Prudent entrepreneurs reorganized their global supply chains into more regional ones, opting for reliability, access to a local workforce and a reduction in carbon footprint rather than the lowest available cost. Multinational industrial companies increased their embeddedness in regional economies, spreading know-how and gaining acceptance.

Concepts of wealth had been rethought by some of the best academic minds, the value of material reality and local productivity rediscovered. Foreign aid, for too long simply a mirror image of an exploitative global economy, had been abolished in favor of careful investments in local urban economies and infrastructure, even charter cities.

Deep tech start-ups, combining business models in software and service with sophisticated hardware in fields as diverse as life sciences, agriculture, aerospace, mobility and energy, focused the attention of investors back on physical products and long-term development processes beyond the easy profits of what was once called the new economy. Just like the larger, already established firms, they sell their highly specific and targeted products and services worldwide.

While material flows, travel and logistics have been reduced, scarcity is not a topic. Energy from diverse renewable sources is plentiful. Computational power and data storage are freely available. Knowledge is open source. The infrastructures for knowledge and communication had been established by private interests, but they have become so essential to these new times, much like the railroads and highways during industrialization, that they now function as ecosystems and organize the world into large cloud economies. A digitally enabled civil society in turn established some degree of local data sovereignty and digital subsidiarity.

Global conglomerates and city states in the form of large functional metropolitan regions, but also cooperatives, open source activists and the pre-capitalist commons and communes that still persisted in the Alpine rim, use nested sets of smart contracts, essentially creating their own currency of trust beyond what was once called money, replacing it with more intelligent forms of data.

Technological advances democratized the tools for industrial production while the know-how to operate them blossomed in urban cultures close to academic centers. A complex and resilient, local and increasingly circular economy developed hand in hand with social equity. Cooperative models of living, producing, even farming have been reducing the ecological footprint of individuals and are increasing social interactions in self-organized productive urban neighborhoods.

And finally, a new market of urban makers developed, producing local, authentic products at a premium. They sell locally from their workshops, but also globally via digital channels. The role of cities as distribution centers for global manufacturers of commodities, however, has largely been taken over by online markets that are more efficient at linking supply to demand.

Urban production became inextricably fused with urban culture, much like in the example of the medieval town where we started our journey. Only this time, the complexity is much larger.

An unprecedented degree of co-dependency asked for a revolution in governance. The start-up culture meant that large firms were externalizing their innovation costs, spreading risk to the public sector. The knowledge economy required workers with expensive academic educations paid for by taxpayers. Agile, just-in-time production allowed firms to save storage space and reduce capital locked in parts and materials, but also pushed the burden of logistics beyond their system boundary onto the public infrastructure, prompting the development of new private infrastructure projects, highly automated and data driven underground package delivery systems for example. Sharing, co-working and the gig-economy finally meant that firms were externalizing social costs to the state. After decades of liberalizing and globalizing markets and the additional acceleration by digitalization, the fragility of the system became so obvious, local problems so intractable and private and public interests so co-dependent that local virtuous circles and forms of collaboration had to be rediscovered. Industrial production and urban economies fused into industrious cities.

While "industrial" came to stand for the means of production, including their potential abstraction and extraction as capital, "industrious" – closer to the term's Latin root – stresses the know-how and zeal immanent in people and localities, neither abstract nor extractable. Add to this the infinite pleasures of material reality – the tangibility of things and the authenticity of spaces – and you have the Industrious City we want to describe in this book.

SWITZERLAND – SPACE AND INFRASTRUCTURE

Géraldine Recker

pp. 15–23
Switzerland – Space and Infrastructure

18, 19, 21
Made for the project *Wasserschloss,* with Saida Brückner

Markus Schaefer

THE INDUSTRIOUS CITY

Brownfield Development
Co-Evolution
Connectedness
Data Commons
Deep Urbanism
Digital Craft
Economic Complexity
Embeddedness
Emergence
Entanglement
Machine in the Garden
Nested System
Productive City
Subsidiarity
Systems Ecology
The Great Transformation
Urban Industry
Urban Landscape
Urban Resilience

Why would we want industry in our cities? After all, industrial production takes place in large halls filled with noisy machinery and, due to automation, increasingly fewer people. It requires massive infrastructures to supply materials and move goods. Large amounts of energy, resources and capital are consumed, emissions and waste produced. Industrial production, confined to industrial zones, outsourced and offshored, happens out of sight of its consumers. It is an abstract process, taken for granted when enjoying the material pleasures of our everyday life. And the private interests and global capital running such industries are seemingly at odds with an idealized conception of cities dedicated to their citizens and their "right to the city."[1]

And yet, since the onset of industrialization in eighteenth-century England, the histories of industry and cities were always closely intertwined. We will see that they are not so much opposites as two often-interwoven manifestations of the same principle. They both rely on the power – and pleasures – of connectedness, the ability of a network, or a system, to achieve more than the sum of its parts. And both of them are heterogeneous, ordered amalgamations, "entanglements," of spaces and people, things and protocols, matter and information, acting on and transforming a place, a territory, even a planet, and bringing forth a system – us – in all our tangible and transcendent, collective and cultural, mesmerizing and messy glory. But we will get to that in due time.

Trying to understand the role and the future of industry in cities, therefore, requires more than a simple list of policies or urbanistic ambitions. We need to understand both cities and industry better if we want to navigate an uncertain and volatile future. We also need to understand their interdependence. We will see that industry and its urban counterpart, infrastructure, is a prosthetics to the city in a similar way as technology is a prosthetics to our bodies and minds – not as an antithesis, but as an extension in the service of connectedness. The question, then, of course, becomes "Who is in charge?" Much of literature and cultural criticism since the onset of industrialization revolves around the question of whether the resulting connectedness is in the service of people, or whether, on the contrary, people are forced into the service of connectedness.[2]

The great critic of such all-consuming technological progress devouring people, cities, societies, or even the biosphere as a whole, is of course Lewis Mumford. In several books, he wrote of the dangers of technology for its own sake. He understood his work as a call to action directed toward culture in balance with its natural environment. Mumford's choice of the word "technics" throughout his work was deliberate. For Mumford, technology is only one part of technics. Using the broader definition of the Greek *tekhne*, which means not only technology but also art, skill and dexterity, technics describes how things are done in a society – socially, technically and industrially.[3]

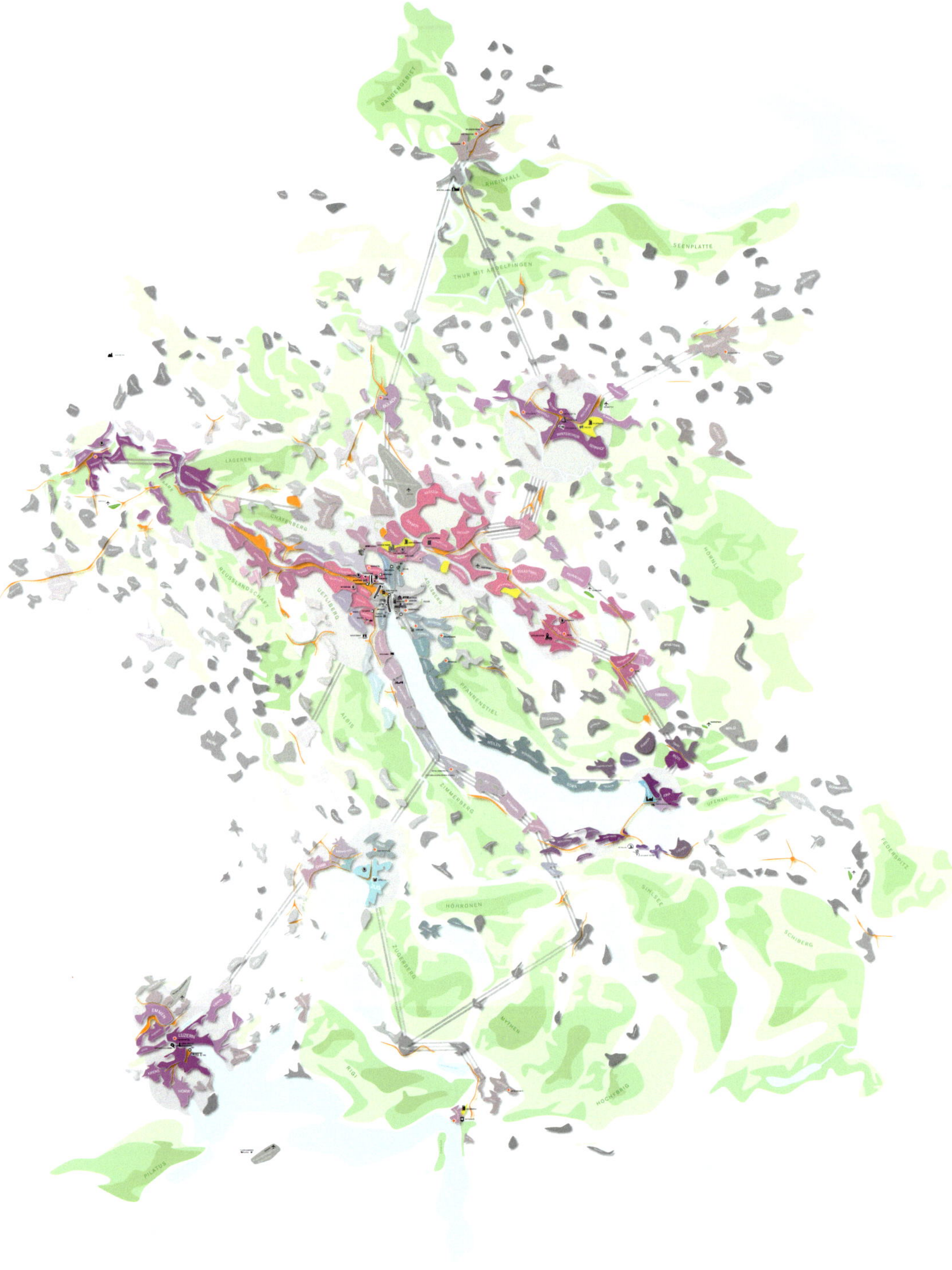

Metrobild 2011, Metropolitan Region Zurich, legend: see page 42
Analysis and visualization: Hosoya Schaefer Architects

In the same way, the term "industrious" we are using in this book attempts to bridge between technological processes and collective productivity. While "industrial" came to stand for the means of production, including their potential abstraction and extraction as capital, "industrious" – closer to the term's Latin root – stresses the know-how and zeal immanent in people and local communities, neither abstract nor extractable.

There are several reasons why it is possible and important to discuss this now: After a century of systemic separation, of zoning out and scaling up, of globalization and offshoring, the pendulum is swinging back again. Digitalization, new production technologies, the knowledge economy, start-up culture, new mobility and the Internet of Things, but also a sense of global fragility and a "new localism"[4] bring industry and cities back together. In the process, cities might become more productive, and industry more urban again. This development is full of potential and instability, which we need to shape and govern well. New building typologies, spaces and infrastructures are required, but almost more importantly, new methods of cooperation, systems thinking and narratives – an understanding not only of form, but also of performance.

But this essay, and the book as a whole, would be incomplete without a specific context, as it is precisely the abstract and generic that we are critiquing. Cities are social, political, economic and spatial realities. We build and inhabit them collectively. By definition, when working on cities we act from within a specific system. In this book, we are looking at the Central European, or more precisely the Swiss cities as case study and model. Industry and industrial policy, vocational training and higher education have a long tradition in this country. Still, cities are dense and contested. Many parties and opinions are involved in planning decisions, historical and environmental contexts are to be considered, leading to impasses and instabilities, but also to resilience.

For exponents of industry this can be frustrating. While they are struggling with global competition, disruptive technological progress, changing customer behavior, new demands from their workforce and the volatility of capital markets, all resulting in ever shrinking decision timeframes, processes in cities, specifically in our democratic, digitally emancipated context, are becoming increasingly more inclusive, but also more complicated and unpredictable.

In the following chapters, we will first venture outwards, exploring where increasing connectedness will lead us, from the economy of cities, its scaling-up by industrialization, digitalization and globalization, and the concurrent transformation of cities, to the fragilities of a possibly overextended connectedness and its planetary limits. Increasing connectedness liberates us from the constraints of the local, and yet in turn creates just another constraint – less apparent and delayed in its effects, maybe. In the second half of the essay, therefore, we will return from our exploration and look inwards again to the specific, local reality in which we are embedded, before ending up with a sketch of an Industrious City assembled from the contributors to this book.

Connected

The Economy of Cities – understanding connectedness

There is a longstanding academic tradition of understanding productivity and innovation as a result of proximity. Already at the end of the nineteenth century, Alfred Marshall described the advantages of the spatial clustering of industries as "agglomeration economies." Industries are more successful when they are close together, and synergies develop between them.[5] Jane Jacobs followed a similar line of thought in her book *The Economy of Cities*, describing how in cities new work is added to old work through continuous innovation and how in turn cities become increasingly independent of other, older or larger cities by "import replacement."[6] Edward Soja wrote about the "self-generating economic culture of cities," an emergent process characterized by organized complexity.[7] Paul Romer won the 2018 Nobel prize for his work on endogenous growth, explaining how local human capital, knowledge and innovation function as drivers of long-term economic development.[8] And, finally, César Hidalgo formalized these ideas in his Principle of Relatedness.[9] Using national trade data, he and his colleagues described the range of products originating from a region as its "product space" and showed that this product space is highly predictive of the development of future products. To describe the quality and diversity of that product space Hidalgo introduced the term "economic complexity" and the Economic Complexity Index (ECI).[10]

Japan, Switzerland and Germany, for example, the three countries with the highest ECIs, export many goods that are rare in the global market and produced only by highly diversified countries with vibrant urban economies, while other countries, also with sizable GDPs, might export raw materials, resources or more ubiquitous industrial commodities such as textile products. New work builds on old work as local knowledge and know-how increase and differentiate.

All of these authors have in common that they understand cities as productive, learning systems that are spatial and localized. César Hidalgo speaks of "sticky knowledge" and writes, "knowledge continues to be embodied in networks of people, and is concentrated in a few places, while bits and products travel swiftly around the world."[11] The reason is that a lot of that knowledge is tacit.[12] It is not explicit and formalized, but rather "how things are done here." Consequently, economic complexity also correlates with income equality, or technically speaking, a low Gini co-efficient.[13] Knowledge and the know-how of its application are embedded in people and their relationships, and arguably in the spaces and infrastructures enabling those relationships.

Cities are quite literally ecosystems of connectedness, of ideas and infrastructures, of stories and spaces that bring us together. They are social reactors fueled by interactions and transactions between people – the exchange of information and of goods – that in turn produce social differentiation and division of work. Cities are agglomeration economies that grow more competitive with increasing integration. They are markets of exchange that are better able to link demand and supply with increasing size. They are breeding grounds for innovations that generate more ideas with increasing interaction density and higher diversity. And they are motors of growth as they create more potential, with less infrastructure the larger their size, in a self-reinforcing positive feedback loop. Scaling connectedness is therefore an important factor in competitiveness and industry the key for it.

The Industry of Cities – scaling connectedness

Industrialization advanced in several phases correlating to major technological breakthroughs, referred to in hindsight as Industry 1.0 to Industry 4.0. It started in Britain in the seventeenth century, very much as a process of import replacement as described by Jane Jacobs. At that time, Mogul India was the largest producer of cotton textiles, rich in natural resources and skilled, cheap labor. Its products were imported into Britain by the English East India Company. By the early nineteenth century, Britain had surpassed India as the world's most important cotton textile producer, despite not having any cotton plantations on its own shores, dominating world export markets and even exporting back to India. This was not due to British labor costs, which were quite high at the time based on the productivity in already established tradable goods and services, but due rather to a completely new way of going about work.

At the core of this reinvention of work was a variety of labor- and time-saving inventions. They in turn came from a particular entrepreneurial and innovative climate bolstered by a series of unique historic factors – from the dissolution of the monasteries by Henry VIII in the 1530s[14] that freed capital and minds, the enclosure acts (e.g., 1773) that consolidated land ownership and drove newly landless farmers to the cities, and an entrepreneurial gentry, to the rise of science and modern capital, perfectly exemplified by Isaac Newton – revolutionary of science, dabbling alchemist and later Master of the Royal Mint perfecting British currency. A highly reliable currency based on science generated trust and desirability, allowing capital to be abstracted from individual landholdings and readied for investment in everything from a national fleet dominating the seas and highways opening up and controlling the English hinterland[15] to private industrial enterprise. The invention of the steam engine by Thomas Newcomen and later James Watt, finally, abstracted work from the physical toils of humans and animals. A self-reinforcing industrial system was set in motion, built on mechanized, efficient mining, the use of that mined coal and iron to work with metal and steel, the development of machinery to execute specific repetitive tasks and new transport systems. Social relationships were reorganized, serfdom and the slave trade abolished, wage labor introduced, social mobility increased, and a liberal outlook on politics developed. The great divergence, the difference in the economic development of East and West, commenced, ensuring the dominance of the Western World for the next centuries.

Between 1840 and 1914, the second industrial revolution was made possible by applying the results of the first in scale. Extensive railroad networks and the telegraph spread people and ideas. The ever more present electricity allowed for factory electrification and the production line. The modern nation state developed hand in hand with the modern market economy, not without growing pains. Karl Polanyi, a Hungarian-American political economist, described this co-development of state and market in his book *The Great Transformation* as a single human invention, which he called the "Market Society." In a somewhat idealized form, he saw society and its economic relations prior to the great transformation as based on reciprocity and redistribution across personal and communal relationships. Industrialization not only changed work, it changed everything. It even changed the way we think about the individual and their relationship to society. Polanyi deplored the loss of "embeddedness," the split of social and economic relations that was to haunt society in the years to come. But arguably this abstraction from embedded, local reality was the price we had to pay for the increase in productivity, competitiveness, wealth, and – in systemic terms – the increase in connectedness we could enjoy.

Once set in motion, industry was made increasingly more efficient with methods such as scientific management, or Taylorism, introduced by Frederick Winslow Taylor. Henry Ford perfected the assembly line where standardization allowed unskilled workers to produce complex products. With factories such as Ford's, where rubber and steel entered on one side and cars drove off the assembly line on the other, it became possible to think of industry and the people working in it as a seamlessly connected and efficient system, sustained by flexible investment capital allocated in a rational financial market.

In the third industrial revolution after the world wars, themselves incubators of industrial development, industry received an additional boost through digitalization. Those standardized assembly lines could now be taken apart, spatially separated (abstracted again) and, together with their supply chains, reconnected with digital tools, managing logistics and financial flows. Connectedness reached a new level. The relative stability after the wars, the efficient control of information, reliable long-distance transportation and the increased division of labor combined with automation brought about a dramatic shift in manufacturing to places where production costs were lowest and labor cheapest. Industry moved to the edge of towns, freeway junctions and cheaper land, and eventually abroad. Suburban campuses developed while industrial areas in inner city locations were abandoned. And much of the low-value-added and toxic work was shifted offshore.

After the oil shock of the seventies, ecological concerns led to attempts to decouple economic growth from environmental pollution. The American economist and Nobel prize winner Simon Kuznets described not only income equality increasing with rising prosperity, but also environmental quality expressed in his so-called "environmental Kuznets curve." The more prosperous a country, the healthier its environment. This effect can be clearly seen in some national statistics, as in Germany and Switzerland.[16] This might be partially attributed to externalizing environmental costs beyond national boundaries to hinterlands of extraction and waste. But it is tempting to think that a mature, highly diversified and "complex" economy (as described by Hidalgo) is able to rely on and generate qualitative growth. Industrialization, then, might be a messy process of maturing, a kind of teenage rebellion of urbanization, but will eventually result in a resilient and inclusive urban economy. Through import replacement industrial capability then spreads globally. We could even hypothesize that such an economy could overcome some of the problems described by Polanyi and become re-embedded into a local context – environmentally, socially, economically and spatially.

And, maybe, we are witnessing such a development right now. Moore's law resulted in integrated circuits cheap enough to embed them anywhere, and in computers powerful enough to use them for anything, from compute-intensive analyses to extensive networking. Computing has become ubiquitous and embedded in the material realm. Or in the terminology we by now established, connectedness is more seamlessly bridging between the real and the virtual. With Industry 4.0, the trend toward automation and data exchange in manufacturing technologies and processes increased. Cyber-physical systems (CPS), the Internet of Things (IoT), cloud computing, cognitive computing and artificial intelligence make industry smarter. Advanced robotics and additive production are increasing flexibility and democratizing access to production, while open data, open source, open algorithms and cloud services are doing the same for access to information and computational power. Automation allows companies to re-shore production in reducing the role of labor in the process[17]. We could envision a future where information flows remain global, while material flows become more local and circular.

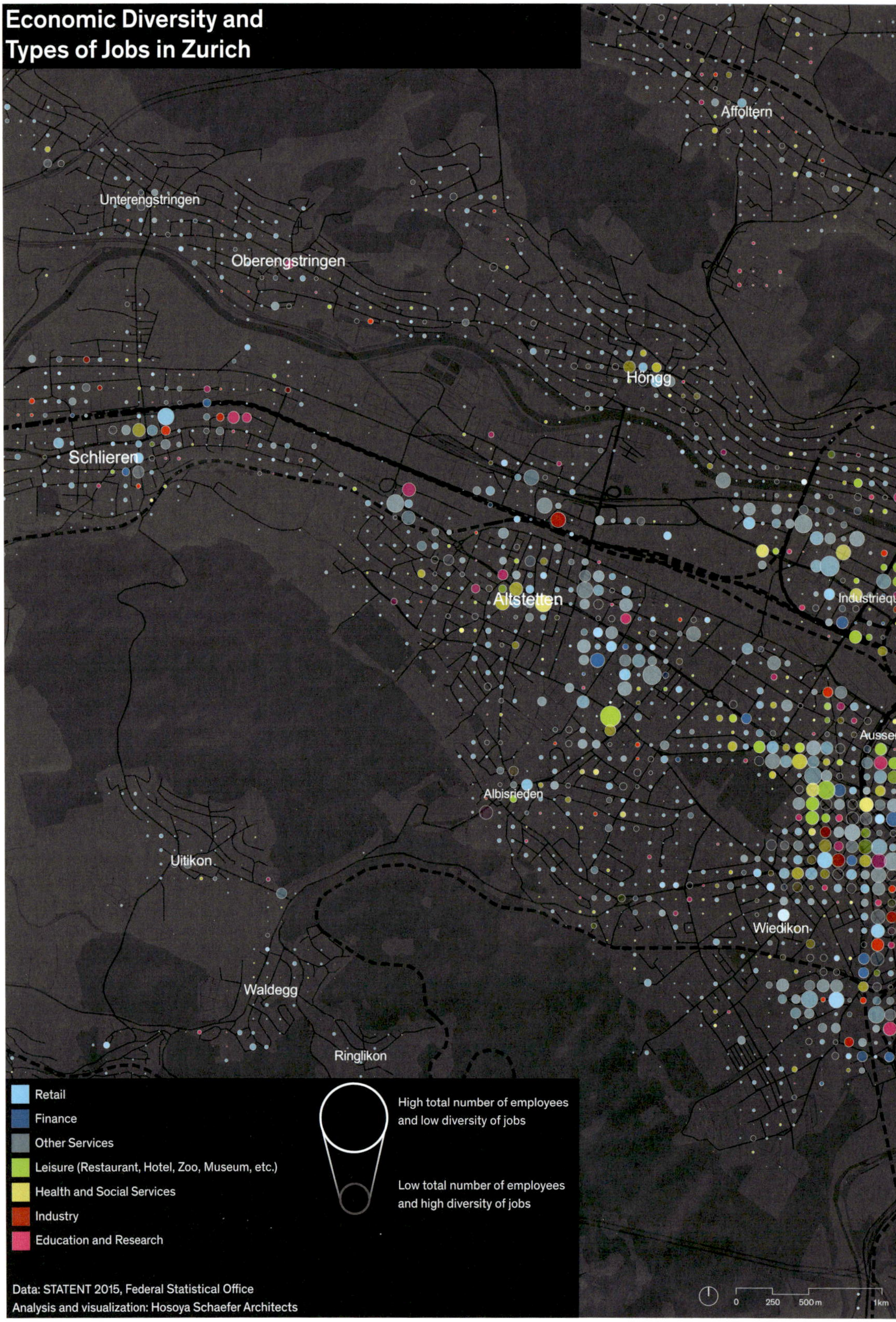
Economic Diversity and Types of Jobs in Zurich
Affoltern
Unterengstringen
Oberengstringen
Höngg
Schlieren
Altstetten
Industriequ
Ausser
Albisrieden
Uitikon
Wiedikon
Waldegg
Ringlikon
Retail
Finance
Other Services
Leisure (Restaurant, Hotel, Zoo, Museum, etc.)
Health and Social Services
Industry
Education and Research
High total number of employees and low diversity of jobs
Low total number of employees and high diversity of jobs
Data: STATENT 2015, Federal Statistical Office
Analysis and visualization: Hosoya Schaefer Architects
0
250
500 m
1km

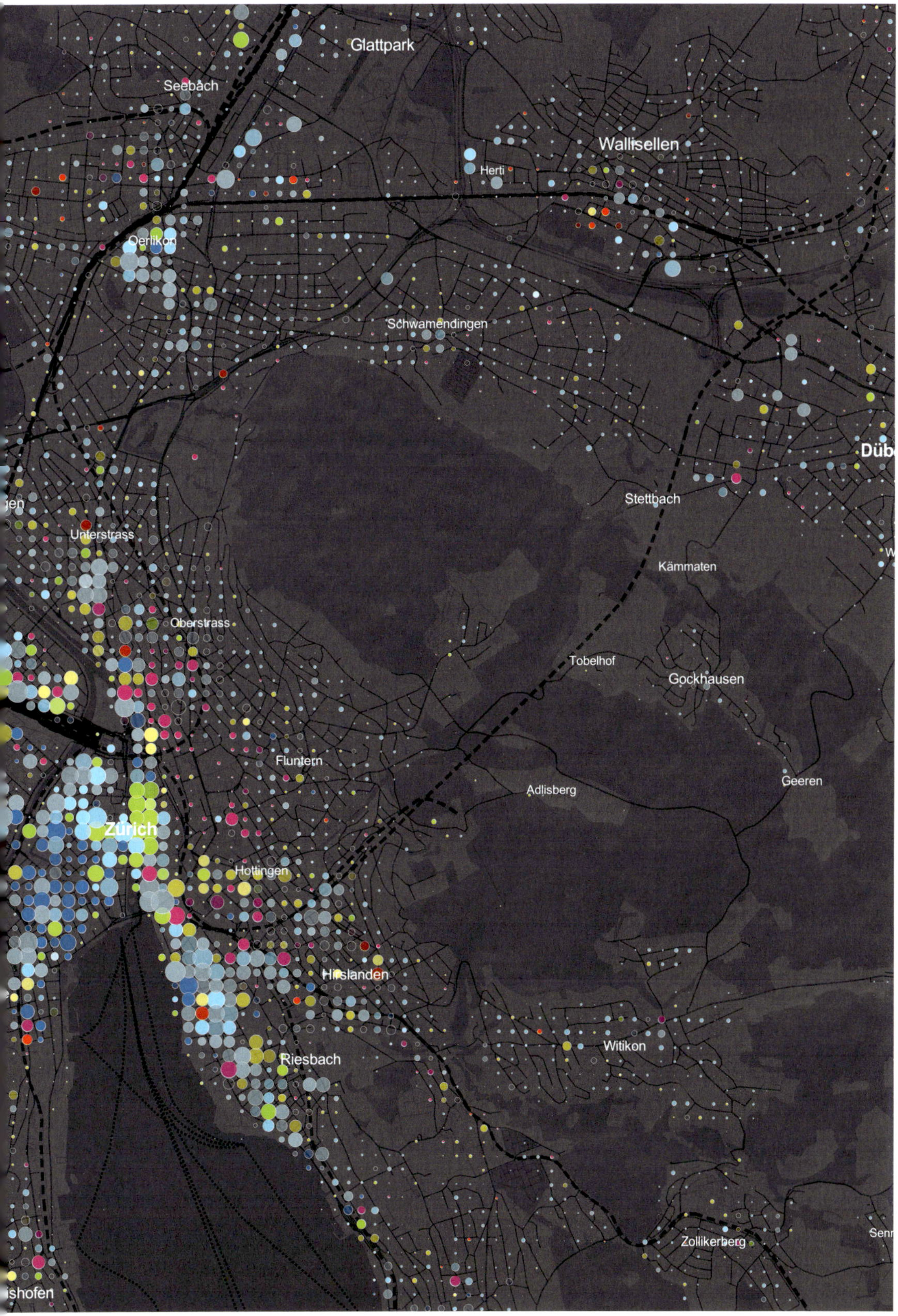
Glattpark
Seebach
Wallisellen
Herti
Oerlikon
Schwamendingen
Dübe
Stettbach
Unterstrass
Kämmaten
Oberstrass
Tobelhof
Gockhausen
Fluntern
Adlisberg
Geeren
Zürich
Hottingen
Hirslanden
Witikon
Riesbach
Zollikerberg
shofen

Environmental concerns, the requirement to reduce CO_2 emissions, unstable political environments and a volatile global economy are motivating firms to bring production back and consolidate it. Each technological advance has reshaped the cities and the societies living in them, as is happening now again.

The Transformation of Cities – reshaping connectedness

Cities are made for exchange, and exchange is based on the interplay of diversity, proximity and mobility. An attractive city combines different things, opportunities and people across various scales and stabilizes their interaction with spaces and stories, infrastructures and institutions.

Attractiveness results in growth, and growth increases attractiveness – mostly. With the technologies emerging from the process of industrialization, growth has been achieved by increasing density. Cities grew vertically. But more important over the last century has been the rise in mobility, enabled by the increasing reach of transportation infrastructures regionally and globally. Mobility enabled cities to extend from their pedestrian cores before industrialization, the bourgeois city with its streetcars and the sprawling post-war city dependent on the automobile, to the polycentric urban region of today, linked by convenient forms of mass transit. Most European cities are a mix of all these modes of transport and the resulting urban typologies: dense historic cores, *Gründerzeit* quarters often extending over former city fortifications, green sprawling suburbs and pearl chains of regional nodes around mass transit stations. Form follows infrastructure.

This continuous transformation was mirrored in the changing reputation of the downtowns. In the 1960s, European cities generally had the highest population density in their modern history. They felt crammed and could not satisfy the spatial appetites of the emerging consumer culture. Everybody who could afford it left the centers and moved to the suburbs. The resulting mobility needs, at that time often met by car, put an entirely new burden on cities – to provide access and transit for automobiles – and made them even less attractive. Cities were perceived as places for the poor, the jobless, the old and the alcoholic, or, in German, the "A-people" (*Arme, Arbeitslose, Alte und Alkoholiker*).

Since the 1980s, new infrastructures, this time on a global scale, have allowed industry to move to countries with lower salaries and land rent. Industrial areas emptied out and logistical demands dwindled. Because the industry of the nineteenth century had been built close to train or harbor infrastructures, the ensuing brownfield sites were often in central locations. Soon these sites were redeveloped for the rising service industry, for retail, leisure and some housing. In the building boom of the eighties, cities were transformed for the consumer society.

In the late 1990s, the cities became attractive again for urban pioneers with modest budgets and enterprising lifestyles. The biggest problems of a car-based transport regime were being fixed, new policies allowed for a more flexible use of public spaces, creative new forms of urban living had developed in empty niches, the fall of the iron curtain opened up Europe's east, and the real estate crash of the mid-nineties and additional brownfield sites provided some quantitative easing in the real estate market. New development models, some proposed by cooperatives, showed the advantages of urban life.

After this phase of experimentation, the next real estate boom took off. Cities blossomed and an increasingly service-oriented, creative, highly mobile, young and global segment left their parents' suburban mansions to live in the city yet again and gain access to its cultural offerings and lifestyle. And maybe they brought with them a suburban desire for urban chic and excitement, but also for green and quiet that newly built housing developments happily catered to. After the consumer city, the creative city emerged, proselytized by Richard Florida and others. Creativity was needed to satisfy the consumer city's insatiable desire for social differentiation and leisure. Design, advertisement, branding, new forms of gastronomy and entertainment, along with consulting and financial services, created added value for consumption. Cities, at least those with access to education and infrastructure, became hotspots for a global kinetic elite. In turn, cities earned taxes and development revenues, gained political weight and sharpened their policy skills. All over the world, post-industrial success stories appeared, as portrayed by Bruce Katz in his book *The Metropolitan Revolution*.[18]

At the same time, land prices and housing rents started rising. The increasing attraction of cities, globalization, individual mobility and economies flooded with cheap money by central banks (trying to counteract the slowing growth of productivity) turned some cities into gentrifying global hotspots, while leaving many others behind. Even Richard Florida acknowledges that the global creative cities are overshooting. Gentrification not only brings about a less diverse society, but also a less diverse set of functions, less difference. Continuing to provide affordable options to settle in the city is not easy and requires political will. Most brownfield sites have already been converted and all the straightforward area developments completed. If the city is to grow further while remaining inclusive, and if urgent housing needs are to be met, then new solutions need to be found. City governments, emboldened by the policy successes of the last decade, but also overwhelmed by the still ongoing growth, will need to work together with real estate owners and developers in entirely new ways to tackle the next wave of transformation.

And this transformation has already begun. With the digital revolution, the economic base of cities is changing again. While retail and entertainment were important drivers of the consumer city of the eighties and nineties, digital platforms prove to be much better at satisfying some of these demands. Rents for retail areas are dropping, locations remaining empty. The ground floors in urban developments, which well-intentioned city planners dedicated to shops and commerce to create a lively city, remain vacant. And yet, while much of the market moved to the virtual, there is a real demand for authenticity, local experiences and community, while at the same time the new generation cannot afford the conspicuous material consumption of their baby-boomer parents. Collective living, live-work arrangements, sharing, concepts of self-sufficiency are not only desirable, but for many also inescapable.

The Digitalization of Cities – supercharging connectedness

Let's take a quick break and look at the larger picture: Over the course of history, technological change, social emancipation (sometimes revolt) and institutional reorganization always went hand in hand. Cities once were sovereign mercantile islands in a topography still ruled by the patchwork of feudalism, lifting their new citizens from serfdom. Industrialization and infrastructure connected cities into a new topology for which over time new system boundaries were established – the territory, laws and rules of the sovereign modern nation state, protecting its citizens from exploitation by means of social welfare. The digital revolution is bringing change yet again, which in its final consequence might be as fundamental as industrialization itself. For our purpose here, it is important to understand that urban industry is not happening anymore in large production halls linked by rails, protected from international competition by national custom borders, but in heterogeneous spaces linked together by data and agile logistics, attached to the cloud and all its material and digital services, cooperating and competing globally in ever-shifting constellations. Digitalization infuses cities with new dynamics for which we need to find new rules, system boundaries, forms of sovereignty and social cohesion.

Smart Cities are only a partial answer. Smart originally connoted embedded computational capabilities, such as in a smart phone or smart device, allowing those to operate to some extent autonomously and interactively, rather than relying on a distant server. That purely technology and industry-driven concept of smartness (Smart City 1.0) has been extended to include citizen consultation (Smart City 2.0), and, more recently, bottom-up formats for participation (Smart City 3.0).

By now we have learned, however, that cities are always "entanglements" of spaces and people, things and protocols, matter and information. Technological progress is never simply additive, but inherently transformational, as we have seen in Mumford's writing on cities or Polanyi's *Great Transformation*. The biggest challenge for cities is not smartness embedded in the city itself, but in its actors and their devices. This simple fact results in an entirely novel, algorithmically and freely addressable connectedness much more versatile than what the infrastructural city was ever able to provide. Mobility, for example, becomes less a question of physical transportation infrastructure than of providing mobility services based on the ability to register demand. Local services, from public transport to taxis are all of a sudden in competition with new global actors. And were these new services to scale up with fleets of autonomous cars, for example, public roads would carry the burden. Or take logistics: agile, just-in-time production allows firms to save on storage space and reduce capital locked in parts and materials. On the other hand, the demand for logistics increases. Instead of few trips with large quantities, many trips with small quantities are necessary, essentially pushing the burden of logistics beyond the system boundary of a factory onto public infrastructure. Cloud services support individual creativity and entrepreneurship, but also reinforce the gig economy and its atomization of work relations, with the public left with funding co-working locations and taking care of social welfare. Social media enables communities, but also serves as a vector of fake news, even aggressive trolling, disrupting local cohesion. Digitalization brought us a further increase in connectedness, but also contributes to its fragility.

Cities, which have been infrastructures of connectedness for millennia, are experiencing competition from the cloud. And the more frictionless and accessible the cloud's services, the more they will absorb demand and concentrate wealth and power. The same is true for user data and the ability to analyze and capitalize on it in prediction markets of all sorts. We pay for connectivity and convenience not primarily by a service fee, but by selling our choice patterns. Data on citizens used to be the prerogative of states. Today it is harvested as Big Data on users by private companies, extracted often far out of reach of local jurisdictions and individual control.

Industry is returning to the city not only to participate in urbanity and innovation, but also to profit from access to infrastructure and talent, markets and data. This is not without potential for disruption. An agenda for an Industrious City, therefore, must be more than just support for urban manufacturing, co-working or Smart City policies. It must be based on a systemic understanding of the opportunities and risks inherent in contemporary technology and processes and their effects on spaces and people, the connected and the embedded.

Embedded

Somewhere between mountains

Looking at Google Earth, hovering somewhere over the Mediterranean Sea, the Italian peninsula stretching to the south, Scandinavia recedes behind the blue-green curvature of the globe to the north, the Alpine Rim is clearly visible, stretching with a playful curl from Southern France to Austria, where – as in a surrealist science experiment – the Italian boot was grafted crudely onto Europe's belly, wrinkles of scar tissue developing along the graft line.

When zooming closer, a fractal compression of specificity appears, a densification of difference with each crease uniquely shaped and separated by crests, some white and gray, some green.

At night, there are no large bright spots to be seen in that area, none like Paris, London or Moscow, but rather a constellation of tiny dots, a cluster of speckles forming a fragile nebula interrupted only by the dark bands of the most prominent of Alpine ridges.

This nebula of urbanity, nestled into the folds of the Alpine Rim, is Switzerland.

Machine in the Garden

When looking at European cities as a network, this urban web is densest along the axes of the Po and Rhine rivers. Their waterways were the continent's main transportation routes. Their basins were the canvas of history where exchange was most likely to occur and diverging interests most often to collide. Exchange and conflict both led to the founding of towns, at the time enclaves in a feudal patchwork, their walls protecting a market and people free to do business.[19]

Today this close-knit, polycentric network of towns and cities is the most prosperous region of the European Union, known as the "blue banana." At the very core of this polycentric network of towns and trade routes was the early Swiss Federation, an alliance between those cantons that, as city-states, formed the nodes, and those that controlled the connections, both, in their very different ways, eminently urban. If you imagine a big cross, the Alpine Rim stretching from east to west and the main urban axis through Europe from south to north, then Switzerland sits in its exact center. Its regions are differentiated by the topography of the Alpine Rim and connected by the topology of Europe's urban system. Its valleys and niches were settled in several waves by people of different languages, religious affiliations, ethnic origins and trades, and fertilized by the interactive density of the continental urban network.

In terms of economic development, the difference between cities and countryside never was as large as in other countries. From the eighteenth century onward, Switzerland saw a proto-industrialization that started in the countryside.[20] Out of reach of the powerful urban guilds, local entrepreneurs gave rural families additional work producing linen cloth or embroidery. Small towns, such as Herisau, Langenthal and Rüti, became centers of the Swiss textile industry. Herisau with 9,500 inhabitants at that time, was the eleventh-largest municipality in Switzerland, whereas Zurich, the largest Swiss city today, before annexing its immediate suburbs in 1894 and 1934, had only 20,000 inhabitants.

The actual industrialization in the nineteenth century proceeded in an equally decentralized manner. There were no raw material deposits that led to a concentrated industrial development as in Belgium, Germany and England, no shipyards around harbors, nor industrial towns founded by an emperor as in Russia. The only resources available were running water as a source of energy and a growing population eager for work. Both were abundant in peripheral locations, for example in the valleys of Glarus and in Serrières near Neuchâtel where Philippe Suchard started his chocolate manufacturing firm.

The first spinning machines, originally made in England, were installed in St. Gallen in 1801 and Winterthur in 1802. Wool and later imported cotton were at the origin of both the mechanical industry, based on building looms, and the chemical industry based on the development of dyes. With industrialization progressing, local industry became an important advocate for building roads and the first private railroad lines. Customs between cantons were abolished, time zones standardized and the first precise national map produced, based on the triangulation of the entire country by quartermaster-general Guillaume Henri Dufour. The development of infrastructure in Switzerland in the nineteenth century was driven as much by the periphery as it was by the urban centers. This was very different than the process in Great Britain, for example, where infrastructure was first funded by a centralized bureaucracy to keep crusading Scottish warlords in check.

With the advent of steel, coal, the steam engine and most importantly the railroad, heavy industry could be located close to large cities and their rail infrastructure. The large industrial complexes of Oerlikon-Bührle and Escher Wyss in Zurich, Brown Boveri in Baden and Sulzer in Winterthur developed adjacent to the historic cores. The landlocked factory of Escher Wyss, for example, was a global leader in hydraulic equipment and steam turbines and produced more than 500 ships exported worldwide. But these concentrations were always balanced by tiny yet productive industrial locations far in the countryside. In 1870, for example, three quarters of all watches sold worldwide were produced in small, hidden towns in Western Switzerland representing two-thirds of the global turnover.

Combining and recombining expertise, building on local skills, crossbreeding them with new technological possibilities, often imported, and then developing them further – this was the beginning of many of the industrial core disciplines for which Switzerland is known today. Good rules and regulations allowed for low marginal costs for cross-company collaboration, political stability for a predictable business environment and reliability in the exchange between firms. Swiss industry is based predominantly on small and mid-sized, agile companies producing highly specialized, globally competitive products. And even the few large industrial companies excel globally in various specific niches with competitive market shares.

Today's largest Swiss companies, however, are not in the manufacturing industry anymore, but in resource trade, food, pharma or retail. Still, Switzerland has a strong and competitive industrial sector, employing about ten percent of the Swiss workforce. While the share of manufacturing in the total GDP modestly expanded to twenty percent from 1990 until today, productivity per employee grew dramatically from around CHF 70,000 to over CHF 200,000. An increase in automation and productivity has offset the pressures of a strong currency and high salaries. The large companies (two percent of all firms) export almost all of their products, while the medium and small enterprises that employ two-thirds of the industrial workforce still export eighty percent[21] with forty-five percent of all exports going to Europe, forty percent to Asia, and twelve percent to North America.[22] Switzerland is almost entirely dependent on exports. It needs to be connected to the world.

Embedded and Connected

This essay, and the book as a whole, argue for a local embedded reality that can competitively produce complex products with all the economic, social, political and spatial benefits we heard about earlier. And inevitably, as we have discussed, complexity requires connectedness. Industry returning to cities, with smaller spatial footprints and based on knowledge and network effects, profits from the connectedness cities provide. Cities in turn benefit from urban production by the rich mix of skills, ideas, people and economies it generates, as well as by the concurrent attenuation in the urban land market.

Three factors threaten this optimistic picture: Our cities are spatially dense and politically diverse. Space is lacking and individual voices can stop entire projects, however systemically important they might be. An excess of embeddedness, therefore, could bring development and innovation to a grinding halt. All the more important are a prudent combination of policy and politics, understanding and communication to prevent the local from turning provincial. Too much connectedness, on the other hand, liquifies everything – capital, knowledge, people and increasingly data, rendering them extractable or locally uncontrollable. Obviously, the skill will be in navigating

1 Here, see chapter "The City as an Ecosystem," p. 105 in this book.
2 Whether it is the piercing intellect of Marx unmasking capital, the bumbling charm of Chaplin humanizing the assembly line in *Modern Times*, or the cyberbio-kung-fu fighting skills of Neo pacifying the Matrix, all are tales of emancipation, overcoming the de-humanizing and alienating compulsions inherent in the respective technologies of their times.
3 Mumford, Lewis: *Technics and Civilization*, London: Routledge, 1934.
4 Katz, Bruce and Nowak, Jeremy, *The New Localism: How Cities Can Thrive in the Age of Populism*, Washington: Brookings Institution Press, 2018.
5 Marshall, Alfred, *Elements of Economics of Industry*, London: Macmillan, 1892.
6 Jacobs, Jane, *The Economy of Cities*, New York: Random House, 1969.
7 Soja, Edward, *Postmetropolis: Critical Studies of Cities and Region,* Oxford: Blackwell, 2000.
8 Romer, Paul M., "Increasing Returns and Long-Run Growth," in: *Journal of Political Economy* 94, no. 5 (Oct. 1986), pp. 1002–1037. Romer, Paul M., "The Origins of Endogenous Growth," in: *The Journal of Economic Perspectives* 8, no. 1 (Winter, 1994), pp. 3–22.
9 Hidalgo, C.A., Balland, P.-A.; Boschma, R., Delgado, M., Feldman, M., Frenken, K., Glaeser, E., He, C., Kogler, D.F., Morrison, A. et al, "The Principle of Relatedness," in: *12th Chaotic Modeling and Simulation International Conference*, Berlin: Springer Science and Business Media LLC, 2018, pp. 451–457.
10 Hidalgo, C.A., Hausmann, R., "The building blocks of economic complexity," in: *National Academy of Sciences,* 2009, *106 (26)*, pp. 10570–10575. Hausmann, R., Hidalgo, C.A., Bustos, S., Coscia, M., Simoes, A., Yildirim, M., *The Atlas of Economic Complexity*, Cambridge, MA: MIT Press, 2014.
11 Hidalgo et al, "The Principle of Relatedness," in: *12th Chaotic Modeling and Simulation International Conference,* Berlin: Springer Science and Business Media LLC, 2018, p. 454.
12 Polanyi, Michael: *Personal Knowledge*, Chicago: University of Chicago Press, 1958.
13 Hartmann, Dominik et al, "Linking Economic Complexity, Institutions, and Income Inequality," in: *World Development* 93, pp. 75–93, 2017.

these scales with a solid understanding of systemic relationships and dependencies, and a keen sense of subsidiarity.

The third factor, however, might be the most consequential: While we enjoyed an ever more integrated global economy and an increasingly complex material life in the past, this trend cannot be taken for granted anymore. Global markets and political alliances are less stable than they used to be. The climate crisis and environmental degradation call the global economy itself into question. Over the last few years, and specifically with the Covid-19 crisis, confidence in globalization has fallen. If a locally embedded, globally connected, complex economy is the basis for prosperity, then restructuring it to organize material and energy flows closer and more circular, to keep information flows open and global, to increase resilience while keeping connectedness is the goal. The Industrious City is therefore also an agenda for retaining local economic complexity in a changing context. And maybe then this ability is again a skill to be exported.

Bruce Katz describes a new localism based on a more tangible sphere of concern and increased problem-solving ability accompanied by a shift in power from the national to the local. "Cities must think like a system and act like an entrepreneur."[23] There is perhaps no more important collective task at the moment than to get these delicate organisms, the cities and their urban regions, ready for the future. We might not be able to exactly predict the outcome of the transformations and disruptions we are currently experiencing, as the very connectedness we currently enjoy increases volatility and accelerates change.

We will need to navigate basic systemic questions yet again – large scale versus a network of many, autonomy versus dependency, global versus local, virtual versus material, information versus reality, prosperity versus sufficiency and collective versus individual. Of course, the solution is to not let ourselves become entrapped in a binary choice but rather yet again define that specific mix which, based on the context we inherited and the technologies and resources at our disposal, will define the character of the city and its society emerging before our eyes.

14 Heldring, Leander et al, "Monks, Gents and Industrialists: The Long-Run Impact of the Dissolution of the English Monasteries," NBER Working Paper No. 21450, August 2015. www.nber.org/papers/w21450.
15 Guldi, Jo, *Roads to Power. Britain Invents the Infrastructure State*, Cambridge: Harvard University Press, 2012.
16 Waslekar, Saahil Sundeep: "World environmental Kuznets curve and the global future," in: *Procedia – Social and Behavioral Sciences* 133 (2014), pp. 310–319.
17 World Bank World Development Report 2019: "The Changing Nature of Work." www.worldbank.org/en/publication/wdr2019.
18 Katz, Bruce, *The Metropolitan Revolution: How Cities and Metros Are Fixing Our Broken Politics and Fragile Economy*, Washington: Brookings Institution Press, 2013.
19 Dincecco, Mark and Onorato, Massimiliano, "Military conflict and the rise of urban Europe," in: *Journal of Economic Growth* 21 (2016), p. 259.
20 Hermann, Michael, *Was die Schweiz zusammenhält: Vier Essays zu Politik und Gesellschaft eines eigentümlichen Landes*, Basel: Zytglogge, 2016.
21 Here, see interview "Swiss Industries," p. 63 in this book.
22 www.oec.world/en/profile/country/che.
23 Matthew Taylor, quoted in: www.thenewlocalism.com/research/the-new-localism-think-like-a-system-act-like-an-entrepreneur/.

Metrobild 2011, Metropolitan Region Zurich

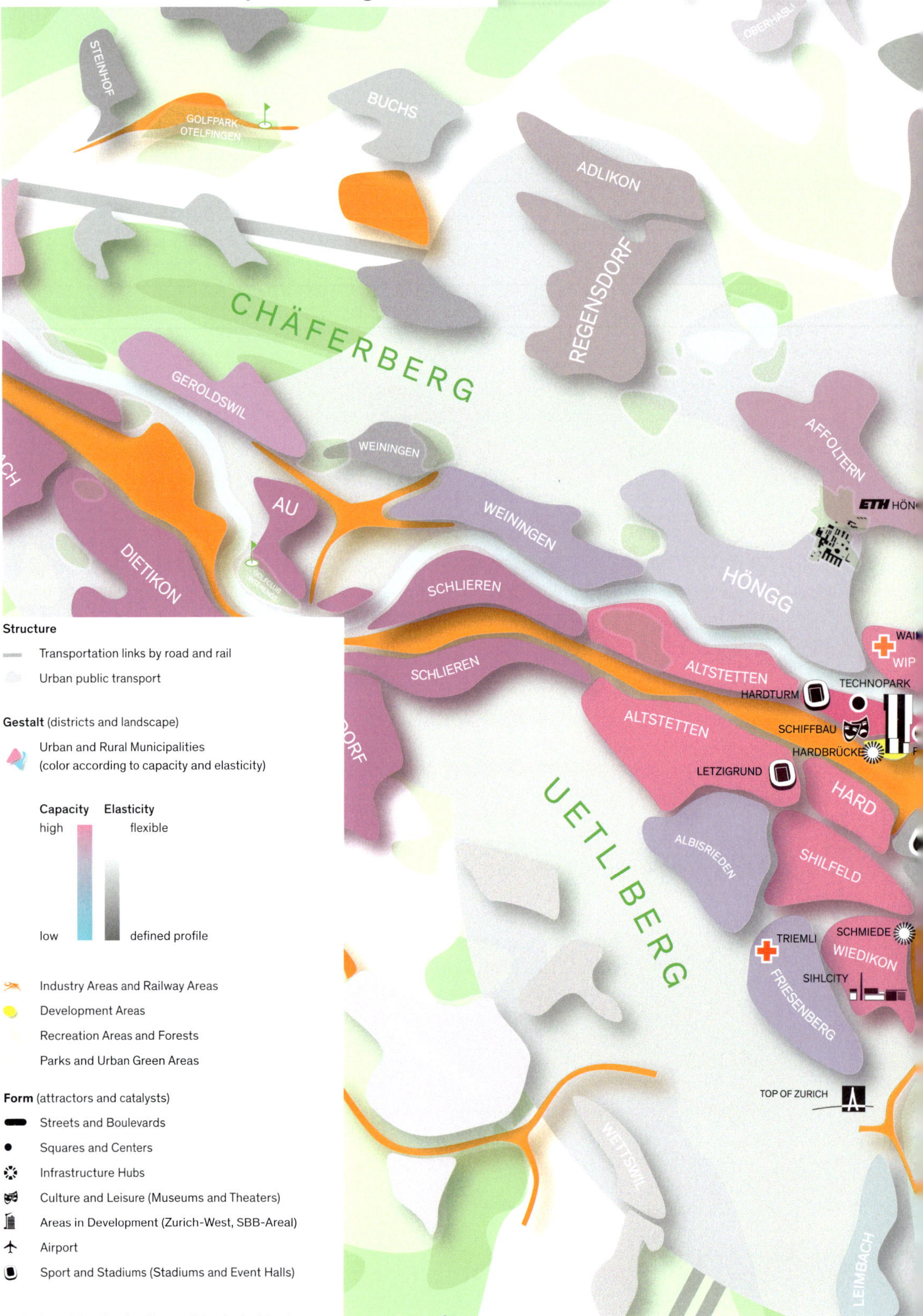

Structure

Transportation links by road and rail

Urban public transport

Gestalt (districts and landscape)

Urban and Rural Municipalities
(color according to capacity and elasticity)

Capacity	**Elasticity**
high	flexible
low	defined profile

Industry Areas and Railway Areas

Development Areas

Recreation Areas and Forests

Parks and Urban Green Areas

Form (attractors and catalysts)

Streets and Boulevards

Squares and Centers

Infrastructure Hubs

Culture and Leisure (Museums and Theaters)

Areas in Development (Zurich-West, SBB-Areal)

Airport

Sport and Stadiums (Stadiums and Event Halls)

Analysis and visualization: Hosoya Schaefer Architects

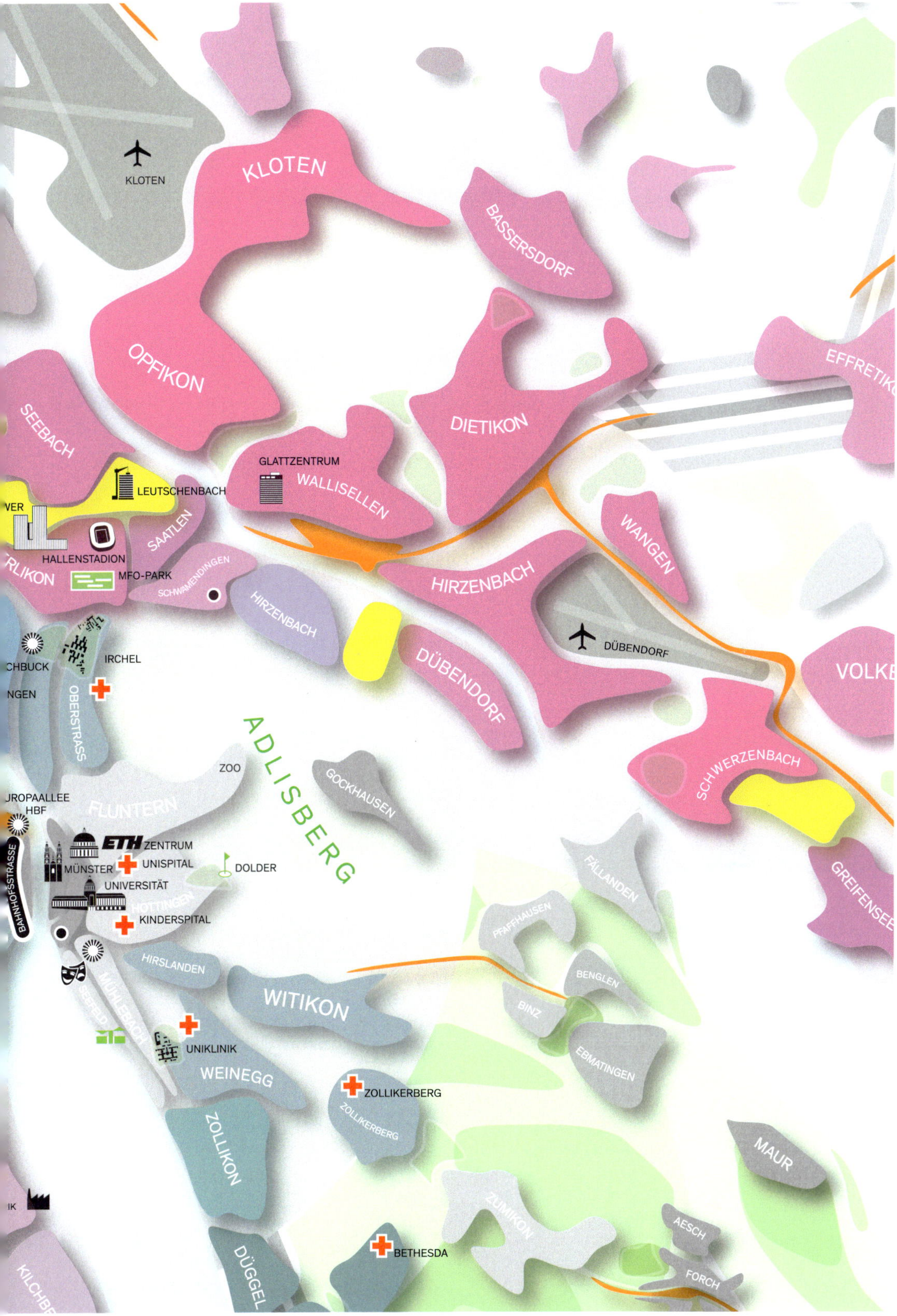
KLOTEN
KLOTEN
BASSERSDORF
OPFIKON
SEEBACH
DIETIKON
GLATTZENTRUM
WALLISELLEN
LEUTSCHENBACH
SAATLEN
HALLENSTADION
MFO-PARK
SCHWAMENDINGEN
HIRZENBACH
HIRZENBACH
WANGEN
DÜBENDORF
DÜBENDORF
IRCHEL
OBERSTRASS
ADLISBERG
ZOO
FLUNTERN
GOCKHAUSEN
SCHWERZENBACH
HBF
ETH ZENTRUM
UNISPITAL
MÜNSTER
DOLDER
UNIVERSITÄT
HOTTINGEN
KINDERSPITAL
BAHNHOFSSTRASSE
FÄLLANDEN
PFAFFHAUSEN
BENGLEN
HIRSLANDEN
WITIKON
BINZ
SEEFELD
MÜHLEBACH
UNIKLINIK
EBMATINGEN
WEINEGG
ZOLLIKERBERG
ZOLLIKERBERG
ZOLLIKON
MAUR
ZUMIKON
AESCH
BETHESDA
FORCH
DÜGGEL

TOWARD AN INDUSTRIOUS CITY

This book assembles the work and ideas of practitioners and thinkers, it shows references and scenarios of an Industrious City. The following chapter collects these insights into a preliminary framework, not a blueprint yet, but maybe an agenda for an Industrious City and its many facets.

Urban Industry

Exporters face stiff global competition and are forced to focus on their competitive advantages. They need to deal with currency fluctuations and flexibly control sourcing and production based on data. Well-educated people are essential for running these increasingly complicated processes, and they want access to urban culture **[Interview: Industrial Operations, p. 169]**. There is an increasing trend to relocate to cities in search of talents and synergies with other firms **[Essay: Industrious Labor in the Second Urban Age, p. 98]**.

Some clusters emerge naturally, as they facilitate logistics and communications. In other cases, clusters are actively planned. While industry used to operate in fenced-off areas belonging to individual companies, firms are now actively looking for co-location. At the same time, prudent entrepreneurs are reorganizing their global supply chains into more regional ones, opting for reliability and political stability, access to a local workforce and a reduction in carbon footprint rather than the lowest available labor costs **[Scenario: Tech Cluster Zug, p. 317]**.

Urban Manufacturing

An urban industry is developing with fewer workers per factory but more companies **[Essay: Urban Manufacturing, p. 175]**. Physically, the ramifications are seen in densely textured cities where former factory buildings or areas previously owned by one company are divided up for smaller companies to co-locate. This new form of urban manufacturing is not only based on new cooperations, but also on new customers looking for authentic local products and an urban experience **[Essay: Urban Production Is Not Utopian, p. 258]**. In turn, it can offer jobs for a diverse staff, local or immigrant, academically educated or self-taught.

Urban manufacturing is deeply networked with various contracting and subcontracting chains all dependent on an urban location. In turn, these networks have a multiplier effect and result in the retention of firms. Leaving the ecosystem would be detrimental. Companies are searching for small units and for collaborations. They are willing to share equipment and spaces, including personnel and clients. Cities are actively supporting networks of technological firms and educational institutions so that such clusters of knowledge and production can prosper **[Scenario: Werkplatz Zurich, p. 283]**.

Urban Innovation

These networks of producers and consumers, together with the proximity to knowledge and culture, in turn are attractive for larger firms interested in bringing part of their production, or at least their research and development, back to the city. Research institutions such as the ETH are creating demand for innovation areas in urban contexts to bridge academic and industrial research **[Scenario: RAD Areal Oerlikon, p. 303]**. In an economic environment where innovation, the differentiation of products and mass customization are increasingly important (and possible), it makes sense to be where both the customers and the talent are. Production is returning to the city in the form of urban industry, urban manufacturing and innovation in a combination of new and old, large and small, high-tech and craft-oriented firms **[Interview: Production Space, p. 159]**.

Maker Culture

At the same time, urban culture is changing. Aging creatives, do-it-yourself-savvy suburbanites who returned to the cities, as well as a younger, often academically trained generation looking for business ideas in a relocalizing economy and meaning in a de-globalizing world profit from new technologies. Already having a strong ethic of making and sharing, albeit digitally, software coders are discovering material culture, the ability "to make stuff." Together, they make up the maker movement. From their diverse backgrounds, its members bring various professional skills and the respective authority and combine that with an appetite for exploration and personal development. Maker culture emphasizes informal, networked, peer-led and shared learning motivated by fun and self-fulfillment. It is a social movement with an artisan spirit. With maker spaces, fab labs and hackathons, it appropriates the pieces of a technological culture, making it useful for a local collective.

All over the world, local entrepreneurs are working on saving the planet with new electric cars, drone projects, logistics and farming robots, all disrupting the old behemoths of industry, too complex both in their technology and processes. New industry is based on simple, open, modular technologies and networked clans with a mission.

The Industrious City offers a wider range of jobs and occupations. Lifestyles can be experimented with, but also less educated labor integrated. Alternative lifestyles are becoming popular and, in a sharing economy, whether in cooperatives or based on digital platforms, also possible. Industry has learned to cater to customers interested in low-cost items in an exchange for contributing personal labor. Hardware and software development fuse with sensors, drones and 3D printing into a new concept of craft with all its social and philosophical connotations. Add a dose of steampunk, a subgenre of cyberpunk, and you have STEAM – the combination of science and technology, interpreted through engineering and the (liberal) arts, and based in mathematics – each disciple enabled once again to understand a life's occupation holistically rather than in forever more narrow professional disciplines.

As retail is transformed by the rise of digital platforms that are better at linking supply and demand than shops or markets, large areas in prime locations will empty out and require new functions. Retail connected to production, conveying the authenticity of the product, could be one of the solutions. In this secondary form of industry, secondary resource flows could also blossom, reusing materials and used products in a form of urban mining and upcycling them locally. It fits a desire, both from producers and consumers, to be more sustainable.

Urban Land Economy

While re-embedding itself into the value chains, culture and "ecosystem" of the city, however, industry also brings its liabilities – logistics, emissions, waste – and its needs – most importantly affordable space that can be used flexibly to accommodate the often very exacting demands of industrial production. In some ways, this means a return to Swiss roots. In Switzerland, industry and its history are deeply embedded in the urban structures and landscapes [Swiss Cases, p. 184]. To retain this structure in the land economy of a gentrifying global city, however, authorities need to actively protect it. The city of Zurich achieved this with the 2014/2016 Building and Zoning Ordinance (BZO) and in 2017 launched its strategy for urban production, "Werkplatz Stadt Zurich," realizing that market forces alone would not cover the demand, which clearly exists as long as locations are affordable.

Urban Policy

The city is now actively keeping industrial zones in its zoning plans. In such zones industrial production, including noise emissions and logistics, is allowed, even required, while housing and similar functions are forbidden.
This prevents the increase in land prices associated with developing for housing, offices or retail and keeps rents affordable for small businesses. It also avoids residential demands that might make industrial uses impossible. For landowners, this in turn means a reduction in land value on the company's books. And development is more challenging since industrial business cases are less profitable than those for the housing or office market. There is a need to invent new processes and business models, more gradual and cooperative transformations working with existing building stock, which in turn questions the exacting building standards required by Swiss law. Certainly, the Industrious City requires that the municipal government actively intervene in the land market, as it already does in the housing market with its support of cooperatives.

With public-private initiatives such as Made in Zurich, these developments are acquiring a shared platform [Interview: Swiss Industries, p. 63]. Still, it is unlikely that this local cottage industry can shore up Swiss prosperity so strongly reliant on industrial exports. The aim always needs to be one of co-existence, small next to large, local next to global, tinkering next to high-tech.

The industry returning to the city is very different from the twentieth-century industry that left it. While industry used to be associated with foundries and presses, assembly lines and ovens, today it also includes semiconductors and nanotech, materials sciences and chemistry, software, design and art. It employs not only the traditional local blue-collar worker, but also experienced professionals with a variety of backgrounds, degrees and disciplines, from all over the world. Its spatial requirements are closer to the human scale. Not only is the city becoming more industrial again, but industry is becoming more urban – mature, agile, networked, polycentric – industrious, not only industrial. Still, this industry makes demands on logistics, resource flows, energy, financing and data.

Urban Logistics

Agile, just-in-time production allows firms to save on storage space and reduce the amount of capital locked up in parts and materials. On the other hand, the efficiency of logistics drops, as many more trips are taken with smaller batch sizes and less pooling. The railroad was ideal for an urban industry of mass production. Trucks solved the mobility needs of a suburban industry [Interview: Urban Logistics, p. 143]. For a granular and networked urban industry, additional logistical solutions need to be developed, organized as full service offerings, from efficiently organizing trucking and storing, and data-based mobility chains linking trains and cargo bikes, to projects like Cargo sous terrain, a private venture that promises to solve just-in-time delivery with tunnels linking cities and urban logistical centers **[Essay: Disappearing Infrastructure, p. 240]**.

Urban Flows

Logistics is not only required to move parts, but also resources and waste. A more tightly connected and efficient industry will need to better control its resource flows. Secondary resource flows, formerly treated as waste, can become raw materials for other industries. And also for this increasingly circular economy access to data is critical **[Interview: Resources Rethought, p. 73]**. With local hubs for highly automated production, parts shipping might be replaced by moving information and possibly very specific production equipment, for example proprietary effectors for otherwise generic robots. Advanced manufacturing and open-source codes for production reduce shipping and strengthen local production **[Interview: Digital Materiality, p. 249]**. While information flows remain global, material flows could become increasingly local and circular.

Energy from diverse renewable sources is becoming increasingly plentiful, but its management, storage and distribution, however, increasingly challenging. In a highly networked, interdependent urban industry, system boundaries might need to be redrawn so that energy users contribute to energy stability rather than increasing its volatility. The Multi Energy Hub in the Tech Cluster Zug, for example, is a partnership between an industrial infrastructure and a public utility, using groundwater, lake water, photovoltaics and clever control systems to increase the autonomy of a production site. Emerging software solutions such as EnergyOn combine energy management with financial tools, both to optimize energy costs for an area, and to increase stability in the larger energy market **[Scenario: Tech Cluster Zug, p. 317]**.

Urban Data

Data is essential to running contemporary industry, both industrial processes and real estate, with concepts such as Industry 4.0, the Internet of Things (IoT), cloud computing, cognitive computing and machine learning. Advanced robotics and additive production, at least in part, reduce the bulk and weight of equipment, increase flexibility and allow for smaller lots and more customization. In the case of the Tech Cluster Zug, planning data will be collected in a digital twin that supports the master plan (Urban Design Information Modeling, UDIM), real estate development, construction (BIM), facility management (CAFM) and innovation based on open data **[Scenario: Tech Cluster Zug, p. 317]**.

The infrastructures for knowledge and communication are being established by private interests, but they have become so essential to these new times, much like the roads and railroads during industrialization, that they now function as ecosystems and organize the world into large cloud economies. Computational power, tools for machine learning, artificial intelligence and data storage are available almost for free. Knowledge is open source. But behind this are global business cases that inevitably extract data from local networks. Accordingly, there needs to be increasing awareness of the value of open data, open source and open algorithms with the aim of a higher degree of data sovereignty. This specifically includes data commons in the service of communities and their local ecosystem, an important goal of start-ups, such as cividi – civic data intelligence. Data needs to be in the service of stability rather than volatility, local value rather than extraction. And this requires concerted, systemic thinking, economic incentives and the respective policies.

Large conglomerates such as IBM or Maersk are including partner firms into their networks of smart contracts, essentially creating their own currency of trust beyond what was once called money, replacing it with more intelligent forms of data. CO_2 markets are developing, as are crowdfunding and forms of microfinancing. Close-knit productive ecosystems might need new technologies for trust beyond money, and the emerging Swiss cluster of cryptocurrencies and smart contracts might provide solutions that are more visionary than bitcoin trading.

Urban Deep Tech

When services and data are linked to hardware, they are less prone to extraction. Also, customer retention becomes easier. Deep tech start-ups, combining business models in software and service with sophisticated hardware in fields as diverse as life sciences, agriculture, aerospace, mobility and energy, return investors' attention to physical products and long-term development processes beyond the easy profits of what was once called the new economy. While Switzerland is not particularly strong in software development, it is predestined to work on deep tech. Combined with topics such as security, data governance, reliability and the life sciences, countless business cases are thinkable **[Interview: Material and Innovation, p. 231]**.

Cities are a form of deep tech themselves. Cities and their inhabitants are increasingly understood as partners in innovation – for example, in the form of urban living labs.

Companies such as Google (or its parent Alphabet and the range of companies in that conglomerate) are aiming at developing entire urban neighborhoods. Increasing urbanization worldwide also makes cities important markets for solutions in the areas of mobility, energy, systems controls and artificial intelligence. But to prevent the dominance of commercial applications, new forms of urban governance are required so that new tools such as Urban Data Hubs or Digital Urban Twins are truly in the service of local communities and at least partially under their control [Essay: The City as an Interface, p. 150].

Urban Governance

Urban economies and value chains make local economies more resilient in the face of global market turbulence. And yet, considering the degree to which Switzerland is export-dependent, it cannot adopt a strategy of isolation or retreat from globalization. Accordingly, Swiss multinationals are currently actively embedding themselves in both foreign and Swiss cities, understanding that local networks and legitimacy are essential [Essay: The City as an Ecosystem, p. 105]. Embeddedness requires new forms of collaboration and mutual learning that are less conducive to the scale of a state but require concrete on-site collaboration with a city or at most a functional urban region.

These new forms of collaboration are also generating new dependencies demanding a revolution in governance. The start-up culture means that large firms are externalizing their innovation costs, spreading the risk to the public purse. The knowledge economy requires workers with expensive academic educations paid for by taxpayers. Agile, just-in-time production allows firms to save on storage space and reduce capital locked up in parts and materials, but it also pushes the burden of logistics beyond their system boundaries onto the public infrastructure. Finally, sharing, co-working and the gig economy mean that firms are externalizing social costs to the state.

Local system sovereignty might be increasingly important. This will only work when the local collaboration is close and enlightened [Essay: The City as an Interface, p. 150]. In turn, an industry that is close to its customers almost inevitably will be transparent and accountable, environmentally friendly and "fair," even allowing for the inclusion of enterprising immigrants [Essay: Urban Manufacturing, p. 175].

We are standing on a ridge and can go in different directions [Interview: Event Horizon, p. 361]. Globalization might be on the wane or reinvented in digital terms. Certainly, it has left each of the cities it touched with the ultimate import replacement – technological knowledge and resources from all over the globe, with industry and infrastructure, with digital links and great stories. At this moment it is important to understand the system we are in and know what we need to look for: a city built on access and redistribution of opportunities, not for moral reasons but to avoid instability; a city with a common story, not for ideological reasons but to contain centrifugal forces; and a city embedded in a local context but still connected to the world.

HISTORY OF PRODUCTION SPACE
ESCHER WYSS AREAL

Jos Schmid

Gion and Turi van Roon
Turning plant, MAN Diesel & Turbo AG
Zurich, 2016

Shipbuilding hall / workshop
Escher Wyss AG, Zurich, 1953

Shipbuilding hall, Schauspielhaus Zürich
Zurich, 2016

LASILLE
LASILLE

General view. Foundry, machine factory and tower
Escher Wyss & Cie., Zurich, 1891–1894

Hardturmstrasse with rail tracks
Escher Wyss & Cie., Zurich, ca. 1924

General view. Puls 5, MAN Diesel & Turbo AG machine factory,
Water tower and Schauspielhaus Zürich, Zurich, 2016

Hardturmstrasse with cycling route
Zurich, 2016

Shipbuilding hall / workshop
Escher Wyss AG, Zurich, 1953

Shipbuilding hall / Schauspielhaus Zürich
Zurich, 2016

Turning plant, Escher Wyss & Cie.
Zurich, 1900

Turning plant, MAN Diesel & Turbo AG
Zurich, 2016

8000 kg

Administrative building, new trainees
Sulzer-Escher Wyss AG, Zurich, 1983

Administrative building, trainees
MAN Diesel & Turbo AG, Zurich, 2016

CONVERSATIONS

Interviewers

Hiromi Hosoya is a founding partner of Hosoya Schaefer Architects. She has bachelor degrees in English Literature, Fine Arts, and Architecture, as well as a Master in Architecture from Harvard University Graduate School of Design. For five years she worked at Toyo Ito & Associates in Tokyo until she became independent in 2003. She taught interdisciplinary design studios at Cornell University in 2005 and 2006 and was a professor at the Academy of Fine Arts in Vienna, Austria from 2007 to 2012. In addition, she taught an advanced architecture design studio and an urban design studio at Harvard GSD in 2011 and 2018.

Markus Schaefer is a founding partner of Hosoya Schaefer Architects. He has a Master in Architecture from the Harvard University Graduate School of Design and a Master in Neurobiology from the University of Zurich. He worked for OMA / Rem Koolhaas in Rotterdam for five years and was a director and co-founder of AMO (1999–2003). He was a studio critic at the Berlage Institute (2005–2007), a professor at the Academy of Fine Arts in Vienna (2007–2012) and a main tutor at the Moscow Graduate School of Urbanism at the National Research University Higher School of Economics in collaboration with the Strelka Institute, teaching Advanced Urban Design (2017–2018). In addition, he taught an advanced urban design studio at Harvard GSD in 2018.

Hosoya Schaefer Architects

Artisanalization
Attracting Talent
Campus Thinking
Digitalization
European Industrial Powerhouse
Industrial Clusters
Industrialized Landscape
Land Scarcity
Made in Zurich
New Industrial Scale
Niche Player
Urban Ecosystem
Urban Production

Interview by Hiromi Hosoya
September 2, 2019
Swissmem, Winterthur

SWISS INDUSTRIES

Johannes Eisenhut / Hans Hess

Dr. Johannes Eisenhut is a managing partner at Senn Development AG and co-founder of the X27 Expo initiative and the Made in Zurich association. He was a managing partner of the advertising and corporate design agency /DEPARTMENT United Creative Forces (now FCB Zurich) and Head of Marketing Europe for Burton Snowboards. He holds a PhD in cognitive linguistics and has studied linguistics, German literature and journalism in Fribourg (lic. phil. i, dipl.-journ.). He has been a snowboard professional since his childhood while being schooled in Mexico, the United States and Switzerland.

Hans Hess is the chairman of the Swiss industry association Swissmem, and Vice-Chairman of the national organization of the Swiss economy, economiesuisse. He is also Chairman at Reichle & De-Massari Holding AG, and Vice-Chairman at dormakaba Holding AG. From 1996 to 2005 he was CEO of Leica Geosystems AG. In 2006, he founded Hanesco AG, which provides international management services to industry. Hess holds a master's degree in Material Science from ETH in Zurich, and an MBA from the University of Southern California.

We want to think about the role, value and future of urban industry. Let's talk about three broad topics: the organizational structure, the spatial requirements and the compatibility of contemporary industry with urban space. Can you give us an overview?

Hess

In Switzerland, manufacturing industries employ about 700,000 people, some 15 percent of the total workforce. We can split them into two roughly equal groups. One is the mechanical and electrical engineering sector represented by the Swissmem employers' association, and the other is the pharmaceutical and chemical sector. In the machinery industries about 45 percent of employees work in production, which means that if you want to set up a company in an urban environment, you have to accept the fact that there will be production there. About 20 percent work in research and development, and this percentage is increasing because simple manufacturing is being outsourced to Eastern Europe, China and India, and the jobs we have here are becoming increasingly specialized and sophisticated. Another 20 percent are in marketing and sales, and maybe another 10 or 15 percent in administration. That's from the point of view of employees. If you look at the structure of our industrial sector, only about 2 percent is comprised of large companies. The majority are small and medium-size enterprises (SMEs). However, if you look at the total number of employees, a third of the people are employed by large companies, a third by medium-sized and a third by small companies. The fact that SME's are predominant in the industrial sector is important. It's also especially important that the average industrial company in Switzerland exports 80 percent of its output, with only 20 percent for domestic use.

We are very export-oriented, which means we face strong global competition. We have to make conscious decisions on where to locate our various activities, taking into consideration operating costs, the proximity to our customers, and particularly the availability of skilled people. With today's demographic changes, finding enough sophisticated people is a challenge. Sophistication does not mean they all have to have university degrees. In industry, only 10 percent have a research university degree, 25 percent have an applied university or equivalent degree, and the rest come out of our famous work-study programs (apprenticeships combined with vocational school). It's important for us to have not only the best scientists but also very good industrial professionals.

Maybe 20 percent of the employees in our industries live in large or medium-sized cities. The rest are located in small cities and villages distributed around the country. Since Switzerland is so small, it's easy to commute from a rural area to the city. Where I live, Zürcher Oberland (the "Zurich highlands"), is quite industrialized and it takes only 15 minutes by train to get to Zurich, or half an hour to Winterthur. Switzerland is densely populated, so everything is kind of urbanized around here.

Many of the large industrial companies we had here in Winterthur are gone. When I was 20 years old, I started my career with Sulzer, a fantastic employer. Now it's been split up and sold off to a large degree. But in Upper Winterthur, some industrial companies have successfully remained and are well integrated into the urban environment. For the last 12 years I've been with Burckhardt Compression, in the Upper Winterthur area, and all kinds of residential areas have been popping up next to our factory. What's left is a small industrial zone, in a sense, in the middle of a residential zone.

Are there industrial clusters in Switzerland and how are they connected?

Hess

That's a very good question. I think there are some manufacturing centers, and I would say this has to do with tradition. Industry began to develop in Switzerland when Napoleon blockaded Britain, and Swiss textile mills could no longer import British machinery. Instead, they made their own weaving and spinning machines based on British models. These manufacturing clusters developed in Zurich, Winterthur and the Zürcher Oberland. Another big and highly concentrated cluster, the chemical industry, sprang up around Basel at the same time. And then in the Jura area, there are the watch and precision mechanics industries.

What about the connections between these industrial clusters?

Hess

They're totally connected. For example, if you take a large company in Winterthur, their suppliers may be located all over Europe. However, proximity is still important. Switzerland and its neighboring areas – Bavaria and Baden-Württemberg in Germany, and Lombardy in Italy – represent the biggest industrial powerhouse in Europe. There's nothing comparable anywhere else. But within that region, the industry is very scattered; there is no one location where everything is concentrated like in the Silicon Valley.

You said Switzerland has its own kind of industrial system, and that's been true historically.

Hess

Right. For instance, take Escher Wyss and MAN Diesel & Turbo, now MAN Engery Solutions, in Zurich. Why are they there? Because that's where Swiss industry was born in 1800. At that time, the first textile machinery companies were located outside of the city. But the city grew and surrounded them until they found themselves in the city center. They have to deal with the challenges, the advantages and disadvantages, of this urbanization.

Then, what would you say about the role of urban centers? Do urban centers have a specific role?

Hess

It's contradictory. On the one hand young people like to live in an urban environment, so that's an advantage in attracting talent and keeping commuting time to a minimum. On the other hand, if you are in the center of Zurich, and you don't already own the land you need, there's no way. It's too expensive and there are all kinds of constraints. It's in the urban agglomeration where you find a compromise between proximity to the city and lower land costs.

Mr. Eisenhut, what makes a brand such as Made in Zurich necessary? Is it more than niche marketing to a very local and urban clientele?

Eisenhut

Mr. Hess already touched on some factors, like getting talent to work for companies. I look at it from the other side. And I say there's a certain corporate culture that calls for being in the city or near the city. It was an interesting experience to build NŒRD, which is the Freitag building on the periphery of Zurich. For Freitag and their corporate culture, it was important to be a Made in Zurich brand. Still, from the point of view of people living in the city, Oerlikon is in the suburbs. And the question was, can we get that culture, the inner-city culture, out to Oerlikon? I think that as employees become a scarce commodity, it becomes more important to know where you want to position your company geographically. In Switzerland's spatial planning we are still chewing away at the Athens Charter and the separation of functions it mandated – live here, work there. But today you have to look at issues like mobility, sustainability and quality of life. It is important that there's life where you work, and also work where you live. I like the title of your book because it's not the industrial city but *The Industrious City*. It is a different term. It's a city that does stuff, that's in movement.

Another trend we are seeing is the digitization of the manufacturing process. We read, a couple of months ago, that the Oerlikon Group is thinking of decentralized industrial units with highly robotized, digitized production. The hypothesis is that the entire robot paradigm and 3D printing can reduce the space needed for production, with increased added value per square meter. Maybe then production can be moved back into urban centers because companies will be able to pay more per square meter of production space.

On the other hand, there's what I call an "artisanalization" – an increase in artisanal fabrication, manually producing things like sausages, belts, shoes and jackets for niche markets. There is a market for locally produced items.

For Made in Zurich, the way this all came together was basically that Markus Freitag and I, who first thought of the label, said to each other, let's go to the city officials and talk about this. Then we found out that they have a guideline called "Strategic Focus Urban Production" (Strategieschwerpunkt Urbane Produktion). And they didn't have a proper name for it, so we approached them and said, "How about we call it Made in Zurich?" And we founded an association together. The interesting thing about Made in Zurich is that it's probably not a label you would use for export purposes... We went from zero to 70 members in no time because there is a need for community. These mostly small enterprises finally have a platform where they can talk to each other.

Hess

From a purely export industry point of view, I would say "Made in Switzerland" is a big advantage. However, we don't use that label anymore because we don't make all our goods in Switzerland. We try to communicate other attributes associated with "Swissness," like quality, reliability, responsiveness and customization.

I would agree that as the structure of our industries changes to achieve an even higher level of optimization, digitization will help us make the next steps. Technologies like 3D printing can make it possible to separate the location of the factory and the location of design work. I think you're right in envisioning that the necessary space will become rather small. I don't envision big plants here in Switzerland. Instead, I envision a bigger number of smaller high-tech plants and R&D centers. Even our larger companies have become much smaller. Sulzer used to employ maybe 20,000 people here in Winterthur. I think there are around 600 now. There has been tremendous structural change and other companies have picked up; yet, all of them are smaller companies.

Since we have high labor costs here, we try to concentrate on value-adding businesses that require knowledge and brainwork. I think the structure and demand for facilities will change. And the social changes that we envision will lead us to urban centers. People don't want to commute anymore. They want to be closer to their work and the cities where there are other activities. I think there's been a change. And if we cooperate well, we might find some interesting recipes for how to integrate this. In Winterthur there is still heavy production, but right next door there are now residential buildings. People live there and walk 100 meters to their office.

Why the focus on urban production? Is it a real estate development strategy or does it cover a real demand?

Eisenhut

I wouldn't call it a strategy. As real estate developers, we are pretty opportunistic, honestly. Because the scarcest element in developing real estate in Switzerland is land. In the bid for the development of the Koch Areal in Zurich, for example, the city made it a prerequisite that one building be dedicated to urban production. Teaming up with two cooperatives, we were able to match this to a functioning and ultimately winning concept.

This is something we realized when we started in Zurich, and I think it's probably true for anything "Made in Switzerland" as well. People who produce things in Zurich, they've got to be crazy because of the high labor and production costs. They have to spend so much time making everything extremely efficient and precise… they have to have so much courage to position their product at the upper end of the price scale and say, "We are premium. And it will work. And we're going to be able to sell it because we're better." That's why people who are part of the Made in Zurich initiative feel like a great community, because they all know everyone here is a bit crazy.

What is the relevance of urban production on an economic level?

Hess

Swiss industries are fundamentally niche players. Only few can play on a large scale. Almost nobody really produces huge volumes. We create something that has a certain level of uniqueness so that people are willing to pay for it. We're not shy about producing one thing for one customer. Being niche players and doing that straightforwardly is a strategy that has worked really well in Switzerland, and it's the reason why we are so successful.

Is urban industry scalable? Will the re-emerging focus on urban production support the standing of Swiss industry in the global context?

Hess

These are some of the reasons why the structures of Swiss industry have changed. But I would say scale is not an issue. It's more about increasing sophistication, leading-edge technology and the Internet of Things. Automation was a necessary change due to the high labor costs in Switzerland. Over the last 30 years, we automated everything we could. Today there may be one person supervising five machines. We may not have as many workers as before, but industry will remain here. And industry will prosper here, because I think we have some uniqueness. The proximity to first-class universities, the fact that international people like to live here, clean air and a safe environment. We try to attract international specialists to come and help us change industrial structures.

What are the new spatial needs of firms, then?

Hess

I envision multipurpose facilities, buildings where you can set up a little machine shop somewhere, then offices in other areas, maybe a little lab. Flexibility is the key thing. You know you want to use your space to move people around and even change the purpose of their jobs. Having a building that gives you the flexibility to adapt is key. For example, if you have a project involving ten people, once they complete the task you can dissolve the team and move on to the next. You need to have flexibility; and you need people to interact. People need to see and hear each other. We see value in people having coffee and chatting together. About 20 years ago, I was CEO at Leica. I had a big site, tore down half the buildings, and added easily accessible outdoor space and childcare in a central location. You have to adapt your space to the needs of the company and also the employees there. As employers and builders, we have to adapt, and space has a lot to do with that; how people move and how they get to work.

Eisenhut

There are new solutions in the making. Our latest production building has double height spaces. As tenant you do not rent area, but space, and you can organize your workflow by adding mezzanine floors. Another large project near Basel, called the "Grid," is meant as a campus of collaboration. The 50,000 m^2 are planned as a large rectangle with a park in the middle the size of a football field. It's designed like a large monastery with cloisters connecting everything and an exoskeleton so that the structural footprint in the floorplan is minimal. The Swiss Innovation Park is the anchor tenant with education, innovation and industry coming together.

There's a word that pops up every once in a while. It used to be called *Industriequartier,* and today the word is "Ecosystem." You want to be a part of an ecosystem… and that ecosystem implies work, off-work, quality of life, sports… There was a time when it was considered dangerous to have a competitor close to you, because they could copy your product and steal your best people. And today, you can be next to your competitor because that gives everybody a bigger pool of employees to fall back on… and that's campus thinking.

What are the requirements regarding the urban context and collaboration with the city authorities?

Eisenhut

In the case of the redevelopment of Koch-Areal, the city authorities were very important. They brought down the price of land and encouraged competition based on the best concept and not on maximizing land value. Although we had to submit a land value estimate for the land lease, it was not a top priority. It was not top price that wins you the plot, but the best concept. And obviously now, after we won the competition, we are held responsible to deliver affordable spaces.

Hess

I'd say it's a different protocol. We have the same thing here in Dübendorf; they have to fight with local communities which tend to see the question of redevelopment narrow-mindedly. Usually, people abandon an industrial site because it's worth so much more money if it's used to build commercial real estate. There needs to be a conscious decision to counteract this and not maximize the price of this land! We need to zone it in a way that allows mixed use, industrial companies with residential areas and schools.

What are the opportunities for urban production in the future and what kind of city does it let us envision?

Eisenhut

I would say integrated thinking. Trying to integrate vertically. Trying to integrate value-added services and integrate with the city in terms of work and life.

Hess

I would say that technological development offers many opportunities, but so does social development. People don't want to commute anymore; they would like to live near where they work. However, people need to interact with one another. If we take the different kinds of technological developments together with the social developments, and work with the responsible communities on how to change the model of the city of the future, I think we have a chance. I think it's an opportunity for us to have a more Industrious City.

Circular Economy
Digitalization
Industrial Clusters
Secondary Resources
Side Streams
Urban Mining

Interview by Hiromi Hosoya
September 19, 2019
RethinkResource, Zurich

RESOURCES RETHOUGHT

Linda Grieder

Linda Grieder is a lawyer by training and an entrepreneur at heart. In 2016 she founded RethinkResource, a Swiss upcycling innovation agency that also offers a pioneering cross-industry marketplace for industrial waste and side streams. Secondary materials and the circular economy have become her main area of interest and expertise. Before becoming an entrepreneur, she specialized in IP law and mainly worked on the way social change impacts jurisprudence.

In the context of the Industrious City, I would like to raise questions about the flow of resources and materials. Can you explain what you are doing with RethinkResource?

RethinkResource is on a mission to implement an industrial circular economy. It started through my fascination with the question of how to combine sustainability and economic value. In RethinkResource we work together with industrial producers in any field and together with them develop new products made from secondary resources. We also help them position themselves in the circular economy environment. While working on these projects we learned that companies are not getting engaged in circular economy as much as they would like to because secondary resources are very difficult to manage. We realized the need to open that market and give companies access to these resources. They need to understand what's available on the market and what's accessible. Until now secondary resources have been perceived as worthless waste materials that nobody really thought about a lot or maybe didn't care about. This prompted us to develop Circado.io, an online trading platform for secondary resources.

What is the difference between RethinkResource, Circado.io and other start-ups?

Our second company, Circado, is a digital trading platform that allows us to scale up. Without digitalization, you're lost today. But something I learned is that the "digital thing" doesn't just happen by itself. It needs people to create it, writing code and enabling machines to do what they are doing. Our people writing code for our trading platform need to understand our customers' needs. We see Circado as a bridge between digital and people. When we talk about people, it's more about enabling them to do what they're good at, and a big part of today's work is digital.

Where are the best business opportunities for you at the moment?

We operate in Europe. That's the market we serve best, at the moment. We are ten people. And we work with companies of different sizes. We have customers that are still very small, developing a new product that is just now coming to market. But we have also worked for big companies. For them, too, it's crucial to understand how they can get engaged in this whole field. Also, consumers are starting to demand solutions.

How does your business make money?

We get orders from our customers. They pay project-based fees for our services. Depending on the customer, if the project involves a clear product development, we get paid for results. If they say, "We want to create a, I don't know, a bread made from a side stream," then once the bread is on the market, we get a fee. And with the other company, Circado[1], where we do trading of side streams, we get a transaction fee when a connection is made between two partners.

Why is your company better than other start-ups?

There are a lot of companies engaged in this line of business. But most of them have either a very specific product that they are developing or a very specific industry that they're working with. We, however, want to leverage the synergies that are created when you connect different industries and also leverage all the know-how hidden away in universities and research institutes. We see ourselves as facilitators or enablers.

Can you give us an idea of the opportunities that arise from managing secondary resource flows?

We are very strong in the food sector. Until now many food producers had to pay a lot of money to get rid of their side streams or waste materials. In the beer brewing process, for example, you have spent grain as a side stream in huge amounts on a daily basis. It's hard to get rid of and needs to be picked up by trucks. And yet, that spent grain is very rich in protein and fiber. And there are emerging industries, for example, insect farming, that have a high interest in materials like these and are willing to pay a respectable price for it. We can connect new, emerging companies with old industries burdened by these recurring waste streams.

Are clusters and physical proximity relevant to your way of thinking and work?

We certainly want side streams to become more valuable, but still, when compared to primary resources, they are low-value materials. This means you need to limit the transportation involved. For most materials, it makes little sense to transport them too far. It's very important for the industrial partners to be close to each other so they can easily connect. For example, in industrial parks there's a lot of potential for recirculating materials within the park. Companies can support each other and circulate resources. There's a huge potential, if clusters of industries are in proximity to production sites.

Is an industry's urban location advantageous for a circular economy? Or are the flows too specific and transportation unavoidable?

That's an interesting question I've been thinking about a lot. For me, just from the material or resource point of view, it matters if the industries are close to one other. The urban location in itself is probably not crucial. But since train stations and connections to highways are often in cities, it can make sense to build these clusters near to or in them.

Would it make sense to actively collocate industries, and do you think this is possible in an urban environment? Or would a greenfield site be easier to handle?

Here's where the people argument comes in. We placed our company in the city, even though that's much more expensive. Everyone thought we were crazy. If you're funding your own company, an urban location is too expensive, they said. I don't think so, because people live here for a reason, and they very much value their environment. All our colleagues live within half an hour of our office, even though it's very expensive. But they have their family and friends here. And I think for most companies it makes sense to go where your people are. If your people live in the city, that's where you need to go. Employees aren't happy if they have to travel two hours a day. I have friends whose commute means an hour-long train ride each way. They spend so much time on the train that they don't have time for their families anymore. And that makes them unhappy, thus less productive. I think this impacts a company. If you want to be close to your people, I think it's clear that companies should stay within the structures of a city.

Are there opportunities to think in terms of an urban material economy? There are concepts of urban mining, of material certificates (Madaster). Has urban waste already become a resource today?

The building industry offers great potential in that context. I think there are a lot of old buildings that need to go away. There are a lot of new buildings being built. And taking a circular economy into consideration definitely makes sense and would contribute to an urban economy.

1 www.rethink-resource.com, www.circado.io.

TANGIBLE PRODUCTION
SITTERWERK, ST. GALLEN

Jos Schmid

pp. 79–81
Ohne Titel, Alex Hanimann, Kunstgiesserei St. Gallen, 2019

82–84, 85 above, 88–89, 91, 94–95
Kunstgiesserei St. Gallen

85 below, 86–87
Stiftung Sitterwerk

90, 96–97
White Snow, Party, Paul McCarthy, Kunstgiesserei St. Gallen, 2014

92–93
Kesselhaus Josephsohn

DIMS (inches):
H 77" L 36" D 31"
WEIGHT
(kgs) 176 kg
FRAGILE
ALL SIDES
REMOVABLE

KUNST

FALCON GRIP

HoTo
Spoon
2 kg

553
492
587
554
443
A34
Löschpapier
558
444
559
Wabenplatten
560
561
562
Papyrus Tapa Amate
601
467
468
584
812
748
587

MATERIAL
ARCHIV

MATERIAL
ARCHIV

KUNSTGIESSEREI
WERKHALLE 2

KUNSTGIESSEREI
WERKHALLE 2

Alex Krieger

INDUSTRIOUS LABOR IN THE *SECOND* URBAN AGE

Industrious City Zone
Industrious Labor
Live Work Play
Local Entrepreneurship
Urban Age

As digital fabrication, artificial intelligence and robotic processes become more common and pervasive, soon (hopefully) powered by renewable energy sources, the traditionally negative impacts of "industry" on daily life – pollution, noise, the hauling and distribution of material and products, and the reservation of extensive areas for a single purpose – will continue to diminish. While certain manufacturing processes still require distance from city centers, much contemporary "industry" is no longer incompatible with daily life. Indeed "manufacturing" today is as much about the manufacturing of ideas as about assembling machines and products. In considering the contemporary place of industry in relationship to the city, it is equally important to ask where today's "industrious worker" might wish to be This is not as new a question as it may seem, as a review of locational decisions regarding work environments in the American experience illustrates.

First, from a historical perspective it would be more accurate to refer to ours as the *second* urban age. It was the emergence of new industrial processes that propelled the first urban age now more than two centuries ago. The rise of the modern city was a direct result of those processes – the concentration of capital, workers and markets was required to support the new expansive modes of production In turn, industries grew dependent on ready access to capital, trainable workers, markets and the transportation and energy infrastructure provided by growing cities. There was a symbiotic relationship between the growth of modern cities and the growth of modern industry, as no doubt existed in less complex ways during prior eras.

While modernizing in tandem, both industry and cities encountered substantial challenges and incongruities (not all entirely overcome). Recall a haunting Charles Dickens passage about mid-nineteenth century London: "It was a town of red brick if the smoke and ashes had allowed it, but as matters stood it was a town of unnatural red and black like the painted face of a savage."[1] That was hardly testament to a humane urbanism. Across the Atlantic circa 1900, to live in the tenements along the edge of Chicago's enormous Union Stockyards was to experience the deleterious effects of 40,000 animals being slaughtered every day.

Such evocations remind us that in those rapidly industrializing cities of the first urban age, industry as it was then experienced was hardly consistent with healthy urban living. The emergence of zoning and other regulations to separate incompatible uses was necessary, even if they are overused today. Memories from that first urban age still linger, apprehensions readily aroused when the subject of mixing industry and urbanity comes up, especially in residential areas, with issues of "scale" being among the concerns.

Skepticism: The Value of Live/Work/Play

Of course, urban centers today encompass few slaughterhouses or massive assemblies of noxious and noisy industrial enterprises. And the nature of most work – we used to say labor – has changed dramatically since the flowering of the Industrial Revolution. It seems easy to conclude that whereas conditions during the first urban age regularly *demanded* the separation of industrial and living spaces, this is no longer the case. Instead we hear a common refrain among urban pundits: Let's make more "live, work, play, 24/7 active environments." The phrase underlies a contemporary sensibility to reduce the distance between human activities, including some of those deemed necessary to separate during that first urban age. Skepticism does remain, even about "clean" (non-polluting, non-noisy) enterprises, and certainly about their size.

Let's raise an emblematic (if extreme) example: Few might be concerned about a neighbor spending night and day in the garage next door inventing the next digital wonder. One might actually be intrigued and supportive, and even feel a neighborhood pride. But sometime later, when a mile-in-circumference corporate headquarters becomes necessary to maintain the enterprise (as Apple recently built in Silicon Valley), one's relationship to that enterprise as a neighbor might be different, even if the actual manufacturing of that digital wonder takes place across oceans. Similarly, we may appreciate the convenience of getting near-daily deliveries from Amazon but are unlikely to enjoy living near one of the company's colossal distribution facilities, and maybe even next to a large office complex.

In 2017, only recently relocated to downtown Seattle, Amazon announced its intention to build a second headquarters, and 238 cities initially submitted their case for why Amazon should come to them. The prospect of up to 50,000 jobs was awfully tantalizing. Amazon's challenge to those cities was sort of "What are you offering us to induce us to come to your town?" Having chosen two cities, Amazon was then unexpectedly rebuffed by a cohort of activists from the Queens area, the New York City site offered to Amazon. In effect the opponents were turning the tables on Amazon's request. They were not interested in how Amazon would benefit, but asked how the company's arrival would enhance their local public realm, benefit their parks and open spaces, help reduce rather than add to local congestion, encourage diversity and opportunity in careers, assist in the provision of affordable housing and control the pace of gentrification. They argued that all this would be great for the neighborhood and the wellbeing of Amazon employees, too. These were not old worries about smoke and noise. Instead they were concerned about soaring property values, displacement, congestion and the specter of too rapid a change arising from so large an enterprise landing all at once."

Industry's Reception

Yes, the maker economy, the return of respect for craft, local entrepreneurship and talent, proximity among producers and customers preferences for authentic local products, indeed, the number of start-ups not headed to become the next Apple, are all on the rise. Nonetheless, the issue of enterprise scale, and more precisely how a modern industry evolves from its formative periods through its phases of growth, is not unimportant to that industry's reception within various urban settings.

The Industrious Laborer

Let's shift the discussion from consideration of the impacts of industry on adjoining areas to a discussion of what the modern "industrious laborer" might expect from their workplace and its context. Where does the contemporary worker wish to be? How did American companies, across the past century, select their locations while often arguing that they were doing so for the benefit of the worker?

Around the turn of the nineteenth to the twentieth centuries (and periodically since), company founders sought more controlled environments for their enterprises, so they set out to build their factories and related services at the edge of urban centers. The advantages included cheap land, room to grow, fewer conflicts with abutters, access to energy sources and the expectation of being able to better manage workers away from the unruly distractions of the city. In such complexes and company towns, maximizing productivity while monitoring worker wellbeing were important goals. Benevolent or naïve paternalism among company owners aimed for establishing physical settings that might produce a more content and thus more productive labor force.

Labor and/or Living

Among the most notable such towns were Homestead, Pennsylvania (1880) and Gary, Indiana (1906) – both massive and longstanding steel production centers – and the short-lived Pullman, Illinois (1880), the dream of the railcar industrialist George Pullman, who sought an all-encompassing and controlled environment for his workers. Overstating only slightly, one might say that what such historical examples and the present campuses of Silicon Valley titans such as Google, Apple and Facebook have in common is the ambition of creating amenity-rich settings to keep staff happy at or near their workplaces, now mostly computer monitors. Facebook's new headquarters, designed by Frank Gehry, has been described as "a cross between high-art, twentieth century corporate thinking, and a child's candy-fueled daydream."[2] An Apple executive anticipating the completion of the company's vast circular headquarters (dubbed the "spaceship," four stories tall and a mile in circumference) predicted, "Once the campus is open, Apple employees will have relatively little reason to leave the building."[3] Note that this is for a type of modern worker growing in percentage: educated, well compensated and industrious. The actual assembly of iPhones is largely performed by others far removed.

Then, early in the twentieth century, industrialists built on the ideas of the City Beautiful and Garden City movements to create what they hoped were garden-like industrial communities. Noteworthy towns included Kohler, Wisconsin (1913), named for the still-active plumbing manufacturer; Morgan Park, Minnesota (1917), built for a US Steel subsidiary; Tyrone, New Mexico (1917), created for the Phelps Dodge Copper Mining Corporation; and Kistler, Pennsylvania (1918), built for the Mount Union Refractories Company.[4] Located on open, undeveloped sites, an underlying hope was to create a more favorable relationship between labor and living while encouraging the growth of a town around the core established by the company.

Push – Pull

At mid-twentieth century, the predecessors of today's digital-age corporate enclaves appeared. These sprawling suburban campuses were laid out on spacious, well-landscaped grounds away from city centers, though tethered to cities via circumferential urban highways. Those campuses, like the newer headquarters of Apple, Facebook and Google, may not be classic company towns. With the advent of ready personal mobility, companies no longer felt obliged to provide employees with housing and civic services. But they still share their predecessors' goal of crafting an environment with qualities conducive to job satisfaction (today including the ambiance of "a candy-fueled daydream"), and thus better performance.

Corporate Landscapes

Three defining projects of the era were the 1954 General Foods Headquarters in White Plains, some twenty miles north of Manhattan; the 1957 Connecticut General Life Insurance Company site near Bloomfield, Connecticut; and the 1960s Deere and Company Administrative Center in Moline, Illinois. The Deere complex was perhaps the purest archetype, taking brilliant advantage of a beautiful bucolic location, and enhancing it further with a remarkable landscape design and striking modern architecture. The main building actually straddles a ravine and overlooks a lake. The most distinctive aspect of many of these corporate campuses – and often the most appreciated by workplace users – was the relationship between the landscape and the buildings. A mobile, car-owning demographic enjoyed working in welcomed daily isolation from both home and urban stress. But for a future generation, such isolation would become dull and tiresome.

"Pastoral Capitalism" is how historian Louise A. Mozingo labels these archetypal bucolic office and research parks, along with their upwardly mobile and nearby suburban citizens.[5] In the decades prior to the rise of Silicon Valley, Boston's Route 128 was heralded as "America's Technology Highway." Along that new highway, actually a segment of an interstate designed to bypass central Boston, the Digital Equipment Corporation, BEA Systems, Lotus, Raytheon, Data General, Computervison, GTE and Analog Devices, among others, were spawned. They were the digital-age parents of Microsoft and Apple. A main advantage for these companies would be the proximity to their labor pool, already nestled in nearby suburban Edens, eliminating the need to commute downtown. Between the mid-1950s and 1980s Boston's population decreased by some 250,000 people, most of whom moved to suburban areas around and beyond Route 128. The number of companies along Route 128 increased from 100 to over 1,200.[6] This shows that while workers chase jobs, modern industries often chase people, especially those with needed expertise or talent. These are examples of companies leaving the city for that reason, not due to noxious incompatibilities between industry and other city functions.

Back to the Hip City

But as the twenty-first century approached and is now unfolding, a move back to the city has been gaining momentum. Suburban business parks are being vacated due to the appeal of urban innovation clusters. Corporate America has been discovering how hip, dynamic, entrepreneurial-focused and fun cities – or at least select portions of them – can be. And so a certain type of company leadership has become attracted to such environments. Amazon, determined to locate its headquarters in downtown Seattle rather than suburban Bellevue, constructed several skyscrapers surrounding a spectacular greenhouse-like structure that invites staff to descend, unwind and interact. A *Seattle Times* headline declared: "Lush Nature Paradise to Adorn $4 Billion Urban Campus."[7] Staffers can still experience nature, but now indoors rather than amid crafted suburban vistas. The timber giant Weyerhaeuser Co., too, opted to leave its striking woodland headquarters south of Seattle for downtown. Even the very icon of the suburban strip, McDonalds, has relocated its headquarters from suburban Chicago to downtown.

The City of Boston has welcomed General Electric, a move that *The Wall Street Journal* reported with an eye to changing times: "General Electric Co. will relocate its headquarters from leafy suburban Connecticut to Boston's busy waterfront."[8] This was a representative move; GE's headquarters has migrated several times to reflect the trends we noted above. Its leafy, modern Connecticut headquarters was the result of the 1970s relocation from one of Pastoral Capitalism's early examples, the famous Electronics Park in Syracuse, New York. Before that was GE's 1940s move from its massive, concentrated Schenectady Works, an early twentieth century industrial icon.

Current business setbacks at the company have, for the moment, prevented the construction of a shiny new headquarters in Boston.

Why such shifts? The CEO of the chemical company Chemours offered a succinct answer: "They don't want to be confined to a building with a cafeteria, and be next door to a shopping center."[9] "They" are today's generation of college-educated, culturally active, aspirational seekers of exciting careers and lifestyles, more readily settled in urban contexts. A corporate move to a lively city center is thus somewhat strategic. GE's move, for example, involves several hundred executives, researchers and supporting staff, not its legions of mid-level managers, much less the rest of its thousands of employees.

An Industrious City Zone?

After a century and more in which employers and valued employees, along with concerned neighbors, sought to separate work from town centers, and companies sought environments conducive to worker productivity, a bustling city center has become this era's idea of a desirable realm for the industrious worker. But in a way, not as much has changed as might appear. Certain incompatibilities between work and living environments remain, now less about noise or pollution and more about conflicts in scale or density. Cities must still zone areas for "industry" so as to ensure that rising land values do not preclude the ability for industry to come, remain and grow, or adversely affect other uses nearby. Transport logistics and traffic management issues remain.

A Growing Demand: Balance

Here, however, is the difference: the industrious worker's growing desire and demand for quality of place and life-work balance. Whether it is the hopeful inventor in their proverbial backyard garage, the aspiring start-up operation sharing a WeWork suite for the moment, those embarking on a second career determined to pursue a dream (an idea) long held in abeyance, or the driven software coder at Google, they want a life more *in balance* between living, working and playing in a 16/7 (rest being essential too) animated, active urban environment. Such expectations will drive the role and place of much industry as our urban age evolves.[10]

Portions of this essay have been adapted from a chapter in *City on a Hill: Urban Idealism from the Puritans to the Present,* Cambridge, MA: Harvard University Press, 2019.

1 Dickens, Charles, *Hard Times*, chapter 5. Originally published 1859, New York: Simon & Schuster, 2007.
2 Fiegerman, Seth, "Facebook's glamorous new headquarters will make you hate your cubicle," MashableUK, www.mashable.com/2015/03/31/facebook-new-headquarters-photos/, published March 31, 2015.
3 Allen-Price, Olivia and Kim, Mina, "A Sneak Peek at Apple's New Cupertino Headquarters," KQED, ww2.kqed.org/news/2015/02/11/a-sneak-peek-at-apples-new-cupertino-headquarters/, published February 11, 2015.
4 Excellent overviews of the American company town include: Crawford, Margaret *Building the Workingman's Paradise: The Design of American Company Towns,* New York: Verso, 1995; Garner, John S., *The Model Company Town: Urban Design through Private Enterprise in Nineteenth-Century New England,* Amherst: University of Massachusetts Press, 1984; and Reps, John W., *Town Planning in Frontier America,* Columbia: University of Missouri Press, 1980.
5 Mozingo, Louise A., *Pastoral Capitalism: A History of Suburban Corporate Landscapes*, Cambridge, MA: MIT Press, 2011.
6 A full account of Route 128 has yet to be written but an excellent brief history is found in Tsipis, Yanni and Kruh, David, *Building Route 128: Images of America,* Portsmouth, NH: Arcadia Publishing, 2003.
7 The article continued: "...the so-called Spheres will serve as a haven of carefully tended nature geared to letting Amazonians break free from their cubicles and think disruptive thoughts. It's an internet-era, Pacific Rim answer to the architecturally astounding gardens set up by European monarchs during the Enlightenment era." Gonzalez, Angel, "Amazon's Spheres: Lush nature paradise to adorn $4 billion urban campus," *The Seattle Times,* January 3, 2017.
8 Eliot Brown, "Casualty of Cities' Resurgence: The Suburban Offices Left Behind," *Wall Street Journal*, January 13, 2016.
9 Mark Vergnano, cited in: Nelson D. Schwartz, "Why Corporate America Is Leaving the Suburbs for the City," *The New York Times,* August 1, 2016.
10 Another future for the industrious worker, anticipated since the dawn of the digital age, has unexpectedly been accelerated by the Covid-19 pandemic in 2020: the separation of work from places dedicated to work. How transformative this will be on work-life balance and on cities overall, especially once the pandemic abates, remains a fascinating question.

Philipp Aerni

THE CITY AS AN ECOSYSTEM

Corporate Expats
Embeddedness
Entrepreneurial Migrants
Globalization
Industry 4.0
Manorial System
New Work from Old
Urban Age
Urban Economics

Global Business and Migration as Forces of Urban Transformation

The twenty-first century will likely become known as the century of global urban development. There are several forces that point in this direction: The world has to cope with more people who primarily aim at becoming more affluent. They do so by moving from areas with few economic opportunities, mostly located in disconnected rural regions, to areas with more economic opportunities, mostly found in growing and globally connected cities. The result will be increased migration, and with it, more migration-induced urban growth in high and low-income countries alike (Saunders 2011, Aerni 2016).

Unfortunately, the current public discourse on urbanization trends rarely takes into account the question of trends in global migration. Many urban planners and designers in affluent countries are primarily concerned with social and environmental issues related to the "built environment" of their cities and "the modes of life and place attachments" within these cities. The urban sociologist Richard Sennett calls the former *ville* and the latter *cité*. In his most recent book, *Building and Dwelling: Ethics for the City* (2018), he argues that great urban planners have tended to be too focused either on the built environment, ignoring the needs of the people who live there, or on the people who contribute to the lived urban environment, ignoring the long-term challenges faced by urban development. In this context, Sennett and many other contemporary urban planners promote mixed neighborhoods, citizen participation, improved environmental quality, public and recreational spaces, urban densification and affordable housing to create an "open city." Sennett associates this term with an ideal place where everyone talks to everyone and global business has been successfully banned from local streets. Nehru Place, a chaotic and semi-informal site in New Delhi, India, seems to represent such an ideal urban settlement. However, it is not clear whether local people doing business there would agree with Sennett's rather romantic views. They probably associate openness more with being open for business and attractive for investment.

Especially the city's new arrivals, migrants in search of economic opportunities, may not regard global business as a threat to "the right to the city," the rallying cry of established urban dwellers engaged in cultural self-defense. Instead, they may rather prefer to advocate their "right to make a living" (Sandefur 2010). Moreover, it is also not clear who is entitled to claim a right to the city. Henri Lefebvre originally defined "The right to the city" in his seminal book *Le droit à la ville* (Lefebvre 1968) at a time when there was a clearly defined distinction between urban and rural, and when globalization was still constrained by the geopolitical standoff that marked the Cold War period. Moreover, Lefebvre understood that the main drivers of the continuous transformation and renewal of prospering cities are economic and social relations not confined to the city itself.

Migration today[1] reflects the decision made by millions of educated rural residents to abandon their disconnected villages in search of improved economic opportunities in urban settlements. They have tended to settle in the kind of suburban areas that emerged in the twentieth century widely disparaged in affluent societies as "urban sprawl" because of their car-oriented, low-rise lifestyle and the generic and monotonous character of their architecture. However, for migrants they provide most of the amenities missing in the regions they came from, and rents are still affordable (Angel 2011). As a result, population growth in recent decades has been concentrated in urban peripheries rather than inner-city areas. This "great suburbanization" (*The Economist* 2014) also contributed to new life in these areas through cultural and economic diversification.

Migrants vs. Expats

The decision made by migrants to settle mostly on the urban fringes produced extended landscapes of urbanization and increased investment in the expansion, operation and maintenance of urban infrastructure, housing and mobility. Both the political right and the political left in affluent countries criticize this situation. The former claims that migrants are unable to adjust to local values and norms, and argues that they are driven by selfish motives such as taking advantage of the social security system. The latter sees globalization as the root of all evil, leading to urban expansion at the expense of the natural environment and the quality of life of residents engaged in defending the urban commons against commercial interests. Depending on their economic circumstances, residents of affluent cities may either see poor migrants as vulnerable and traumatized victims or resent them for taking undeserved advantage of institutions and infrastructures. Both views are mistaken. Most migrants arrive in cities for economic, not political reasons. As such, they must be understood as active entrepreneurs rather than passive victims of political and economic distress elsewhere. They are mainly driven by the hope of earning a better living in places where well-paid jobs are available. In most cases, their primary motivation is not to exploit the social security system for personal enrichment. Instead, most are prepared to accept whatever jobs are on offer, seeking to gain local acceptance and respect and support their extended family left behind. In addition, they expect this move to increase their chances for a good marriage and an increased ability to invest in the future of their children. International migrants forego their political rights, since they are not entitled to vote in the host country. In return, they benefit from new economic rights by taking advantage of improved economic opportunities, mainly serving the needs of local residents and enterprises in return for a decent salary, which they may eventually invest in their own future business (Saunders 2011).

The other type of migrant is often called an "expat." Their motivation is not to escape poverty but to seek employment that best matches their skills and personal expectations. They are highly educated and work in well-paid economic sectors associated with "the creative class" (Florida 2003, 2017). As internationally coveted "talents," they may substantially contribute to the prosperity of the city where they work. But they have also become a major target of criticism by left-wing activists for appropriating inner-city living spaces and thereby forcing out established residents who can no longer afford the rent in expensive redeveloped urban residential areas. This trend has been associated with neoliberal urbanism leading to gentrification and more segregation in cities (Yip 2019, Cardullo and Kitchin 2019). It also has allegedly made urban social movements more politically oriented. Often they direct their hatred at external agents blamed for making urban life more expensive (see the current protests in Santiago, Chile, and Quito, Ecuador) or suppressing local freedom and autonomy (see Barcelona, Spain, and Hong Kong, China) (Karaliotas and Swyngedouw 2019). The urban scholar Sennett interprets these urban uprisings as part of a global resistance movement against the enemies of the "open city." Sennett argues that the latter prefer enclosed compounds, and consequently destroy the city's porous and informal character.[2] Since expats tend to work for multinational companies linked to global capitalism, they are often also associated with those enemies of the open city or the external forces endangering the urban commons and the viability of established urban small-scale businesses.

How Critical Is Critical Urban Theory?

Urban studies scholars are quite ambitious in that they are not content with merely understanding urban development in its historical and socioeconomic context. They also want to unveil the underlying power structures shaping the built environment (*ville)* and the way people live in the city (*cité).* As such, critical urban theory understands itself as the critique of power, inequality, injustice and exploitation within and among urban areas. Neil Brenner, a well-known urban theorist, defines it as follows: "It [critical urban theory] insists that another, more democratic, socially just and sustainable form of urbanization is possible, even if such possibilities are currently being suppressed through dominant institutional arrangements, practices and ideologies." (Brenner 2009, p. 198.)

This quote brings to mind the movie *The Matrix*. Its thesis is that an external power has taken over all human beings and hidden this control from them, but paradise can be restored if people come together to cast off that power. Whereas in the movie it is a classic Hollywood hero who liberates them from heteronomy by eliminating the external evil power, critical urban theorists like Brenner believe that organized urban resistance movements must assume this task by breaking the hold of the external power (mostly associated with agents of global capitalism) and then reconstructing the urban commons. Thus these urban resistance movements can restore a socially just urban society based on common property management and the protection of human rights against business interests. His narrative reveals the underlying mythical structure that critical urban theory has in common with ecosystem models (Rangan 2000). It implies that self-sufficient systems are harmonious unless they are disturbed by an externality. Identifying and removing the source of this disturbance may restore the original state of harmony. This narrative is especially attractive to adolescents who tend to believe that the world revolves around them rather than the other way around. It is also popular among citizens who long for a less complex world that provides meaning, orientation and identity (Aerni 2018).

In the current global debate on sustainable urbanization, the people who actively drive urban transformation, namely poor migrants and entrepreneurs connecting local with global business activities, do not shape the narrative. Their cultural background, concerns and anxieties are judged irrelevant because in the mythical portrayal of the urban struggle, they are confined to the role of poor passive (and disparaged) victims, stooges of the perpetrator (global capitalism). It is assumed that they have no agency themselves but instead should be thankful for the urban struggle against global business. The fact is, however, that cities are and always have been primarily a product of trade and technology driven by global business (with the exception of garrison towns). The prosperity of cities depends very much on the real agents of change, not the protesters but the entrepreneurial migrants.

The City as a Means to an End

The above Brenner quotation may be based on a mythical baseline assumption, but the challenge is real: How can we create more "democratic, socially just and sustainable forms of urbanization" in the twenty-first century? The answer lies in understanding how nineteenth-century urbanization and industrialization created the foundations for democratic, social and sustainable societies in twentieth-century Europe.

Some people confuse economic development with a zero-sum game by arguing that this progress came at the expense of the exploited countries in the South. However, this does not explain the rise of Asia in the twenty-first century global knowledge economy. Asia's success can hardly be exclusively attributed to some external force (Aerni 2019). Instead, it has much to do with intelligent domestic industrial policies that take advantage of foreign direct investment from the Global North. Such policies have enabled the build-up of the necessary domestic human and non-human capital stock in local business-oriented urban clusters (Special Economic Zones) that, in turn, lay the foundation for countrywide economic and social development (Aerni et al. 2016). The rise of Asia challenges the Western claim of intellectual and economic supremacy often associated with “the white man’s burden” (Easterly 2007). One may object by arguing that more prosperity has not led to more democracy or sustainability, especially in China. That may be true for the time being, but the same was true for Europe during its nineteenth-century industrial and urban transformation.

Why Urban Planners Need a Better Grasp of the Urban Economy

Urban theorists (Sheppard et al. 2013, Brenner and Schmid 2017) have so far primarily focused on the downside of the rise and expansion of business-oriented Asian cities. They may be right in the sense that many Asian urban planners have put too much emphasis on the built environment and too little on the actual needs of its dwellers – consequently many Asian metropolises have a lot in common with Le Corbusier’s vision of cities as machines with no history. Sennett criticizes these city governments for limiting themselves to the execution of distinct functions for their tax-paying inhabitants while not allowing them any say. These municipal administrations completely ignore what Sennett considers an urban system’s primary task: to foster interactions between the *ville* (the built environment) and the *cité* (the urban mentality). In his view, connecting the built and lived environments is more difficult if cities are erected and shaped to conform to closed systems allowing no role for urban residents to co-shape their neighborhoods. Such closed systems mainly serve the powerful interests of global business and its local agents, real estate developers.

Yet Sennett does not explain why global business cannot be compatible with local urban culture, and why foreign direct investment would prefer closed systems. Global business, in fact, thrives on open markets, shared platform technologies and the free movement of knowledge, people, capital and goods.

In essence, Sennett fails to grasp the economic foundation of the city, which, according to Jane Jacobs, is all about constantly adding new jobs to old ones (Jacobs 1969). In other words, entrepreneurs create new markets through innovation. In this regard, they may primarily consider the city a means to an end. They significantly shape the urban mentality and the lived environment – much more than the post-material urban flaneur Sennett has in mind. Business-minded local residents are not particular about whether their customers or suppliers represent global or local business. What matters to them is the customer’s ability to pay for products or services and the supplier’s ability to deliver what has been agreed.

As an elderly socialist who grew up in the Cold War period, Sennett finds it hard to connect the pursuit of business with “ethics.”

But when he argues that urban planners should be less concerned about the perfect design and focus more on serving the practical needs and preferences of its residents, one wonders why he does not use the term "business-oriented." After all, the story of the semi informal entrepreneur at Nehru Place meant to illustrate his point in his recent book (Sennett 2018) reveals a business-oriented mindset rather than an attitude of urban resistance. The semi-informal entrepreneur probably could not care less about whether he operates in an open or a closed city as long as he can make a living. He probably would be happy to do business with a multinational company that enabled him to attract more investment in the upgrading and professional management of his shop. Would that be less ethical than joining the resistance movement? The fact is that global businesses often abide by stricter environmental and social standards than their local counterparts, and they bring in new knowledge and networks that help a city and its dwellers prosper in the long run (Aerni 2018) In other words, cities that make an effort to connect local and global business may contribute more to inclusive growth, and consequently to the UN Sustainable Development Goals (SDG), than those that try to keep external forces at bay.

This UN project calls for sustainable cities and communities (goal 11). How that is interpreted will be crucial to effectively addressing the challenges of population growth and rural-urban migration in many low-income countries. After all, the more marginalized segments in society want more investment in controlled urban expansion that would make it easier for them to do business (Angel et al 2016). Some low-income countries are establishing new cities with business-friendly infrastructure and various forms of encouraging investments and local entrepreneurship (charter cities, smart cities, industrial zones, free trade zones). The aim is to replicate the success of the special economic zones (SEZ) established in China to jumpstart endogenous economic development – while also more effectively addressing the numerous shortcomings of that experience.

The idea of charter cities, however, comes not from China but medieval Europe. At that time, the so-called manorial system, governed by local land-owning aristocrats, was the foundation of the strictly hierarchical and static feudal society. Its subjects benefited from social and military protection in return for paying their dues to the landlord, serving in his army and providing a certain amount of unpaid labor. Although subjects had no economic or political rights, they could at least count on a certain material security since the manor was run primarily on the basis of autarkic production and consumption. It was a self-sufficient arrangement designed to care for all the estate's dependents. However, a growing share of the population was not integrated into such settlements – merchants, outcasts, refugees, scholars, beggars and the surplus offspring that poor families could not feed. These people were forced into a precarious life as migrant workers or mercenaries. In the twelfth century, the German Duke of Saxony, Henry the Lion, was the first to recognize that new cities could offer a future for this entrepreneurial surplus population if these settlements were run by institutions favoring trade and market creation. Henry eventually helped found Lübeck and numerous other towns in Northern Germany and Bavaria that became important merchant cities. Lübeck's economic success in particular led to the creation of new cities with similar charters along the Baltic. These cities formed a commercial and defensive confederation of merchant guilds and market towns that became known as the Hanseatic League. The League came to dominate trade along the Baltic coasts for three centuries and laid the foundation for the economic rise of Germany. This urban transformation in late medieval Europe did not, however, affect the self-sufficient manorial systems in the countryside until the nineteenth-century industrial revolution led to rapid structural changes in rural areas (Aerni 2015b).

The Industrious City

The term "fourth industrial revolution" was coined by Klaus Schwab (Schwab 2015). It refers to the convergence of different technologies in the fields of robotics, artificial intelligence, nanotechnology, quantum computing, biotechnology, 3D printing and the emerging Internet of Things, and the consequences of this convergence for communications and connectivity in twenty-first century societies and the global economy. Doomsayers predict it will lead to the destruction of traditional industries, the devaluation of practical skills, the end of privacy and widespread unemployment because robots will execute almost every function that humans currently perform. Yet this line of argument ignores one crucial fact: human knowledge did not evolve through individuals solving problems on their own but through collaboration – individuals thinking and working in conjunction with the thinking and working of others. The group intelligence that emerges from the shared intentionality of people in pursuit of a common purpose transcends the physical and intellectual capacities of the individuals involved – and it is this shared intentionality that robots will not be able to imitate. Advanced deep learning techniques may enable robots to do any job faster and better than humans, but they will never be able to create new markets that result in new jobs. These markets are always the result of a shared intentionality – the combination of different human mental and physical skills to achieve a particular outcome (Sloman and Fernbach 2017).

Therefore, if new technologies can be harnessed to improve the ability of humans to translate ideas into concrete and safe products and services to meet specific demands, then these technologies are more likely to become tools of economic empowerment – provided that the institutional framework and the physical and digital infrastructure are supportive and inclusive.

New urban spaces for the creation of a new type of Industrious City may become platforms designed to re-empower local business – taking advantage of advanced technologies, specialized business services and standardized modules of production that have become user-friendly and affordable.

Such an Industrious City may emerge in a former industrial zone of a larger established city, existing industry-owned land in a relatively central urban location, or in cities with lower land values.[3] The location can be envisioned as a special industrial zone offering all the amenities and institutions necessary to attract long-term investments, which then result in technology transfers, capacity development and further investment in the production of domestic goods and services, for the city itself and its rural hinterland as well. Industrious cities must therefore be conceived in the context of extended urban landscapes. They revive such landscapes as public-private initiatives mobilizing various levels of governance to support the shared facilities. This requires the political will to set up an institutional framework that enables an Industrious City to thrive. Industrious cities may prosper and expand if they can achieve their purpose – to reinvent urbanity as a site for productive exchange directed toward the constant creation of new markets and adding new jobs to old. Achieving this purpose requires overcoming the binomial mindset that sees new technologies only as a threat to traditional practices, and global companies only as a negative external force undermining local business and culture.

Global Business in Local Culture

Global companies are no longer exclusively focused on producing uniform, cheap goods for local markets in direct competition with local alternatives, as was the case in the era of mass production. Instead, they increasingly set up local subsidiaries that seek local partners to produce goods for the local market, tailored to local needs. This trend toward embedding global business activities in the local economy is supported by new technologies that make mass customization viable. Another factor encouraging this trend is the growing uncertainty provoked by the US-China trade war and the increasing complexity and fragility of global supply chains. Finally, a principled embeddedness approach makes sense for a multinational enterprise because of the need to invest in one of today's essential non-tangible assets: social capital. Social capital is earned by building up a local reputation as a reliable and trustworthy partner. Multinational enterprises reach this stage when they are no longer perceived as external stakeholders serving foreign interests at the expense of domestic concerns. This means they must become an integral part of the domestic economy and address domestic challenges that may also affect them in the long run. Once they are perceived as local stakeholders, their cost of doing business decreases and local revenues increase due to lower transaction costs, greater popularity with local customers and employees, and a secure long-term operating license.

A Return to the Manorial System?

In this light, an Industrious City that mainly uses its global connectivity to produce and sell locally may be seen as a return to the goals of the old manorial system. Like this base unit of the former feudal economy, it aims to ensure that locals do not just passively consume goods produced elsewhere, but are co-involved in production, which is then tailored to local needs. There are, however, two big differences. While the manorial system had nothing to offer those operating outside the system, the Industrious City mobilizes skills from outside to fulfill needs inside the system. Consequently it serves as an engine of local development, offering economic opportunities and more secure employment to migrants, as well as global job creation. Moreover, because the medieval manorial system was strictly hierarchical, it offered neither social mobility nor economic or political freedom. The landlord assumed the role of *pater familias*, taking care of his subjects while they were meant to remain loyal and dutiful to their master. In contrast, the Industrious City is characterized by flat hierarchies, openness and extensive economic freedom – and, depending on the country, also political freedom.

Concluding Remarks

The UN Sustainable Development Goals recognize the challenge of creating more inclusive, resilient and sustainable cities (SDG 11) that are well prepared for migration-induced urban growth. By offering migrants not just shelter but also economic opportunities, inclusive cities also contribute to the reduction of inequality within and between countries (SDG 10). However, solution-oriented practitioners are not shaping the current discourse on sustainable urbanization. Instead, this role is being played by urban theorists who interpret the current phase of urban transformation from an ideological point of view. They make use of a mythical narrative to interpret the global expansion of urban landscapes. It starts from the binomial baseline assumption that global business is an external force threatening urban lives and livelihoods. This dark force is supposedly being confronted by the good force – namely urban residents engaged in organized resistance to reclaim their right to the city, a vision that in most cases does not include migrants. Migrants' cultural backgrounds and personal concerns and anxieties are deemed irrelevant, because, in the mythical portrayal of the urban struggle, agency is only attributed to the incumbent class of urban residents involved in organized resistance. In most cases, however, these protesters represent the consumption-oriented, privileged class of urban society. Their concern is all about cultural identity, not economic survival. Consequently, they fear the true agents of change, namely local entrepreneurs and migrant workers involved in the transformation of urban landscapes, people who regard the city as a means to an end rather than an end in itself. This is in line with the views of the interdisciplinary urban scholar Jane Jacobs. Her theory of how cities evolve and contribute to either exclusive or inclusive development inside and outside the city (Jacobs 1969, 1985), has been empirically validated, yet it remains ignored in academia (Talbot 2019). Perhaps this is because it dispenses with the popular myth of an urban struggle between good and evil that tends to exclude the real drivers of local change.

The global economic and technological changes driving the fourth industrial revolution are likely to lead to a rediscovery of Jacobs in the twenty-first century. The resulting urban transformation may create additional threats to urban inclusiveness and sustainability, but it will also produce new urban spaces that may herald the reinvention of the Industrious City to address global social and environmental challenges. Now, however, the term Industrious City no longer means mass production factories and company towns, but a concentrated and coordinated diversity of economic activities. It must be understood as an innovation ecosystem that constantly adds new jobs to old, making use of new, user-friendly technologies to better cater to the needs of the local economy. As a consequence, the new Industrious City is very versatile and responsive, and may therefore lead to a far greater embeddedness of global business in local culture. It will also offer great opportunities for the creation of new productive and inclusive cities in developing countries, able to attract educated migrants and connect them to a larger economy. Eventually, this new reality will be reflected in the academic discourse, and hopefully lead to more inclusive and creative theories of urban development more in line with the UN Sustainable Development Goals and Agenda 2030.

1 In 2018, 55% of the world population lived in cities and the percentage is expected to increase to 68% by 2050, mainly due to internal migration within low-income countries, as well as international migration mostly within the regions of the Global South.

2 See Sennett's speech at the Harvard Graduate School of Design on October 17, 2017: www.youtube.com/watch?v=7PoRrVqJ-FQ.

3 The Industrious City could also be understood as the urban landscape as a whole. A requirement for urban production is a form of land rent (price) control to make investments more attractive. In Switzerland, the prevailing political will is against rezoning (e.g. Zurich, with SBB-Werkstätten). Further, some land already belongs to an industrial developer (e.g. V-ZUG), and land values are lower in some cities (e.g. Biel, Yverdon).

References:
Aerni, P. (2018). *Global Business in Local Culture: The Impact of Embedded Multinational Enterprises*, SpringerBriefs in Economics, 2018, pp. 1–122. (doi.org/10.1007/978-3-030-03798-7)
Aerni, P. (2019). "Langfristige Direktinvestitionen als Chance für lokales Unternehmertum und Beitrag zu inklusivem Wachstum," *Almanach Entwicklungspolitik 2020: Afrika zwischen Aufbruch und Armut*, Caritas-Verlag, Lucerne, pp. 171–180.
Aerni, P. (2016). "Coping with Migration-Induced Urban Growth: Addressing the Blind Spot of UN-Habitat," *Sustainability 8* (8). www.mdpi.com/2071-1050/8/8/800/pdf.
Aerni, P. (2015). *The Sustainable Provision of Environmental Services: from Regulation to Innovation*, Springer Series on CSR, Ethics and Governance, Springer, Heidelberg, July 2015.
Aerni, P. (2015b). *Neue Städte für Migranten*. NZZ Feuilleton, 2.12.2015. www.nzz.ch/feuilleton/kunst_architektur/neue-staedte-fuer-migranten-ld.3368.
Angel, S., Blei, A. M., Parent, J., Lamson-Hall, P., Galarza-Sanchez, N., Civco, D. L. and Thom, K. (2016). *Atlas of urban expansion – 2016 edition. Areas and Densities*, NYU Urban Expansion Program at New York University, UN-Habitat and the Lincoln Institute of Land Policy.
Angel, S., Parent, J., Civco, D. L. and Blei, A. M. (2011). *Making room for a planet of cities*, Lincoln Institute of Land Policy, Cambridge. www.lincolninst.edu/sites/default/files/pubfiles/making-room-for-a-planet-of-cities-full_0.pdf.
Cardullo, P. and Kitchin, R. (2019). "Smart urbanism and smart citizenship: The neoliberal logic of 'citizen-focused' smart cities in Europe," *Environment and Planning C: Politics and Space* 37, no. 5 (2019), pp. 813–830.
Brenner, N. and Schmid, C. (2017). "Planetary urbanization," *The Globalizing Cities Reader*, Routledge, pp. 479–482.
Brenner, N. (2009). "What is critical urban theory?" *City*, 13 (2–3), pp. 198–207.
Brenner, N., Marcuse, P., and Mayer, M. (eds.) (2012). *Cities for People, Not for Profit: Critical Urban Theory and the Right to the City*, Routledge.
Easterly, W. (2007). *The White Man's Burden: Why the West's Efforts to Aid the Rest Have Done So Much Ill and So Little Good*, Penguin Books.
Florida, R. (2003). *The Rise of the Creative Class,* Basic Books, New York.
Florida, R. (2017). *The New Urban Crisis: How Our Cities Are Increasing Inequality, Deepening Segregation, and Failing the Middle Class – And What We Can Do About It*, Basic Books, New York.
Jacobs, J. (1969). *The Economy of Cities*, Vintage Press.
Jacobs, J. (1985). *Cities and the Wealth of Nations,* Vintage Press.
Karaliotas, L. and Swyngedouw, E. (2019) "Exploring insurgent urban mobilizations: from urban social movements to urban political movements?" *Handbook of Urban Geography*, Edward Elgar Publishing.
Lefebvre, H. (1968). *Le droit à la ville*, Anthropos, Paris.
Ma, Y., Rong, K., Mangalagiu, D., Thornton, T. F. and Zhu, D. (2018). "Co-evolution between urban sustainability and business ecosystem innovation: Evidence from the sharing mobility sector in Shanghai," *Journal of Cleaner Production*, 188, pp. 942–953.
Sandefur, T. (2010). *The Right to Earn a Living: Economic Freedom and the Law*, Cato Institute, Washington.
Saunders, D. (2011). *Arrival City: How The Largest Migration in History Is Reshaping Our World*, Vintage Press.
Schaefer, M. and Hosoya, H. (2018). "The Industrious City: Rethinking Urban Industry in the Digital Age," option studio, Harvard Graduate School of Design, Boston, May 1, 2018.
Schwab, K. (2015). "The Fourth Industrial Revolution: What It Means and How to Respond," *Foreign Affairs*, December 2015. www.foreignaffairs.com/articles/2015-12-12/fourth-industrial-revolution.
Sennett. R. (2018). *Building and Dwelling: Ethics for the City,* Allen Lane, London.
Sheppard, E., Leitner, H. and Maringanti, A., 2013. "Provincializing global urbanism: A manifesto," Urban Geography, 34 (7), pp. 893–900.
Sloman, S. and Fernbach, P. (2017). *The knowledge illusion: the myth of individual thought and the power of collective wisdom*, Pan Macmillan.
Talbot, D. (2019). *Who the hell is Jane Jacobs? And what are her theories all about*? Bowden & Brazil.
The Economist (2014). "A Planet of Suburbs," December 4, 2014 (available online).
The Economist (2019). "Special Report: Global Supply Chains," July 11, 2019.
Yang, F., and Xu, J. (2018). "Privacy concerns in China's smart city campaign: The deficit of China's Cybersecurity Law," *Asia & the Pacific Policy Studies*, 5 (3), pp. 533–543.
Yip, N.M., López, M. A. M. and Sun, X. (eds.) (2019). *Contested Cities and Urban Activism*, Palgrave Macmillan.

SWISS FACTORY

Joël Tettamanti

pp. 117–125
Untitled images from the studies “Chemicals,” 2006–2007

126–132
Untitled images from the studies “Freitag,” 2013

133–141
Untitled images from the studies “Victorinox,” 2009

SCHICHT
1

Clariant

Swiss Factory

TECNORAMA

Swiss Factory

Vakuum Ltg. K10
Kondensat

Swiss Factory

Swiss Factory

FREITAG
SHOP
ZÜRICH
TIPHOOK
SUPERMARKET

Swiss Factory

Swiss Factory

3410-30

Swiss Factory

RASTER

Automated Transport
Human Smart City
Intelligent Urban Logistics
Just-in-Time
Logistical Partnership Models
Permanent Logistics
Three-Dimensional Logistics
Verticalization

Interview by Markus Schaefer
October 17, 2019
Rapp Trans, Zurich

URBAN LOGISTICS

Danny Riedel / Thomas Schmid

Danny Riedel is Deputy Managing Director of Rapp Industrieplaner AG and is responsible mainly for clients from trade and industry. Prior to this, he was a member of the Executive Board at OTB AG in Basel. He specializes in logistics and factory concepts and the implementation of major projects. In addition to being a member of the Logistikleiter Club Schweiz (Logistics Manager Club Switzerland), the Verband Intralogistik Schweiz (Swiss Intralogistics Association) and the Bundesvereinigung Logistik (Federal Logistics Association), Danny Riedel is also involved in the field of Building Information Modeling within the Rapp Group.

Thomas Schmid, Senior Consultant and Associate Partner at Rapp Trans AG, has been working in the traffic and transport industry for twenty years. At present, his main focus is on management consultancy in the field of freight management and logistics for clients from industry, trade, logistics and real estate, and for the public sector with regard to cargo handling. He teaches at the Institute for Transport Planning and Systems at the ETH Zurich, at the Zurich University of Applied Sciences in Winterthur and at the Lucerne University of Applied Sciences and Arts.

Perhaps we could begin with you briefly explaining what each of you does and in what way you complement each other.

Schmid

In simple, classical terms, logistics consists of haulage, handling and storage operations. As transport engineers, we specialize in haulage and handling. Our colleagues are responsible for anything to do with the interior of the buildings and the architecture, the processes in the buildings and intralogistics. And that's where we complement each other. We face specific challenges at logistics sites, especially a certain degree of displacement pressure as well as other types of outside pressure. If someone from area development or property development comes to us and asks: Does this company need so many tracks? Can this be optimized, so that new developments are possible in the neighborhood? – then we have to devise solutions: how can something be enhanced so that, on the one hand, the site can continue to operate normally and, on the other hand, urban development can be carried out, for example planning track crossings, improving junctions and releasing potential.

A company's main concern is being easy to reach, so transport is key when it comes to its location. It's a very tricky task, as is working together with area development. If you include transport, utilities and the functions for loading and unloading right from the outset, you arrive at new or different solutions for the positioning of functions and buildings on a site.

The first stage of Switzerland's industrialization took place mainly outside the cities, until the railways made it possible to settle near the cities. When the truck revolution came along, the suburbs gained importance, and industrial parks that could only really be reached by road. There's constant talk of how these things are changing now. Is something as fundamental happening in transport at the moment?

Schmid

There's a theory being promoted, for example, that goods are the best thing to use automated transport for, as opposed to people, which is why tests are being conducted with drones and parcel robots. These are the first signs of automated dispatch in the small volume sector. The digital connecting of trucks, "platooning," is also being tested. Automation is especially noticeable in this area.

The problem we're having is that the existence of Swiss Railway's cargo service is under threat from digitalization and the impact of structural changes in freight: more and more freight is being dispatched, but it consists of smaller units. That's the result of just-in-time and lean management strategies. No one has the space on their premises, or the time, to store all these individual units until there's enough to fill up a whole cargo train or even just a container. Those are the relevant criteria. We're talking here about permanent logistics, something we're seeing in business everywhere. Goods are supposed to be available quickly, wherever and whenever they're needed. Ideally, industry should be avoiding waste and only producing what there's demand for. So there are no large warehouses, no stock, etcetera, everything is in a flow and logistics is moved from industrial parks onto the transport network instead. These are trends that oppose the railway system and the use of trains, and are making it difficult to consolidate many small orders into mass dispatches.

If we look at the buildings and architecture: are we seeing a paradigm shift in organizational and technical terms? And what does this mean for inside and outside the site boundaries, the building and the company?

Riedel

Industry is facing different types of issues, though I might add that it wasn't industry but the consumer that triggered the demand for small orders. Industry sees itself forced to react, and with all of the upstream and downstream processes in the supply chain. One important point is lean management, process optimization, which of course is especially affecting Switzerland because it's an expensive location. Swiss companies are innovative and just as keen when it comes to keeping their processes under control and optimized. And they have to do this because of demand, which has changed from the large batches previously produced to one-piece flows, where customers can order a product that they've practically designed themselves out of modules. That naturally poses a challenge for the production system. The increased need for retooling the machines, which wasn't necessary before, costs time, and this time has to be minimized. I have to be able to create a larger number of variations. This means that I have a completely different inventory than before; the range of possible versions is almost infinite. And that of course affects the building. Another aspect is that customers order today and it's actually too late if they don't receive it until the next day, because they want it right away. So what does that mean? Order cycles are getting ever shorter, which means that productivity needs to become ever higher. I can increase productivity in two ways: either by taking on more staff, though at some point my system will still become overloaded, or by automation. Automation will therefore continue to increase, but even then there's a limit.

A second point is storage. Thomas, you said that we're only really producing the things that have been ordered or that there's demand for. That's somewhat wishful thinking. It works for companies who have got their processes under control, but most of them haven't yet. This means that we're still dependent on storage space, and that's dead capital. Warehouses are big, they need space. And that's the second impact on industry in the city: space. In the past, and you can see this clearly in older industrial areas, storage halls were built that had one, two or perhaps three stories, with a relatively large footprint, which no one could afford today. So you have to build upwards, go vertical. From my point of view it's a good strategy, even though there are different risks involved, of course, especially regarding the flow of goods and intralogistics, because this is how bottlenecks arise. There's a major focus now on the logistics systems that are needed for transporting freight vertically.

Let's take V-ZUG as an example, which is currently modernizing its factory premises with its new Tech Cluster Zug, a company operating in a sector that's not particularly innovative and where a certain volume must be produced in order for them to survive. What does it mean for such a company when it has to reduce batch sizes and push ahead with verticalization?

Riedel

It's clearly visible in V-ZUG's old structures: in their large factory, all their assembly lines are suitably arranged side by side. If we had the space, then of course we could build like that. But we haven't. So we layer the individual lines and connect them to the upstream and downstream production processes. To do that, we not only have to be able to connect the machines to each other, for example, but also link the data. It requires a seamless inventory management system where all these highly complex processes can be controlled.

If we define V-ZUG as a self-contained system: everything that happens on the site is dealt with by the information system and the vertical transport chain. Now, of course, changes on the site are having an impact on the town of Zug and its infrastructure. And public space cannot be controlled. In other words, this is where the technically ideal industrial process chain comes into contact with the much more chaotic urban space. What is your opinion on this issue?

Riedel

Today's customers want to order today and take delivery tomorrow. The consequence, from my perspective, is that the volume of freight per truck or vehicle is decreasing, but the vehicles have to go on the road with growing frequency. That means that in the future, the road network is going to come under a different degree of strain. Where outgoing goods are concerned, this will be caused less by heavy vehicles and more by vans and small trucks.

Currently, deliveries actually occur on a business-to-business basis; in other words, I get goods delivered one-to-one from ten or twenty suppliers. That's a huge waste, because one pallet is delivered by a thirty or forty-ton truck up to thirty times a day. One solution here would be consolidation – creating urban routes and that way reducing the volume of traffic in the city. Especially heavy goods traffic.

If we now supply this site, this enclosed V-ZUG system, with these small batches, and then on the one hand I have trucks that are coming in more frequently, and on the other hand small delivery vans that are going out more frequently. What impact will this have on traffic in the city and for the city? Is it sustainable and intelligent? How must cities adapt to this?

Schmid

There are already companies offering platforms where different customer volumes are bundled and distributed on urban tours to reduce the number of trips. Other companies advertise for business by stating that they deliver in the city energy-efficiently and with zero CO_2-emissions using various environmentally friendly means of transport: by cargo train to the City Hub, then by electric truck to the Micro Hub and from there by cargo bike to the city centers. This is how logistics chains develop, which leads to further reloading or location issues: where do the reloading and transfers take place? These are vital issues, which are currently undergoing intensive discussion in cities under the heading of intelligent urban logistics.

Riedel

I'd like to add to that: I think what will be necessary for the next phase is partnership models. Today, classic haulage companies make their own plans and then, because of these much shorter cycles in demand, make rather inefficient use of trucks. It doesn't matter whether it's a three-quarters-full or half-full truck or a van. If the individual carriers formed a network, an exchange could take place about what capacity is still available in which vehicle. But of course this requires cooperation between the individual players. I believe we are a long way from achieving this at the moment.

Schmid

Yes, we're observing a consolidation in the corporate landscape of logistics, which means that network players are emerging. Companies that can secure such networks, can integrate further partner companies, have redundancies in their systems and can choose from many alternatives – they'll be the winners in this development.

Does any type of Google or Uber Freight exist? A company which owns absolutely nothing itself but is just a network or a platform?

Riedel

I think there will be partnership models in the future. At the end of the day, it's a question of resources and who they're owned by. The resources belong to the large companies that have the vehicles, and those are much more expensive than the private cars owned by Uber drivers. Companies would have to more or less outsource a portion of their work, namely their entire fleet management – a key element of their know-how, their core competence, actually – and then provide only the infrastructure. I don't know whether the business would be worth their while.

Still on the question of resilience, you referred to it as robust supply chains at one point: How will this work in the future? What does robustness mean and how is it being pursued right now?

Schmid

The pressure is caused by this lack of flexibility. Because everything is strictly timetabled, if a disruption occurs then I have to have an immediate alternative. And that leads to plans, alternative plans, and agreements. So you anticipate those alternatives and you safeguard yourself. That's the way to deal with this need for flexibility.

Riedel

The haulage problem is currently more of a two-dimensional issue. In Switzerland and in the cities, goods are mainly transported by rail and road. Porsche and Boeing are currently working on a type of urban aircraft. That could be interesting. I think that in the future we'll be able to handle some of the small-volume business, but possibly also some of the heavier freight by air. Transport drones are a beginning, but their maximum load is only about two and a half kilos. If we succeed in developing aircraft that can also transport larger loads, up to one or two tons, like Cargo sous terrain, but in the air, not underground, that would be very interesting.

If we assume that industrialization is the reason why we have a liberal country, is it then true that digitalization and automation will inevitably lead to an authoritarian state, since a basic democratic order cannot deliver the necessary process management?

Schmid

No. In my opinion, this is where digitalization will reach its limits. Not everything that is technically feasible will be accepted by society and the economy. It will become evident what is acceptable, and what society and industry are prepared to invest or to give up in favor of digitalization. Even if digitalization can facilitate a central and controlling authority, I don't think it requires an authoritarian state.

I'm rather Marxist in that respect: technological change generates new institutional requirements, and institutions either move with the times or they don't. If you could imagine a liberal civil-society solution, what would it look like?

Schmid

Smart City concepts have already gone through various phases. These days it's all about Smart City 3.0, the Human Smart City, where the focus is not on technology but on people. This is where opportunities are opening up for participation, involvement, codetermination and so on. There are a great many possibilities, including in the democratic process, which can be simplified thanks to digitalization. I tend to support this approach, too. It's a chance to use information and communication technologies to shape development processes by involving and networking the different stakeholders. It provides transparency, makes processes visible, generates an understanding of the facts and communicates them. I actually see a great many opportunities for democracy and for the shaping of our future.

Gesa Ziemer

THE CITY AS AN INTERFACE – ANALOG AND DIGITAL ASPECTS

City as Interface
Civic Tech Society
Decision Support Systems
Digital Urban Twins
Industry 4.0
Internet of Things
Onlife

Digitalization

Cities around the world are not only getting bigger, they are mainly becoming denser. According to UN counts, there are now more than thirty megacities in the world with a population of more than ten million. In a time of global extreme urbanization, cities are having to face many challenges if they are to continue to function at all as a form of organization. One solution recommended for the current issues of urbanization – even in much smaller European cities – is that digitalization would ensure the smooth running of many processes. Digitalization means first of all transferring analog data into digital storage. It also means the analysis, systematization and curation of data sets and processing them further in the form of products and services. Cities have always been places of technological innovation, where material and dematerializing processes have been connected. Just as building a house has evolved from pure craftsmanship to machine-controlled construction, our mobility has also changed from analog walking to high-speed movement. However, technologies are never successful because they are technically innovative; they become so when people make use of them and this use enables new ways of living together. The interesting question that therefore arises is how the interfaces of analog and digital practices are shaped and how this changes urban development.

Today's Industrious City is often thought of as a smart city, the aim of which is to make cities more efficient, technologically more advanced, but also ecologically and socially more sustainable with the use of "technical-informational infrastructure."[1] It should be emphasized that this definition is not only about efficiency, but also about ecology and sustainability[2]. However, whether a city meets this requirement is something that has to be critically reviewed on a case-by-case basis. There is no doubt that digital technologies are having a major impact on cities and, above all, on their inhabitants today: we use apps instead of analog maps to find our way around; we rent and share bicycles or cars via sharing or mobility-on-demand systems; we travel with digital booking systems that hardly require us to plan our travel anymore; our public authorities are increasingly switching to digital services so we no longer have to go along in person with every form; and we use social media and images, which then generate new images, to navigate ourselves and others through our environment. Cities are being equipped with sensors that provide real-time data, and more and more homes are being built as smart buildings. Urban development and the building industry are also increasingly based on data that enables dynamic scenario development and promises interdisciplinarity, such as in Building Information Modeling (BIM). The city is constantly producing data, but the citizens themselves are also generating more and more, for example with the use of apps or social media. The question arising in the discourse about smart cities is therefore not only how the city's data flows, but also how people can become more conscious of their own data and retain access to it.

However, the city has not only become a big-data producer but also an interface that we are heavily involved in due to our use of it, and which we constantly help to shape. The Internet-of-Things technologies have connected our material possessions such as our cars, refrigerators and wristwatches to the virtual world of the Internet, and the city has also become a big Internet-of-Things platform. Intelligent traffic lights, streets and buildings, which constantly scan and evaluate our driving, living, consumption and social behaviors and then generate new offers, have long since determined our everyday life. This exchange between the material and non-physical world leads to objects communicating with each other, such as our apartment door, which automatically recognizes whether we are authorized to enter and causes the heating system to raise the temperature in the room slightly. In the field of science, this development is currently being dealt with under the banner of New Materialism. The key message is that data should not be perceived as rigid objects, but as dynamic beings that are developing a will of their own to which we, as consumers, constantly react. The more data is available and the better its quality, the more intelligent the applications become. This credo applies not only to the field of artificial intelligence, but above all to every instance of data capture, systematization and processing in a city. It becomes absolutely clear from this that dealing with large amounts of data and applications always creates ambivalence: on the one hand, digitalization makes it possible to provide practical services for users, while on the other hand almost any tool can be misused to monitor and centrally control a society. This ambivalence must be withstood where digitalization is concerned; it is therefore all the more important to develop the highest possible level of data consciousness in people and help them become technologically adept.

Transitioning from Analog to Digital Practices

If we summarize the major aspects of a city's digitalization, then growth can be expected in the areas of automation and networking, the spread of digital terminals (modularization), increased data generation and improvements in computing and storage capacity. If we take a close look at the processes in a city, however, we have not yet reached the age of digitalization, but are rather at the transition stage from analog to digital capturing systems and applications. The philosopher Luciano Floridi emphasizes that we are currently operating neither completely offline nor completely online, but are living more of an "onlife,"[3] which means that we are online but still living a physical life. We are, then, at the transition from digital to analog practices. There are many examples of this in urban life: for example, in some places, civic participation is still being carried out using pen, paper and cards, while in others it is already modularized in the form of online surveys or touch-tables, so that all results are directly available in a digital format.

The extent of digitalization varies not only from city to city and country to country, but also within a city. Depending on data protection, security requirements, the political situation, legislation or user data culture, a city or region will have a certain data situation. In Germany, for example, health and financial data are subject to a higher level of data protection than area data, which is why, though there is a high level of personal privacy protection, there are also fewer digital innovations in these areas. The fluctuation between the tangible and intangible world applies to the city in general. Even if a building is planned and constructed using a BIM program, at some point it will have a physical existence. Even if architectural competitions are increasingly evaluated on data-based scenarios, the design must ultimately be realized. Even if civic participation changes with online procedures, the citizens will still be riding their bicycles from A to B through the city. Digital technologies do not simply replace analog actions; instead, we are constantly called upon to cooperate with machines and critically examine whether the use of these technologies will also lead to the improvement of processes and tangible products.

New Forms of Cooperation – CityScopes in the CityScienceLab

The rhetoric that many cities use in relation to digitalization is often driven by business more than by the genuine demands of citizens. Certainly, this should provoke critical reflection; however, it should result not only in the deconstruction of naïve promises that technology will save us. It is also just as essential to use case studies to analyze in detail whether the use of technologies has a sustainable, ecological and social impact on the inhabitants of a city. There should be differentiated consideration of where a city's digitalization really generates non-profit added value for the inhabitants, because this is precisely the decisive criterion of a meaningful digital city.

This is the goal that the CityScienceLab[4] of HafenCity University of Hamburg has been trying to achieve for several years in cooperation with the MIT Media Lab in Cambridge, Massachusetts. The research lab builds what they call CityScopes – interactive, data-based city models that can be used to visualize and model the current state of a city and its future scenarios. "What if…?" is a question that is discussed with citizens and stakeholders from the public administration, civil society, business, politics and science. A good-quality data situation and a transparency law make it possible to productively discuss topics such as housing construction, social infrastructure and mobility with all of Hamburg's stakeholders and subsequently arrive at suitable solutions that are always compromises. We also call our tools Decision Support Systems, which not only facilitate decision making, but above all make it easier to understand. The reason is this: if it is clearly recognizable how a compromise was reached and what consequences it has, then the acceptance of all the parties involved is much greater. As cities become more and more densely populated and the pressure on land increases, conflicts between the various interest groups also become more intense. In this respect, the interdisciplinary team from the fields of architecture, computer science, urban design, cultural and social sciences also sees its work as a contribution to a lively and constructive practice of democracy, as it aims to minimize simplifications, angry citizen's protests and unproductive populism in favor of a dialogue-based discussion culture that permits multicausality. Every research project is therefore based on three aspects: new forms of collaboration, scenario building and data visualization. In the Finding Places[5] project in the winter of 2015/2016 for example, when around 40,000 refugees arrived in the city within the space of four months, we discussed temporary accommodation with Hamburg residents. The city council was faced with the enormous challenge of providing dry and safe accommodation for the many people – and in a growing city with almost none to offer. The availability of good-quality and transparent area data made it possible for us to hold workshops with citizens and stakeholders and discuss with them the distribution of refugee housing on public areas. This project – alongside many other political activities – helped to prevent a referendum that could have led to the complete closure of the city's borders and subsequently to the polarization of its citizens.

This example shows the potential that the use of spatial data can have. Having digitally collated many urban planning criteria such as development plans, zoning, nature conservation requirements and the ownership of public spaces, it was possible to apply this project to other future topics of urban development. An extended version of civic participation is currently taking place within the framework of the Digital Participation System (DIPAS)[6] on the subject of housing construction, transport and nature conservation. We can already see that with the use of online surveys and CityScopes, many more people from different social groups participate and make surprisingly informed and constructive contributions. These are now being summarized and evaluated by a Natural Language Processing application. The comments are machine-analyzed and clustered, meaning that as the number of responses increases, the citizens' opinions can be read in a more differentiated way. This represents a new challenge: how can one filter and standardize the data that the comments produce without levelling out too much of their meaningful language expression, which is characterized not only by content but also by linguistic style? Such applications are still very much embedded in research but must be put to practical use in the long term.

Urban Data Hubs – Digital Urban Twins

If a city is to have access to such data in the first place, it is necessary to set up Urban Data Platforms or Urban Data Hubs. Open and collaborative platforms ensure that relevant data is made available to people, authorities and innovation hubs with small and large companies. In data portals, urban data such as statistics, geodata, reports and contracts are made available as open data for further use at municipal, federal and international level. Data on particulate matter pollution can be accessed, as can walking and driving times, school locations, or information such as a tree cadaster that geographically locates street trees. Urban data platforms are systems that combine different databases and sources that often exist separately. In many cities, for example, there are different websites for administrative and geodata, whose structure is often incomprehensible to the layperson. Interoperability is a central aspect of data usability: for data to be linked easily and well it is essential that standards are met. Digitalization as well as processes for the acquisition and processing of new data – statistical data as well as data from the rapidly growing field of real-time acquisition – must therefore meet clearly defined requirements. We can still see today how authorities sometimes continue to store their data in data silos that only they can access. Urban data hubs, on the other hand, attempt to free data from these silos, thus enabling more interdisciplinary work between public administration departments.

The aim is to use this structure to significantly improve the findability and the usability of existing urban data, which involves a high degree of conceptual work. Many open data platforms suffer from the high usage barrier of what is on offer: people who cannot process data in its raw form and are not data-literate are usually barred from access until applications are developed that can convert the data into a readable form. Consequently, some cities are making vigorous use of data visualization as a means to making data understandable. Good illustration – for example in dashboards or cockpits – supports urban planning and is only possible with cooperation between the disciplines of computer science and (communication) design, so that the interfaces are attractive and can be used at a low threshold.

As part of this development, cities are increasingly developing Digital Urban Twins (DUT). A DUT is a dynamic, virtual, interactive 3D city model and a collaborative city data platform that can be used by experts and citizens alike. Digital twins are – to put it simply – digital replicas of material objects (such as buildings, streets, bodies of water) or intangible process chains (such as administrative procedures, civic participation, traffic control), which are built from data and algorithms and connected to the real world via sensors. Digital twins already form the basis today of the process chains of Industry 4.0. They accompany the entire development, production and operating cycles of a product or service. Thanks to virtual simulation models, processes can be planned, optimized, predicted and adapted. Naturally, setting up a twin for an entire city is much more complex than for a component in a production chain. Research is currently being conducted on the use of demonstrators and simulations that can improve the current state and forecasts by means of future scenarios (housing construction, social infrastructure, new mobility, tourism, etc.) as well as decision making. There will be integration of 3D technologies and mixed reality tools, which open up new possibilities for urban mediation. At the same time, a DUT can be thought of as a business platform onto which local start-ups and companies are docked. Well-developed twins should also provide opportunities for cities to network with each other.

Data and Technology Control for Cities and People

The Digital Urban Twin is a good example of how cities need to work with businesses if they want to offer digital services. So, the question is this: How can cities cooperate with the large global IT companies and still retain control over the shaping of their own digital future? How can citizens develop and maintain technological sovereignty? Another question: How can independently designed data lead to the use of technology for the common good? Technological sovereignty also means empowering cities and people to solve their issues themselves and organize them beyond a "dictatorship of no alternatives," to quote a phrase from the philosopher Roberto Unger.[7] This claim seems presumptuous when you look at a project like Quayside, a smart city at the Port of Toronto, developed by Sidewalk Labs[8] in cooperation with the city. One would expect that a company like Google, which belongs to the Alphabet Group, would collect, evaluate and market data and thus restrict rather than promote possibilities for acting toward the common good. Companies have far more personnel, computing and IT capacities and technical know-how, which cities depend on. Today, cities are often referred to as digital test sites where digital innovations are experimented with under real conditions, such as autonomous vehicles in the city center or on expressways. This generates a great deal of data, which not only the companies should be permitted to store but must also be made usable for the city. It remains a huge challenge for cities to cooperate with companies and at the same time follow a self-determined path that enables them to use technologies and innovations for the benefit of their citizens.

If one looks at the issue in more differentiated terms, then technological sovereignty should be sought at two levels at least: first, cities should try to maintain control over data, sensors and algorithms. Secondly, cities should pursue active cooperation with citizens. Instead of developing new services solely on the basis of technical possibilities, they should be designed more in cooperation with people. This would result in a user orientation, which should be supported, or civic engagement, also encompassed by the term Civic Tech Society. How do cities implement a focus on the common good and technological sovereignty in this regard? The way to get access is for the data to be considered as commons, and for public services to work with open standards and open source, so that data can be shared in the sense of a sharing economy.

Thinking with Data – An Outlook

Interdisciplinary use of data by different stakeholders from civil society, politics, science and business leads to people actually coming together in an analog way and achieving better results, greater acceptance and identification through joint decision making. In contrast to older technologies, in the digital city increasingly large amounts of data first have to be curated, which also leads to higher scaling; and secondly, transparency in the good sense means that there is less domination knowledge. Open data policies ensure that everyone has access to the same data and is equally called upon to creatively combine data quality. This could spark a new way of thinking with data. Data enable new perspectives on old problems, or in other words: horizontal, combinatory thinking – similar to the rhizomatic thinking of the philosopher Gilles Deleuze – has long since found its way into urban development. In the Finding Places project, for example, transparent data portals made it possible to find good locations for refugee accommodation by creatively combining spatial, educational, financial and mobility data. The potential is far from being exhausted, but the example shows what possibilities are lying dormant in such applications. And once again, the meeting of people, the moderation of discussions, the involvement of the districts and so on were successful at both analog and digital interfaces.

On the Productive Aspect of Digitalization

Nevertheless, the question must now be posed more radically and philosophically about the influence of data on future urban development: Will people control cities at all in the future or will the city control its people?[9] Will the networking of objects (such as cars, traffic lights, streets, apartments, etc.) via the Internet result in technologically intelligent urban control that is largely independent of people? According to the philosopher Yuval Noah Harari, the use of technology causes intelligence and consciousness to become detached from one another and the belief in intelligence to grow out of all perspective.[10] This means that human subjectivity, sensuality and experience, qualities that we associate with consciousness, will no longer play an important role. Consciousness also develops in relation to materiality, because sensual perception (and thus learning) takes place on the basis of materials. Will we come into contact with material less and less through digitally autonomous controls? Why do we still need a taxi driver who can skillfully drive us through the city, converse with us, show us the sights in passing, and in doing so remind us of the materiality of monuments and buildings, when autonomous vehicles can independently anticipate traffic jams and take us quickly and safely to our destination? Intelligent technologies are sufficient for collecting data, and process it using algorithms and artificial intelligence, optimizing our lives in the cities and making them more efficient. So why use subjective evaluations, memories or (sensual) experiences of materials to appropriate the city?

Such considerations are of course nothing new; they sound like science fiction to the ears of some and arise with regularity when technical upheavals are at work. The image of Charlie Chaplin in his factory's clockwork mechanism in the 1936 film *Modern Times*, which reflects the influence of new work methods in the age of industrialization, demonstrates impressively how man becomes appropriated by new technologies. No one can predict whether cities will ever relatively autonomously control people and make many workers superfluous. At present, I believe it makes sense not to consider the issue from such polar angles, but to launch combinations of consciousness and intelligence that address dangers and potentials equally – and thus do justice to the topic's high degree of complexity. This also means that the abstractness and intangibility of data should always be seen in relation to the material city. The robot on the building site will not replace the craftsmen and women immediately, but it will continue to change the work. People who perform this craft will, like many others, eventually be working with semi-autonomous machines. Historically, reference has been made repeatedly to the great adaptability of us humans, who will perform combinations of analog and digital activities.

The good digital city will never be an optimized and efficient city only in *quantitative* terms; more than anything it must consider *quality* of life. Or, to use Harari's words once more: Is there perhaps a way to bring intelligence and consciousness together in urban development after all? We are at the transition point between analog and digital and thus, once again, at the crossroads where we have to negotiate between man and technology. The crucial question is how we can enrich intelligent urban systems with subjective experiences, consciousness and materiality, because the digital city has to offer more than just increased efficiency. Homo digitalis still has components of a homo materialis and must configure this interaction – with all its ambivalences.

1 Christoph Bieber and Peter Bihr, *Digitalisierung und die Smart City. Ressource und Barriere transformativer Urbanisierung. Expertise für das WBGU-Hauptgutachten Der Umzug der Menschheit: Die transformative Kraft der Städte,"* Berlin, 2016, p. 4.
2 Cf. Wissenschaftlicher Beirat der Bundesregierung Globale Umweltveränderungen (WBGU), *Digitalisierung. Worüber wir jetzt reden müssen,* Berlin, 2018.
3 Cf. Luciano Floridi, *The Onlife Manifesto. Being Human in a Hyperconnected Era*, Cham: Springer International Publishing, 2015.
4 Cf. www.hcu-hamburg.de/research/csl/.
5 Cf. www.findingplaces.hamburg.
6 Cf. www.hamburg.de/dipas.
7 Evgeny Morozov and Francesca Bria, *Die smarte Stadt neu denken. Wie urbane Technologien demokratisiert werden können,* Berlin: Rosa Luxemburg Stiftung 2017, p. 50.
8 Cf. www.sidewalklabs.com.
9 Cf. Nina Hälker and Gesa Ziemer, Digitale Stadtpolitiken. Wie Daten Städte steuern," in: Ingrid Breckner, Albrecht Göschel and Ulf Matthiesen (ed.), *Stadtsoziologie und Stadtentwicklung. Handbuch für Wissenschaft und Studium,* Baden-Baden: Nomos 2020, (currently in press).
10 Cf. Yuval Noah Harari, *Homo Deus. Eine Geschichte von morgen,* Munich: C. H. Beck, 2017.

Area Development
Continuous Reinvention
Densification
Generic Space
Hybrid City
Industrious Architect
Live Work
Maag-, Löwenbräu-, Sulzer-Areal
More Software Less Hardware
New Sensibility
Rural Modern
Serendipity
Systems Thinking

Interview by Hiromi Hosoya
September 23, 2019
Hosoya Schaefer Architects, Zurich

PRODUCTION SPACE

Mike Guyer / Momoyo Kaijima / Markus Schaefer

Mike Guyer founded the Annette Gigon / Mike Guyer Architekten practice together with Annette Gigon in 1989. He was a guest lecturer in 2002 at the École Polytechnique Fédérale de Lausanne (Swiss Federal Institute of Technology Lausanne) and at the ETH Zurich (Swiss Federal Institute of Technology Zurich) in 2009. Since 2012, Annette Gigon and Mike Guyer have been professors for architecture and design at ETH Zurich. They have received various awards for their work, including the City of Hamburg's Fritz Schumacher Prize, the International Fellowship Award of the Royal Institute of British Architects, and the most prestigious architecture prize in Switzerland: the Tageslicht (Daylight) Award.

Momoyo Kaijima founded Atelier Bow-Wow with Yoshiharu Tsukamoto in 1992. Since 2017, she has been a professor of Architectural Behaviorology at the ETH Zurich. She has taught at the Harvard University GSD (2003, 2016), as a guest professor at ETHZ (2005–2007), and at the Royal Danish Academy of Fine Arts (2011–2012), Rice University (2014–2015), the Delft University of Technology (2015–2016) and Columbia University (2017). While engaging in design projects for houses, public buildings and train station plazas, she has conducted numerous investigations of the city through architecture in endeavors such as Made in Tokyo and Pet Architecture. She was the curator of the Japanese Pavilion at the sixteenth International Architecture Exhibition – La Biennale di Venezia.

Let's talk about production spaces and how to build a productive city. To start, Markus, can you explain the title of this book? What does it mean?

Schaefer

The book came about for two reasons. First, Mobimo asked us to support them in rethinking the RAD Areal in Oerlikon. This historic industrial site is half-empty and yet the city of Zurich refuses to have it rezoned, with the aim to keep the site affordably priced and dedicated to urban industry and manufacturing. At the same time, Harvard asked us to teach an option studio in urban design. We decided to combine the requests as we have a couple of industrial projects in the office and believe that industry – in terms of production, material flows, its gritty reality and the typologies it requires – is an interesting program for an academic studio as it makes the city real. If you think that cities have become increasingly service-oriented, and therefore increasingly digital and abstract, industry is a counterbalance to that. The title *The Industrious City* is meant to describe a city that is industrial, in that there's still industry there, and at the same time, industrious in that the people are productive, have access and agency. We think that there are three factors that come together. There is the remaining old industry, like the Man Group, Bombardier or RAD. Then there are new high-tech industries like biotech, health and new energy, triggered by the proximity to the ETH. Finally, there is urban manufacturing, a sort of service industry for the service industry in the words of Saskia Sassen. For example, Freitag produces shoulder bags and other accessories bought by bankers, or you have craft beer consumed by creatives. In the sixties, everybody wanted to leave the city, and now people are flocking back, especially creatives and young people seeking access to a globalized world. At the same time, retail is shrinking, because the digital is much better at linking supply and demand than city centers. All these inner-city developments, which were organized around retail, must be rethought now. These factors require us all to reinvent the city yet again. After the leisure and retail-city of the eighties and nineties, or the creative city of the last two decades, we might now see the productive or, as we would call it, the Industrious City.

Why is it critical to what we do in our studio?

Schaefer

Our studio is very much organized around systems thinking. If we work on a building, then we also ask what's happening around the building, which leads you to urbanism or transportation. The budget leads us to economic questions. We attempt to understand a city holistically, as a complex system where we actively look for relationships with all other disciplines. With our spin-off cividi, we raise questions about big and open data. And the book *The Industrious City* is an effort to understand the city as a productive ecosystem.

Mike, your office has a wide variety of projects, also on a range of formerly industrial areas, such as the Maag-Areal, the Löwenbräu-Areal and the Sulzer-Areal. Can you explain the context, and the urbanistic and architectural opportunities of these projects?

Guyer

Zurich-West is one of the industrial areas of Zurich that was transformed very quickly over the last years into an open, mixed-use neighborhood. Zurich-Nord was the first one, Zurich-West the second, and now, Zurich-Süd, and the areas along the rail tracks owned by the Swiss Railway Company the most recent. In the nineties, there was a big demand for large office spaces located on representative sites, closely linked to the public transportation system. There was a huge political discussion about how you can open these industrial areas for other uses. And as the city and the Canton could not agree, there was an up-front change in the zoning law by the Canton. That is how the discussion started.

At the beginning there were some round tables. On a site of more than 7,000 square meters, Swiss zoning law allows for locally rewriting the zoning regulations based on certain obligations but also with benefits – a certain freedom in terms of height, an unusual proximity of buildings, or a hybrid mix of functions. When the urban competition for Zurich-West started, there was a concept of a core comprising three or four buildings that should be conserved as a reminder of the industrial past. Now the last segment of this area is being developed, and it turned out that this idea, which the clients strongly resisted at the beginning, is very valuable in that it provides the area with historical richness. In the end there was no problem in renting out these preserved buildings after they were refurbished.

The Maag-Areal was important as the client was ready to build a high-rise, a typology that was not discussed in the eighties. It took five years of intense negotiations to realize this aim. The height finally was determined politically and a hybrid function with housing and offices was out of the question. However, the city was quite precise in demanding at least a public atmosphere on the ground floor and a public function on the top of the tower. They could not really demand this by law, but by a gentlemen's agreement. Interestingly, now with the development of the second part, where the Music Hall Tonhalle is located, the owners have learned that they really need to go for a hyper-hybrid building. They want to keep even more of the old structure, and they're no longer interested in high-rises or corporate towers.

Löwenbräu, another site, was a former brewery. It was then sold several times, first to Migros and then to a series of developers. Part of it was even turned into an art cooperative. The interesting thing is that the site's temporary use before reconstruction became very important for the town. It was a famous contemporary art location, putting Zurich on the international map in the nineties. The city realized this immediately, while the private developer took a little longer to see it. The then mayor of Zurich made a quick deal. He offered the developers more square meters if they would sell all the so-called difficult parts, where the art is installed now, to a community of art stakeholders – galleries, museums, etc. It was also clear that about sixty or seventy percent of the existing buildings should remain. Imagine that! Since they are horizontally organized, they occupy a lot of ground space, making it difficult to reach the total FAR – the floor area ratio – allowed for this plot. There was even a serious discussion about positioning high-rises on top of the old buildings, although this is a non-high-rise zone. It was also interesting that the other part was the Swiss Mill, which remained an industrial parcel and even got an extension for its 110-meter-high silo. There was a public vote in favor of it. The Löwenbräu may be a more interesting example for the idea of an Industrious City, as it is characterized by a concern for the existing qualities of the site, transforming it within the context of a vision of the future. Now it's active on almost every level of the city's daily life. There are residences, offices, media use, a radio station and shops, and there is the whole part of the historic environment that was left intact.

And the third one, the Sulzer-Areal in Winterthur, is also interesting as it was the last one of these large areas. Jean Nouvel won that competition in the nineties, I think, with a concept where he proposed to demolish most buildings. But that project just didn't happen. The city was too small and the resources lacking. A more gradual approach had to be taken, that allowed the area to absorb the new interventions and change slowly over time. I think they made quite an interesting decision to keep some industrial halls. In our competition contribution, we doubled the number of halls, which the jury and developer considered positive. But again, the important part of the competition proposal was the transformation timeline, based on the idea of replacing some of the buildings while others continued to function as before. The site had to be developed gradually. I think that's the difference. While Maag and Löwenbräu were about architectural issues, Sulzer-Areal was purely urbanistic.

Both of you teach architecture at ETH Zurich. When you observe the ideas currently being discussed at the university, what new developments and opportunities do you see?

Guyer

Our urbanistic issues in Switzerland are not a popular topic at the ETH anymore. The ETH looks now at really large cities in Africa, South America and Asia. What we are talking about here at this table is a very focused look at Swiss or Central European cities and their development. Swiss cities are even more specific as they were not demolished in war and continued to develop in a very natural, very human way. And I think we should draw as many qualities out of that as we can. After the last industrial areas have been transformed, the cities will be fully built up within their urban limits. Then the issue will become how to deal with neighborhoods destined for both residential and industrial use. How can we densify this situation?

Schaefer

Then there is the urban agglomeration. In contrast to the organized and controlled urbanity in the inner city, there is nothing like that in the suburbs and the wider built-up area. It's quite a challenge to transform it into something that's not just a brutal transplant of urbanity, as so often happens. We want this outer city to retain a kind of village quality. Instead of experimenting with this, architects tend to think we need urbanity everywhere. I think an important task will be to find a new sensibility and toolbox to allow for a more measured approach.

Guyer

Take the example of a start-up, a group of young people who for personal reasons don't want to leave for Berlin, Tel Aviv or Paris. As of now, they can't afford to stay here. Prices per square meter here in Zurich and even the surrounding area are very expensive. So, they might think about moving to a more peripheral area. They don't care, because they are digitally linked to everywhere. They operate within their network. And they can profit from these abandoned areas where they can more or less do what they want. That's the opportunity offered by such areas, and young entrepreneurs are now relocating to places like Bülach, Thurgau, Rheintal and Glarus.

Momoyo, your and Yoshiharu's life work established a very unique and strong standing position in the field of architecture in Japan. Can you explain your concept of the city?

Kaijima

We really believe in living and working together. After World War II, there was a housing crisis in Japan. Families were living together in one house because they were poor. Maybe from a European perspective (laughs), this idea of several generations living together is messy. At that time, Japanese businessmen worked in central Tokyo, but couldn't afford a house there. Instead they bought suburban houses and spent an hour commuting to work every day. It was exhausting for everyone. That's why most of our first commissions came from the younger generation. Most of the families who want to live in the city are creative people, intellectuals, teachers, professors and artists who want an urbanized space to live and work in together. I think this trend has developed over the last two decades. Their first decision was to buy a tiny plot of land in central Tokyo and build a tiny house where they could live and work. This generation is now getting older, but another, younger one coming up is demanding new solutions. Now we have a lot of abandoned houses we need to renovate for this mix of living and working, often in rural areas, where land is much cheaper, and people can invest or even self-build.

Does urban industry and urban manufacturing play a role in your work? And since you have a good overview over global trends, do you see something emerging?

Kaijima

Maybe the ETH invited me to teach here because the way we see the city as a hybrid is very useful for teaching students. Even more so because most urban planners still plan cities as a residential area, an industrial area and so on, an obsolete approach today. In our studio, we look at hybridized or mixed use, and for the students this is different and interesting. Japan is a strange country in terms of hybridization, and that's helpful in thinking about new opportunities.

Even in small things we need a philosophy about our future. Not a clear philosophy, but future images. The mix is one thing, sharing is another recent popular word, along with commonalities and behavior. These things always embrace movement; they're not fixed. There is always a next thing coming. This kind of relay thinking is an important driving force. It's something for people to develop, enjoy and evolve.

Schaefer

One reason we were interested in having you here together was to start a discussion about scale and constant transformation. I think the Industrious City should, ideally, be a place able to continuously reinvent itself. How can we get away from rigid, monolithic ideas about urban design?

Guyer

I can speak from an experience last week. I was a member of a jury in Geneva for the Acacias area. The program was mixed use, and public participation was required. It was strictly defined but very unclear about how the uses can work together. The jury meeting was quite frustrating and completely different than a jury would have been fifteen years ago. It was difficult to get to the real architectural issues. There were half a dozen very different projects, almost like urbanistic schemes.

The architecture of the Europaallee, for example, is not on the same level as its urban planning. In my view, these buildings have not been developed as envisioned. I'm not so sure these hybrid buildings will be successful, as you can see now in the discussion about the multi-functional development of "Kosmos." Hybrid or multi-layered projects are interesting fields of possible battles, especially when parts of this hybrid usage will vanish because they just don't work. I also think we should avoid seeing this situation in an emotional or ideological way.

What do you think, Markus? I mean, in a way you work both on architectural projects and designing on different urban scales.

Schaefer

The reason they asked us to work on the RAD Oerlikon is that we like to think of content/context, program/programming and urban design/architecture at the same time. In our project for the V-ZUG Areal, for example, we are serving in an advisory capacity, as members of the steering committee, as client representatives, as master planners and as architects. In a way, we are a part of everything. We also often take part in projects like the Engadin airport, where we support the client in the definition of the program and development processes. I believe this is a niche for which you need the right clients, and where you can break out of the rigid, guild-like understanding of what architects do.

Architects should generate more environments that are flexible and allow differentiation in "open typologies." Buildings could become simpler if architects stopped trying so hard. A strong, simple structure where the specific identity has more to do with programming, usage and accessibility. More software, less hardware. I am not sure it is a good idea that hybrid use is hardwired into a building.

What do you think about the opportunities in the countryside?

Kaijima

Switzerland has a very interesting potential. It could become very rural, and at the same time very networked and urban. That is very different than other countries, and maybe this is really a core potential. That's why if the young generation has an interest in moving to a rural area with a new vision for a business or an idea for an organization or program, it can work.

I think some people want to stay here longer and they like their homeland. But unfortunately, there are no jobs, and life is too expensive. That's why the mission is to create new jobs for young people. What Switzerland has to offer is very limited; it is a rare hybrid between very rich, very rural and very modern. Consequently, I think, people need new design ideas so that even a very rural area can look new and very contemporary.

Schaefer

Maybe the Industrious City is not only in the centers? Because Switzerland is like a large decentralized city. I think that's one good conclusion. And the other conclusion, Momoyo, you were talking about the architect as a kind of social advisor in the sense of linking things together based on common sense. Mike mentioned the idea of the architect as an entrepreneur. Perhaps we could position an Industrious City architect as a maker of connections to keep our cities productive, social, collective and so on.

Finally, we come to the question of how to build a productive city.

Guyer

When talking about how to build a productive city, I think it's interesting to take flexibility into account. That leads me to the idea of generic space. If an Industrious City is to be a productive environment, how can a generic space be a space with atmosphere, where people feel at ease and able to develop? Where they have freedom to act as individuals, while at the same time, this is architecture, so it's part of the public space, the streets, squares and so on.

Kaijima

That's why, perhaps, we need different scales and different architectures. This kind of use, thinking and management requires a paradigm shift. I think Zurich has a lot of potential for large-scale developments, for example. In Tokyo we have a very dynamic small house development but also a huge infrastructure. Because we work on different scales simultaneously, we're developing a city with a lot of potential for change. We could maintain this kind of diversity of scales as much as possible. It might be helpful.

Automation
Empowerment
Industrial Clusters
Make or Buy
Near-Sourcing
Urban Transformation

Interview by Hiromi Hosoya
September 19, 2019
Rheinmetall Air Defence, Zurich-Oerlikon

INDUSTRIAL OPERATIONS

Reinhard Flückiger

Reinhard Flückiger is a former COO at Rheinmetall Air Defence AG. He served twenty years as executive board member and has extensive experience in the management of international supply chains, with ten years of international postings in Nigeria, Canada and Saudi Arabia. Although retired, he continues to do consulting work.

Mr. Flückiger, you have been running operations at RAD on the site in Oerlikon for many years. What does it mean for an industrial firm to operate in the city? What are the biggest benefits and the biggest problems?

From my experience of more than thirty-three years in this industry, it's all about people. Whether I look for the roots of a problem or a success, I will always end up with people. For me, really, the biggest question is motivation. You can have very fancy tools to try and motivate people, but it's not that easy. I think it takes a personal approach. People not only work at this company, they have lives at home and families. You need a holistic approach to people. Most of all, they need to feel appreciated for what they do.

We have to give people roads forward. You often hear about empowerment. Let us take the classic example of a worker who was introduced to working with a computer, which was originally not his task. Now he is very proud to have an impact by reporting back on his job himself instead of handing it over to a foreman who reports back. In the end it all comes down to leading by example.

Is a location in the city desirable?

I have lived through what has happened in Oerlikon over the last twenty years. We were skeptical at the beginning. But then it turned out to be wonderful. Many new stores and restaurants opened in the area. For example, we have a sushi restaurant, drug stores, cleaners and hotels just around the corner. The business works great. We even have an elderly home just across the street and everything is very close. And throughout these transformations our place is still intact and we still have our operations and jobs here.

From the operational point of view, what is the benefit of your firm being in Oerlikon? How important is location regarding access (e.g., for workers), visibility (e.g., for clients or partners), or participation in an industrial cluster?

Operationally, it doesn't really matter much whether we are here or in Dielsdorf or Oberwinterthur. But as long as you can afford it, it is a benefit to have your factory in an urban environment. If I have a super new factory in an anonymous industrial estate outside of the city that does not motivate people for whatever reason, then I have a problem. I'd rather be in a mature place with people who are motivated. In addition, our location in Oerlikon is part of our brand, so clients expect to come to Oerlikon to see their product. And they like to see this place in a certain light, and they have certain expectations. An urban environment for a factory comes at a price, however, and with certain restrictions, such as access. But as long as we can get a forty-ton truck to our location, we can operate. The more important aspect is how people get to a site. The closer the site is to where they live, the better. And international clients expect a state-of-the-art infrastructure close to the airport. They don't want to travel for two hours by road in addition to the air travel just to end up in a small village with no hotel. And they would like to see their product presented in a fashionable way.

How do we have to imagine the logistics required to run an industrial company, specifically RAD? Can you give us an overview?

You have to manage the whole supply chain. A company needs to concentrate on core competencies. You have to focus your investments on human resources, equipment or infrastructure. As the chessboard becomes more complex, you really have to focus or you will not survive. It's a competitive environment, with targets everywhere.

Today's supply chains are very complex. We work with different currencies that fluctuate. We moved everything outside Switzerland, only to find a couple of years later that the Swiss franc had become weaker again. And actually, Swiss suppliers match European suppliers on pricing. So, it's very dynamic, and part of my job is to correctly manage the so-called "make or buy" strategy. And then you have offset requirements – some customers require a hundred percent offset. That means we have to economically offset the whole purchase price in their country. That's another challenge.

What components and pieces are produced on-site, and what components come pre-assembled?

We concentrate on what we call the core or critical components, which are the most complex parts. They have to be reliable and we need to have full control and traceability back to the raw material. All other electronic components, cables, motors, drive systems, optical systems and other structures, we try to purchase globally with the best (not lowest) cost in mind.

The amount of the waste you have in your factory is surprisingly little. Why?

We don't buy the actual raw material, like crude aluminum, and then shape it. We go to a casting company that masters the art of casting and then we buy the complete cast. We just do the machining of those critical casts to guarantee the precision of the final system.

Can you tell us about your data management system?

This is the brain of the company. Data becomes increasingly important in our production and managing processes, especially as you probably won't find a place where labor costs are higher than here in downtown Zurich. They ask us why do you stay here? If our competitors would like to have us fail in the market and they know that our owners will challenge us, they wonder how can we still produce here and sell our products on the market with a profit. Since the labor content is expensive, as you can imagine, we have to work on efficiency. Data in this respect becomes increasingly important to manage our complex processes. We continuously endeavor to automate processes and make them safer.

The aim is really to have an optimized ratio between people in production and those in administration. We are talking millions of data records, and if you don't have the right system, you have many people tinkering with Excel sheets. I primarily look at the ratio between our management and indirectly productive people compared with our productive people. Sometimes you find the ratio is about 50:50. So, for one person who makes something you have another person who just manages the data. This burdens your cost and ultimately, if you want to stay in business, you have to optimize that. We want as few indirectly productive people as possible and we want to automate all this data management as much as possible.

Do you think there's an advantage to locating industry in the city? When thinking about the future of the RAD site, do ideas of clustering companies in the city that have synergies or even are part of value chains make sense?

Zurich is known for its banks and finance industry. But you know, not everybody can work or wants to work in a bank. I think it makes the city much richer if it has a vital industrial sector. Not only the banking industry, but real industry, which I think is certainly worth preserving. The other thing is that people don't like change. If you take them out of the city and put them in an industrial zone somewhere it would almost certainly impact their motivation.

I think it is worth talking about operating clusters. For example, there is a cluster in Schlieren where they work on biotechnology. It's important, especially when a company is just starting out, that it finds the right place, an incubator where it can grow. You have a lot of effects in a cluster; people can talk to each other and exchange information. They also use the same facilities and equipment in certain aspects. That helps to bring costs down. We never actually strategically planned to have a "techno park" here in Oerlikon; however, I think we might go in that direction sooner or later.

Is near-sourcing at all an option for you? Or are the high-tech products for which Switzerland is known made from components that are inherently globally sourced?

Yes. I will give you an example. When it comes to a paint shop, as you just saw, we don't run that paint shop ourselves anymore; we have a service provider do that at our location in Oerlikon. However, we need to closely monitor the quality because we still have to do the final touch-up before the client receives the product. We cannot transport the product halfway across the country to have it painted. Maybe that would be cheaper, but we need this source to be very close for flexibility. In fact, the more complex an activity, such as development and engineering, the more important communication becomes. With these activities our engineers feel more comfortable if they can speak their native language.

For things that are well defined, on the other hand, – and we have a lot of repetition – I can go further out, as far as China. For things that need a lot of communication until we get the right material and the right product and the right service, the closer the better. Sometimes, it is paramount to have them basically on the same site.

Nina Rappaport

URBAN MANUFACTURING

Equitable City
Flexible Specialization
Hybrid Manufacturing
Informal Economy
Neo-Cottage Industries
Process Removal
Vertical Urban Factory

Since the First Industrial Revolution, a global spatial system based on economic flows has followed parallel patterns in numerous countries, from crescendos to diminuendos, embedding an urban production process that encompasses local consumption and international export. From small, urban cottage industries to mega-industrial spaces in hinterlands, spreading out across greenfields as suburban industrial parks, production across different scales is parallel and simultaneously occurring. Each scale and typology of urban manufacturing – from large to small, heavy to light – relies on connectivity through virtual and physical networks. From the local to the global, in what can be called the "glocal," goods are distributed in an international consumption space where challenging questions arise about social justice, material versus immaterial labor, trade regulations and ways to support a democratic workplace both at small and large scales and at different skill levels. Ultimately, the question becomes how these social, political and economic aspirations will induce a paradigm shift in the space and places for urban production[1]. The nuances of urban manufacturing and its economic complexities relating to land use and spatial organization provide a focus in cities including Philadelphia (once called the "Workshop of the World") and districts in New York, Detroit and Turin – all former industrial bastions with similar social and economic concerns at all scales.

Broadly defined, urban manufacturing encompasses raw making, assembly, repair, prototyping, distribution logistics and storage. In the wake of the new networked technologies, emerging businesses – often making products related to urban lifestyle – have been reinvigorating cities as new more popular places to live. This is happening in the context of the transition to cities of over seventy percent of the world's population by 2030. Such new urban companies include fashion, food, fabrication and furniture. But since all things are needed by urban dwellers, including even some farm tools and beekeeping supplies for urban farms, any consumer good can be made locally in a new productive, sustainable urban paradigm. We can observe that manufacturing and assembly methods considered light rather than heavy are able to flourish and have a place in cities, as they do not pollute, and they take up less space. Nonetheless, heavy and large-scale manufacturing operations are still visible at cities' edges, where metal work, food production and open-air production such as gravel and concrete still actively occupy vast volumes and grand sites.

As entrepreneurs in the new economy create companies to make things in cities, the reality of legacy (or long-lasting) large-scale firms and mass production continues to need attention from policy makers and economists. Economic policies need to support legacy companies in their transition to advanced technologies so they can adjust machinery for CNC and augmented robotics in Industry 4.0, and thus remain in place. While much production has moved to Asian

Economic Production Zones, Mexican maquiladoras and the Global South in general, where labor costs are cheaper and working conditions unsafe, other companies, both large and small, maintain their historic continuity in situ. These companies continue to rely on their urban locality for their skilled and unskilled workers and remain committed to their city, even as the impact of one economic and health crisis after another and trade regulations shifts their networks to distant places and changes their relationships with their supply chain that we are seeing in a new light with Covid-19. The companies best able to survive these fluctuations are those that might be considered higher end manufacturers and producers. Shifman Mattress in Newark still makes high-end comfort mattresses by hand. Lighting companies such as Edison Price Lighting and Modulighter in New York rely on urban design communities that need to be in proximity to their consumers for precise specifications. Other companies such as Shinola a leather goods and watch producer using Swiss technology, have moved to declining Rust Belt cities, thus supporting the local workforce. Shinola has even built a hotel in Chicago, indicating the company's expanding investment but also its focus on "lifestyle." While these high-end businesses cater to an elite clientele, they provide jobs and skills training for urban residents, and have growth potential.

Larger-scale urban factories are often forgotten, considered gone, of no use or not interesting because they are not part of the new economy. From the urban edge to urban sprawl to the hinterlands that we pass through on trains and highways, behemoth factories have merged with the post-industrial landscape. Their sheer massiveness creates an awesome raw beauty, as did the early twentieth-century factories of AEG designed by Peter Behrens, Hans Hertlein's Siemenstadt plants in Berlin, Albert Kahn's massive factories for Chrysler Tank Arsenal and Willow Run, a site occupying 975 acres of farmland originally owned by Henry Ford. There is something sublime in their capacity to make an array of goods through spatial mechanization and an organization in which form follows flow in an isomorphic fashion. Our somewhat nostalgic attitude toward their massiveness requires recognition of the often-paternalistic hegemony and harsh working conditions imposed on those who labored inside, while we continue to appreciate their architectural design and production power voided of their social impact.

These mega-factories required acreage that is unobtainable in cities today, due not only to cost but also residential and commercial development pressures, as well as pollution. For example, the North Philadelphia Industrial Park, developed in the 1970s, stretched across 651 acres, something that would be impossible to initiate today. These single-story factory buildings were built primarily by a few companies in a limited architectural configuration focusing primarily on flexible, open space, and housed bakeries, meat processing, rubber and metal production, printing and paper manufacturers

Constructed of concrete, brick and steel, with long rows of loading docks and parking, these sites subsumed greenfields at the city's edge. In the industrial park setting, the entrance was controlled, and trucks could deliver and pick up goods without interference from pedestrians. They could operate in an enclave without required good neighbor behavior in terms of noise and nuisance laws. Increasingly isolated, their industrial network was not as interconnected as manufacturers in the denser part of the city. And with new trade laws favoring nations with cheaper labor, many of these mass-producing companies were totally removed from the city in what I call "process removal" – subtracting the process of making things from everyday view. By removing factories from the urban realm, factories become societies in and of themselves, heterotopias in Foucault's terms, leading to oppression through both their work environments and the removal of the process from daily view.

However, closer to the edge of many cities, such as the Port Richmond area of Philadelphia, legacy companies continue as they did in the early twentieth century. Their larger-scale products tend to correspond to larger-scale manufacturing spaces. The architecture is tough and raw, often with unfinished and uninsulated walls, meant to be used and abused, with machines organized systematically for production flow with configurations specific to the products. Whether the factory is box-shaped, L-shaped, E-shaped or linear, processes impact the factory floor and its layout. Since the 1980s, a new relationship between R&D and production places engineers in proximity to workers for constant feedback. With the need for sustainable production, factories strive to configure water, heat and waste systems to be more efficient and respectful to neighbors, especially in the former heavy industrial area along the Delaware River.

These factories in Philadelphia are passed down from family member to family member, as I observed at a window company, a metal recycling container fabricator, a cardboard box company, a food packaging firm and a canvas supply company, all factories where I interviewed workers in my ongoing ethnographic study, *A Worker's Lunch Box.* Visible in the window manufacturer's three contiguous buildings are glass sheets and extruded aluminum bars stored on high shelves to be used to make windows for commercial and residential buildings. Workers like Maria, a recent immigrant from Ecuador, cut the glass with CNC computer machines, controlling robots housed in metal cages to contain the process and keep it clean and safe. She gets teary-eyed when discussing how much the company has helped her make her life. Other workers finish the glass sheet edges by hand, smoothing them out, and carry them on trolleys to a production line where workers insert them into an aluminum frame and move them to a packaging and logistics area.

The steel company sells large recycling containers to major shopping centers and supermarkets, among others. They organize their heavy production in a vast brick shed illuminated by natural light from large steel casement windows. There, Mark, a dedicated metal worker, refines his corner of the factory floor, organizing the smaller steel pieces he cuts on a shearing machine following the designers blueprints. The pieces are then moved on skids that he has set up and welders merge them into hefty steel containers. He feels he has a legacy too. He describes his pride in making something that will exist "longer here than me." The company owner often speaks at gatherings of high school parents to tell them that factory jobs still exist and pay more than jobs at McDonalds and other retail venues. The high value that owners and workers place on these jobs is hard to imagine without walking down the city streets in this mixed manufacturing neighborhood and entering through their doors.

Formerly in a multistoried brick-and-concrete vertical urban factory, Tastykake, a longtime baking company, moved from North Philadelphia to the Navy Yard. In this renewed manufacturing center where naval ships were once constructed, they bake their goods in a new sustainable building. Their neighbors include the Aker Philadelphia Shipyard, which still builds ships, as well as smaller pharmaceutical and technology companies. These factories employ a few thousand workers. While not on par with the numbers of the past they are still a major economic link for the city and workforce.

A similar economic phenomenon is taking place in Long Island City in Queens, New York, one of the country's most dynamic industrial areas. Legacy companies continue to produce plastics, lighting fixtures, frames, baked goods, engine parts, steam machines and garments, and do printing and repair work. Simultaneously, new start-ups include advanced electronics technology manufacturers 3D printing, stage set design and breweries. A district once solely industrial has been converted to mixed use, with the idea that this will encourage more overall development. However, the development that has occurred has been primarily residential. This has gentrified the local community, which vocally objected to and successfully blocked a new Amazon headquarters. The few remaining manufacturing blocks inland from the waterfront are struggling against displacement. One legacy company is a lighting fixture manufacturer where workers puncture large metal sheets with flatbed CNC milling machines to create housings for lights and pack products for distribution to museums and galleries. In one corner, a metal turner uses traditional metal blades with wooden handles to spin and refine the metals. Yet now surrounded by residential towers, the company is struggling to keep its location even though it has adapted to new technology processing.

In the new economy of flexible specialization in an increasingly networked system, numerous production methods based on information systems support smaller, cleaner technology manufacturers. The companies' footprints are similar to the cottage industries of the eighteenth century when piecework predated mass production. These "neo-cottage" industries impact jobs in that there are fewer workers per factory but more companies. Physically, the ramifications are seen in densely textured cities where former factory buildings previously owned by one company are divided up for co-located smaller companies that only use between 1,000 and 5,000 square feet each. Such setups now exist in New York, Philadelphia, Turin, Toronto, London and Paris, with its emblematic *hôtels industriels* – new purpose-built, mixed-use factory buildings that are a model of the contemporary Vertical Urban Factory typology.

At Globe Dye Works, in North Philadelphia, committed developers readapted a former thread-dyeing company. The brick-and-concrete gridded structure held dyeing tanks and processing facilities on four floors. Now the building holds companies making products such as ice cream, coffee and pottery, with some space for artists, as well as woodworking enterprises that produce in smaller spaces with a handful of employees. The central hall still houses the rusted vats and machinery, providing an "irresistible ruin" atmosphere ideal for event backdrops.

In Turin, Italy, thousands of workers once walked through entrance gates to their hands-on, physical jobs at the 35,000-square-meter train maintenance structures of the Officine Grandi Riparazioni (OGR)[2]. Today, the Politecnico occupies a corner of the space where an additive manufacturing factory, Avio Aero, has installed its operations. This company builds parts by adding layer upon layer of fine aluminum dust to create elements for GE's turbo airplane engines. Four-million-dollar machines are housed in a small corner of the former high-bay train factory with only fifteen staff. The additive processes are also harnessed to repair components in a way somewhat similar to the nineteenth century American system of interchangeable parts. These small parts can be made in smaller spaces connected to technology and educational institutions so that the cluster of knowledge continues to expand in a new hybridization of manufacturing and research. The location provides shorter commuting time for workers, proximate shared resources and a local supply chain that contributes to reduced energy use for companies and the city as a whole. As manufacturing is reintegrated into the urban fabric, intensified physical and virtual networks can resolve urban economic contingencies while also maintaining legacy industries.

Constellations – Large and Small

The nuanced interrelationship between large and small companies is evident in cities where small companies feed into mega-firms in a complex ecosystem. Large-scale factories often require physical proximity to smaller companies and vice versa; business-to-business relationships are not only virtual. The clustering of firms, as discussed by Marshall and Von Thünen in 1930, continues today, whether it is a more informal relationship between a metalworker who needs a wood frame for a piece of furniture, or the formal relationship between automotive companies and suppliers of fixtures such as windshield wipers and car seats. While many production situations are connected by virtual logistics – emailing and uploading design files for mass customization or for 3D printing on demand – physical proximity increases bodies of knowledge and of worker skills.

In Turin, Fiat (like Ford) began with a small factory in 1912 and expanded to Lingotto in 1926 and then Mirafiori in the 1950s. It collaborated with smaller, more specialized suppliers that crafted (and still craft) leather car seats, fine metal components and carpentry thus forming a non-linear production line. Ford, however, wanted to control production in what is called vertically integrated manufacturing, so that Henry Ford even owned rubber farms in Brazil for his tires and created a short-lived town called Fordlandia for his workers. But in surrounding Detroit, spin-off companies employing highly skilled workers made his car body parts (such as the Dodge brothers' chassis), valves, heating systems and wood trim, combining distributed networks of workshops and integrated in-house production.[3]

This physical network of distributed constellations still matters today. Its impact is seen in the 2019 UAW strikes in Lansing and Detroit, Michigan, which affected suppliers as well as the GM factory Some 6,000 workers in everything from advertising to bumpers and windshield wipers to metal parts stopped work.[4] The network is co-dependent, relying on larger companies to keep smaller ones in business and vice versa. In Turin, car seats are still made in nearby workshops. Auto upholsters such as the Lear Corporation supply what is now the Fiat/Chrysler Group in the US Electric motor companies, metal wire fabricators and die-casting companies such as 2A have expanded to other industries in their business-to-business networks.

The efficiency of a physically linked manufacturing community retains value and is necessary for company organization in which the production line encompasses a neighborhood. For example, in garment districts in numerous cities, pattern making, fabric outlets cloth cutting, sewing, button and zipper suppliers are in close proximity to each other, to a strong workforce and to designers. The supply chain may not be long, but it is wide, circulating throughout cities and responding to different demands. This is the case in Detroit Turin, Philadelphia, Hong Kong and even Dharavi, for instance.

Informal

In addition to formal networks, informal commercial and maker enterprises, more often dispersed than clustered by trade, comprise yet another ecosystem extending across an entire city. We can still learn from the informal economy in terms of these constellations formed by proximity and curious mixes.

Informal urban districts such as Hong Kong's Kowloon Walled City – until its demolition in 1993 because of the prevalence of crime and poverty – also fueled small cottage industries. Residents developed their own food production chain through informal networks made possible by extreme urban density. About 33,000 people lived in a 6.5-acre self-organized housing system, with basic needs such as water and electricity often supplied by covertly tapping into city systems. In terms of making things, anyone with a good tool could make a profit. Women lucky enough to have a sewing machine might work as subcontractors for a shoe factory, sewing the tops of canvas sneakers or completing piecework.

In Dharavi, India, a three-square-kilometer area that is home to 800,000 people, numerous production networks of small entrepreneurial workshops have agglomerated into areas according to trade and expertise, such as leather, clothing and pottery making. Though threatened by demolition, the community has held on. The leatherwork industry is particularly strong in its informal organization, with family-run workshops that sell to larger distributors, like the more commercial garment industry.[5] These small, flexible cottage industries with no permanent workforce are subcontractors for other suppliers in the formal economy. They provide a strong backbone for the local leather goods infrastructure while simultaneously being part of a global industry.[6] The global economy and its traditional stance does not recognize the power of this informal market despite its importance. For example, in Brazil, in 2014 the informal market was worth $826 billion, equivalent to 16.1 percent of the country's gross domestic product.[7] This success is often due to the interdependence of various production methods and the ingenuity of the workers.

In an organized way, the cities of Paris and Geneva have been investing in new spaces for manufacturers since the 1980s. What are called *hôtels industriels* flexibly mix, in one building, fabricators and services to assist their development. Because these companies do not pollute or create invasive noise or nuisances and can thus be good neighbors, the city has enticed them to stay in Paris. An intensive and productive atmosphere is evident in these integrated projects, which return jobs to residential districts. The government has recognized the need to blend housing with suitable light industrial spaces building on community needs and values. Here we see the potential for hybrid manufacturing spaces, naturally occurring industrial areas in former factory strongholds like Detroit, Brooklyn and Turin where a transition to new fabrication culture is taking place.

Hybridization

The hybridization of manufacturing with other uses encourages a transformative, dynamic city. New types of zoning and building codes can encourage mixed use, combining residential and light manufacturing at the district and building scale. Buffer zones can be created to mitigate manufacturing and other issues, both spatially and environmentally. These buffers can be dual purpose – for instance, in new or renovated buildings they can be fire stairs and elevators for vertical circulation. In terms of public space, factory districts are notoriously uninviting, but new public spaces in such districts can serve as a defining yet porous edge to open up factories to cities.

Many companies that occupy mixed-use spaces are artisanal smaller brands or suppliers for other companies, as happens in the automobile industry. Despite the new urban culture's embrace of a small-batch lifestyle, newer, often self-financed companies making artisanal products like chocolate, crafts, handmade jewelry and organic goods have not yet proven their longevity. Companies start small, and in a way innocently, as entrepreneurs with an emphasis on authenticity and knowledge of where things come from in their supply chain, but often their expensive niche goods gentrify communities. The diverse mix of class and culture in the former industrial neighborhoods then disappears as lofts are converted first for artists and artisans and then the upper classes. New York's SoHo in the 1980s is a notorious example of this scenario.

But some smaller companies incubated in mixed-use spaces grow into major enterprises. Advanced and nano-manufacturing and 3D printers and printing services are expanding. MakerBot, for example, a 3D printer company that produces kits for home assembly, was so successful that it was purchased by Stratasys. While the company is still based in Brooklyn, its production is not. Another example of a new spatial configuration for manufacturing is Voodoo Manufacturing, which prints goods from stacked arrays of 200 plus 3D printers in a high-bay space in Brooklyn, which was even able to scale up and produce shields during the Covid-19 pandemic. Advanced technology and augmented digital production have the potential to create new kinds of jobs in a new hybrid spatial flow. Companies can achieve longevity if they can scale up like the legacy manufacturers of yore.

New spaces for advanced technologies have wider ramifications for the growth of cities and their social organization, especially for recent immigrants who need jobs. When the numbers of employees in the industrial network comprising an ecosystem are combined, they have increased and, in some instances, even approach their former heights. City administrations must reconsider methods and means to reclaim industrial space through zoning changes to encourage mixed use and the maintenance of industrial space in what I have called Mandatory Inclusionary Manufacturing.[8] They need to promote an awareness that productive companies and their architectural typologies can be part of the urban mix needed to support unknown future forms of manufacturing and provide opportunities for new knowledges to produce things locally and sustainably. This paradigm looks backward and forward to a resilient city in a vibrant atmosphere of making things locally. Such manufacturing processes can connect up with each other in a waste-to-production stream for a circular economy.

As urban thinkers such as Jane Jacobs have frequently noted, the intensity and diversity of human endeavors is what makes cities vital and strong, equitable and open, and together the large and small industrial processes can return manufacturing to its central place in the urban fabric, cultivating complex and layered ecological networks that underpin a more equitable city.

1 All the more evident in the recent Covid-19 pandemic.
2 It was turned temporarily into a hospital during the Covid-19 pandemic.
3 David Hochfelder and Susan Helper, "Suppliers and Product Development in the Early American Automobile Industry," in: *Business and Economic History* 25, no. 2 (Winter 1996), pp. 39–51, Cambridge University Press.
4 Ian Thibodeau, *The Detroit News,* September 24, 2019.
5 Marie-Caroline Saglio-Yatzimirsky, *Dharavi: From Mega-Slum to Urban Paradigm,* New Delhi: Routledge, 2013.
6 See Robert Neuwirth, *Stealth of Nations, The Global Rise of the Informal Economy,* New York: Penguin Random House, 2012.
7 Jay Forte, "Informal Economy in Brazil Worth R$826 Billion in 2014," *The Rio Times,* June 26, 2015. www.riotimesonline.com/brazil-news/rio-business/brazils-informal-economy-was-worth-r826-billion-in-2014/.
8 This is a concept developed for requiring spaces for urban manufacturing in the same way that affordable residential spaces are required for new developments. I first presented this at a 2015 City Council hearing as a way to support urban manufacturing space, and subsequently wrote about.

SWISS CASES

Industries have continuously been agents for urban change, from the creation of the first urban manufacturing sites in the eighteenth century in Neuenburg, to the first industrial compounds on the outskirts of the cities and corporate global campuses like Roche in Basel. The examples are unique to the polycentric urban landscape of Switzerland and explicitly show how industries relate to or have been embedded in the urban fabric. The industrial compounds have seen, in most cases, radical transformation over time through the constant renegotiation and blurring of the boundaries between the industrial and the urban. As such, these areas are examples and concrete sites for a future Industrious City.

CLASSIFICATION MATRIX

BUILDING STRUCTURE

Existing
The existing buildings are still intact.

Refurbished
The existing buildings have been refurbished or transformed.

Newly Built
The existing buildings have been erased and replaced.

URBAN EMBEDDEDNESS

None
The industry represents a closed island.

Partial
The industry is partially open to the city.

Fully Embedded
The industry is fully intertwined with the city fabric.

AGENTS

Industrial
The existing industry is main initiator of transformation.

Commercial
Private investors have initiated the transformation.

Communal
Residents have initiated the transformation.

Legislative
A legislative authority drives the transformation.

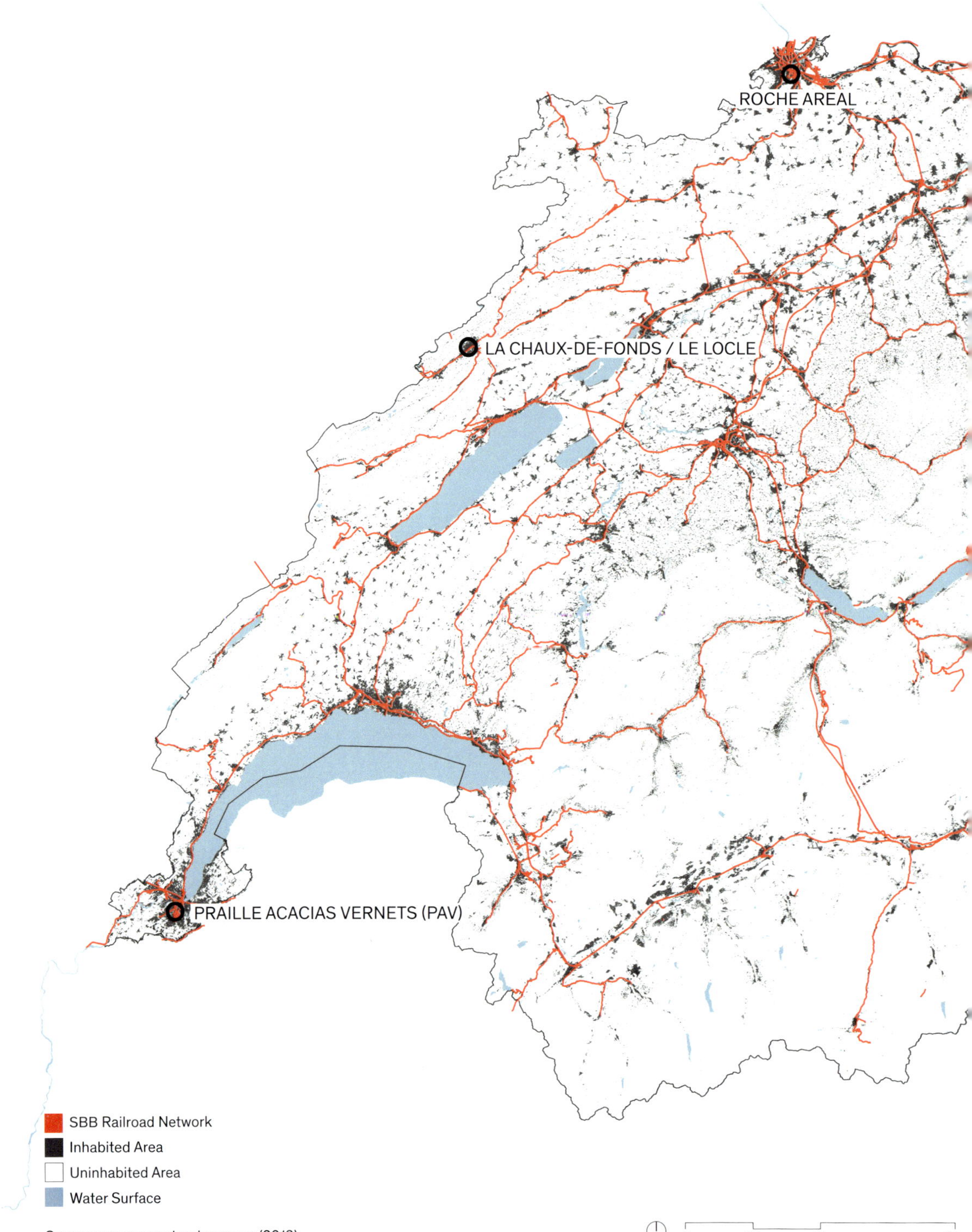

Source: www.openstreetmap.org (2013)

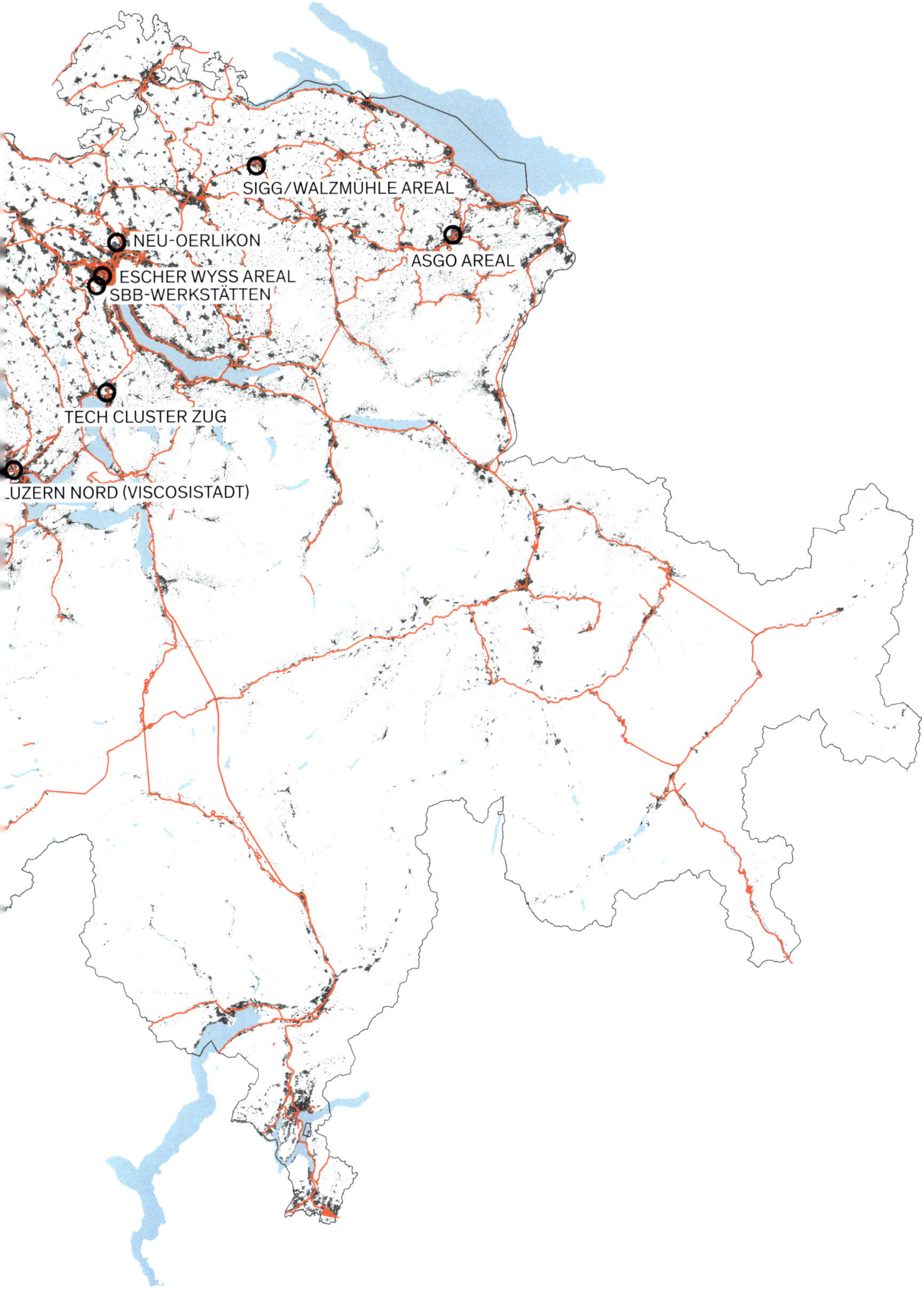
SIGG/WALZMÜHLE AREAL
NEU-OERLIKON
ASGO AREAL
ESCHER WYSS AREAL
SBB-WERKSTÄTTEN
TECH CLUSTER ZUG
UZERN NORD (VISCOSISTADT)

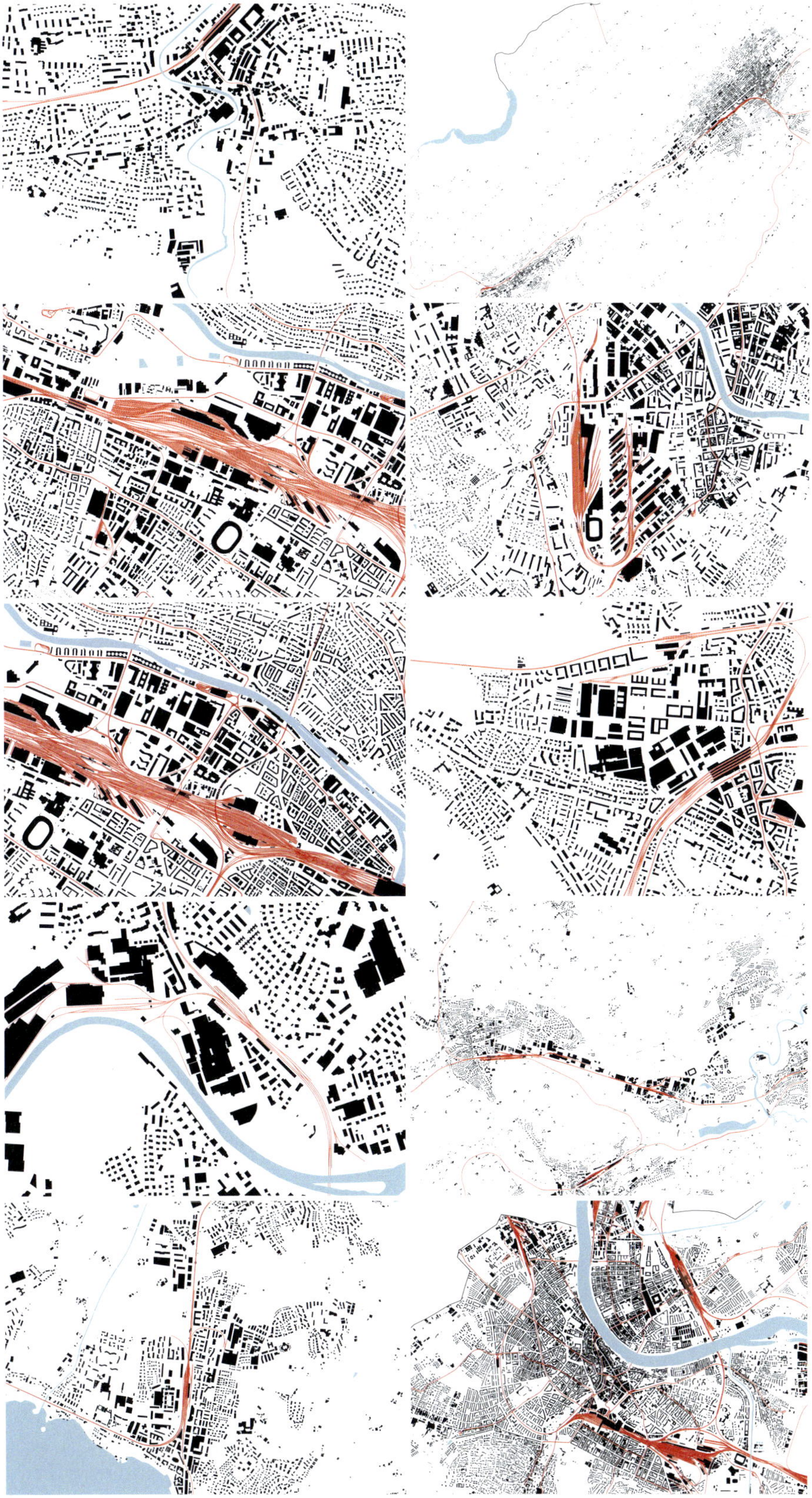

SIGG/WALZMÜHLE AREAL

Frauenfeld

The Walzmühle Areal, located in the southern part of Frauenfeld on the Murg River, is a former mill established in 1831. It has a long and successful production legacy. In 1917, it was turned into an aluminum products factory by the famous Ferdinand Sigg, who further expanded its premises. The Areal was bought by HIAG Immobilien in 2013 and transformed into a mixed-use area. Most of the existing buildings have been declared heritage sites because of their architectural value and refurbished. Although it is still an isolated island, today it consists of office and commercial spaces, apartments and loft buildings. The SIGG AG bottle factory, today an integral industrial part of the area, is located just opposite the old Walzmühle compound.

Data
Established: 1831
Transformation Plan: 2013
Site Area: 15,000 m^2
Agents: SIGG AG, HIAG Immobilien

Classification Matrix
Building structure – refurbished
Urban embeddedness – partial
Agents – industrial

Sources
www1.annualreport.hiag.com/uploads/tx_dlcenter/HIAG_GB16_de_Arealentwicklung.pdf
www.walzmuehle.ch

0
100
300
500 m

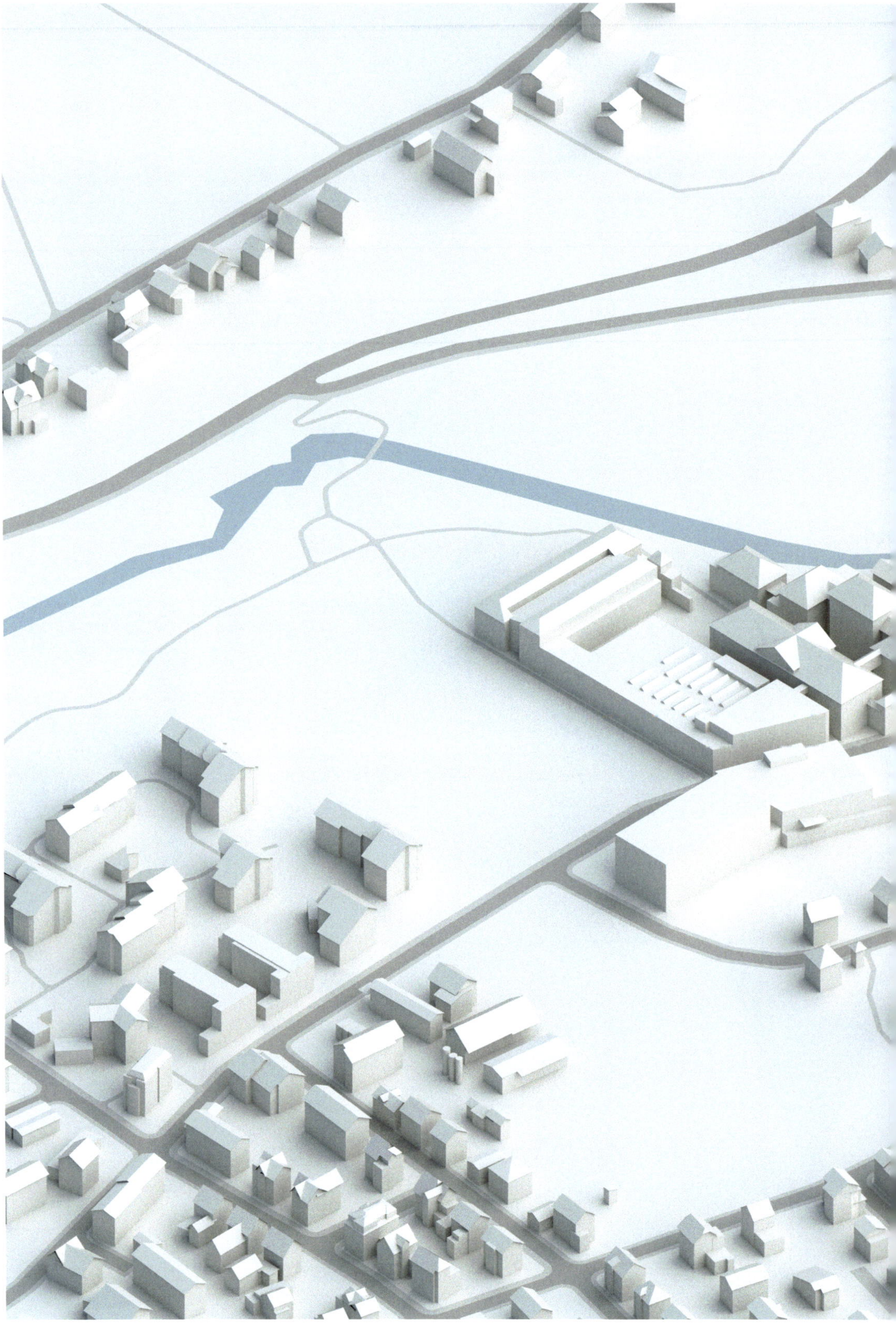

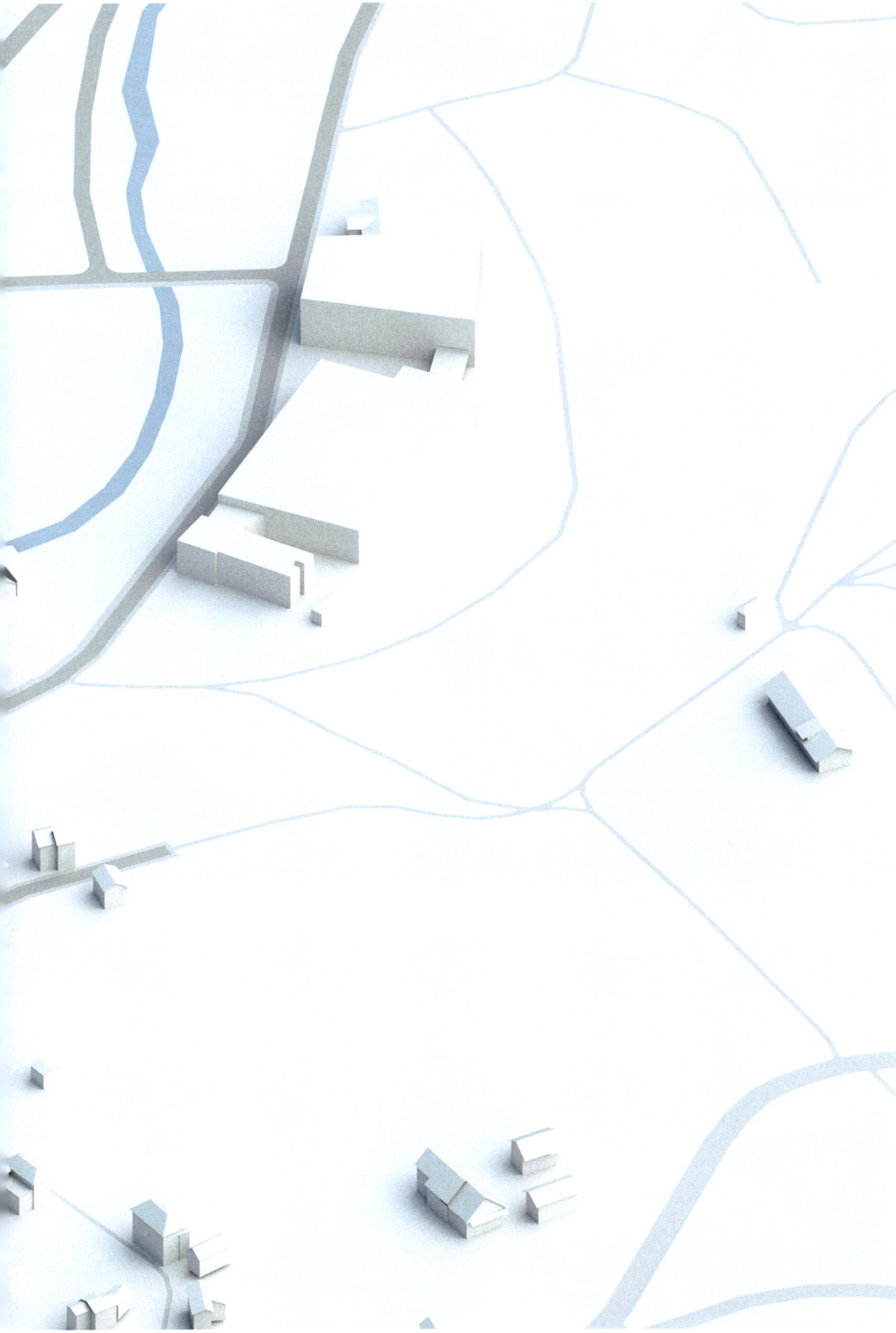

LA CHAUX-DE-FONDS / LE LOCLE

Neuchâtel

Nestled into the Jura Mountains, Le Locle and La Chaux de Fonds have a long history of watchmaking. By the 1840s this was their main industry. City officials recognized this and hired Charles-Henri Junod to plan the cities according to the needs of the industry after a fire almost destroyed La Locle. Both cities owe their character and urban structure to watchmaking and were designed in a rational manner to accommodate the industry as a primary function. The industry brought prosperity to a region ill-suited for farming. Karl Marx even mentions it in *Capital* (1867), writing: "This whole town is a factory." The watchmakers built their own houses for living and production, giving both cities a distinct urban character. In this sense, the production, living and public spaces are completely merged, forming a coherent urban whole. These unique cities are listed as UNESCO world heritage sites.

Data
Established: Eighteenth century
Site Area: 283.9 ha

Classification Matrix
Building structure – existing
Urban embeddedness – fully embedded
Agents – industrial, commercial, communal, legislative

Sources
www.j3l.ch/en/P34069/watchmaking-town
www.watchonista.com/articles/industrial-watchmaking-heart-housing
whc.unesco.org/en/list/1302/
www.urbanisme-horloger.ch

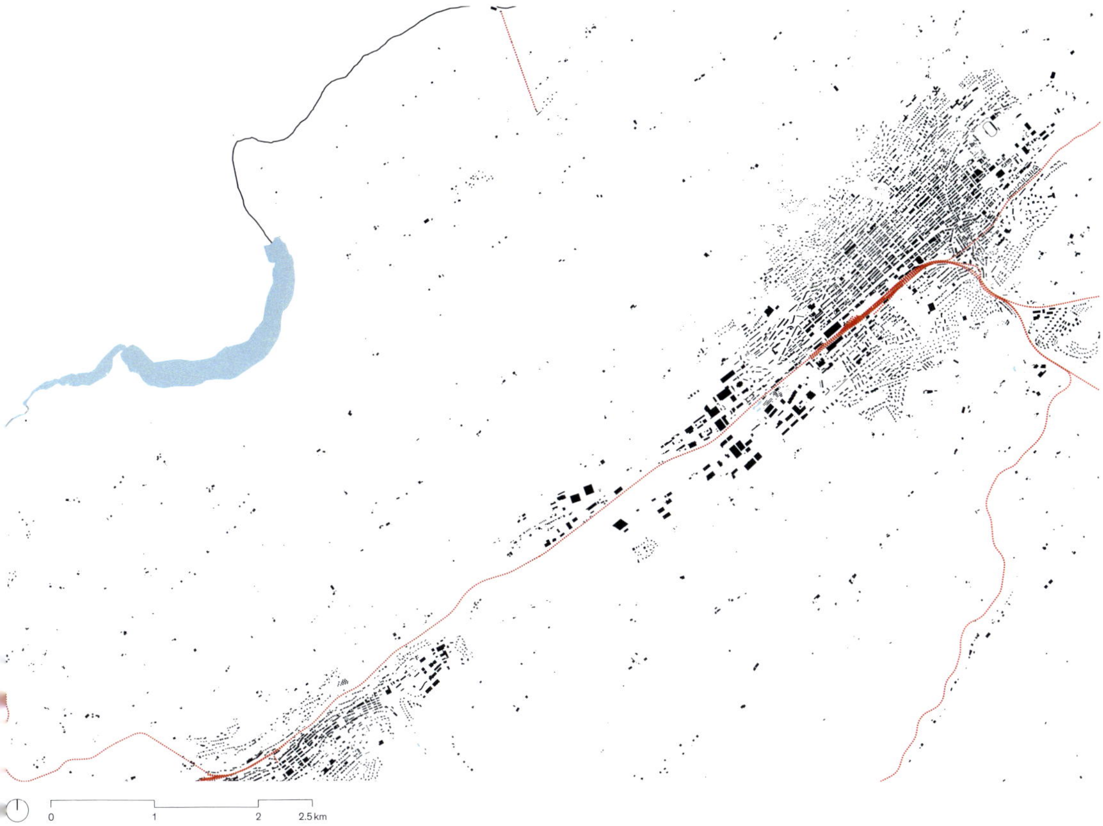
0
1
2
2.5 km

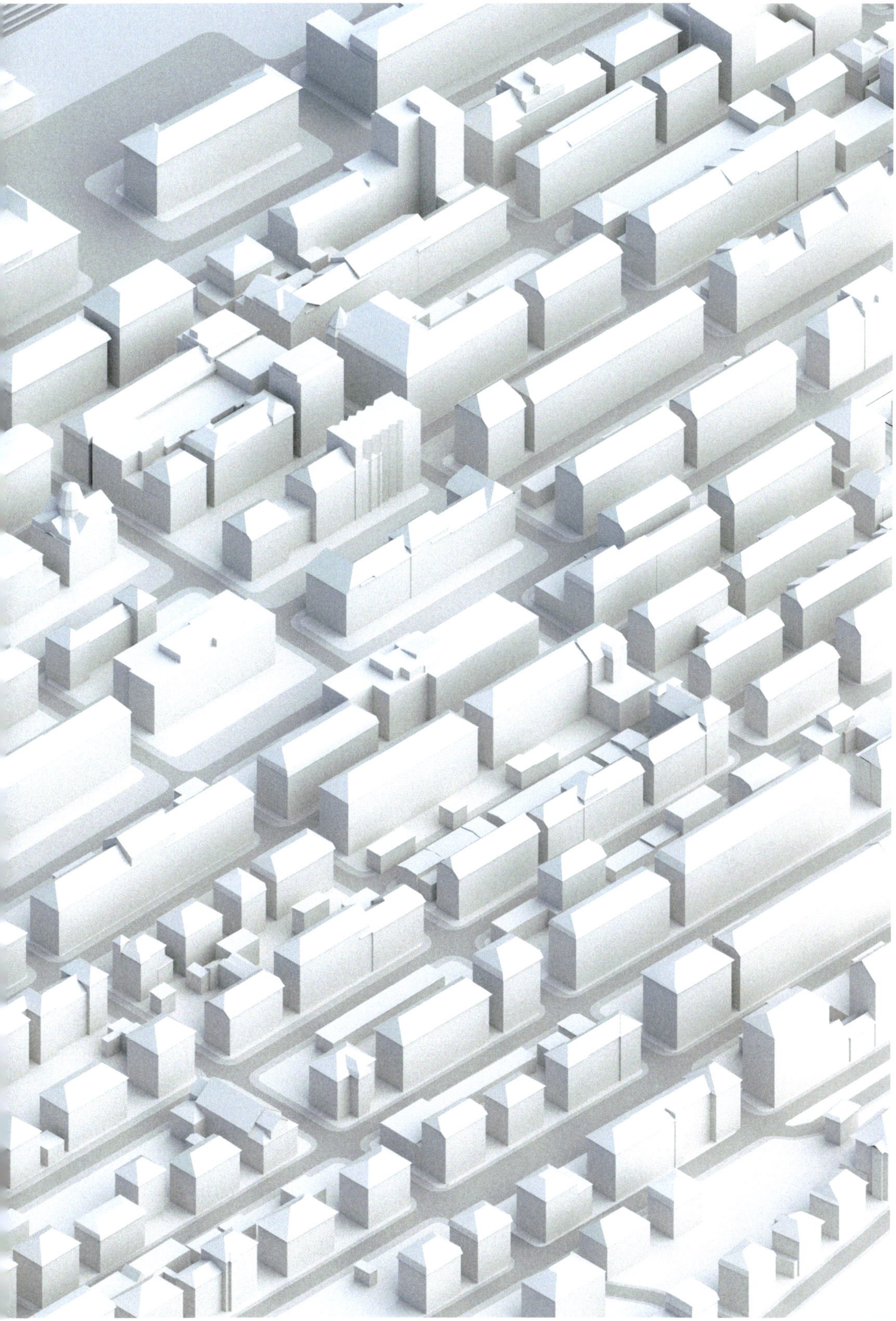

SBB-WERKSTÄTTEN

Zurich

The area along the railway tracks between the Zurich main train station and Altstetten is one of the last major urban development areas in Zurich. The area consists of workshops and a service center for the SBB railways company and is still in use today. It consists of a paint workshop, an inspection center for locomotives and railway cars, a turning and milling workshop and a large warehouse. It also has a spacious dining hall for the workers and an office area. The buildings have grown into an ensemble of streets and courtyards with recognizable yellow brick facades and the potential to be listed as a heritage site. The latest transformation plan was developed in 2016 and encompasses an industrial area of 42,000 m^2. It will turn into an attractive location for commercial and industrial innovation, start-ups and a place for culture. Under the name "Werkstadt Zurich," a lively area for work and leisure will emerge over the next twenty years. Together with the neighboring quarters it will form a new and recognizable city district open to the public.

Data
Established: 1905
Transformation Plan: 2016–2025
Site Area: 42,000 m^2
Agents: SBB AG, City of Zurich

Classification Matrix
Building structure – refurbished
Urban embeddedness – partial
Agents – industrial, legislative

Sources
www.werkstadt-zuerich.ch
www.sbb-realestate.ch/projects/zurich-werkstadt
www.tagesanzeiger.ch/zuerich/stadt/zuerichs-beste-abstellgleise/story/25351748

0
200
600 m
1 km

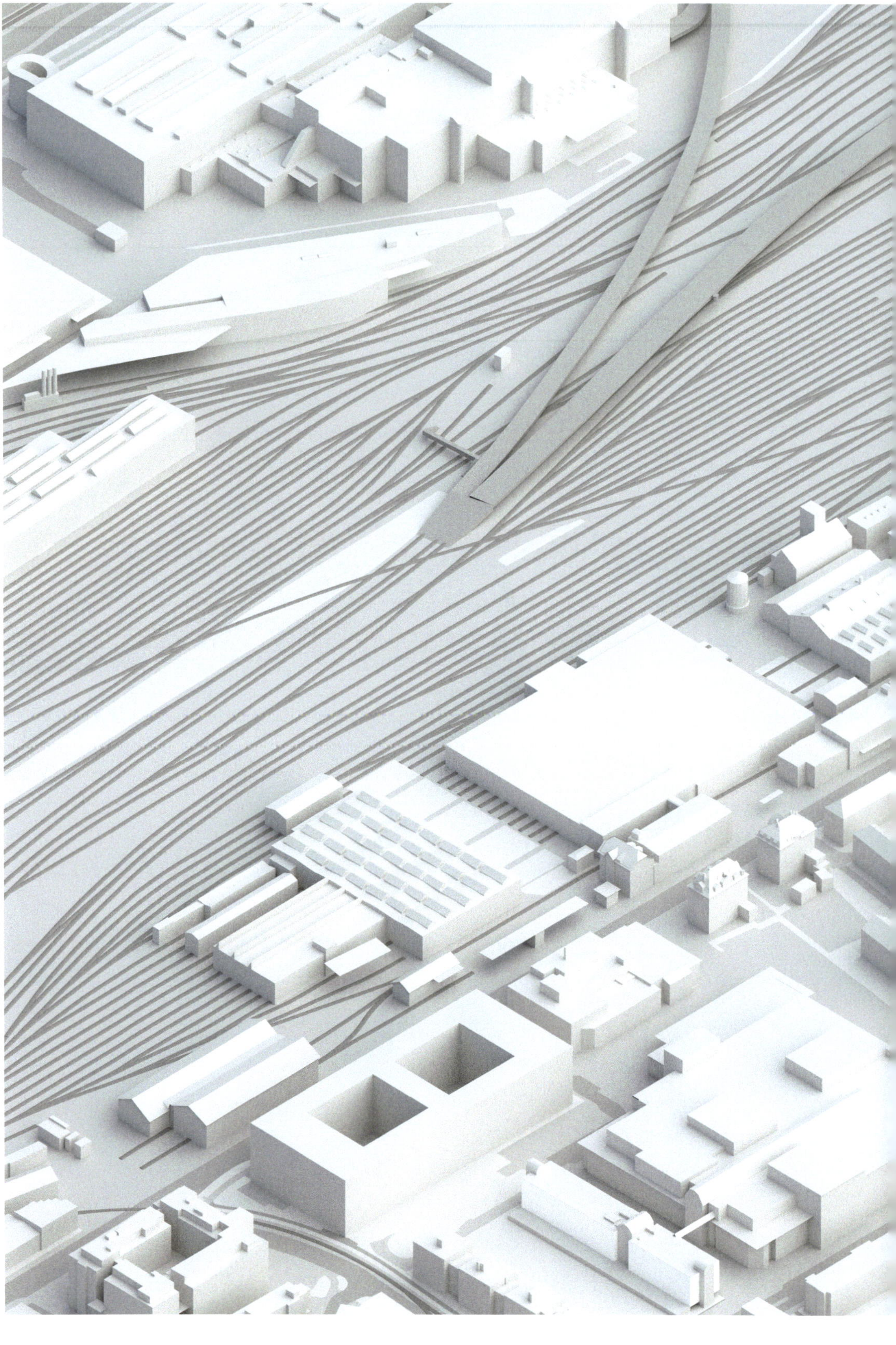

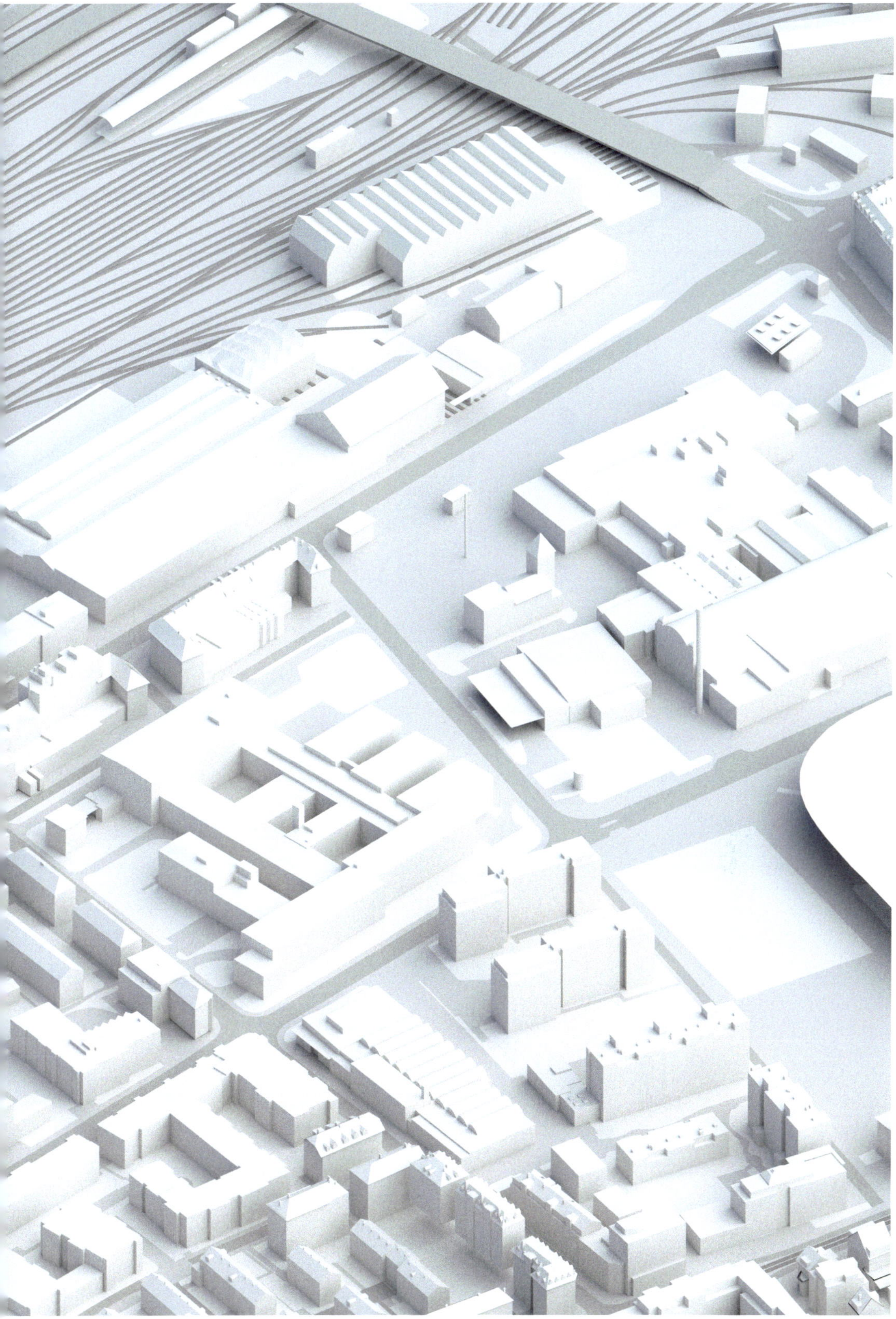

PRAILLE ACACIAS VERNETS (PAV)

Geneva

The Praille Acacias Vernets (PAV) Areal covers 230 hectares extending over the Praille, Acacias and Vernets districts, and at the same time, it is in the heart of metropolitan Geneva. This is one of the largest industrial areas in Switzerland and the focus of the Canton of Geneva's development over the next few decades. The PAV is heterogeneous in its use. Besides the predominant industry, logistics, commerce and housing are present on-site. The PAV will eventually restructure Geneva and offer over 11,000 new residential units and 6,200 additional jobs as well as new infrastructure and public facilities. Cultural facilities, various outdoor and indoor gathering and sports facilities, services, entertainment and many other uses will be accommodated in the area. The PAV district master plan (PDQ) is designed as an evolving and dynamic tool aimed at establishing a vision and an implementation strategy over a long-term period.

Data
Transformation Plan: 2005–2050
Site Area: 230 ha
Agents: Canton of Geneva, Department of Planning

Classification Matrix
Building structure – existing, newly built
Urban embeddedness – partial
Agents – legislative

Sources
www1.annualreport.hiag.com/uploads/tx_dlcenter/HIAG_GB16_de_Arealentwicklung.pdf
www.ge.ch/dossier/opportunite-developpement-unique
www.ge.ch/dossier/praille-acacias-vernets-pav

0
200
800 m
1 km

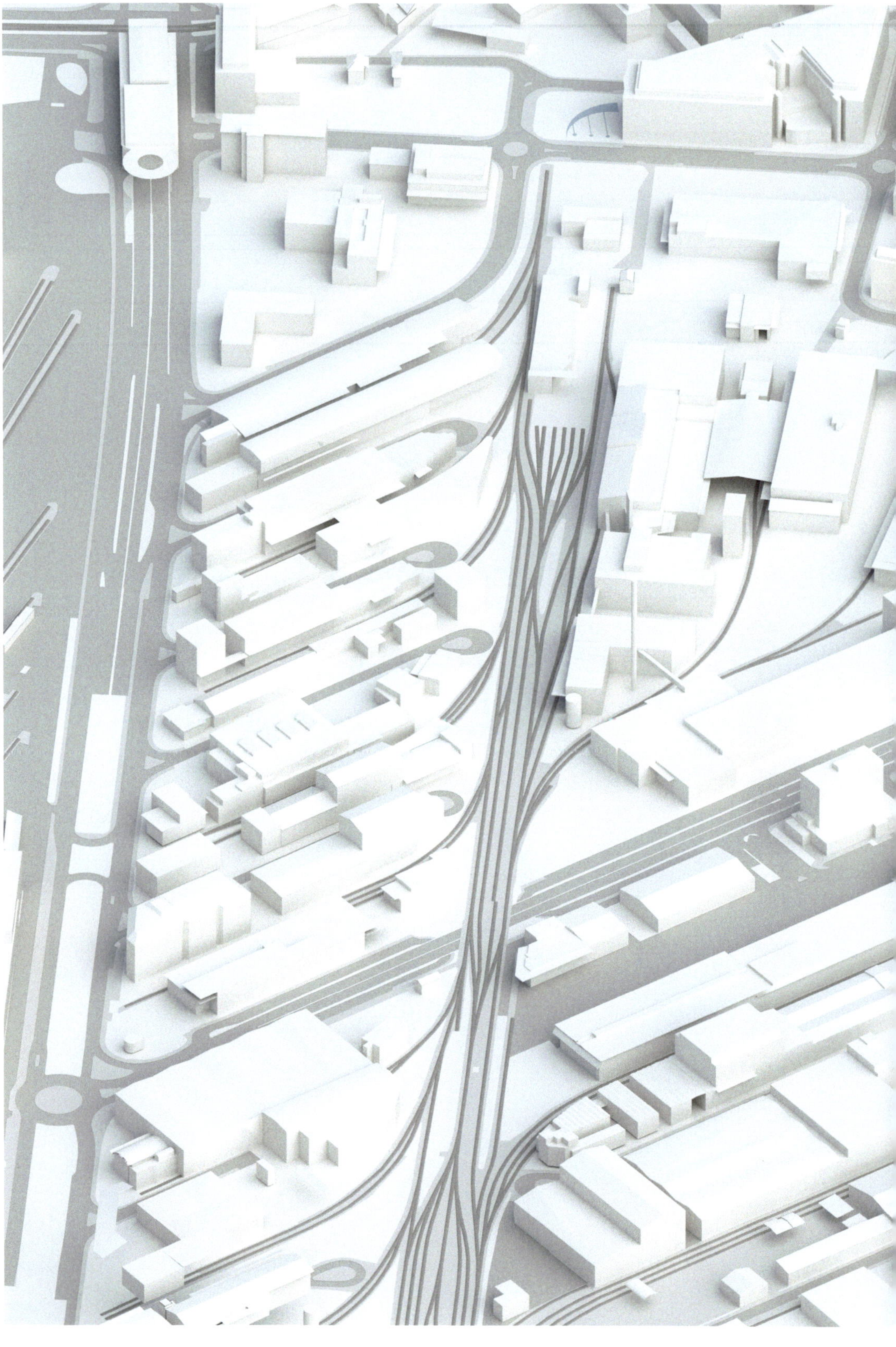

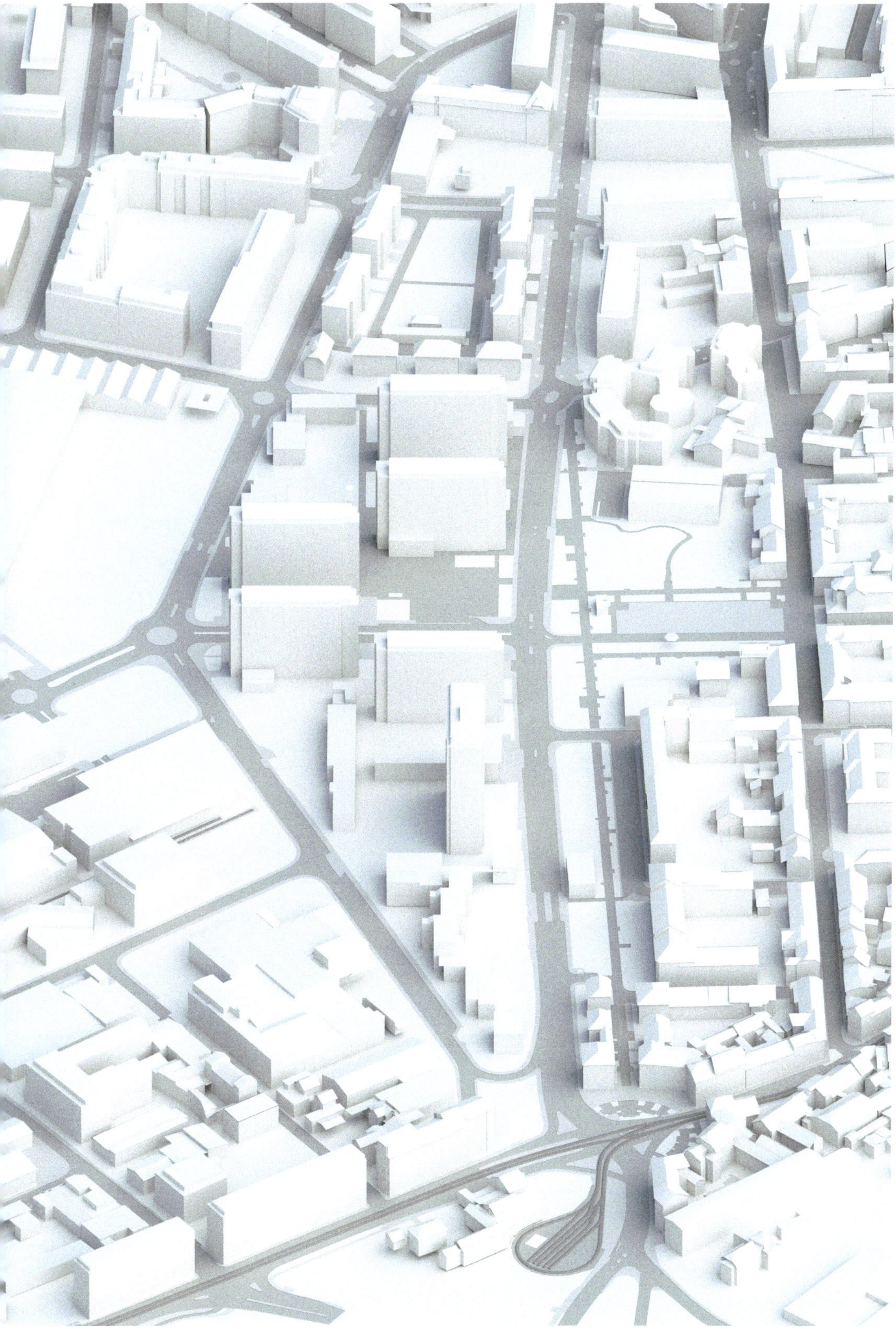

ESCHER WYSS AREAL

Zurich

The Escher Wyss Areal was established around 1889 for the then-thriving engine and turbine building industries. It represents a former outer-city industrial area that is now considered an integral part of the city center. Today, it unites industry, housing and cultural amenities. In 1999, the Sulzer turbine and pump plant, located in the middle of the Areal, was sold to the Austrian VA Tech, and in 2001, the turbo-compressor business was sold to the German MAN Group, still present and operating on-site. Since the 1990s the area has been redesigned and transformed. The latest development strategy for the Escher Wyss Areal arose in 2005 and provides around 60,000 square meters to be developed further while maintaining industry as a core use to be upgraded with additional uses for the district. Since then, housing, theaters and educational facilities have been constructed in multi-phase developments.

Data
Established: ca. 1889
Transformation Plan: 2005
Site Area: 60,000 m^2
Agents: Allreal, City of Zurich, MAN Diesel & Turbo AG (since 2018: MAN Energy Solutions Schweiz AG), Mobimo

Classification Matrix
Building structure – refurbished, newly built
Urban embeddedness – fully embedded
Agents – industrial, commercial, legislative

Sources
www.escher-wyss-areal.ch
www.stadt-zuerich.ch/hbd/de/index/staedtebau/planung/entwicklungsgebiete/zuerich_west/projekte_realisiert/escher_wyss-areal_realisiert.html
www.allreal.ch/nc/fileadmin/user_upload/publikationen/sonderpublikationen/Escher_Wyss_Areal.pdf

0
250
500 m
1 km

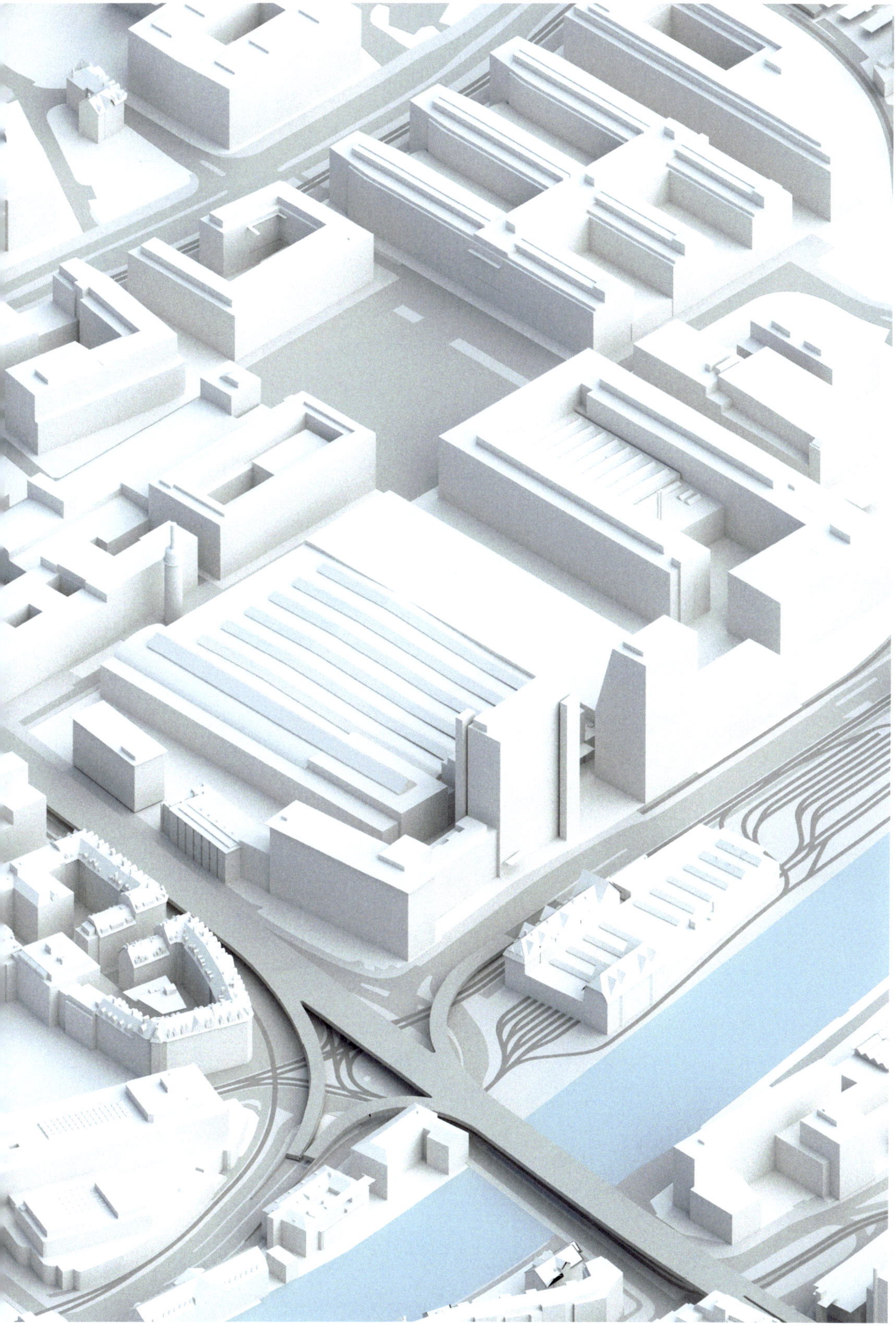

NEU-OERLIKON

Zurich

The former industrial area “Maschinenfabrik Oerlikon” is one of the largest inner-city development zones in Switzerland. The landowners ABB, Oerlikon Bührle Holding and SBB worked together with the City of Zurich over a period of ten years to develop and design a new urban center in Oerlikon. Even before this transformation, the city had already gradually grown up around it. Today Neu-Oerlikon encompasses a lively neighborhood with playgrounds, meeting areas, various cooperatives, artisanal manufacturers and an air defense industry. Rheinmetall Air Defense AG’s local manufacturing site employs around 700 people. The new NŒRD building is home to local manufacturers, most famously the flagship brand Freitag which is part of the Made in Zurich initiative. The open areas have been transformed as well; the most notable example is the MFO Park, a uniquely designed public facility. It is one of four newly created parks in the area. Even though Neu-Oerlikon has been substantially transformed over the years, it is still changing. Most recently it has seen the reconstruction of the area around the Oerlikon train station.

Data
Established: ca. 1876
Transformation Plan: 1988–2022
Site Area: 750,000 m^2 (2013)
Total Production Area: 173,000 m^2 (2013)
Agents: City of Zurich, ABB, Oerlikon Bührle Holding (since 2006: OC Oerlikon), SBB

Classification Matrix
Building structure – existing, newly built
Urban embeddedness – fully embedded
Agents – industrial, commercial, legislative

Sources
www.stadt-zuerich.ch/hbd/de/index/staedtebau/planung/entwicklungsgebiete/neu-oerlikon/kennzahlen.html
www.industriegeschichten.ch/neu-oerlikon
www.nzz.ch/lernen_von_neu-oerlikon_und_baden_nord-1.734752

0
100
200
400 m

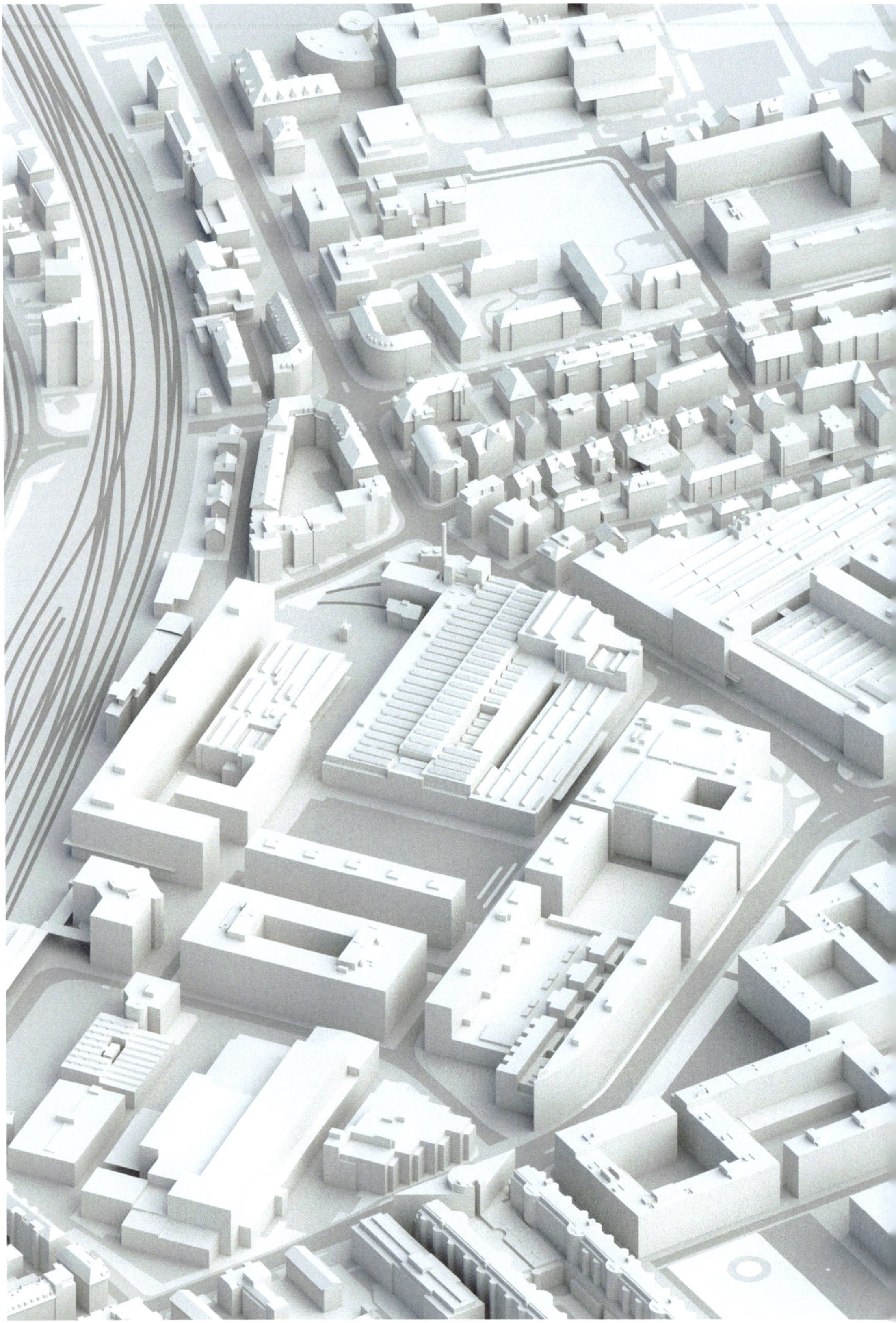

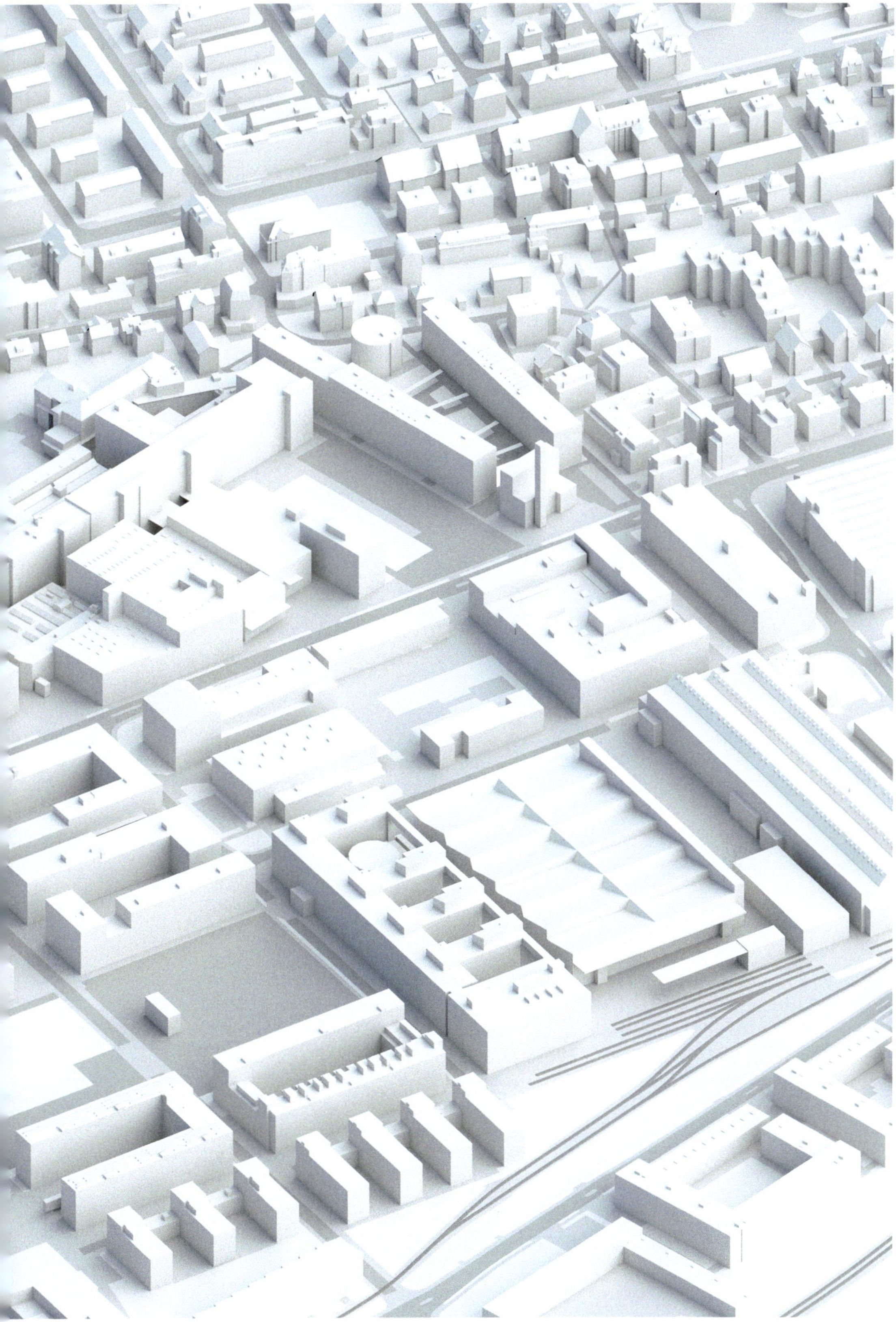

LUZERN NORD (VISCOSISTADT)

Lucerne

For over a hundred years, the area around the confluence of the rivers Reuss and Kleine Emme in central Switzerland has produced threads and synthetic yarn. Today, Monosuisse AG still manufactures on-site, while the Luzern Nord Areal has been a focus for redevelopment by the Canton of Lucerne and the Municipality of Emmen since 2010. The area was named Viscosistadt in 2013, referencing its industrial past, and is already transforming into a part of the city offering space for university, education, culture, commerce, gastronomy, residences and parks. A total of 1,500 new apartments and 4,000 additional jobs will be created here. The Lucerne University Department of Design and Art moved into the area in 2016, with more than 850 students and 200 staff working on-site. Viscosistadt represents joint and coordinated planning among the various stakeholders: the Municipality of Emmen, the City of Lucerne, the transport association, business development companies, area developers and municipal associations.

Data
Established: 1905
Transformation Plan: 2010
Site Area: 73,000 m^2
Agents: Monosuisse AG, Municipality of Emmen, City of Lucerne, Canton of Lucerne

Classification Matrix
Building structure – refurbished, newly built
Urban embeddedness – fully embedded
Agents – industrial, commercial, communal, legislative

Sources
www.luzernnord.ch
www.viscosistadt.ch
www.luzernnord.ch/fileadmin/downloads/staedtebauliches-leitbild-luzernnord_small.pdf

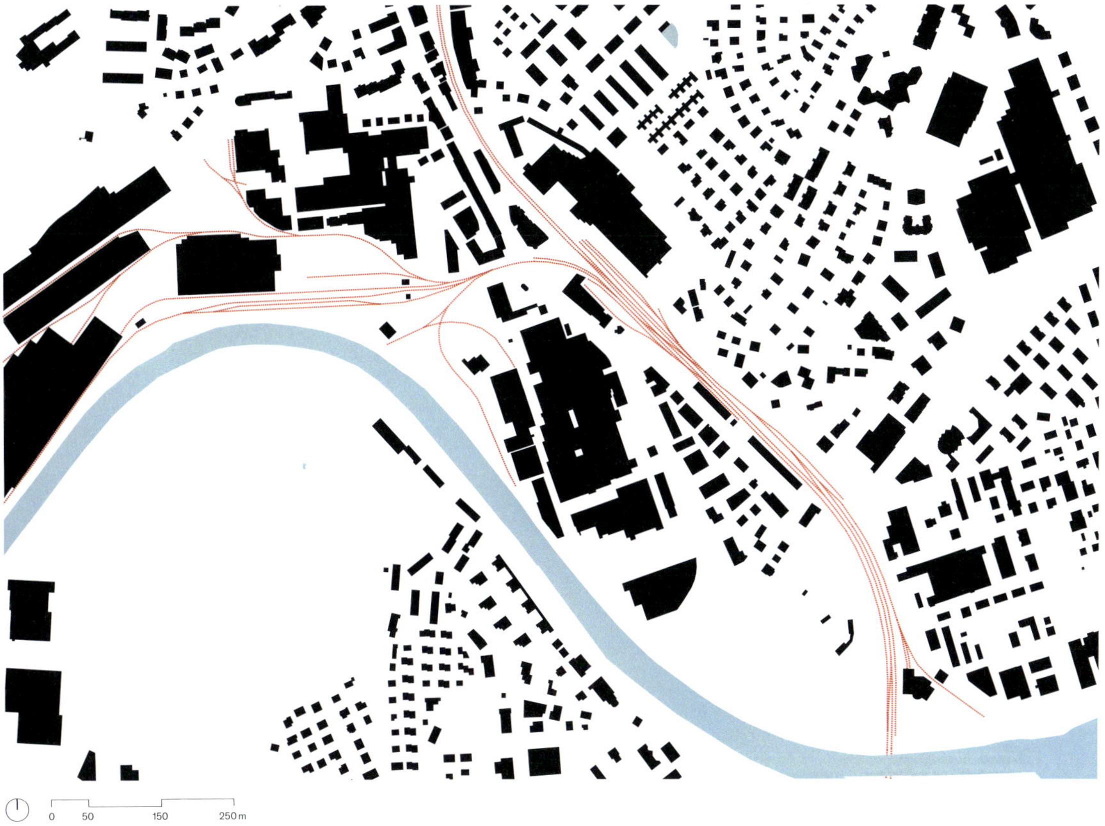

0
50
150
250 m

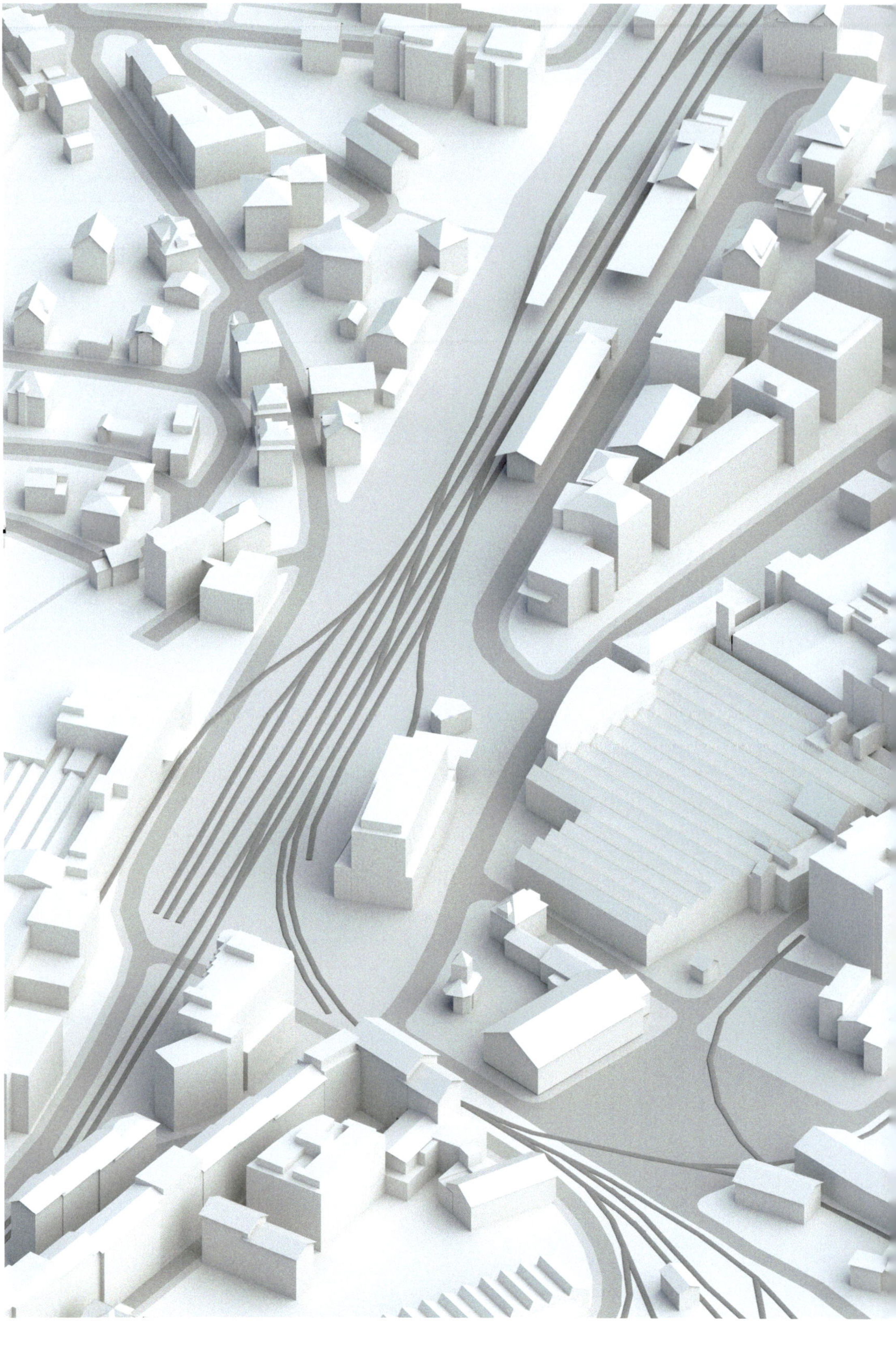

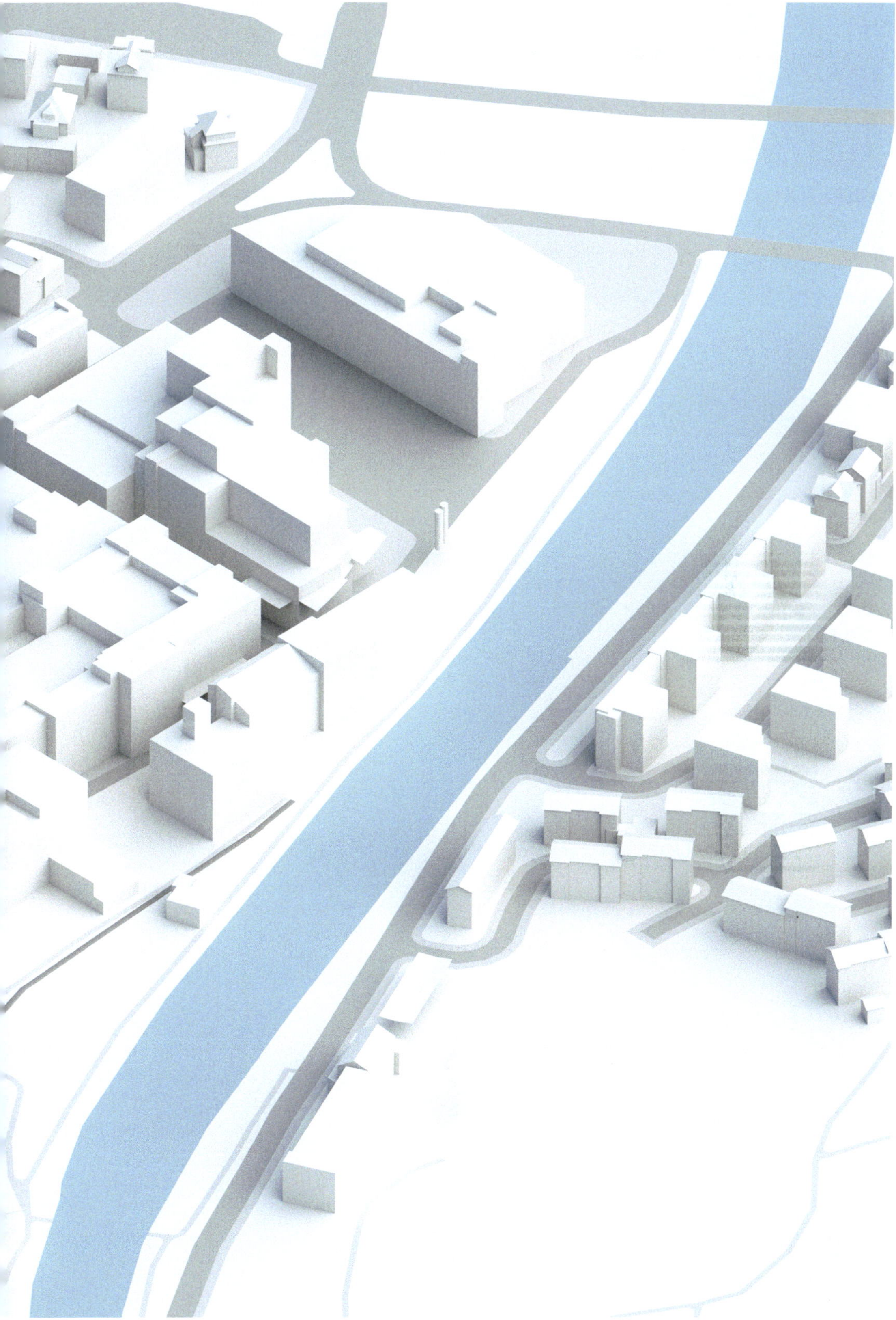

ASGO AREAL

St. Gallen West – Gossau Ost

Since the 1970s, many companies have built their headquarters and production facilities in the region between St. Gallen West and Gossau Ost. The region is wide and heterogeneous, consisting of industries, residential and green areas. Over the years, the area's informal growth eventually prompted the authorities to rethink and plan its further development. It is unique in its configuration on the edge between two cities and has grown into one of the largest economic zones in Switzerland. In May 2017 the Association Areal St. Gallen West – Gossau Ost (ASGO) was founded, with 35 members. Since 2017, they have held workshops with stakeholders from the city authorities, landowners and various companies to draft the further development. In the future, ASGO will remain commercial, but the goal is to turn it into a zone with planned open spaces and connections to the nearby cities. The most challenging project is the transformation of the energy network. It is foreseen that the current and future companies will be energy-independent, while the surplus heat from the industrial processes will be used to heat the residential areas and offices. There are now expert groups studying residential development, urban logistics, train and bus networks, pedestrian and bicycle networks, public and green spaces and energy, working on a bundle of measures for development.

Data
Established: ca.1970
Transformation Plan: 2019–2021
Agents: Association Areal St. Gallen West – Gossau Ost (ASGO), City of St. Gallen, City of Gossau, Industrie- und Gewerbeverein St. Gallen-West, Handels- und Industrievereinigung Gossau SG

Classification Matrix
Building structure – existing
Urban embeddedness – none
Agents – commercial, legislative

Sources
www.asgo.ch
www.asgo.ch/download/medienbeitrag-st-galler-nachrichten-ein-gebiet-im-wandel
www.tagblatt.ch/ostschweiz/stgallen/im-westen-der-stadt-stgallen-gibts-neues-ld.1170388

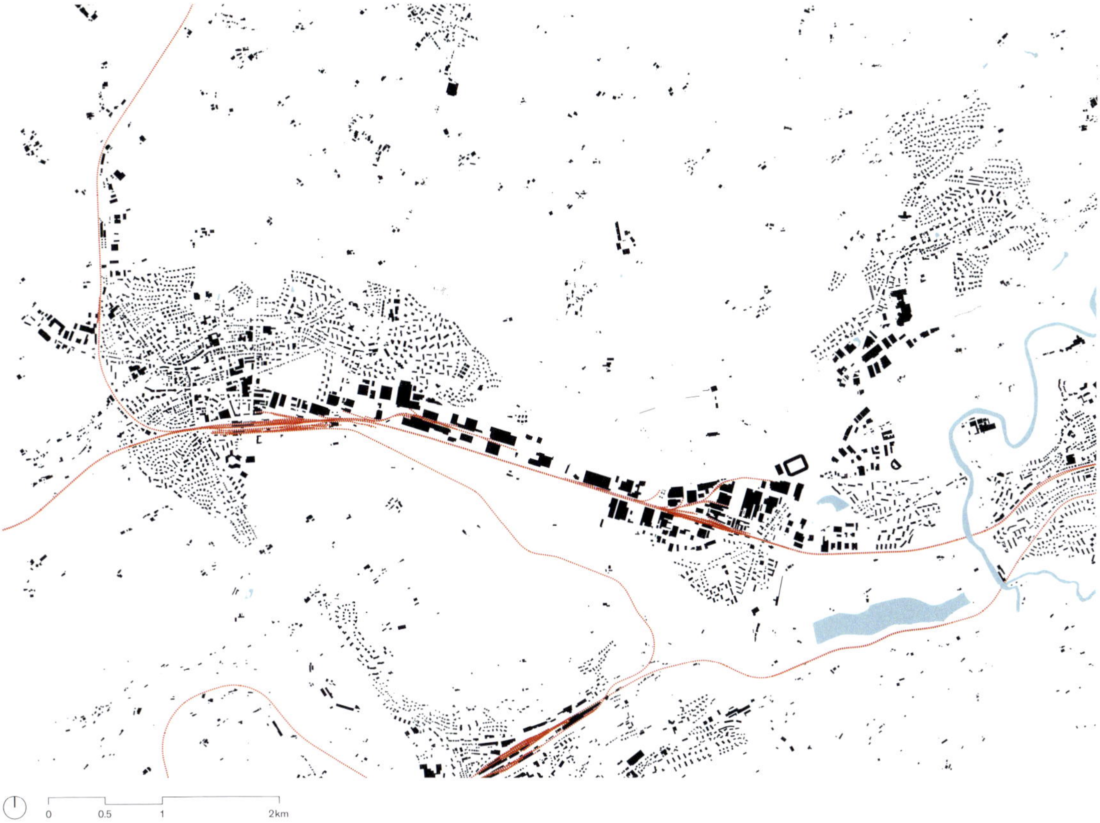
0
0.5
1
2km

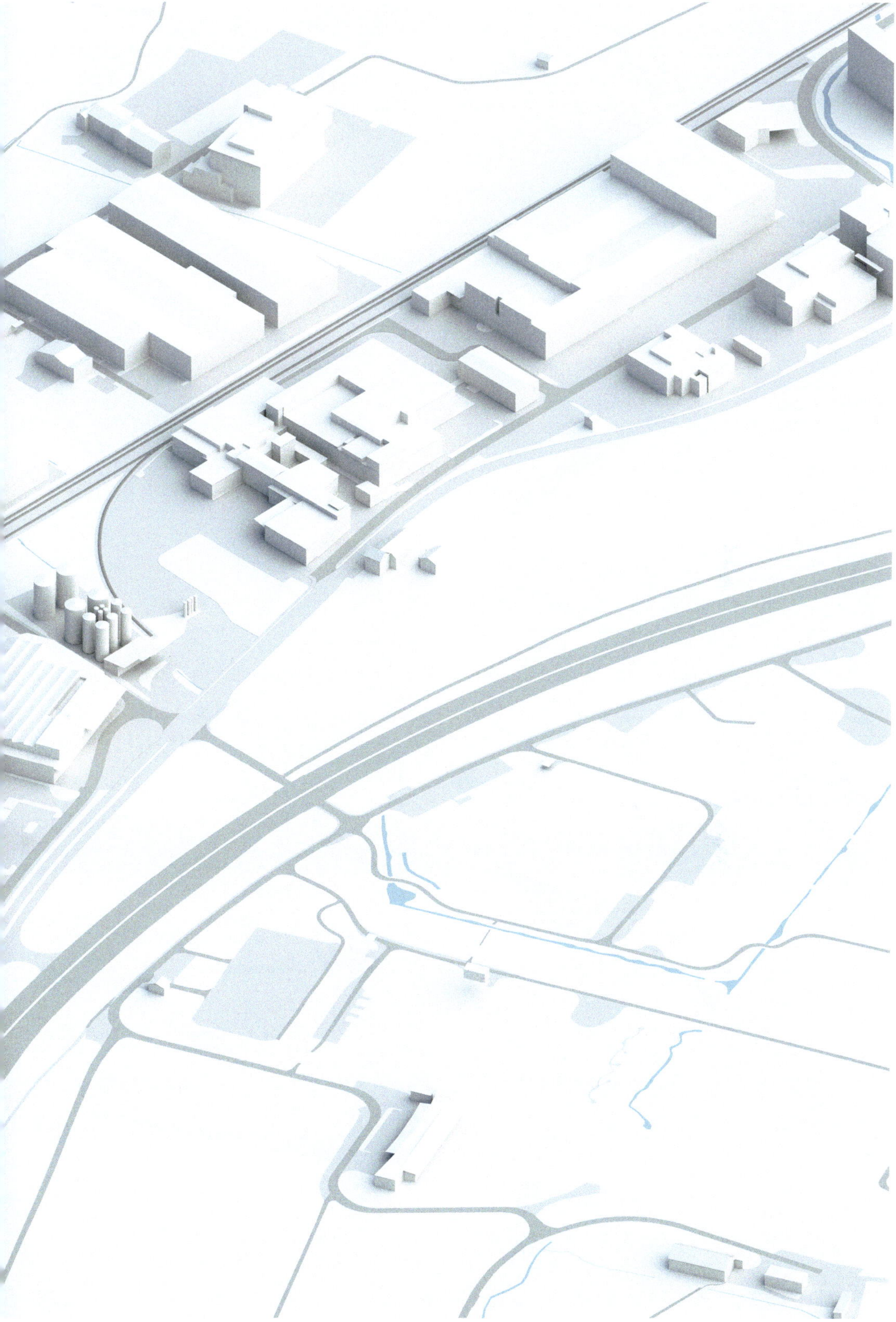

TECH CLUSTER ZUG

Zug

V-ZUG is a household appliance manufacturer established in 1913 in the city of Zug. This industrial area once located at the northern edge of the city today lies in the middle of the new residential area between the cities of Zug and Baar, currently in the middle of radical transformation. What was until recently used exclusively for industry will become a center for technology and innovation, privately developed in close collaboration with the City of Zug. The area will become a part of the city while maintaining industrial production on-site. What is especially interesting is that the process of transformation does not foresee a simple replacement of industrial with other activities; instead, industry will remain fully functional in parallel with the transformation. While the first buildings have already gone up, the process will take place in additional phases projected to last until 2045. These phases are accompanied by temporary uses for start-ups, new industrial companies, workshops, ateliers and laboratories, with the possibility to extend their lease permanently.

Data
Established: 1913
Transformation Plan: 2013–2045
Site Area: 95,500 m^2
Total Production Area: 53,000 m^2
Agents: V-ZUG Real Estate AG, City of Zug

Classification Matrix
Building structure – existing, newly built
Urban embeddedness – partial
Agents – industrial, commercial

Sources
www.vzug.com/ch/de/profile/
www.hosoyaschaefer.com/projects/areal-v-zug-ag
www.nzz.ch/schweiz/ein-industrieareal-oeffnet-sich-1.18226954

0
200
600 m
1 km

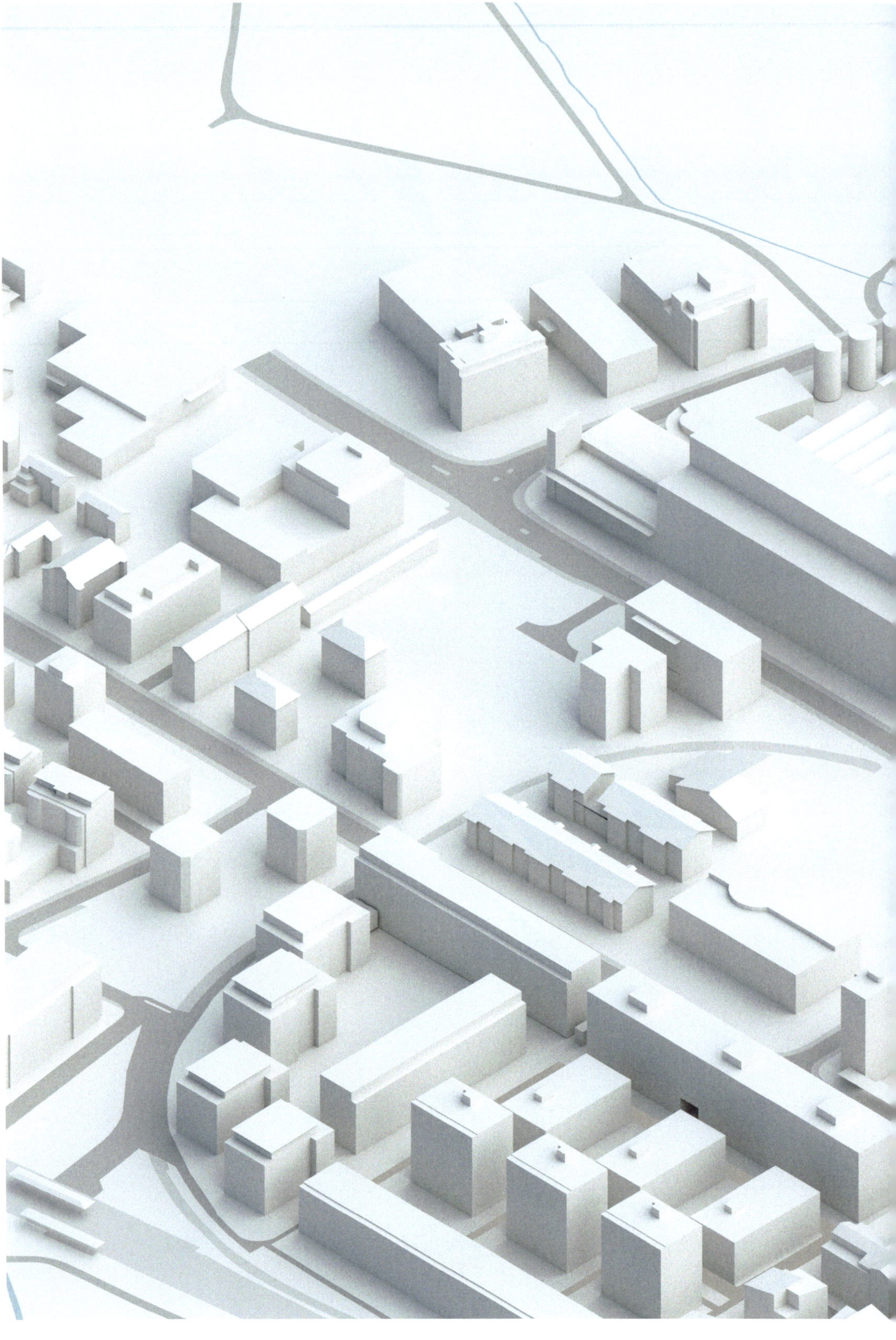

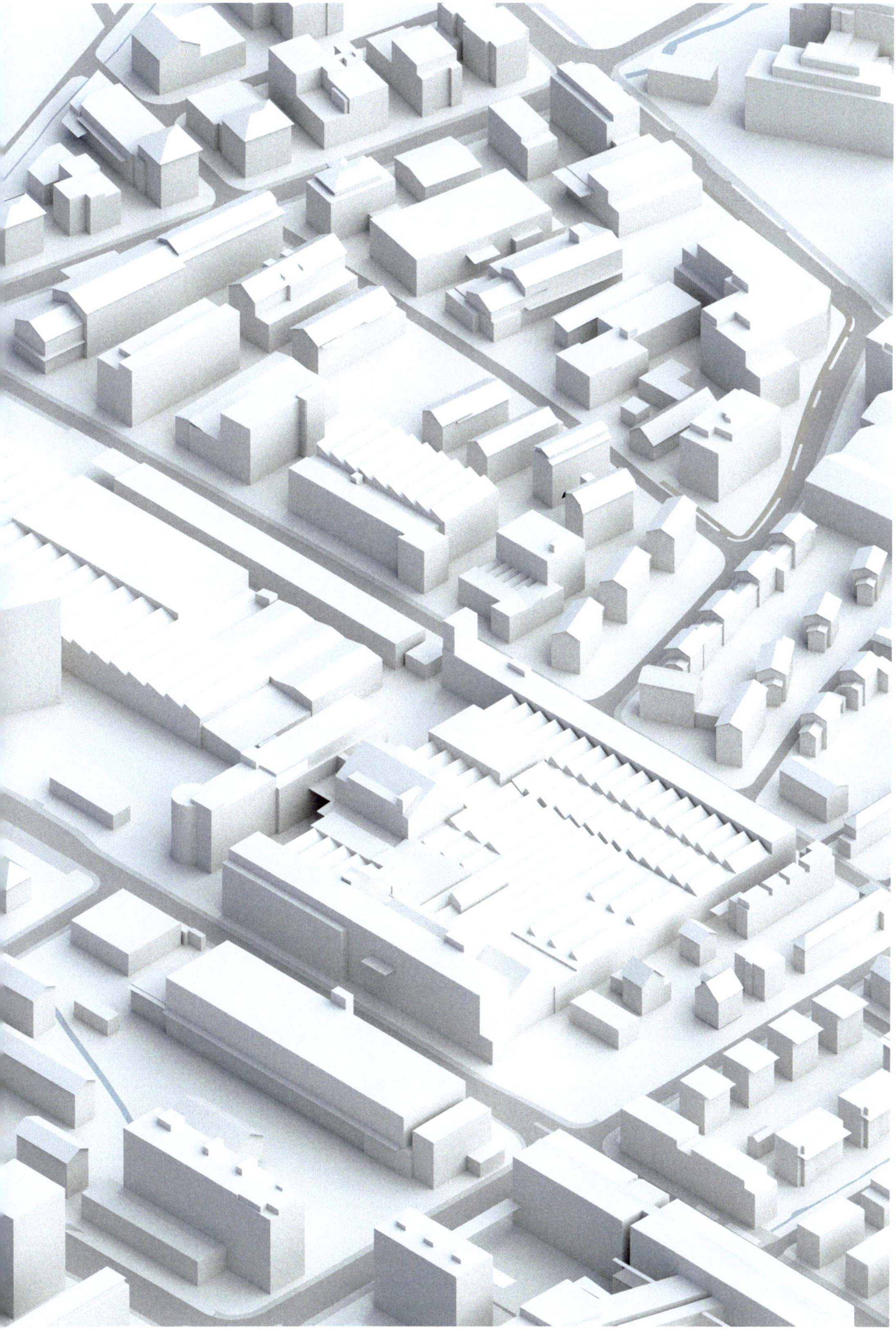

ROCHE AREAL

Basel

The Roche Holding AG, founded in 1896 by Fritz Hoffmann-La Roche, has become one of the largest pharmaceuticals and diagnostics companies worldwide. Its headquarters is in the Roche Areal located on the Rhine River, near the border with Germany and France, in the center of Basel. It consists of production laboratories, research and development centers and offices for its 11,400 employees working on-site. Today the area is surrounded by residential districts on three sides and the Rhine River to the south. Currently Roche is building new research and development centers and radically transforming the area. Their plan is to consolidate production and research in the northern part of the site, thus opening the southern part along the river to the neighborhood by creating a public park and promenade. Because of confidentiality concerns, the company has been a corporate island in the middle of the city. However, with the recent transformations its aim is to open at least part of its perimeter to the city and the public.

Data
Established: 1896
Transformation Plan: 2013–2023
Agents: Roche Holding AG

Classification Matrix
Building structure – existing, newly built
Urban embeddedness – none
Agents – industrial

Sources
www.quartierinfo-roche-basel.ch/quartierinfo/Standortentwicklung/Hintergrund.html
www.architekturbasel.ch/tabula-rasa-am-rhein-roche-plant-neubebauung-des-suedareals
www.bzbasel.ch/basel/basel-stadt/baukraene-auf-dem-ganzen-areal-der-startschuss-fuer-den-zweiten-roche-turm-ist-gefallen-131249301

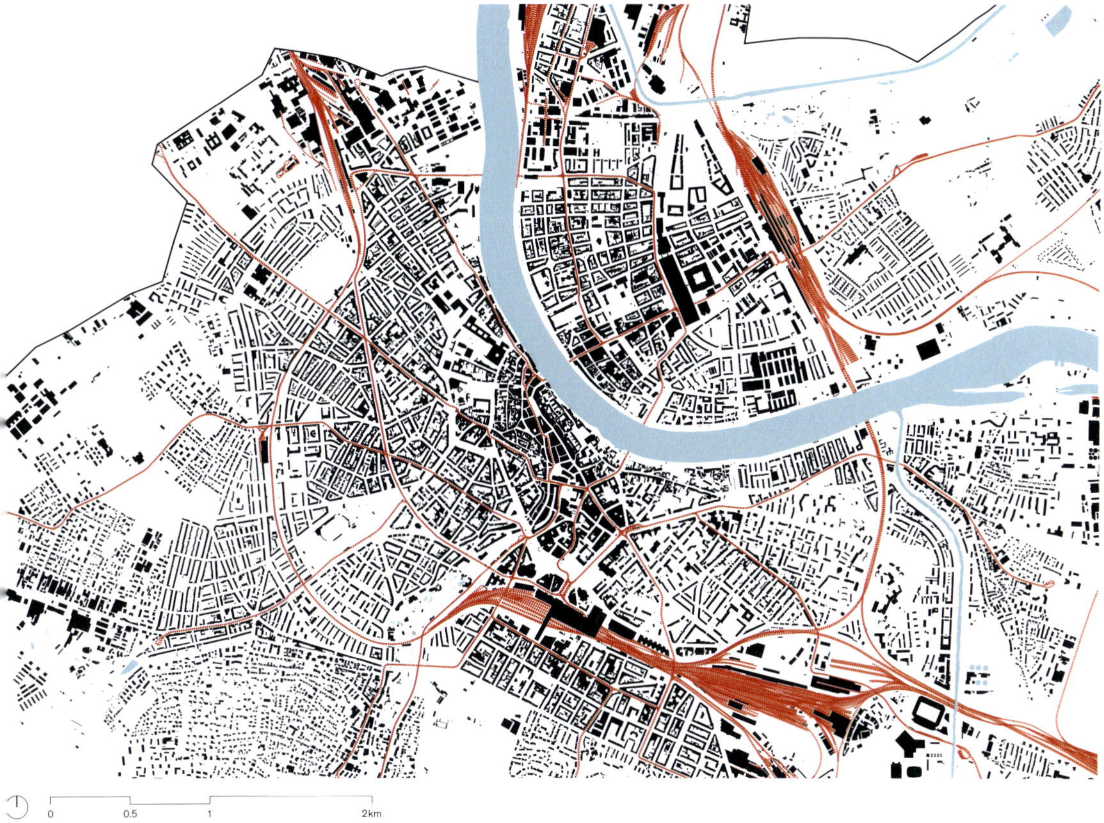
0
0.5
1
2km

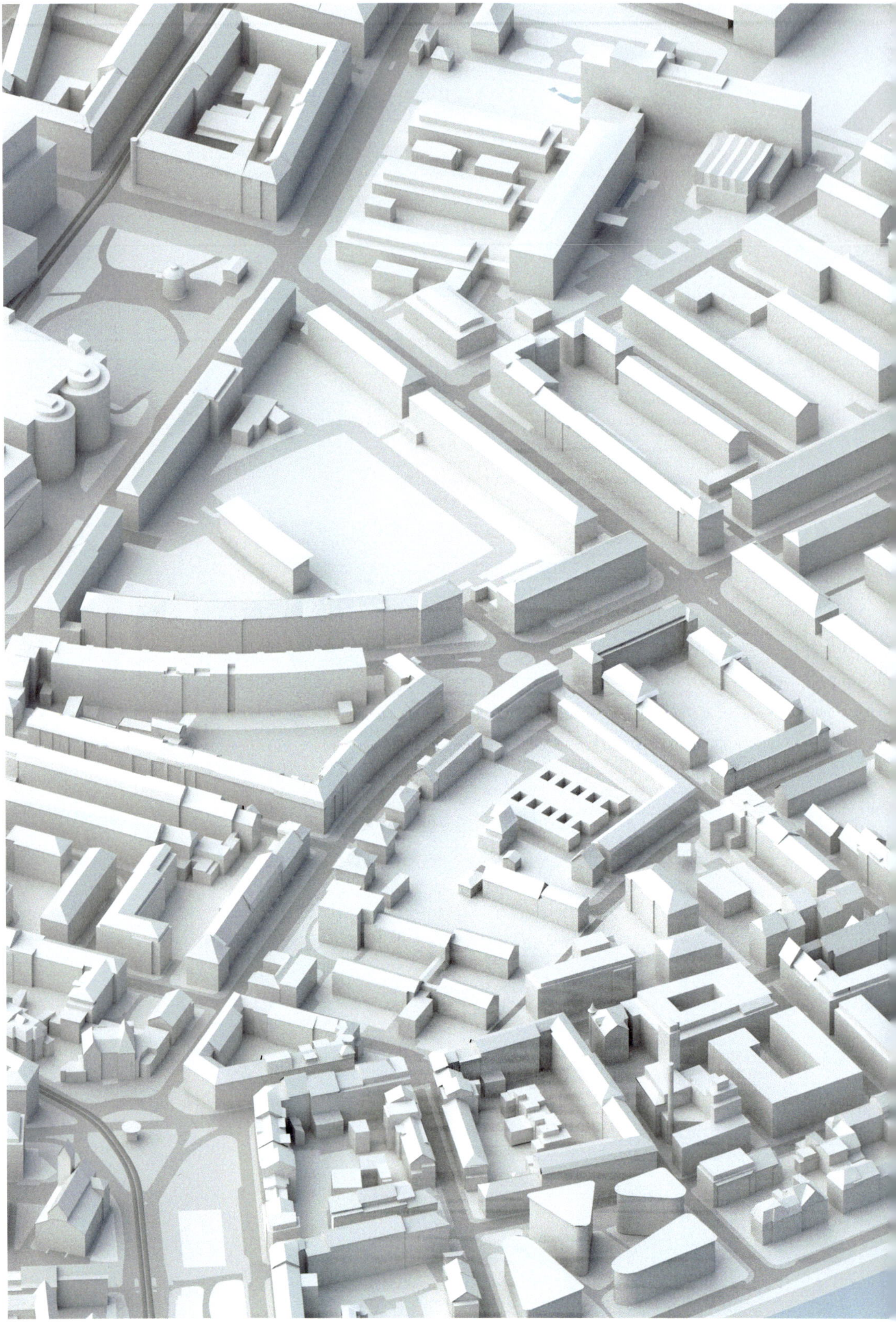

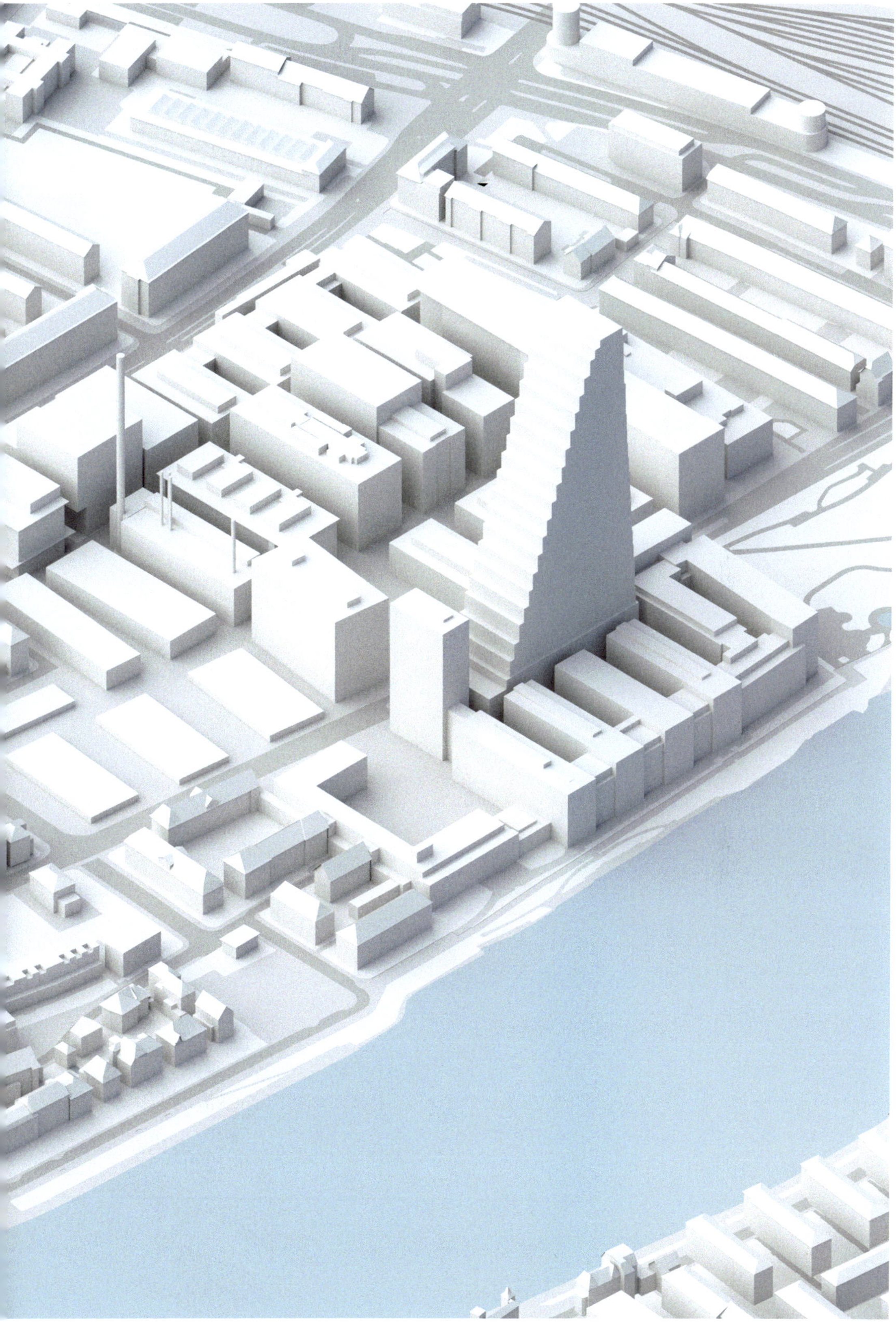

Circular Economy
Deep Tech
Gig Economy
Knowledge Transfer
Maker Scene
Material Pass
Open Source
Producing Prosperity
Scalability
Trade 2.0
Urban Industry

Interview by Markus Schaefer
September 27, 2019
Zühlke Ventures, Schlieren

MATERIAL AND INNOVATION

Marloes Fischer / Patrick Griss

Marloes Fischer is President of Madaster Switzerland and founder and CEO of Circular Hub, the knowledge and network platform for the circular economy in Switzerland. Prior to this, she was a manager for many years in the Lean Operations division at Zurich Insurance and the shipping company Maersk Line. Her goal is to demonstrate ways to improve social, ecological and economic factors for people, the environment and business. For her, circularity is the next logical step to making companies future-ready, while at the same time taking profitability and consumer demand into consideration.

Dr. Patrick Griss is a board member of several disruptive companies, and Executive Partner at Zühlke Ventures, the investment arm of Zühlke Group. As an investor, he draws upon his personal experience to identify and promote exceptional teams, business ideas and technologies in the deep tech sector. His primary focus is on health tech, since the global health industry is at the beginning of a massive transition toward digitalized, customized and automated products and processes.

Could you introduce yourself and say what you're currently involved in?

Griss

I'm head of Zühlke Ventures, the investment arm of Zühlke Group. We invest in start-ups. Our portfolio consists of eleven companies, half of which are located in the US. We're very active there in Silicon Valley and Boston. It's my job to understand market shifts, to analyze costumer requirements and to find the right start-ups to develop the type of products that will be successful on the market. I'm responsible for the entire innovation cycle, above all regarding hardware technologies in the deep tech sector. That's not to say that we don't develop software, but we also look for a solution that's a combination of hardware and software, product and service. The topic of hardware is incredibly important for business in Switzerland. We're still capable of it and we're good at it, especially miniaturized hardware. However, developing these technologies is one thing, but to also scale them up and sell them is very difficult for a start-up company. You need a lot of experience to do that. That kind of experience exists in Switzerland, but what we need now is a platform that brings everything together. There's a huge potential in it, especially in the urban sphere.

Right, and we'll come back to that. Can you give us an example that relates to the city?

Griss

The last investment we undertook was in a company working on the transdermal administration of medication – the very precise dosage of drugs that can be applied locally, completely pain-free. By digitally linking the drug administration systems with a cloud, the doctor can document whether, when and how much of the drug was taken. Tracking is a big problem at the moment. Another example is the spirometer. This technology can measure the respiration patterns of asthma patients and predict when their next asthma attack will occur. If we can detect such attacks early enough, we can prevent them becoming acute. We call this predictive treatment, which requires us to rely heavily on the recording of breathing patterns and their analysis using artificial intelligence (AI).

The main reason for us getting to know each other was the idea of a deep tech accelerator, made up of different partners who help start-ups to scale up production and sales. First to you, Marloes Fischer: Who are you and what are the two companies you represent?

Fischer

I got involved in the topic of the circular economy in connection with social innovation and then took a closer look at it in Switzerland. That was in 2017, when there was actually not much going on. But I thought that Switzerland would be the ideal place for it. Switzerland is strong in high-quality industrial products and processes; the skilled workers are well-qualified – all ideal prerequisites for a circular economy. But what was missing was the knowledge. That's why I founded Circular Hub in 2018 as a networking and knowledge platform whose aim is to generate awareness and highlight problems, challenges and possible next steps. In addition, there was training, courses, applied learning, though not in terms of technology, because every company has its own, but more to do with the transformation to a circular economy. How can innovation, customer orientation, feedback, etcetera, be driven forward? When you consult to companies, implementation support is carried out at the end in order to really work toward actual execution and specific projects. But these processes run for a really long time. I'm actually a rather impatient person and I came to the conclusion that I'd have to do something myself to strengthen the credibility of our approach. While I was looking for a way to do that, I got to know Madaster. The materials cadaster is a digital software used by real estate owners and anyone who works in the building industry – construction planning, facility management, banks or dismantling companies. The Madaster platform creates transparency concerning the materials in the built-up area: What materials have been used for construction and where? What is their value? And how can I best use the material for maximum efficiency and longevity? Where do I need administration, a different product, transparent management? And at the same time: at what point does it make sense to consider a building as a materials warehouse? If we want to work toward a circular economy which is all about closing loops, we have to include the materials contained in building fabric. Our platform has been online since September 11, 2019.

Are cities ever good places for industry? What are the specific conditions industry needs in order to function? And how can cities react to that?

Griss

I think that cities are interesting for industry. There are, however, certain basic requirements. For one thing, there's the environmental factor: industry that stinks hasn't a chance. That means it has to be a clean industry. Second, there's the space factor: railway wagons, for example, can no longer be produced in the city. Third, I think it has to be something to do with either customization, one-off or small series production or the manufacture of extremely high-tech products, because the people you need to develop and make these high-tech products live in the city. Customization in particular is often oriented toward manufacturing or alternative lifestyles. I can see a very distinctive trend there. If we take the Swiss Federal Railways' Werkstadt district in Altstetten as an example, the whole do-it-yourself activity there is extremely interesting. The maker scene has grown exponentially in the last ten years and become a huge business – a new generation that is intentionally non-corporate. That's what I mean when I speak about Business 2.0.

Let me pose a provocative question: Is the maker scene simply the cottage industry of the future? Small, but small-scale? In other words not really economically relevant? Are we overestimating the maker scene? Or does it have the right to exist?

Griss

I think that's the wrong question. Without wealth there would be no maker scene, only industry and minor trades. But when you *do* have wealth, there's a niche for this new type of lifestyle and economy.

Next question, then: How do we maintain wealth? The maker scene alone is surely not enough?

Griss

Right. The thing we call the maker scene is just an aspect of customization. The other aspect is having industrial products in the future that we can and want to manufacture on-site. I think that is soon going to be the case.

And what are the drivers and the possibilities of this? What does it mean for companies?

Griss

If my entire capital is tied up on a cargo ship for three weeks, then it's not doing any work. If I can produce the same product all over the world within a few seconds at the touch of a button, then I've saved three weeks' worth of working capital. Today's technologies are not yet sufficiently far advanced that products can be manufactured on a large scale, but the tendency is definitely in that direction. Another clear trend I can see is the progress of the gig economy. We notice it here in our own company with the freelancers, people who don't want to do coding in a permanent position. It's something we can no longer prevent. When I see how a start-up develops apps or web solutions with a network of self-employed people all working in different parts of the world, I find it amazing. Those people are increasingly turning into small business owners. And the products are being adapted even more precisely to demand – that's progress that's already taken for granted in software and AI. Open-source technology platforms enable me to create a product very easily on a modular basis. The same is happening now in hardware, too.

The information is global, but the material is local. That means we're no longer shipping materials, only information. When you hear that – information global, materials local – is that ok in your eyes?

Fischer

Yes, I think there's no other way. The open-source solutions that are being implemented all over the world and the local resources that can be used for them – they give way to new ideas that are also made available as open source. This development is gaining speed.

But when we think of the circular economy, we're not talking about material but above all about talent and expertise. The concept that we're putting into practice with Madaster is making data available in order to understand where it comes from and how it got there. We want to continue this with a creative approach, for example with municipal authorities, and small manufacturers that make new products out of old ones. At the moment these are isolated initiatives. We need to network in order to involve the local urban environment in generating economic opportunities.

But is it possible to make enough profit with secondary material flows for it to be worthwhile? To what extent must fundamental economic change take place for it to work at all?

Fischer

In construction planning, I have the construction costs and a five, six or ten-year plan. But the costs of the utilization and dismantling phases are not included, because the life cycle isn't taken into consideration from the beginning. Building with recycled materials only then makes sense if aspects such as the CO_2 footprint or health factors in the building environment are included in the costs of a project. However, there are no structured regulations provided for this in accounting terms. I believe it's a matter of internalization, of taking a holistic view of costs into consideration that arise in the various phases of the life cycle from planning to dismantling. It can mean that the construction costs are perhaps ten percent higher, but there's a reduction in the number of days that the users are off sick.

How can you make the internalization of externalized costs sound compelling?

Fischer

The crux of the matter is: who's financing it? And how do I do that? Again, this is connected to wealth. We need a bridge from the current situation, from our assets, from what we do well today, what we live from, to the new situation. Perhaps old aspects will still be a part of it, but there's always something new. And creating the bridge to the new situation, these are our classic Swiss strengths. These strengths, the ones we have today and that we need to advance, are research and training. It's important to strengthen the transfer of knowledge between science and industry. And the great thing is that we are good at clean technologies, and they also fit in well with the urban environment.

Just to go back to the subject of global and digital: Let's assume that a blueprint for a particular machine is sent to a 3D printer and it sets local material flows in motion. The material is local, the information is global. That's obviously a problem because, just as with social media,

data and knowledge are being removed from their local base. How can we ensure that the know-how remains anchored in its place of origin?

Griss

In 3D printing in particular, we have some very interesting start-ups establishing themselves right now in Zurich that are going to become globally relevant. In my opinion, it's not necessarily the case that technology transfer will only be a success if we build up companies employing thousands of people. It's quite possible for a successful transfer to mean that the local investors make a high profit and then reinvest. It isn't just jobs that count. We only lose assets and added value if start-ups accept too much money from abroad and then move out there. That's where the trouble starts. If we allow that to happen, and at the moment it's happening too often, then we lose the money we invested in training and the early stages of the start-up. What we haven't yet understood in Switzerland is how to believe in ourselves and to think big.

What locational advantage would a circular economy offer us? Or to put it more clearly: What advantage would we have if we didn't outsource so much of our production, for example to Vietnam or China, where a circular economy isn't yet a topic of interest?

Fischer

I think that's exactly the issue. Switzerland is unique in northern Europe because its system of universities of applied sciences also produces highly qualified craftsmen and craftswomen, and not just a well-trained workforce with university degrees. And if we assume that not everyone wants to get a university degree, then the circular economy has great potential for practical application. This means implementing local production with local resources, based on the knowledge and quality of the industry and craftsmanship that we already have. This is where we need creativity, and creativity needs space and time. This brings us back to the issue of wealth, that we don't have to worry about initial funding, but that we can really think ahead and ask ourselves what we really need here to realize the practical application of our technological potential.

Griss

Whatever we do, it has to be feasible on an industrial scale. If it isn't, we lose wealth, plain and simple. This also means that we have to achieve this transformation on an industrial scale. The companies I mentioned still make a living by buying many components from Vietnam, China and other countries. At the moment there is almost no other way. But as soon as we have these technologies available that allow us to avoid these unbelievable numbers of components, financially it will become incredibly interesting.

Could we talk briefly about why economies of scale have to be taken into account for this circular economy to really work?

Fischer

The world is globalized and we can't go back. What we need for a circular economy is the creativity to use the available resources optimally. This means taking what we have into a new technological development step by step. A circular economy is unthinkable without the use of the digital technologies that already exist. This also means involving the workforce in this process. It's also about training.

Griss

If we look at the building materials, insulation material for example, we're talking about unimaginable amounts of material that is industrially produced and sent in a centralized manner out into the world at enormous logistical cost. From an ecological point of view, these are absurd flows of materials. It's really a question of industrial scale. On the one hand in terms of costs, on the other hand in terms of people's expectations, consumption. It can't be changed overnight.

For me, prosperity is ultimately also related to connectedness between material and people. The more connectedness we have, the greater our wealth, but also the more CO_2 is produced. Do we need to reduce wealth?

Griss

When I think of urban industry, I don't see the smoking chimneys; I see beautiful, clean Switzerland with clean high-tech products that are sold for large sums all over the world. The materials are increasingly being distributed digitally, but behind them are real, value-creating and value-added products. The pure service economy is an illusion, it doesn't exist. Every functioning economy needs production.

Fischer

This is what I want to achieve. To create transparency about what effect we have when we behave in a certain way, what's really in hygiene products, how food is produced or even how much an Uber driver earns. And this is where data transparency is the only approach.

How can this flow of materials be organized so that it really can generate wealth?

Fischer

How can you create a design so that it can be reused, upgraded in terms of upcycling or recycled in terms of its raw material? This table here with its laminated surface cannot be recycled. It requires technologies and clever, perhaps also traditional, ways of working that we have to bring back. I think it's not just about scalability in production, because the needs are different, but especially about scalability in terms of know-how. And then we're already talking about software technology.

Let's take a device from the field of deep tech that can be recycled: this device is actually only temporary. The software brings it to life; then it is replaced by new technology. But the materials and the software can be reused.

Fischer

I recently spoke to a company in Bern that manufactures small robots that are used in surgery. They have switched to a long-term rental model so that they can take the equipment back, upgrade it and then sell or rent it out again. The complexity of the development process also forces us to think about how to revamp a product again and again so that it doesn't become obsolete. I think there are all kinds of possibilities. What might be necessary, though, in order to document everything that has gone into the development process, is a material passport for each product.

The idea of the city constantly transforming itself, reinventing itself, with this built-in intelligence, is something I find very exciting. What really happens then, we'll see.

Fischer

Exactly. If we look at the migratory flows and natural disasters, then we have to change something. I'm not being idealistic about it. What good is our building energy certificate plus, if suddenly the temperatures here keep reaching thirty or forty degrees? Then we really have a problem with our building fabric. We didn't plan for such situations, because we construct buildings to last eighty years. Why do we build for such longevity? In twenty years we might want or need something completely different. I think we have to incorporate this flexibility into our thinking, even if it's complicated.

Daniel Wiener

DISAPPEARING INFRASTRUCTURE

Automated Transport
Cargo Sous Terrain
City Hub
Collaborative Innovation
Digital Transformation
Digitalization of Logistics
Eco-social Modernity
Repair Economy

Switzerland's first significant national infrastructure, built in the mid-nineteenth century, was financed not by the state but by profit-driven "railway barons." From that time on, trains became the comfortable and efficient alternative to arduous journeys in horse-drawn carriages. Shortly afterward, the construction of hydroelectric power plants – again a private initiative – ensured an independent source of electricity for Switzerland, coal imports no longer being needed. Infrastructure investors were the ones laying the economic foundations for the first Swiss modern era.

In their pursuit of capital returns, they contributed tremendously to the social stabilization of this fragile young state. The Sonderbund War of 1847 left the country marred by religious tensions, broad disparities between the linguistic regions and power conflicts between different cities. The railway network helped Switzerland to achieve cohesion. Hydroelectric power resulted in savings on expensive raw material imports. Relatively democratic conditions ensured that the proportion of the population contributing to economic growth was larger than in the rest of Europe.

An additional factor played an important role in Switzerland's rise from rural poorhouse to rich industrial nation: its liberal immigration policy. The open borders provided refuge to the freethinkers and the persecuted from all over Europe. It gave them the opportunity to escape from the demons of feudalism, antisemitism or colonialism that were rampant in their home countries. This is how my Jewish grandmother came from Lithuania to Switzerland around 1905 after her husband had been murdered. Fearing there would be one pogrom after another, she fled Lithuania without a passport and with her six children in tow. A single mother and a widow, she opened up a hotel for Russian migrants. Lenin is said to have spent time there. It was not rare for these people – today we would call them talents – to found companies, globalizing Switzerland from within. The towns and cities with their mix of languages and multicultural fabric became hubs for production, trade, ideas, art trends and political movements. Their positive influence has continued, until today.

These centers also provided rurally born sons and daughters with work and the chance to shape their lives more independently. Urbanization led to liberation from social and religious constraints, and built acceptance for a secular education system that encouraged scientific thought and innovation: industries such as chemicals, pharmaceuticals, machine engineering, electronics and many others profited from it.

Prosperity and Disruption

This long cycle of increasing prosperity ended with the fall of the Berlin Wall and the entry into the digital age. Since then, economic renewal has stagnated in this country. The Swiss Market Index (SMI) is a good example of the innovation backlog. This index brings together the country's thirty top listed companies. The two newest companies in the SMI, Partners Group (asset management) and Temenos Group (banking software), began their rise in the 1990s, a quarter of a century ago. The third youngest name on the SMI is already middle-aged: Logitech's founders developed their first products in 1976, 44 years ago – and in Silicon Valley. All the other SMI success stories go back further, sometimes more than one hundred years. Switzerland is therefore probably the world champion in continuity. But what is needed now is disruption. It is the defining economic principle in the transition to a new era. In contrast to the nineteenth century, today's Switzerland is obviously shying away from it.

Indeed, our country still has one of the highest gross national products per capita in the world. This is mainly thanks to the pharmaceutical industry. On the other hand, the once leading financial center has had to bend to international pressure and abandon its business model of tax evasion and money laundering. The preferential taxation of international holding companies is also history. So Helvetia, too, has no other way out but through true innovation, if it wishes to maintain long-term prosperity.

Repair Economy

At the moment, however, the lack of routine means that stumbling around in the dark is the order of the day. Switzerland has no plan for reducing the proportion of its total energy consumption based on expensive imports of fossil fuels – namely 75 percent – to net zero by 2050, despite its respective commitment in the Paris Climate Agreement. We are also a long way off from a resource-preserving circular economy, which in turn is prompting the cantons to plan further waste dumps. Every month, the fashion industry launches collections whose production chain leaves a trail of devastation all over the globe, including the oceans. Healthcare costs are rising not only because increasingly sophisticated treatments are coming onto the market, but also because so-called civilization diseases such as depression, obesity, stress and lifestyle-related high blood pressure are on the rise. The industries that exist to prevent and treat the worst excesses of our lifestyle are expanding much faster than any other industries and services. Were it not for the employment effect of this repair economy, Switzerland would probably have the highest unemployment rate in Europe.

The Swiss Start-Up Scene

It is good to know that, in view of the backlog of innovation, there are entrepreneurs who want to take the reins and who have ideas for real, sometimes radical, ways out of the growth dilemma. A thousand flowers are blossoming on the Swiss start-up scene. The majority of them have ideas for saving the world: in mobility, for example, the spectrum ranges from wheelchair technology that enables people with walking difficulties to climb stairs, to two and four-wheeled vehicle concepts that aim to provide climate-friendly transport on a grand scale. Knowledge and skills are there – not least in many agile, small and mid-sized, even long-established companies. However, in addition to political pressure, two elements are lacking for the big picture: specialist staff and money, or more precisely: open borders, and capital for the market-launch phase of innovations (late-stage venture capital).

As soon as their start-up sells its first products and needs a lot of capital for expansion, most successful founders are drawn abroad, where skilled staff are easier to find, and large-scale financing is readily available. Life science/biotech and ICT/fintech companies are the exception to this rule, having absorbed more than two-thirds of venture capital in 2018. For these fields, there are investors in this country who are prepared to jointly bear the growing risk for these companies – and to benefit from the opportunities.

Dormant Money

Money is available for all the other companies, too. But it is sleeping. There will soon be one trillion francs sitting in our pension fund accounts. The money is in fact invested: in listed equities, real estate and above all in bonds. Just not in what Switzerland urgently needs: Jobs at the cutting edge of technology to ensure prosperity for future generations – and in an infrastructure that makes Switzerland sustainable territorially. And the two are interrelated.

Cargo Sous Terrain

A new idea is demonstrating precisely how the two are interrelated, and it may actually succeed in unlocking the current dearth of innovation. Large Swiss companies are working together with small specialist firms to achieve this. The national Cargo sous terrain (CST) project, financed exclusively by private money, has overcome the first technical, financial and political hurdles – technically, with in-depth feasibility studies, financially, with market analysis, a business plan and 114 million Swiss francs in committed funds, which will suffice until building permission is given for the first section. Politically, a Swiss CST law is in preparation: the Federal Act on Underground Freight Transport is currently under parliamentary discussion for 2020/2021 (cf. www.cst.ch).

Switzerland City Underground

CST understands itself as a one-stop shop for the underground transportation of pallets, containers and parcels in a 500-kilometer long tunnel network between Geneva and St. Gallen, and between Basel and Lucerne, with a branch leading off from Bern to Thun. CST treats and services this region like a single large city with almost ten million inhabitants and a high density of jobs. The first CST stage between Härkingen-Niederbipp and Zurich, with a branch line to Zurich Airport, will go into operation in 2031 and cost around three billion Swiss francs. The total investment for the entire network, which is scheduled for completion in 2045, is estimated at 30 billion Swiss francs, a similar amount therefore to that of the New Rail Link through the Alps (NRLA).

CST is building eighty hubs along the tunnel routes for incoming and outgoing goods. With 5,000 square meters of floor space, these modern freight stations take up five to ten times less area than traditional logistics centers. The reason for the massive space savings can be seen in the CST tunnels: they are six meters wide and have three lanes. Two lanes are used to transport pallets and packages in both directions. The middle lane allows goods to be stored and sorted. CST's patented innovation is therefore to simultaneously transport, store and sort goods within one system.

The storage area of the middle tunnel lane totals one million square meters. This is equivalent to ten large logistics centers, which can be managed invisibly and flexibly in the basement of the city of Switzerland. Demand will determine at which hub, at what time and in which order the goods leave the tunnel system and roll to the end customer in purpose-built electric vehicles: these can be branches of retailers, garages, restaurants, factories or private individuals.

CST mainly drives above ground on the public road network for the final mile from the outer city hub to the delivery destination. Its urban fleet, like the small underground vehicles, is powered only by electricity from renewable energy sources. Small containers are delivered by bicycle courier.

Privately Public

The CST Act provides the legal framework for integrating the private freight transport network into Switzerland's territory in an environmentally friendly manner, and for it to be operated without discrimination. The law is the result of an unusual partnership between private parties (promoters, investors, operators) and the State (in the form of the Federal Council and its Department of the Environment, Transport, Energy and Communications). What is unusual is that CST – in contrast to the internationally more common financing by public-private partnerships – requires no state subsidies or guarantees. If the constellation proves successful, it could become a model for the implementation of other infrastructures in Switzerland and elsewhere.

The initiative to develop CST came from private actors, from shipping companies such as Migros, Coop and Swiss Post, whose trucks are increasingly stuck in traffic jams and are then unable to deliver on time. The alternative of the freight train is not flexible enough for most goods. Trains can only transport bulk loads profitably. Besides, passenger transport has priority on the rails. The entire volume of freight is increasing endlessly, driven by prosperity and a never-ending flood of parcels, and it is expected to grow by a further twenty-five percent by 2040, according to the Federal Office for Urban Development's medium forecast scenario.

With its fully automated goods dispatch system, CST is also advancing the digitalization of Swiss logistics. In the final stage around one third of all parcels, containers and pallets in the Swiss Central Plateau region and Northwestern Switzerland will be transported via CST and its partners. Thanks to the large number of individual packages and the corresponding data on customer needs, CST has the potential to act as a platform company with sufficient clout to stand up to international distributors such as Amazon and Alibaba.

CST is therefore playing a key role in the digital transformation of Switzerland. The project also serves as a technical innovation platform for the country for topics such as traffic control and autonomous driving, logistics control, motorization technologies and efficient city logistics vehicles. Another business area is the use of the CST tunnel floor (under the track bed), for example for data cables or as a transport channel for the central storage (sequestration) of greenhouse gases from waste incineration, and cement works in sealed underground caverns.

Eco-social Modernity

Research areas such as this would in turn require that universities, including those of applied sciences, involved themselves – which they already do – and that greater funding were made available for the expansion of technically specialized start-ups. They could develop solutions for CST and also sell them elsewhere. Ultimately this is a mirror image of 150 years ago with the "old" infrastructures: the railways and power plants stimulated inventions, spurred innovation and laid the foundation for export successes such as transformers, inverters, ship propellers, compressors, turbines, and also special building materials and tunnel drilling technology – and for financial innovations.

Private financing, digitalization, platform economy and technological innovation are four examples of the importance of CST for Switzerland's entry into a new, eco-social modernity. Another example which would have a similar impact as the CST, would be an initiative for a brave nationwide expansion of renewable energy.

One more important aspect of CST is its social impact. Poorer neighborhoods blighted by traffic, noise and pollution will become quieter and less encumbered thanks to the CST network and, above all, their citizens will benefit from better health. Networks like this can provide better services to remote areas and increase the efficiency and punctuality of deliveries to villages and other hard-to-reach areas located far away from major infrastructure. The overall job situation for logistics workers will significantly improve with CST, in particular as a result of a cleaner working environment, greater job diversity, and essentially through the creation of more value in the supply chain, which will lead to higher wages.

In its function as infrastructure, CST primarily serves to make freight transport eco-friendly: for the first time, central logistics can be carried out without exhaust fumes and without damaging the landscape. The eighty planned CST hubs at junctions with existing roads, railways, waterways and airports take up very little space. This is also due to private funding. The costs of land and resources have a direct impact on the return on investment and must therefore be minimized. Traditional freight yards have never done this calculation and hence they currently occupy hundreds of hectares of valuable land.

City Hubs

CST's obligation to generate a return on investment is leading to a completely different kind of planning: not only should land occupation be kept to a minimum, but additional functions are also being sought that will allow for a higher density and variety of uses on the same site. This is how the concept of the City Hub as an urban distribution center came about. The freight station of the twenty-first century must be compatible with the city in order to receive a building permit in the first place. The ideal City Hub is a building that is integrated into the urban structure of the quarter. It can accommodate not only cinemas, bookstores, restaurants and medical practices, but also kindergartens, playgrounds and apartments.

The CST Brand

Being integrated into the neighborhood does not mean that CST architecture has to be as inconspicuous as possible or even ingratiate itself. On the contrary, it has the opportunity to set accents throughout Switzerland as a recognizable element, as a CST brand, with variations depending on the location. This makes it possible to repurpose industrial wastelands into CST logistics centers. Emissions that emanated from traditional freight stations are eliminated, as well as the distance from quiet everyday life required. With their mix of uses, the City Hubs are suitable linkages between different land-use patterns and functional spaces in the city and the countryside.

In the countryside, hubs are usually located close to an existing logistics center, such as the Swiss post or a retailer. Here, too, additional functions are conceivable, such as centers for 3D printing. The materials for it can be delivered via CST, just as the printed goods can be directly delivered to customers via CST. CST thus becomes a logistics platform that transports, stores, sorts, consolidates, and generates data for a more efficient logistics, produces goods commercially or industrially, and manages a diverse real estate portfolio similar to the Swiss Federal Railways.

CST – The Future of Switzerland

What does all this have to do with the future viability of Switzerland? CST will definitely be able to finance itself. International investors are showing great interest. However, the sponsors have made a public commitment to retaining a Swiss majority in the shareholder base wherever possible. The prerequisite for this is that the large institutional investors, above all the pension funds, play along. That is what is really required for success.

In addition, CST can become an export product, since many trucks and freight trains in other countries are in much longer traffic jams than in Switzerland. More importantly, CST is the first step toward making infrastructure invisible. Switzerland not only can afford to do this; it must do it in order to prevent built-up areas from taking over even more of the landscape. And in many cases, it will also pay off financially to make alternative use of motorway areas, waste incineration plants, factories, reloading points or normal urban roads in various new ways.

Today's monofunctional large-scale structures with wide open spaces around them (due to emissions) can become huge central land reserves thanks to multilevel structures, built partly underground, and literally turn into usable land what was not previously considered as such. A covered railway cut-off area offers additional space for a park and a quieter, more pleasant view from the surrounding apartments. Building lakeside roads one level lower than usual is not exactly cheap because of groundwater issues, but it can make new bicycle routes, promenades and beaches possible. A sewage treatment plant needs no daylight and can have an office building and solar panels constructed on top it. It is almost standard practice to lay high-voltage lines underground (wind turbines could rotate where the masts would have stood).

The example of CST shows that in the future, local recreation and logistics need no longer be mutually exclusive; they can even be mutually beneficial. The underground, commercial use of a site has the potential for an even more generously designed park above it – because the whole thing can be financed more easily thanks to the income from underground. However, this is not an appeal for the construction of car parks under existing green spaces. It is more a case of repairing and healing inhuman derelict zones in cities by means of a multilevel arrangement of private and public spaces.

The owners of land adjacent to these changes in use have every interest in co-financing such investments, as they will benefit from the upgrade in their environment. This type of added value must be at least partially taxed, meaning laws will probably also have to be adapted.

Collaborative Innovation

The taming of urban infrastructure can only succeed on a large scale if the silo mentality prevalent in public offices, and also amongst consumers, and public and private sources of funds, is eliminated. What we need is a system of collaborative innovation, of which CST is a prime example. Major stakeholders who would normally go head-to-head with each other on the free market are working together and with the government: Migros with Coop, Credit Suisse with Zürcher and Basellandschaftliche Kantonalbank, Mobiliar with Helvetia, Swiss Post with DPD, SBB Cargo with Rhenus Logistics, Marti Group with Implenia, to name but a few. In collaboration, they are taking on the role that individual capitalists played in Switzerland in the nineteenth century, when railways and hydroelectric power plants laid the foundation for an era of prolonged economic growth.

The step from a mentality of economic lone fighters to collaborative innovators is perhaps the greatest disruption required by our economy and society today.

Algorithmic Aesthetics
Architecture Agency
Future Factory
Global Information
Humanistic Agenda
Hybrid Workplace
Knowledge Transfer
Local Production
New Sensibility
Open Source
Production Networks
Scalability

Interview by Markus Schaefer
October 3, 2019
Institute of Technology in Architecture, ETH Zurich

DIGITAL MATERIALITY

Fabio Gramazio / Matthias Kohler

The architecture practice **Gramazio & Kohler** was founded in 2000 by Fabio Gramazio and Matthias Kohler. Their multi-disciplinary interests range from computational design and robotic fabrication to material innovation. Current projects include the design of the Empa NEST research platform, a future living and working laboratory for sustainable building construction. They also opened the world's first architectural robotic laboratory at ETH Zurich. Gramazio & Kohler's research has been formative in the field of digital architecture, setting precedence and, de facto, creating a new field of research merging advanced architectural design and additive fabrication processes through the customized use of industrial robots.

We based the idea for the Industrious City on the observation that industries are once again coming back to the city, but this time they are highly digitized and knowledge-intensive, with reduced emissions. They have smaller footprints and lower marginal costs, so small companies can afford to come back to the city and work in novel and networked ways. They are attracted by advantages like closeness to universities such as ETH, which enables innovation. Another observation is that cities are continuously reinventing themselves. Earlier we saw a trend where industries and people were leaving the city for the suburbs. Then people started to come back, first with the rise of leisure and retail companies, then service industries, and lately the rise of the creative industries. Now, the city can reinvent itself again with industry and production returning, productive, haptic and re-localized. Our idea is to start a conversation around these topics, and I would like to start by asking you to describe your practice and the core idea behind it.

As architects, we push forward the way we think of architecture as a proactive agency. In this sense we include research, innovation and technologies, particularly digital and robotic technologies. Instead of just saying we are architects, we rely on an existing technological base that we use and proactively explore, and push these technological boundaries from an architectural viewpoint. On a conceptual level, for us investigating new things involving technology is part of the design process. Often our concepts start from an observation, a system, hardware or a process, that then radiates into the design itself. These two activities are completely intermixed.

It's interesting that you say you are architects. Because when I come in here, I see you as craftsmen, thinkers, producers. And in some way, if you were truly architects, like really running an architectural company, the percentage of time you could spend on actually producing things would probably be lower.

That's the old model. But we are extremely privileged. This is the ideal form of combination.

My question is actually not so much about privilege, more about the business case and disciplinary model. If you were to leave the ETH for some unlikely reason, would you then go back to drawing plans? Or would you try to scale what you do into actual architectural production?

I don't see us as a production company. But what we've been researching at ETH is how to work in a network with production companies interested in innovation. These projects depend to some degree on the different intellectual contributions to a project. If we were to transpose this to a privatized model, then we would intensify such networks. And we still wouldn't start the design process in a traditional way, which is nonmaterial and conceptual, beginning with a large scale and ending with a small scale. Instead, we combine the conceptual phase with the

Mesh Mould and In-situ Fabricator, 2016–2017

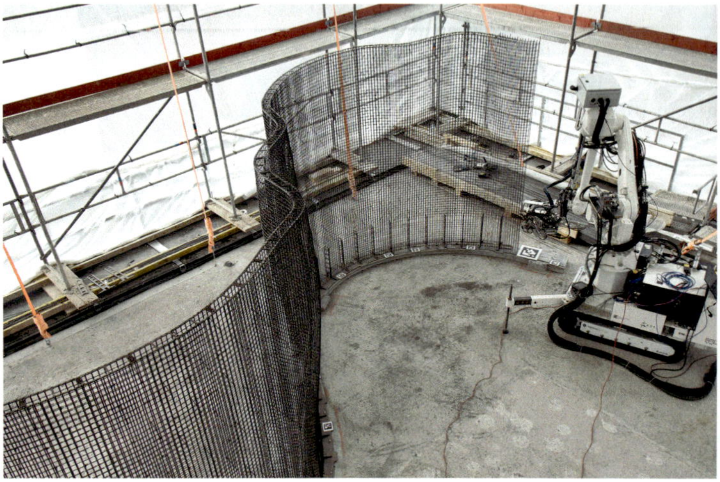

back end, more or less, the factual phase of how we build, how we technologically implement such a project as a chain and how we code it. We work from both ends toward implementation, and basically we work without scale.

Software developers very naturally work in a design-build manner. And they iterate, right? As architects we find ourselves, in a weird way, in a highly abstract situation. Because we don't produce.

I think it's very unlikely that the architect becomes the producer of the architecture. You do not own the means of production, legally. In our case, the plan is a combination between drawing and code. Or only code, no drawing anymore. And then you hand it over to somebody who does the execution planning and all these things. Or you go directly to the machine. And suddenly you need the trust of the owner to give you access to the machine, which is more likely to happen with small, flexible craftsmen and only on a very specific machine.

Because of the digital turn, you now have 3D printing factories, and theoretically you could imagine similar, more bespoke models on a larger scale. What we have here at the robotic fabrication laboratory is an attempt to sketch a factory of the future where craftsmanship and digital production naturally come together. But this factory doesn't prescribe the product. It's basically just a huge printing laboratory.

Generic?

It's a 14 × 15 × 6 meter print space, basically, with four arms. You can print, assemble, mill, you can do whatever you want. So, this generic setup would require producers who could offer this in a commercial framework, which for us architects would be an ideal setting. Currently we work with specialized producers, for example in timber or metal construction, coming from the traditional industries.

Patrick Griss, another one of our interview partners, envisions that instead of transporting goods in shipping containers, we would just send the information and then produce locally – global information, local production.

This was the assumption we had when we started to work with robots. If you have the same system here and in China, it doesn't make sense to produce here and ship there. If you can just send the data and know that you have an identical set up on the other end you can use that just like a 3D printer. Now, this thinking can go further. The receiving end doesn't even have to have an identical setup. It can be done with just some compatibilities and protocols between the two ends. For example, if you take robots, it will be along the lines of end-effectors and materials. Maybe you can send an end-effector that's then mounted on a robot. However, that robot could have a different metric. This seems feasible. For example, in 2008 for the Venice Biennale we sent a container with a robot, and later we sent the same thing to New York, so we are already working with this idea.

That brings me to a core question. César Hidalgo talks of knowledge being sticky. He argues that while information flows freely, while anything can be found on Google, you still need local know-how embedded in people to make things work. How generic do you think these robotic futures can be? And how much is still embedded in local practice? You have local suppliers who can come when the robot is broken. You have assistants and students who know how to use the machine. How much can you abstract what you do from space and matter?

In a global world, this know-how becomes a bit more diffused. But right now, it's clearly bound to a context. It's a thing that has to build up with time. I can imagine that in twenty years there will be big city hubs where this culture can grow. If the culture for this kind of knowledge is present locally, then there will be interoperability. I don't think you will have all this culture concentrated at MIT and the rest of the world would just be dumb hardware. That would never work. The process has to be reciprocal. If certain places have specific knowledge others are interested in, you can trade it, but the trade goes in several directions.

In the long run, every technology we've seen has been kind of broken down and made easier, probably also dumber in a way, by integrating it more. I'll give a technical example. Until now, robots were programmed by telling them the exact motion in space. Now we see a shift toward telling the robot where it should be and what it should avoid. And it finds its own path. I think there are many of these small shifts which in combination make it quite plausible that complex tools and instruments requiring a lot of people, maintenance and knowledge can become more and more easily accessible. So, what you need is a culture that works with these trends, and kind of adapts to them.

For architecture, I think it's worthwhile to be involved in these processes and shape them, so that it's not only industry, for example manufacturing or CAD, driving these developments. But the drive to make processes simpler will remain.

More generic, pure information you can send somewhere in the world and they can work with it, right?

There is another development that Professor Philippe Block launched. We started, for example, to write open source code accessible to the entire institute and now to other universities like MIT. The idea is to bring in an agency at the software level and build alliances. That's a new development for architectural discourse. This means, for example, when people leave this place, if a PhD student gets a professorship, like for example Stefana Parascho who went to Princeton and Kathrin Dörfler who went to TU Munich, they can just implement the shared code base in another location and continue contributing.

I think that's brilliant and closer to the scientific method than an industrial approach implemented in closed silos.

If we work on a project with an industrial company, we would say, "You will profit, and we will profit, by working on a shared code base. It means you will be tracking what's currently happening on the university level. And you'll have support for your development by tapping into that knowledge." Then they develop their custom application on that code base – a kind of plug-in. That would represent a big shift because it promotes the participation of smaller companies that lack the power, size or experience to implement it by themselves. Big industries are frightened by this idea because it goes against their proprietary thinking about processing knowledge or developing software. But clearly things will move in this direction.

Robotic Fabrication Laboratory, 2010–2017

The next big topic is the question of how to scale. You base much of your work on prototyping and open source thinking, and I wonder how you can scale up the means and tools of production toward an industrial and economically viable involvement.

Strangely enough, I'm not so worried about scaling.... We have an unconventional method, aside from the regular academic procedures like disseminating papers, which is to demonstrate our ideas with real buildings like the DFAB house, or the roof of our institute building here. The aim is to say, "Okay, can we push what happens in the research lab out to factual architectural reality?" Although these are small and unique pilot projects that don't transfer easily to industry, they create an awareness that this is a reality now. In the case of the DFAB house, all the structural components were built using different additive fabrication technologies. This demonstrates that right now we can build a house by digitally fabricating all the major components. This is slowly pushing the boundaries of what's possible, and people love it. Not long ago, companies like Google announced their intention to build their new headquarters using robots, but in the end they couldn't pull it off. And in this respect, we're saying, "Our projects are small, they're Swiss, but here they are." I think that's part of a unique method, and probably we will not be able to scale this up ourselves.

Scaling isn't part of academia's mandate; we try to transfer. But increasingly now, larger companies are interested in this. For example, Google is now doing urban development.... I'm more worried about architecture than about scale. I think scale will happen with these technologies, maybe just not in the direction we intended. Then the question becomes what is the role of architecture in scaling up? What is an appropriate architecture for these new industrial processes? I don't think that's been properly answered yet.

If you argue that the digital chain is controllable, then the question becomes, who controls it? Is it the architect, the producer, the contractor, or is it the guy who controls the digitality of it, like Google? In that case, the architect can quickly become obsolete and our way of doing architecture an antiquated model...

From the traditional fabrication point of view, this technology can be applied as a model everywhere, it can scale up, but what about architectural and cultural values that go beyond optimization? This is what's at stake for us. Architects, and not only architects, have a great responsibility to steer this process. We need to ask: Who will drive these developments? And who will engage with them?

The argument for Deep Tech, the combination of software and hardware, is not only that it will be a business model of the future. Deep Tech also means you have a local, material base that could resist extreme globalization. For example, local hot spots of integrated industrial knowledge could allow you to generate a counterweight to pure data flows. The applications we use, like Google Maps, are all globalized; and data extraction happens quickly. We use Google Maps as a convenience, but our data is extracted and processed in Silicon Valley and furthers a Silicon Valley business case, rather than a local business case.

I'm firmly convinced that you have to invest heavily in education and networks that are very local. You have certain specific conditions, and you have to recognize the conditions. This is where we start from. If we think in these terms, then at a certain point architecture becomes valuable again. It can go beyond optimization and rationalization, which probably will drive the first wave of big investments.... I think that the pure service aspect of architecture cannot compete with Google, but you can compete in terms of intelligence and beauty, and with in-depth knowledge of how to put things together.

Architects need to work with the same technologies as other companies. We cannot compete by retracting into a niche because we would become very marginalized. Working with these technologies while combining them with the substantial knowledge of our domain – that's basically winning. I think the slowly changing sensibility of the markets provides another opportunity. Sustainability as a consideration, for example. Here you have a sense that society doesn't look for the same projects it used to. If this trend does not get overwhelmed by marketing agencies for the big players telling us what future we want, it could become valuable. A new sensibility or a big push toward local material resources could turn into economic value, a situation where architects or producers with appropriate ethics are sought after. That is not easy if you come out of an old industrial paradigm.

How inclusive can you be in working in an organization like this? What I am hoping for is a future society where, ideally, a robot lab can be located in downtown Zurich and produce things people actually need in collaboration with traditional craft – for me, that's a beautiful fiction.

Our agenda is extremely humanistic, and I think it's important to have a vision rooted in values. An ideal future, for example, would be to have this local knowledge competing globally with other specializations or flavors of this knowledge, making it possible to exchange and integrate machines and people.

The new workplaces are also production places. They are not only desks for meetings. This is also important for architecture, to enable and bring up spaces that can hybridize the physicality of production and intellectual work. I don't think these two domains need to be disconnected anymore. There's also a technological reason for this: machines are getting smarter, they have more sensors, etc., so they can be closer to humans. Traditionally, this was just too dangerous in many domains. That's not the case anymore.

You have the knowledge worker who is educated, well paid, and wants to live in the city, in a real city with a lot of quality of life. With the craftsman of the future – and I include us in this category – you again have people who are highly educated and don't want to move to the outskirts or the middle of nowhere to produce. You can't do that anymore. It's naïve and socially unsustainable to try to install people who work on computers doing design and other intellectual work, and their machines, in an unpopulated location.

Let's talk about beauty finally. What I find interesting about the roof of the new ITA (Institute of Technology in Architecture) building we are sitting under is that it looks quite imperfect, kind of like digital vintage. It shows the idea that the digital does not need to appear perfect; it can look crafted.

This roof is a deliberate expression of the algorithm that optimized it. There is an optimization of how many nails go into each joint and the width of each slate is scaled accordingly so it can have the right number of connections. This leads to the jagged lines you see if you look across the roof. This is not how we usually imagine the digital – it's a purely algorithmic detail that results in an imperfect – you could say crafty – expression. We want to allow the aesthetics of these processes, be they material or algorithmic, to express themselves.

Exactly. Which brings us to the final idea in this actor network of people and robots, things and spaces we are discussing. If each actor is free and kind of respected for what he, she or it does, then you have this almost ecological aesthetics emerging as a result.

Because it's just happening. It's process driven.

Anna Schindler

URBAN PRODUCTION IS NOT UTOPIAN

Brooklyn Navy Yard
Industry 4.0
Made in Zurich
SFMade
Urban Economics
Urban Manufacturing Alliance
Urban Production
Werkstadt

"Zurich is more than tourism, more than shopping, more than eating and more than going out." This is the opening statement of the film on Made in Zurich's homepage. The camera pans in a wide radius over the area known today as Zurich-West, taking in the Prime Tower and the area of railroad tracks which, in the nineteenth century, was where the biggest industrial companies in the canton of Zurich were located: the machine factory of Escher Wyss AG with its boiler-making facility and foundry, the Steinfels AG soap factory, the Schoeller AG dye works and the gear makers Maag-Zahnräder AG. In 2004 Maag Gear became the last industrial manufacturer to leave the area. The site itself, however, continues to be a production center in Zurich West: Made in Zurich, the movement promoting the interests of the remaining and slowly reviving urban manufacture, displays images from the bicycle-building workshop of Fahrradbauer Stolz, a turbine rotor at MAN Energy Solutions and mentions IVY and Climeworks as examples. Zurich has more capital than just capital. Ships, though, are no longer being built here and coal is no longer burned on the outskirts of Zurich's District 5. Instead, Zurich's production hub now houses, among other enterprises, an industrial-sized greenhouse, the tarpaulin tailors Freitag-Brüder, the Zuriga coffee machine manufacturers, the Turbinenbräu brewery and Mikas, an organic sausage producer (stadt.fleisch.wurst). Watching over it all is the origami lion positioned above this claim: Made in Zurich provides a platform for "urban productivists" from all walks of life, and is also an official designation of origin. "We are what we do," say the people running these modern workshops and with that they mean: What we do belongs (back) in the city.

With Made in Zurich, the city, in collaboration with private producers, has launched an initiative stemming from the trend that has been impacting urban areas, especially in the Western world, since the turn of the millennium. After a long phase of de-industrialization and with a corresponding focus on the city as a place to live and in which to provide services, cities themselves – including Zurich – are rediscovering the importance of manufacturing and industry. The latter comprises three types, the first being the research-intensive and increasingly tertiarized industries, and companies referred to with terms such as high-tech, advanced manufacturing, biotech and others. The second type are the "traditional" manufacturing businesses or those specializing in installation and maintenance work, such as metal processing workshops and plumbing companies. The third are the artisans, who produce tangible goods. The boundaries between these three areas are indistinct, but together they form the local urban production center.

"We are convinced that in an active and vibrant city, the production of goods should and will once again become more important," say the initiators of Made in Zurich, the companies Freitag lab.ag and Senn Resources, and the City of Zurich's urban planning department.

This production is in a state of upheaval: digitalization and automation are making decentralized production and shorter, closed production chains possible in smaller areas and closer to the consumers. At the same time, the artisan sector is encountering a new type of appreciation: the production process itself is becoming part of the experience. People want to be able to watch how something is made – on the sewing machine or in the workshop, in the factory hall or on the assembly line. They now have the chance to see for themselves how value is created. The message here is: it makes sense (again) to produce in the city.

Urban Production and Digital Change

"In many industries, the mobile internet, cloud technology, software and hardware such as 3D printers, laser cutters, multifunctional machines and interactive manufacturing robots are already being used in production," states the Technologiestiftung (technology foundation) of Berlin in its report of 2016.[1] The biggest developments in this area are currently in the digitalization of manufacturing processes. Networked resource planning and the corresponding software are resulting in far-reaching changes for manufacturing. If the machines are connected to the internet and also to each other, value-added chains can be developed in a way that was previously not possible. Products can be made in the smallest of batches, even as one-offs, and at tremendous speed, literally as on-demand orders. Urban production is therefore production not only *in* the city, but above all *for* the city and its dynamics. Thanks to digital innovation, product manufacture can once again take place in urban areas – with lower emissions and in a manner more compatible with the city than twentieth-century industry, but faster, easier and closer to the customer.

The Made in Zurich initiative unites fashion and furniture companies, soap-makers and food producers, and also high-tech companies and industrial firms under a single label that can be displayed with pride. Products manufactured in Zurich now have an official designation of origin which not only distinguishes the goods and their creators and manufacturers, but above all is intended to give a face to Zurich's urban production center. In San Francisco, the non-profit organization SFMade, founded in 2010, has managed in just under ten years not only to place urban production back on the city council's agenda, but also to physically re-establish it in former industrial areas in the Latino/Hispanic quarter. In the southern part of the city between Market Street and the old port, between residential buildings, restaurants, bars, clubs and offices, there are production plants and all kinds of manufacturing companies taking over run-down workshops and filling them with new life. SFMade helps them to find space, places workers and specialists in jobs via its own platform – especially in blue-collar work that is becoming scarce – and offers training opportunities and advice. SFMade provides strategic support to city leaders and local politicians in order to promote the creation of good conditions for local manufacturers and their employees – there have been 630 companies so far, providing more than 4,700 jobs.[2]

By following this example, Zurich's production center can also give itself an energy boost and generate fresh impetus. In addition to its contribution to overall economic performance and prosperity, it fulfills other important functions for the city. It creates economic stability and reduces risk by diversifying the industry structure in what is otherwise a financial center. It makes a significant addition to the variety of jobs on offer, and it makes an important contribution to the dual education system and to a city of short distances. By passing the 2014/2016 Building and Zoning Ordinance (BZO), the City of Zurich has committed itself to securing the last available spaces for the urban production center and to strengthening it in terms of economic policy – less than five percent of all urban land available for development is now classified as industrial zones in various forms. In the 1963 BZO, when the industrial and commercial zone experienced its largest expansion and forty-three percent of the then 289,000 workers were employed in the secondary sector, the figure was around four times higher. After that, the area designated as the industrial and commercial zone was successively reduced with each revision up until the 1999 BZO and at the same time partially opened up for pure service providers. The 2014/2016 BZO has caused the wind to change, and economic and political awareness has also altered: the spaces are currently the same as in 1999, but in some areas the proportion of potential service areas has been restricted again. The result is that the strategic goal of maintaining the sites for industry and commerce, which was decided upon in principal by Zurich's city council in 2007 and established in spatial terms in 2010 is now being put into physical practice.

A Call for Production in the City

What has prompted this securing of space in Zurich, and similar efforts elsewhere, is the reflection back to the times when the city was a place for the production and processing of goods. Social and technological changes made cities attractive again as places to live and less disruptive, small-scale and innovative – urban – production became possible. This revival is driven not only by digitalization, but also by demand in the big cities for high-quality and sustainable products and by the specialist workforce and networks of mostly small firms that are available here. The city of Zurich has a long tradition of industry and commerce. Its name is associated with top-quality goods and first-class innovation, which is promoted in vocational schools as well as at the Swiss Federal Institute of Technology in Zurich. Proximity to research and development characterizes the production center, which in Zurich just as elsewhere is confronted with the challenges of Industry 4.0. The acceleration and continuous adaptation of industrial processes requires a rethink in planning and economic policy. This will in fact be implemented in Zurich, for example at the Werkstadt, a site owned by the Swiss Federal Railways (SBB). The former railway workshops will gradually be converted into a center for crafts, factories, food producers, high-tech and small industrial enterprises of all kinds – depending on what the growing population of the city of Zurich needs and demands in the coming decades.

A Win for the City – And for the SBB

All the companies that have settled in the Werkstadt – but also on smaller sites in Zurich – belong in the category of modern urban production. They can be larger or smaller, focus on custom-made or standard production – historically they are located in urban space and manufacture products with a local connection. In 2006, American sociologist and economist Saskia Sassen was one of the first authors to draw attention to the potential of urban production, and at the same time severely criticized cities' neglect of the manufacturing industry – the small, networked firms that are crucial components of the overall urban economy. As a result of this criticism, the Urban Manufacturing Alliance was founded in the US, with the aim of bringing urban production back into cities that were once industrial strongholds but have been in deep crisis since the 1990s: Detroit, Baltimore, Cincinnati, Milwaukee, Philadelphia and Portland. The organization's credo is that city and production are mutually dependent and mutually beneficial. Supporting the ecosystem of small and mid-sized industrial, manufacturing and commercial enterprises in urban areas can give the economy the kind of boost that primarily benefits the lower middle class and the workers – something that is essential for the cohesion of American society. The new urban economy should "stabilize the social structure of cities and by strengthening local cycles make urban economies more robust against the turbulence of the world market," writes German urban researcher, economist and sociologist Dieter Läpple.[3] The small and mid-sized enterprises of urban production are geared toward local demand and usually manufacture high-quality, often sustainably produced goods. Unlike in the US, many German cities have never lost a critical volume of industry, which favors the revival of urban production. In Zurich, the relative importance of the production center (in terms of employment) remained more or less constant at around ten percent between 1995 and 2014. However, commercial and industrial production and, even more so, high-tech companies declined between 1995 and 2014 – the creative sector, on the other hand, has increased significantly.

Nevertheless: Zurich's production center is thriving. And even if the outlook varies from one sector to another – commercial and industrial production remains under pressure because the city remains attractive for other sectors (especially those with a high proportion of services), and because digitalization has made even less of an impact in this subsector – on the whole, the economic and social trend toward urban production in Zurich means there are opportunities. Promoting them will achieve triple gains for Zurich as a business location: for companies, if economic activities within their own value chain and in cooperation with other companies are strengthened; for the local universities, which can test and implement innovations with various partners from applied research and development, thereby expanding the network between science and industry; and for the public sector, in diversifying its economic structure and creating a range of opportunities for the public within the urban space.

The secret of a successful location lies in the combination of content concept, spatial possibilities and processual skills, according to urban researchers Alain Thierstein and Robert Salkeld.[4] Successful locations are created or transformed by courageous, innovative private enterprises that believe in the potential of their production factors, and by a forward-looking public sector with prudent authorities that ensure accessibility and a high level of interaction with research. One such place is the Brooklyn Navy Yard in New York, a 91-hectare former naval shipyard between the Dumbo and Williamsburg districts. During the Second World War, 700,000 workers were employed there; when the yard had to close in 1966, it was the largest industrial site in New York State. In the 1970s, only a few tenants still used the site, and the industrial buildings were neglected and fell into ruin. After the turn of the millennium, however, the Brooklyn Navy Yard Development Corporation (BNYDC), a non-profit organization, was formed, driven by the vision of building a new type of industrial park on this piece of state-owned land that would primarily provide a home for small and mid-sized enterprises. In 2006, the City of New York promised the necessary funds to rebuild the ailing infrastructure.

Today, New York has 6,000 factories providing 81,000 jobs – over 400 of which are located in the Brooklyn Navy Yard. These businesses provide employment for around 6,000 people, many of whom live in the neighborhood. They are often young start-ups that are committed to sustainability, the sharing community, new technologies, creatively paired with old trades, which benefit from the state and privately supported industrial areas on the harbor front. At the same time, the Navy Yard is planning the future of ecologically focused and technologically advanced local enterprises. A giant rooftop farm bears witness to the trend of urban gardening – another part of urban production – while the building below is entirely devoted to gastronomy. The master plan commissioned by the BNYDC envisages a massive increase in building activity and the creation of more than 10,000 new jobs by the end of 2020. The "Cutting Edge Urban Industry" is currently reinventing itself. Zurich's aspirations do not stretch quite as far as that. There is definitely a future for the urban production center, however. And in the Werkstadt, where all the conditions for success are being met, that future is going to be bright.

1 Anne Caroline Erbstößer, *Produktion in der Stadt. Berliner Mischung 2.0,* Technologiestiftung Berlin, Berlin, 2016, p. 9.
2 In 2018, San Francisco's urban producers generated about ten percent of the increase in jobs in the city and contributed 882 million dollars to the municipal budget. And in the summer of 2019, the city's first Advanced Manufacturing Center opened its doors. Humanmade is more than just a gigantic maker space of 4,500 square meters; it is a training center with a prototype manufacturing facility for wood and metal processing, a laser cutting lab, 3D printers, state-of-the-art textile production and an electronics lab equipped with the very latest in industrial software.
3 Dieter Läpple, "Produktion zurück in die Stadt. Ein Plädoyer," in: Bauwelt, 35, 2016, pp. 23–29, here p. 27.
4 Cf. Alain Thierstein and Robert Salkeld, "Digital, smart, vernetzt? Starke Standorte brauchen mehr!" in: Metall Zug AG (ed.), *Digital: Wirtschaft, Gesellschaft, Chancen, Risiken,* Zug, 2016, pp. 114–118, here p. 117.

Barbara Zeleny

LEARNING-PROCESS-PLAN – FROM WORKSHOP TO WERKSTADT

Industrial Quarter
Learning-Process-Plan
Urban Production
Urban Transformation
Vertical Urban Factory
Werkstadt

In the industrial park in the west of the city of Zurich, the mood is relaxed and creative. In an elongated courtyard, there are small seating areas with colorful shade sails, sunflowers in large wooden boxes and herbs in terracotta pots. Barbecue aromas fill the air, music plays in the distance. A high stele made of four stacked white water-tanks indicates the way to buildings A, Q, U, Y and D: large factory halls of yellow brick with high, arched windows, panes of cast glass, iron trusses and roofs with skylights.

The buildings, planned as one large project, today form an expansive, mature complex. They feature architectural interventions that were made during the last century or so and are as charming as the friendly faces of old people. In the last few years, they have been filled again with new life – forty small to mid-sized businesses have settled into five buildings. The transformation of the former workshops of the Swiss Federal Railways into the "Werkstadt" – a vibrant base for urban production – has begun.

But how does such a transformation come about? What are the challenges, risks and opportunities that an investor or landowner must take into account? How can success be achieved? What requirements and expectations do future users have? And is there sufficient demand to revitalize such a site in the middle of the city? In other words: can the investment pay off?

The new Werkstadt district demonstrates how a 42,000-square-meter industrial site can be transformed into a hub for manufacturing companies and innovative start-ups, as well as for culture and recreation. Over the next twenty years, a production site and a center for creative enterprise and cultural life will emerge, all connected to the neighboring districts. It will be a place to work, or a place to visit – somewhere that people will happily spend their leisure time. A personable place with the power to attract.

The method developed for the transformation is the "learning-process-plan." One might see it as a type of slow planning, one that has a careful analysis of the requirements, getting to know the users, and learning by doing at its core. Working with the learning-process-plan means seeking a path that approaches the goal step by step, away from the conventional planning process – a constant dialogue between today and the future. There is no tabula rasa redevelopment, no large advance investment. Instead, work is done cautiously with what is already there: with the users and with the existing buildings.

One Hundred Years of Railroad History

The site's history begins in the late nineteenth century. When it became necessary to extend Zurich's central station, the workshops of the then Swiss Northeastern Railway (Schweizerische Nordostbahn – NOB), which until then had been situated in the center of the city, had to be relocated. In 1902, after the railroads had been nationalized, the Swiss Federal Railways (Schweizerische Bundesbahnen –

Aerial view around 1930,
view in the direction of Altstetten

Aerial view of the Werkstadt Area in 2016,
view in the direction of Altstetten

Site plan 1910

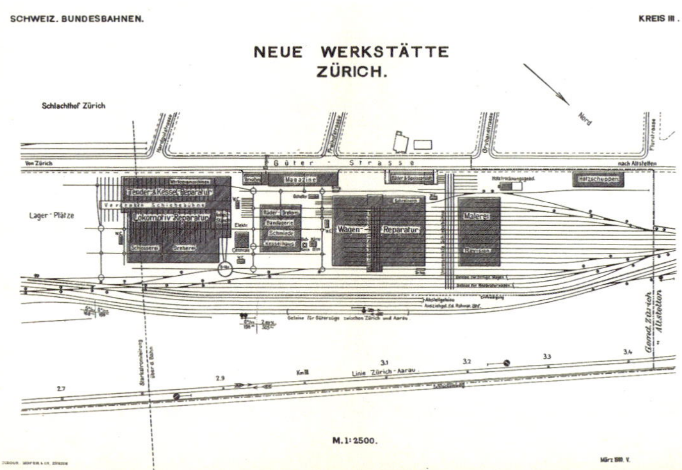

SBB workshops ca. 1930

Smithy in the Zurich workshops, 1941

SBB) took over and continued the construction project. A suitably sized open patch of land was found on the south side of the tracks This site, altogether 1,000 meters long and with an area of 125,000 square meters, runs parallel to today's Hohlstrasse.[1] The new transformer on the neighboring slaughterhouse premises supplied the electricity that was needed, and since the site was located on the outskirts of Altstetten, there was a guaranteed supply of labor. The number of workers in the SBB workshops increased steadily from then on and in 1967 totaled as many as 900 people.[2] Today, the site is still used by the SBB, with around 250 employees in the Altstetten services facility.

The SBB workshops were built between 1905 and 1911 and had slight changes and extensions made to them in stages. Their proximity to the rail tracks defines the site: the work halls are interlinked with them; between the buildings there are views of the rails. The expanse and the dynamics of the tracks contrast with the orderly, administrative world of the linear buildings. As a whole, the buildings form an ensemble in two layers, serviced by Hohlgasse, a rue intérieure parallel to Hohlstrasse. For around 100 years, this world existed separately from the city, which over the years has developed and become denser.

Urban Production as an Opportunity

A lot has changed since the SBB workshops were opened. The site is transforming today as a result of urban, societal and, of course, technological change: for example, the installation of diagnostic equipment such as computers and sensors in locomotives and coaches has shortened standing times and has led to a more efficient use of space. At the same time, trains have become longer and have therefore mostly outgrown the old halls. The type of servicing needed by 400-meter-long trains now takes place in the facility in Herdern, on the opposite side of the tracks.

In addition to technological progress, urban and societal development plays an important role. An essential precondition was provided by the City of Zurich's urban development strategy of 2010, which designated the site as a place of work with a focus on innovation. Jobs are in demand in this part of the city, since Altstetten's population is expected to grow by between 10,000 and 15,000 in the next few years. On the neighboring pieces of land, in the Letzi apartment buildings and in the Letzibach D residential area, 430 units will be ready for occupancy by 2023. What used to be a district on the periphery of the city is now situated in its center and has become an integral part of it. It is a focal point for inner-city consolidation. The transformation of the SBB workshops into the Werkstadt is an endeavor to preserve the area's identity. This is accomplished not only by preserving the old building fabric, but also by using the facility as a production park. Today's key word is urban production – a development that is seen to be part of the transition from an industrial to a knowledge-based society. Along with this change comes a shift in the production of some consumer goods from the urban periphery to the center – from handcrafted manufacture to mass production and differentiated production. The hypothesis of a transformation toward manufacturing was proposed by the US sociologist and urbanist Jane Jacobs around fifty years ago in her book *The Economy of Cities*.[3] In her opinion, the differentiated manufacturing industry is a specific new form of urban service. A service for and in the city, made possible by urban producers, with the aim of increasing added value by shortening the supply chain.

This transformation is being fueled by a demand for genuine, locally made products: the need to know where and under what conditions something has been produced, where it comes from and where it is going. The manufacturing process itself is a part of the identity of the product, which appeals to a socially and environmentally aware customer base. When consumers are in close proximity to where production takes place, it leads to savings in energy and transportation and the assurance of fair social conditions. The role, therefore, that urban manufacture now plays is that of a driving force of municipal development, since it provides jobs to qualified skilled workers that are located near to where they live. In return, the manufacturing businesses benefit from the urban location by networking possibilities, innovation potential, synergies and a ready market for their products and services. The concentration and the diversity of the jobs are a source of enhancement for the city and contribute to its economic foundation.

Urban Transformation – The Learning Process as a Plan

The transformation of the site into the Werkstadt started at the end of 2016 when the SBB's maintenance and repairs facility was moved outwards to the eastern perimeter. As a result of a partial revision of Zurich's 2014 municipal building and zone regulations (BZO), the site was designated an industry and commerce zone (IG I). In addition to that, it is defined as a place of work, so residence there has been basically ruled out as far as future use is concerned. We – the landowner SBB and the City of Zurich – have agreed in the strategy for the SBB Areas West to develop the property with a focus on urban production. Two organizations were founded at the outset to manage the project: one comprises the planners working on the project master plan; the other is made up of the "doers," who are responsible for the immediate measures. We sought agencies for the planning process whose approaches would complement and challenge each other in the development of innovative solutions. Two agencies in particular convinced us of their visions for the site's future: KCAP Architects & Planners, led by professor emeritus at ETH Zurich, Kees Christiaanse, and denkstatt sàrl, headed by repurposing expert from

Basel, Barbara Buser. The team was completed by traffic planners IBV Hüsler, landscape architects Studio Vulkan, and Keoto AG, specialists in energy and sustainability design.

The learning-process-plan – a participatory, multi-track work method – is the joint endeavor of the SBB and this specially chosen planning team. In short, this consists of testing out the ideas spawned by a user needs analysis and feeding the results, after careful reflection and discussion, back into the process. The approach differs from a conventional development project in that it is based on dialogue with the stakeholders at various levels, and the fact that operation and development are being run in parallel. A participatory planning process is necessary, which makes the procedure challenging. It involves the observation of three aspects: the "Here and Now" (the current situation), the "Who and What" (the users and their needs) and the "Then and When" (the urban densification of the area). The prioritization and hierarchization of the different aspects depend on the issue at hand and the point of view, rather like music tracks being highlighted or balanced out in a sampling. This process poses an enticing challenge on account of the dynamics inherent in it.

It all began with a website. There was a brief description of the initial vision for the property. The section "Be a part of the Werkstadt" called upon interested parties to send their requirements to us. During the first few months we received requests from more than 200 artisans, publishers, laboratories, architects, sausage and cheese producers and many other businesses. The extent of demand has proved that the city of Zurich has very high potential. At the beginning of 2017, a section of the site was made available for short-term usage. The respondents' space requirements were analyzed and compared with the existing buildings. The first phase involved looking for businesses that could occupy the buildings without any major refurbishment needed. The industrial architecture of the buildings allows for a variety of spatial configurations. The rows of buildings along Hohlstrasse provide small units consisting of between 50 and 500 square meters (A, U and Y). Many small companies from the creative sector will be operating here until the buildings are completely refurbished for long-term use. The former works halls (Q and D) have units from 500 to 1,000 square meters in which urban producers are currently working.[4]

These businesses make up the "Here and Now" category. The broad mix of cleantech companies, craft businesses and office suites, of interim uses and long-term pioneer occupancies, means that coordinating them is quite demanding. Factors such as the expanse of the site, the condition of the buildings and the assortment of usage types culminate in a complexity so high that it has to be approached in steps. The interim users are only present for a limited period; the pioneers, on the other hand, come to expand and contribute to the site's development. Our role is to act as long-term supporters and curators of the process, in order to enable the companies in the Werkstadt to advance. With time, the site will become denser from within and so, together with the resident businesses, we will devise the most efficient architectural, ecological and economic solution for it.

One of the most valuable parts of this industrial park is the buildings. They create an identity and provide the park with an historical anchor point. The patina on the surfaces, which has gradually appeared during the buildings' hundred-year history, generates a certain atmospheric effect. It has been possible to rent out several of the buildings in their existing state, with no structural work necessary. Others will have to be adapted. The canton's historic landmark assessment is the basis of the plan for each construction phase. Certain of the buildings have been given protected landmark status and their maintenance and future use assured in a preservation agreement. The assessment is an essential tool for implementing renovation measures efficiently and ensuring that none are undertaken unnecessarily. The starting point of each project is an inventory including an appraisal and rating of the structural fabric. This enables us to preserve high-quality buildings.

At the same time, the "Who and What" category needs to be dealt with; this involves the analysis of the different users' specific requirements. In order to facilitate this, the uses are divided into thematic groups: food manufacture, wood and metal crafting, event and artistic enterprise, and mobility. Within these groups there are further varied requirements. They concern space, load bearing capacity, daylight, temperature and logistical needs. We drafted and distributed a catalogue of questions to all interested parties in order to suitably position their businesses. Using the insights gained from this first exercise we created a knowledge pool and narrowed down the direction to take. We invited the thematic groups to a series of workshops in order to understand their wishes and needs as precisely as possible. Most of all, we were interested in finding out what all the users could make mutual use of. To remain cost-effective, urban production requires the disciplined allocation of space and, moreover, the optimum use of the area that supplies rental income. If certain areas are used collectively, synergies can be exploited and costs shared. Furthermore, the tenants' needs can provide the impetus for new services to emerge that can be incorporated into the park's overall usage mix.

The workshops showed that there is a demand for separate storage facilities and a central logistics center. The immediate result is that these services are now provided on-site. Packages are taken to the mobility hub, labeled by the logistics staff and given to couriers with instructions of where to send them and what delivery method to use. The logistics center then bills the businesses for dispatch services. For door-to-door food delivery in particular there has been an increase in the city in the use of bicycle couriers. Having a dedicated logistics facility enables the businesses to focus on their core competencies; it also means that CO_2 emissions, noise and traffic are avoided. Another service that is provided is the storage of generic material such as packaging. Indeed, the range of services on offer within the park is expanding steadily. The creation of common spaces for meetings, events and exhibitions is a further possibility, especially since many of the enterprises are active in urban social networks where informal communication is important. They need places to meet in order to keep their fingers on the pulse, so to speak.

The "Then and When" category concerns the implementation of the vision. It happens in three stages: short term, medium term and long term. The short-term stage involves initial occupancies with no need for building refurbishment of any kind. Medium term refers to repurposing, as in the conversion of Hall Q. Activities pursued with a long-term outlook concern further or complete refurbishment and even the construction of new buildings, as in the case of the factory halls R and S, and the former locomotive repairs hall. Work on the medium-term transformation of building Q began in early 2020. The planned usage will represent a major test case of an ecosystem of urban production on the site.

The Werkstadt master plan summarizes the vision that has existed since the end of 2019 between the landowner – SBB, the City of Zurich and the canton's landmark preservation authorities. It serves as an instrument for further steps in the site's transformation and envisages, for example, integration of the area into both the Hard quarter (District 4, Aussersihl) and Altstetten (District 9). Its well-established structure provides good conditions for this. The longitudinal axis through the area is important, as are the transverse axes which function as points of access to the inner depths. The grounds will gradually be made accessible to the public; the courtyards will be redesigned into urban spaces that invite visitors to linger a while and that make a wide variety of activities possible. The ground floors will be activated by culture, retail and places to eat and drink, every day of the week and at all times of the day, and the factory halls will provide inspiring insights into the types of production being carried out.

The master plan stipulates that the rhythm of the site, which is determined by an alternation of open space and large halls, should be maintained. It bears witness to the industrial history, as well as the industrial character of the buildings, the distances between them, and the geometry of the railroad tracks. The uniform design acts as a connecting element and gives the area a coherent appearance. The draft for future densification is intended to lie on top of the current figure ground plan and interlock with it. The aim is to create a harmonious mix of existing and new buildings, with the possibility of stacking uses in the sense of a vertical urban factory[5]. Due to its location in the high-rise area, the site is part of an urban axis with higher

1 Cf. Hans-Peter Bärtschi, *Industrialisierung, Eisenbahnschlachten und Städtebau. Die Entwicklung des Zürcher Industrie- und Arbeiterstadtteils Aussersihl. Ein vergleichender Beitrag zur Architektur- und Technikgeschichte*, Basel: Birkhäuser, 1983, p. 211.
2 Cf. ibid., p. 213.
3 Cf. Jane Jacobs, *The Economy of Cities*, New York: Random House, 1969.
4 An up-to-date list of the Werkstadt businesses can be found at www.werkstadt-zuerich.ch.
5 Cf. Nina Rappaport, *Vertical Urban Factory*, New York: Actar, 2015.

buildings. The master plan defines what maximum volume is permissible at which location and where urban development accents may be set. The site will be carefully completed in the future in cooperation with the City of Zurich, the cantonal landmark preservation authorities and the users themselves. Each subproject will have an architectural and urbanistic approach developed for it with regard to the granularity and materiality of the annexes.

Learning from Werkstadt

The Werkstadt project demonstrates how the sustainable transformation of an industrial quarter can be achieved by long-term planning, deceleration and a clever methodology. Transformation takes place not only at a functional and spatial level but also at an institutional one. These two transformations – spatial and institutional – are based on two conditions: the political and economic framework, and the needs of the users.

The Werkstadt is a pioneering transformation, but this is precisely what determines its financial reality. The landowner bears the financial responsibility and has to weigh up opportunities and risks. As far as demand for the Werkstadt was concerned, doubts were fortunately assuaged early on. Evidently there is great potential for urban production in the city of Zurich. This potential must be carefully monitored, however, since each subproject means a new start with new conditions. Here is where the learning-process-plan has proven its value as a strategy. Regular feedback from the market ensures that each and every user can determine the best possible conditions in which to thrive. If the conditions for the companies are met, the investment will also pay off.

As with all economic considerations, of course, there has to be a greater vision. The learning-process-plan should – in contrast to the conventional planning process – have a utopian element to it. The approach needs to be accompanied by a continuous process of rethinking to ensure that it remains adaptable and agile. The learning-process-plan is a tool for moving forward collaboratively. The city is not only being physically transformed again by each new generation, it is also undergoing social, political, technological and economic change. These processes of change are an inherent feature of urban life. Thus, the Werkstadt – despite sounding as if it were complete – is not a finished task. Like the city itself, it will never be finished. It will continue to develop as a collective endeavor in a process of continuous construction.

Werkstadt site, Werkhof district, 2016

Werkstadt site, Building D, 2016

Werkstadt site, Gleishof (Track Square) 2016

A peek into the Werkstadt, Vicafe, 2019

A peek into the Werkstadt, the upholsterer, 2019

SCENARIOS FOR AN INDUSTRIOUS CITY

INDUSTRY RETURNS TO THE CITY

This book is about industry returning to the city. For the last twenty years, however, the opposite has happened. All over the world, industry left the constrained and expensive urban spaces it historically occupied for cheaper, more accessible and less contested areas in the urban periphery or offshore. Its abandoned sites, often positioned in key locations in cities, were turned into thriving, but also more profitable mixed-use urban neighborhoods, from chocolate factories to slaughterhouses, from docklands to ammunition factories. In Zurich, over 67 hectares of industrial land were turned into housing, office or retail space. After Zurich-Nord in Oerlikon as the first large urban redevelopment project, soon after Zurich-West and various other sites followed. Only two large industrial areas remain within city boundaries. In the new developments, on the other hand urban production was conspicuously absent, as at the time there seemed to be no demand and low returns to be expected.

In 2007, Zurich's city council decided on the strategic goal of maintaining sites for industry and commerce to keep the city from gentrifying and losing history, talent or resilience. Inspired by examples from its twin city San Francisco, the value of urban production was recognized and with the 2014/2016 zoning law revision turned into practice. This follows a by now well-established larger trend Along with San Francisco, various other cities support urban production, such as Stuttgart and Vienna with their concepts for the "productive city" (*Produktive Stadt*), Munich with its *Gewerbehöfe* Paris with its *hôtels industriels*, Brussels with its recent publication *A Good City Has Industry* and New York with its Brooklyn Navy Yard one of the largest sites for urban industries worldwide.

At the same time, urban development faces new challenges: straightforward area developments are growing scarce and established program mixes are being questioned as both retail and office spaces come under pressure from the effects of digitalization. The concept of the productive city could both meet a need and solve a problem, but it challenges existing regulations, urban ideals and established development and business models. Urban development of industrial sites needs to focus on the use value, not the capital value of urban land holdings, as the residual land value generated in development is small, possibly even zero. Business cases inevitably need to revolve around gradual transformation, low land price appreciation and small investments to achieve affordable spaces, with rentability still acceptable, nonetheless. A city's urban production strategy, therefore, is also a policy tool vis-à-vis the urban land market and its excesses in an era of cheap money. And with its focus on working capital, quite literally, rather than book profits, it also aids in diversifying a possibly overheating urban land market, along with cooperative ownership models.

In 2014, the city commissioned a study from Hosoya Schaefer to show the possibility and benefits of keeping the maintenance

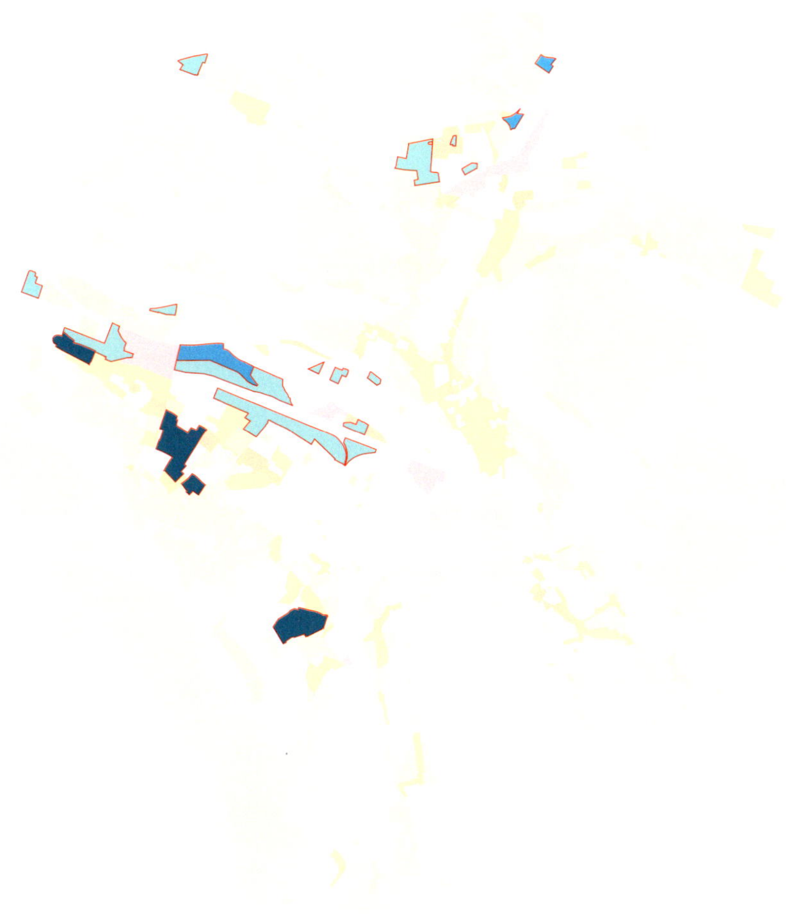

Industrial and commercial zones in Zurich

Industrial and commercial zone IG I

Industrial and commercial zone IG II

Industrial and commercial zone IG III

Source: City of Zurich, land use planning – municipal building and zoning ordinance (BZO) – GeoServer, 2020

workshops of the Swiss Federal Railways SBB, located along the train tracks between the Zurich Main Train Station and Zurich-Altstetten, dedicated to urban production instead of developing the strip into housing and office space. Today, that once secret plan has become a success story with a site fully occupied by various companies, start-ups and makers. A "learning-process-plan" put forward by the SBB and the City of Zurich is the tool that ensures a successful collaboration and long-term transformation of the site.

Likewise in the case of the RAD Rheinmetall Air Defence area located in Oerlikon in the north of Zurich, the city is insisting on retaining its industrial use. This resulted in an academic exercise supported by Mobimo and the city in cooperation with the site's owner RAD in a design studio carried out at the Harvard University GSD in the spring semester of 2018 by Hosoya Schaefer. The Oerlikon area is one of the large urban redevelopment areas in Zurich that has grown into a vibrant part of the city over the last twenty years. The RAD Areal, however, is still a closed industrial island with an uncertain future. The projects envision concepts for merging urban and industrial functions, including the positioning of industry as a civic attraction, cooperative planning, circular and sharing economies, and, finally, reimagining urban and architectural typologies. Here, also, the land economy of urban development needs to be rethought in comparison with the high capital investment and high land value appreciation that landowners, developers and investors have grown used to over the last twenty years.

The Tech Cluster Zug, finally, is a project won by Hosoya Schaefer in 2013 in an international competition for the industrial compound of the household appliance producer V-ZUG in the eponymous city. The company consolidates its production facilities into a "vertical factory" while freeing site area for its gradual transformation and reprogramming into a dense and robust productive urban neighborhood. Here, the main actor is an industrial conglomerate that is developing into a diversified urban asset holding with substantial industrial activities, rather than following other formerly industrial firms who are now primarily invested in commercial, non-industrial real estate.

From an urbanist point of view, all of these projects are confronting the question: How can we conceptualize a productive city that is both resilient and dense and at the same time humane and livable? What parameters and criteria will guide its development and who will be the actors that turn such visions into reality? The following scenarios frame three different takes on the future Industrious City and propose three different modalities for its development.

Urban Development Areas in Zurich

Urban development areas in Zurich by gross floor area (GFA) and use, as of December 2012

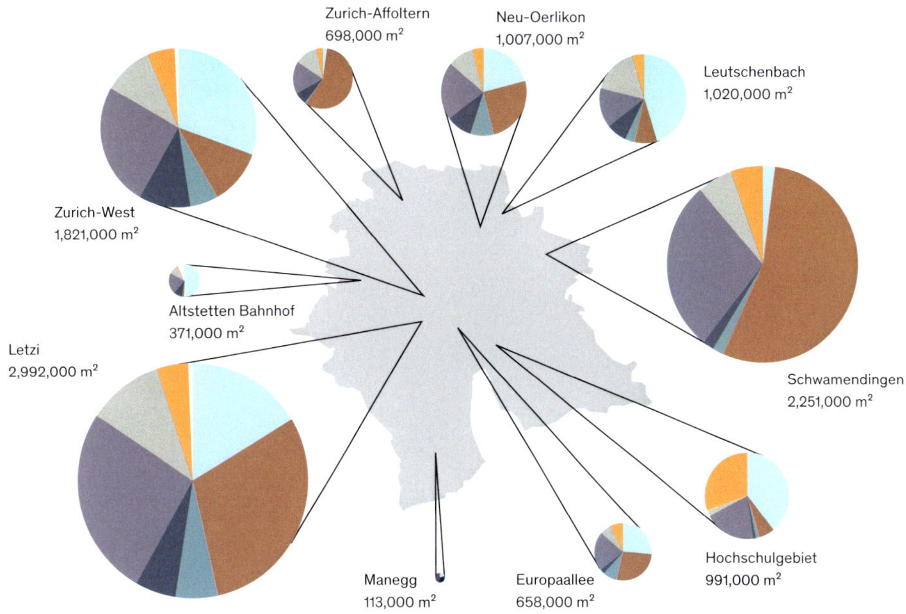

Brownfield Turned Residential and Office Use

Urban brownfields that have been turned into residential and office spaces, as of December 2012

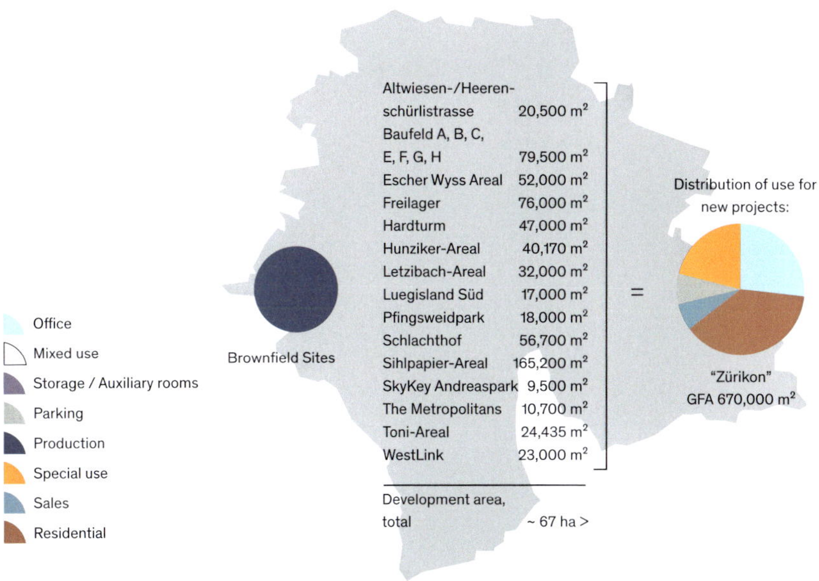

Data: Statistics Office – City of Zurich
Visualization: Hosoya Schaefer Architects

Urban Industry Land Use Grain

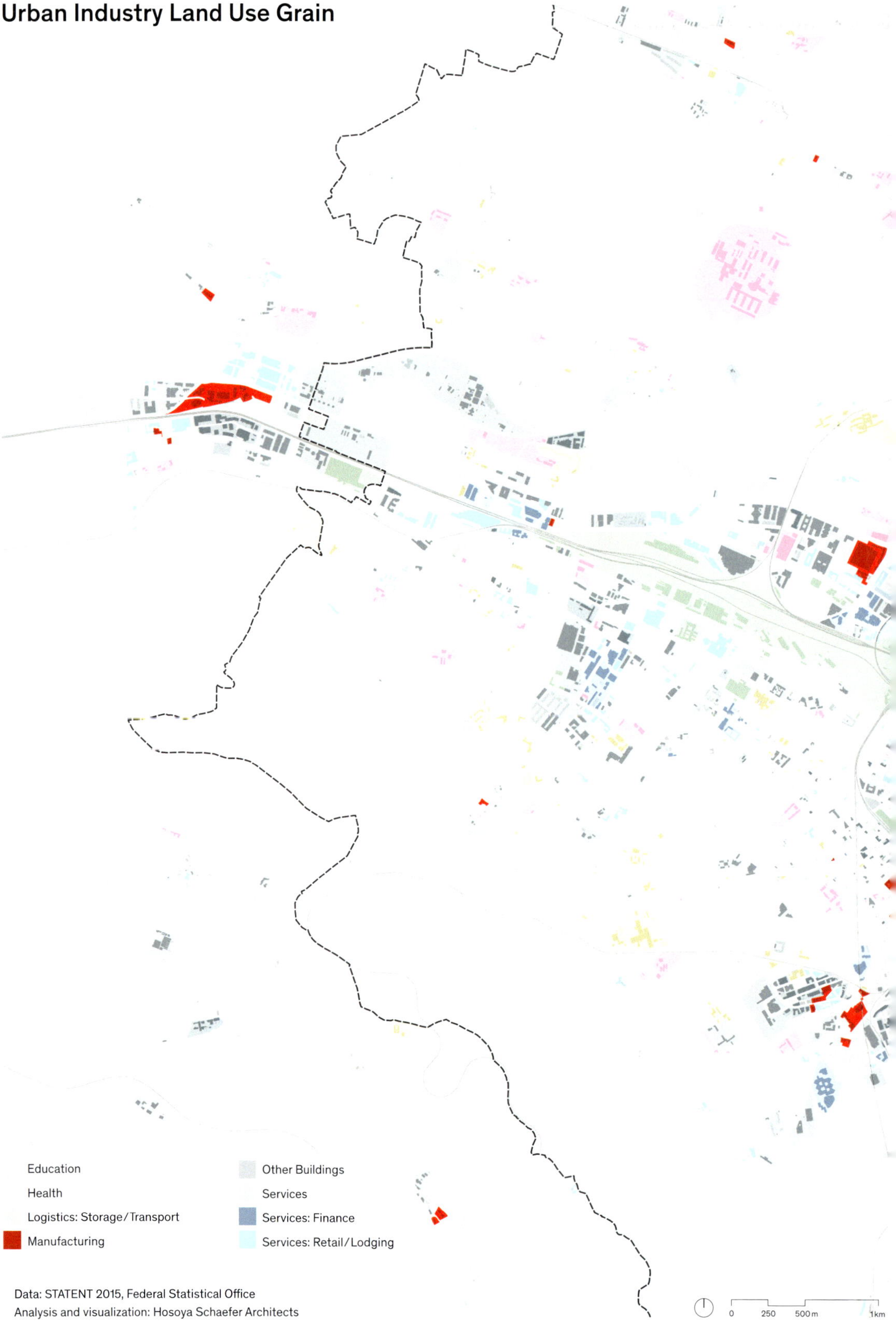

Data: STATENT 2015, Federal Statistical Office
Analysis and visualization: Hosoya Schaefer Architects

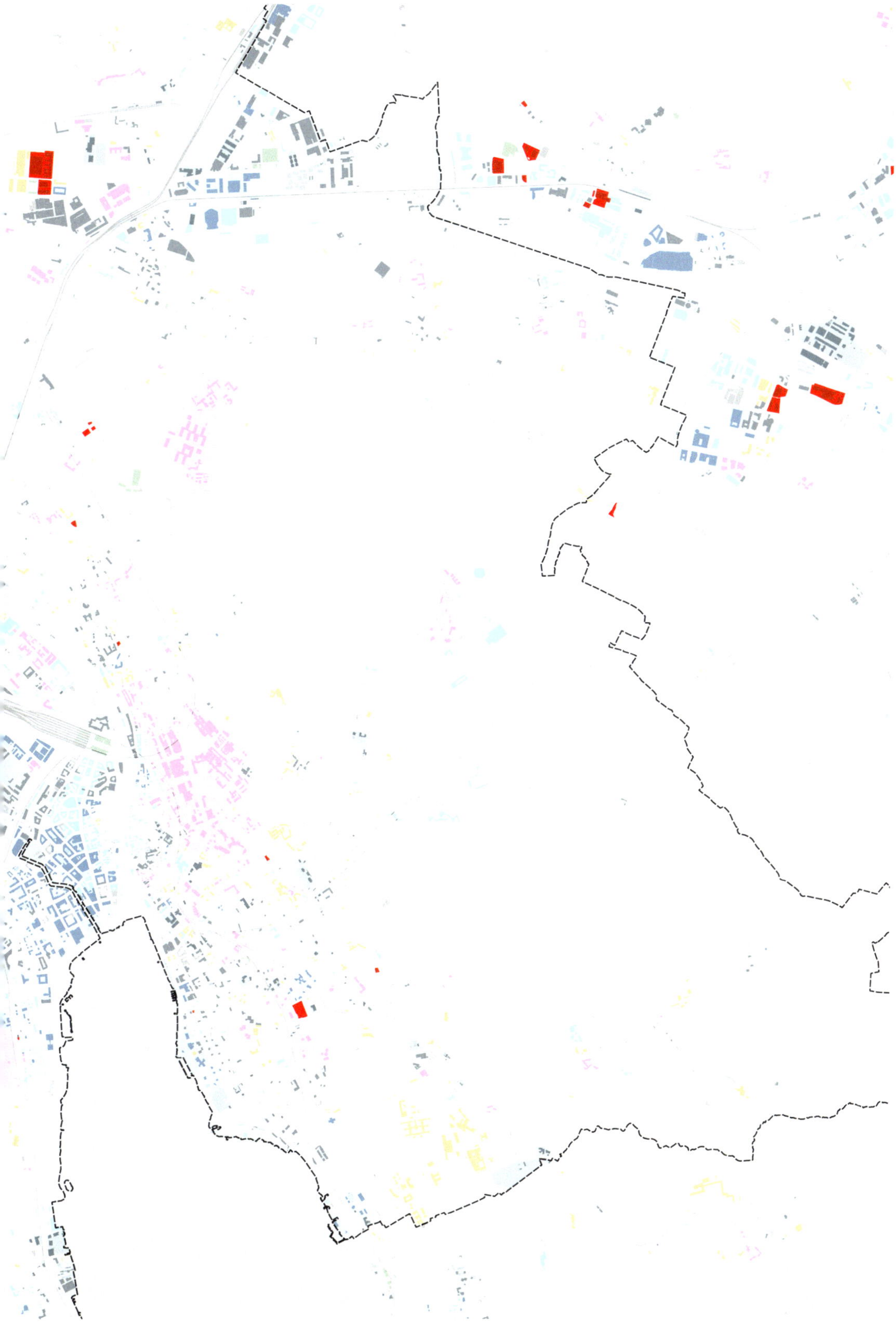

WERKPLATZ ZURICH

Zurich

The sites of the Swiss Federal Railways (SBB) workshops and the adjacent "Rohmbe," a raw materials supply facility, south of the rail tracks cover a total inner-city space of 21 hectares and are among the last major industrial sites in Zurich. In 2016, the SBB's main workshops west of the city were made available for conversion. It was important for the city to align the future use of this space with the spatial development 2010 and Zurich 2025 strategies and to position it as a new place of work for technology companies and industry. How, though? Compared with the land-value increase that results when such sites are converted into accommodation and office premises, there is little profit to be expected from industrial areas. Putting forward this proposal has been difficult, particularly because of the central location of the site, and because the SBB is a state-owned company that uses real estate development to cross-subsidize public transport. Using this area as a model, the city therefore commissioned a study to shed light, at a conceptual level, on the possibilities of urban manufacture in inner-city areas.

Classic business and industrial parks are usually monofunctional. Centrally located manufacturing sites, however, should be developed into a mixed, lively piece of the city. The aim is to create a business and industrial district that also integrates other uses, and thus generates an urban culture of its own. Urban manufacturing should be an incubator, a laboratory, an open space and a niche with an independent profile.

Companies from related sectors are attracted by the wide range of space on offer at various different price levels; this allows clusters to form, and it facilitates synergies and promotes innovation.

Financially healthy technology companies and innovative small businesses complement each other: when profitable companies settle into areas that have not yet been redeveloped, it enables the provision to pioneers of subsidized space in the existing buildings with scope for them to grow. In addition, there are units for small commercial enterprises, niches for the creative industries, service providers and also university ventures. For an innovation hub such as this to successfully expand, it makes sense to have cooperation between the public sector, universities and the private sector (triple helix approach).

In order to facilitate the development of diversity and avoid having to make restrictions from the outset with regard to potential occupants – sectors can be difficult to predetermine for the long run – a range of varied, flexible unit types are created. This also matches the latest space requirements of industry and commerce; often, a modular, flexible construction method is needed which allows, for example, for prototype and small series production combined with offices for management and engineering.

The basic primary unit types for key uses are:
Laboratory – cutting-edge technology
Workshop – industry
Studio/Office – creative
Hall/Arena – service provider / primary

In addition to these are units for secondary uses that enable further synergies and transform the site into a lively district:
Bar-Restaurant/Store – service provider / secondary
Stage – culture
Apartment – accommodation (small scale)

This is how a flexible, innovative business and industrial district evolves.

View from Altstetten toward Zurich main train station ca. 1920. The SBB Areal and the slaughterhouse are visible on the lower right, Escher Wyss Areal is visible on the middle left.

Laboratory – cutting-edge technology

Workshop – industry

Studio/Office – creative

Hall/Arena – service provider / primary

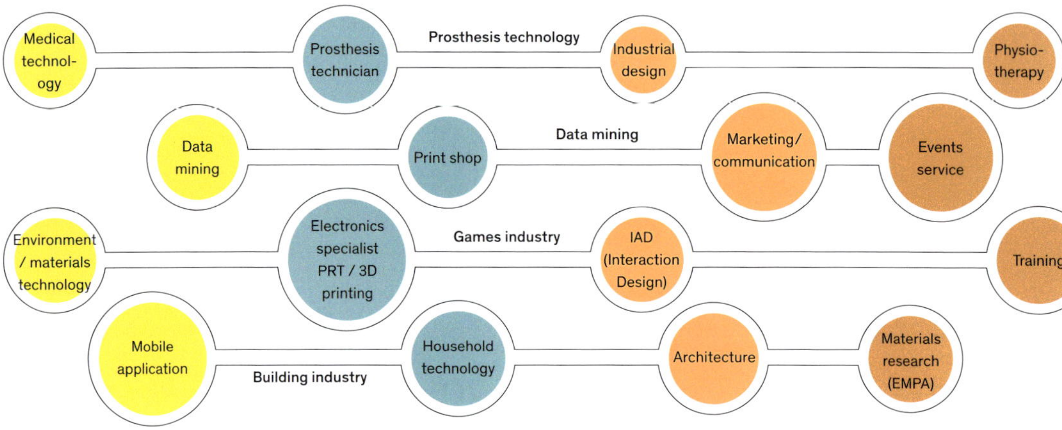

Synergies and innovation within related sectors

In the field of product development, synergies are increasingly important for promoting innovation. The desired type of commercial and industrial companies sought can create synergies within their related sectors, identify financial resources and find talented employees, as well as attract new customers and establish new contacts.

It is therefore important to offer different types of spaces. Companies operating in the same sector, but which occupy different positions in the value chain, can come together and create synergies with the improved possibilities for exchange. The diagram shows synergy scenarios for different sectors according to the different unit types. In the health industry, for example, it is conceivable that in the medical technology sector (Laboratory) prostheses are developed with the involvement of industrial designers (Studio) and produced next door as prototypes (Workshop). In collaboration with physiotherapists, the prostheses are then tested and later sold (Hall).

The different types of unit also promote the coexistence of small, innovative companies and large, profitable firms. This enables knowledge transfer and provides possibilities for new financing models.

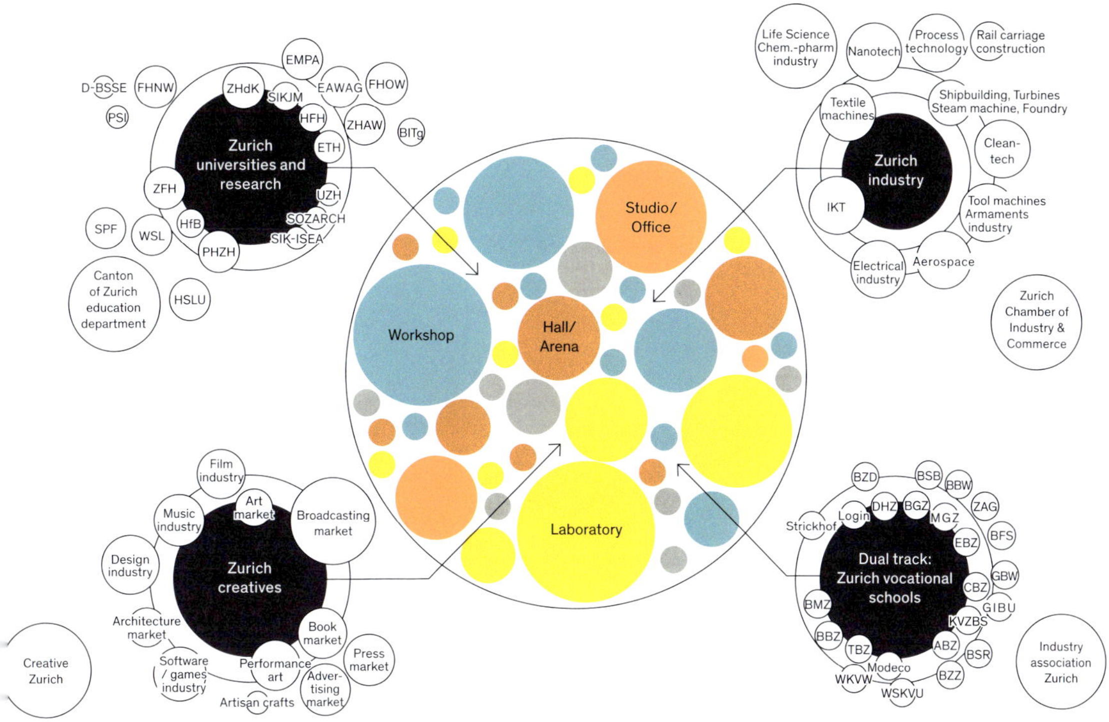

Synergies with Zurich, center of education, and the creative industries

In addition to attracting commercial enterprises, universities can also be targeted to participate so that cooperation can develop between science, industry and trade.

Sites of urban manufacture could be for the universities of applied science what the Technopark is for ETH Zurich: an interface between Swiss crafting tradition and tertiary, practice-based training at international level.

The creative industries also play an important role as a promoter of social innovation and a producer of urban culture. They instill life into the area, while the area gives them opportunities for advancement. A successful example of synergies is the Proekt_Fabrika in Moscow. Here, a paper factory has provided affordable spaces for artists who work primarily with paper; they enliven the area, create a positive image for the factory and take over part of the paper produced.

Concept Gleisraum Süd

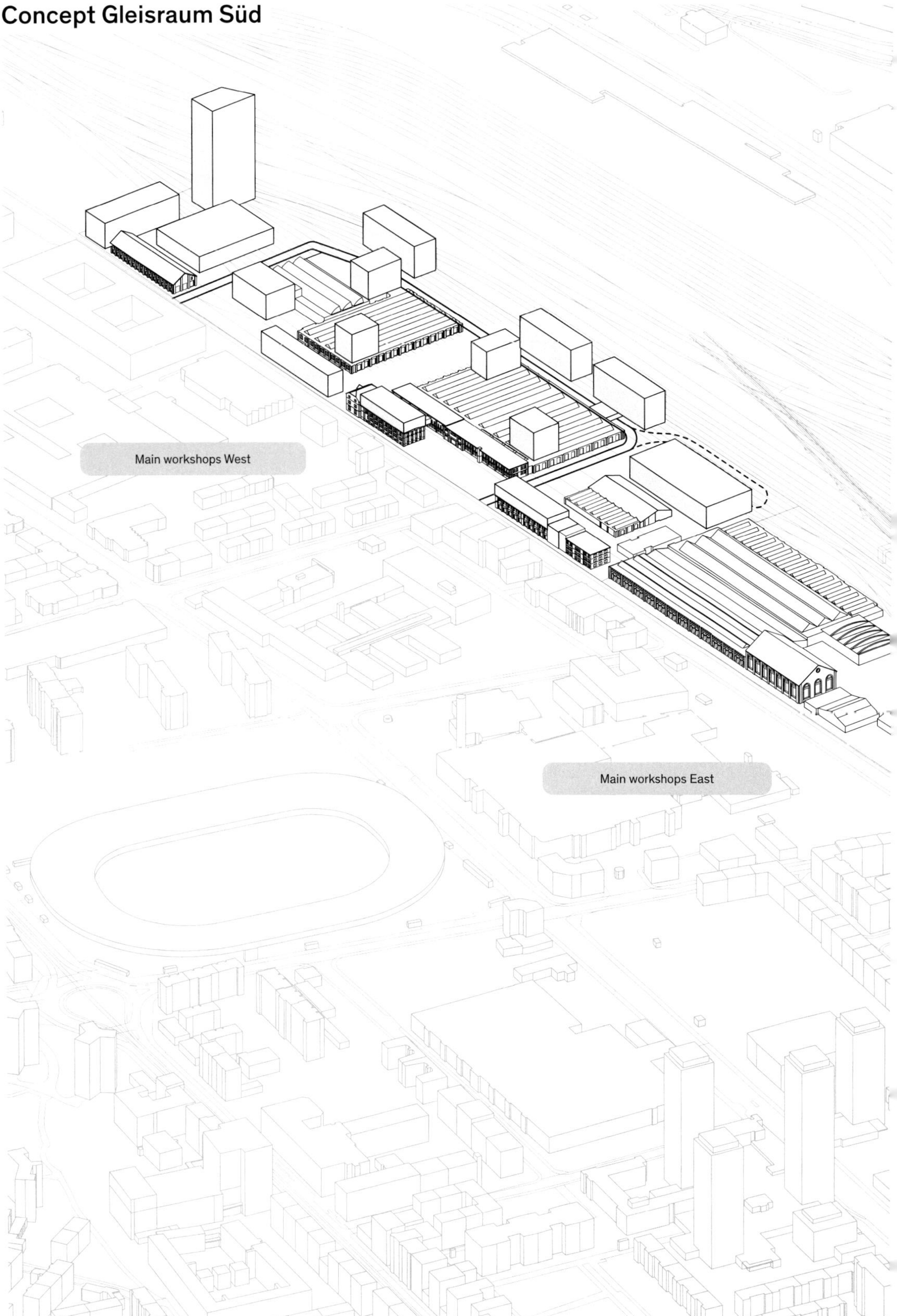

Actors

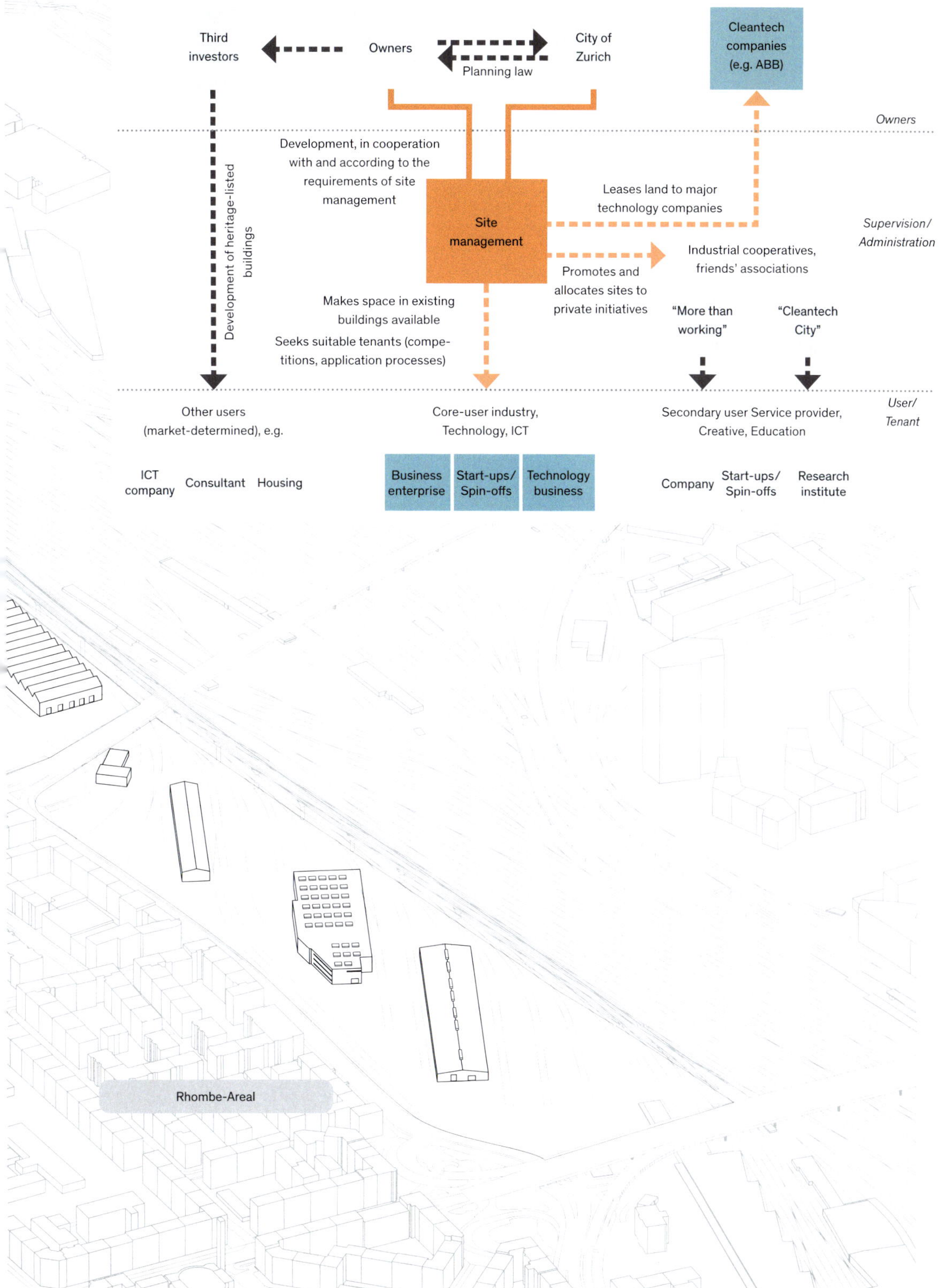
Third investors
Owners
City of Zurich
Planning law
Cleantech companies (e.g. ABB)
Owners
Development, in cooperation with and according to the requirements of site management
Development of heritage-listed buildings
Site management
Leases land to major technology companies
Supervision/ Administration
Industrial cooperatives, friends' associations
Promotes and allocates sites to private initiatives
Makes space in existing buildings available
Seeks suitable tenants (competitions, application processes)
"More than working"
"Cleantech City"
User/ Tenant
Other users (market-determined), e.g.
Core-user industry, Technology, ICT
Secondary user Service provider, Creative, Education
ICT company
Consultant
Housing
Business enterprise
Start-ups/ Spin-offs
Technology business
Company
Start-ups/ Spin-offs
Research institute
Rhombe-Areal

Perimeter block

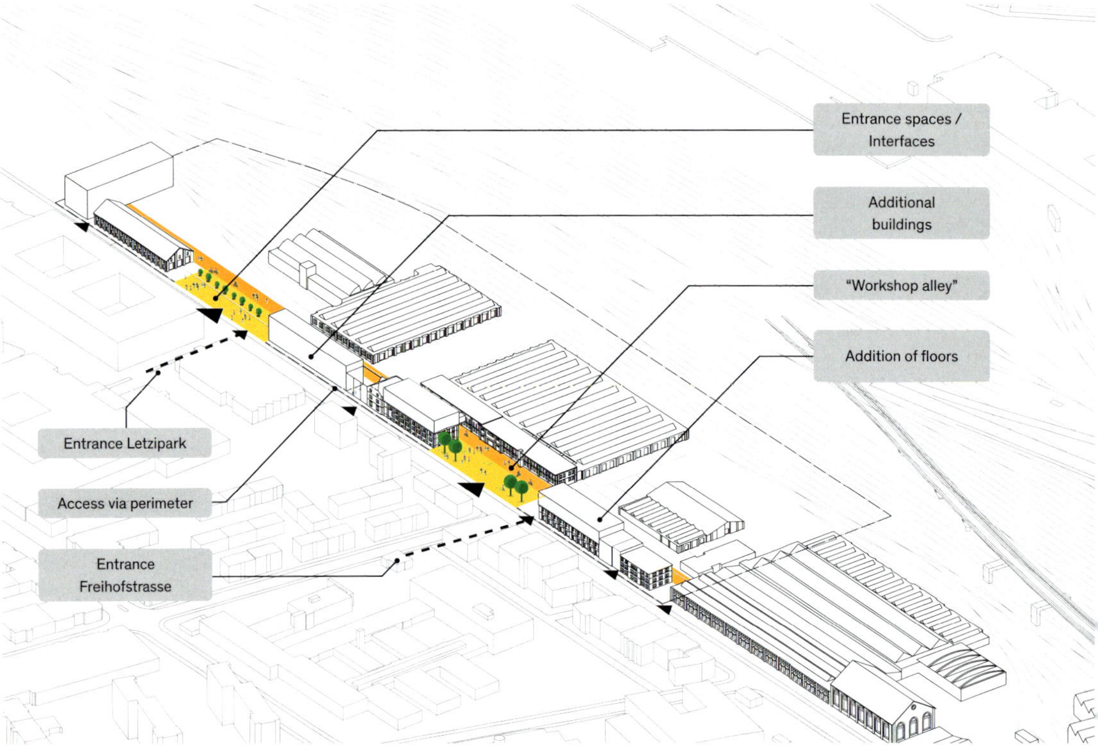

Halls and units

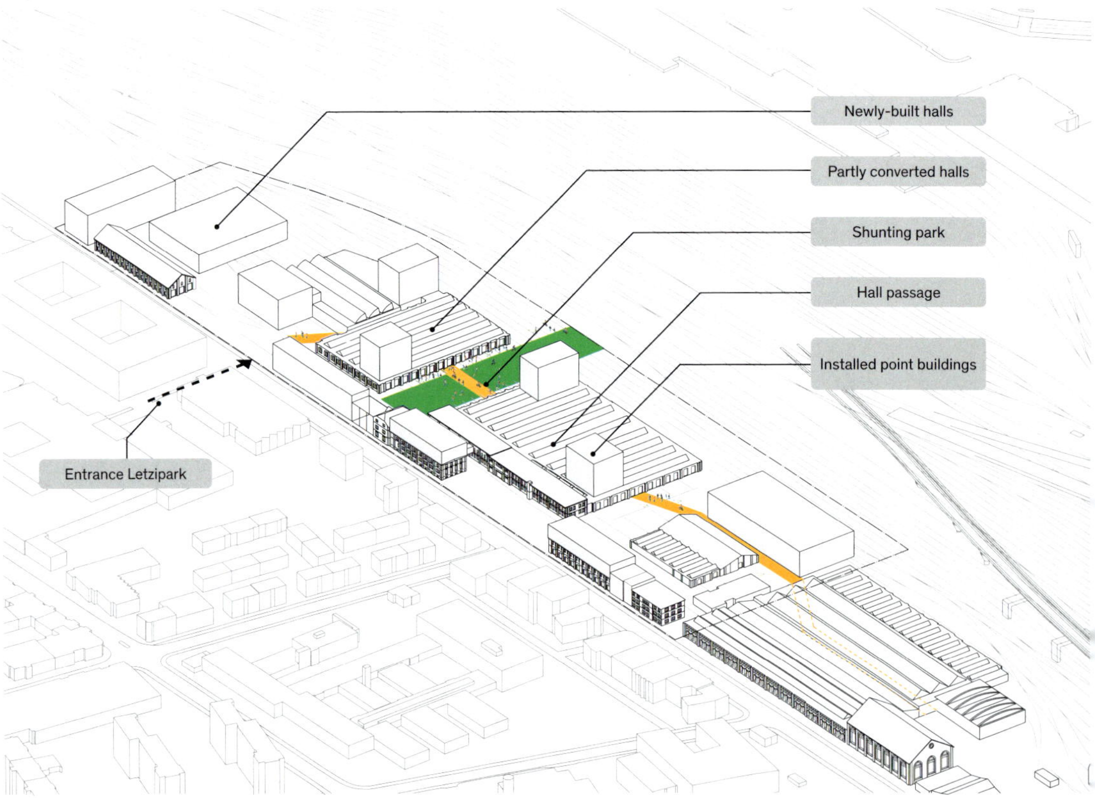

Urban Fabric: Transform the Existing

As part of the study commissioned by the City of Zurich, a structure was devised that allows for flexible development. Today, the site is being transformed and managed by SBB itself with a whole new group of planners [Essay: Urban Production Is Not Utopian, p. 258].

Concept 1: Intensification
Building stock is to be left intact and repurposed. Some of the perimeter buildings are enlarged. The existing buildings can be extended vertically to allow for more intensive use and increased density. The current lines of the industrial buildings must be retained, even if the street areas remain narrow.

Concept 2: Infrastructure
The former internal service alleys should remain and be used as a "workshop alley" for slow traffic and also for deliveries.

Concept 3: Connection to the city
Entrance areas will be created between the buildings along Hohlstrasse, which will act as interfaces between the site and Hohlstrasse as well as the surrounding developments and specific usage zones (Letzipark, Mediacampus). The square situated at the end of Freihofstrasse will be integrated in this open space system.

Concept 4: Halls and units
The halls adjacent to the "workshop alley" are divided into units and are a core component of the new usage concept. A variety of unit types, in particular Hall, Studio and Workshop, can be realized here. New hall-like structures can also be built on the western part of the site.

Individual higher volumes can also be integrated into the perimeter areas of the halls, which complement the range of space types and can accommodate offices and laboratories, for example.

Concept 5: Hall interior – the "Hallengasse," a passage through the halls
A passage can serve as a central element of infrastructure, leading through the halls and providing easier access to the different areas of the site. It enables a more flexible division of the halls and creates a special, covered space that also makes the halls accessible to the public.

In the future, this passage can also be extended to the eastern section of the workshops if the halls there are also converted. In the west, the passage connects to Hohlstrasse and also the entrance to the Letzipark.

Landmarks and buildings along track edge

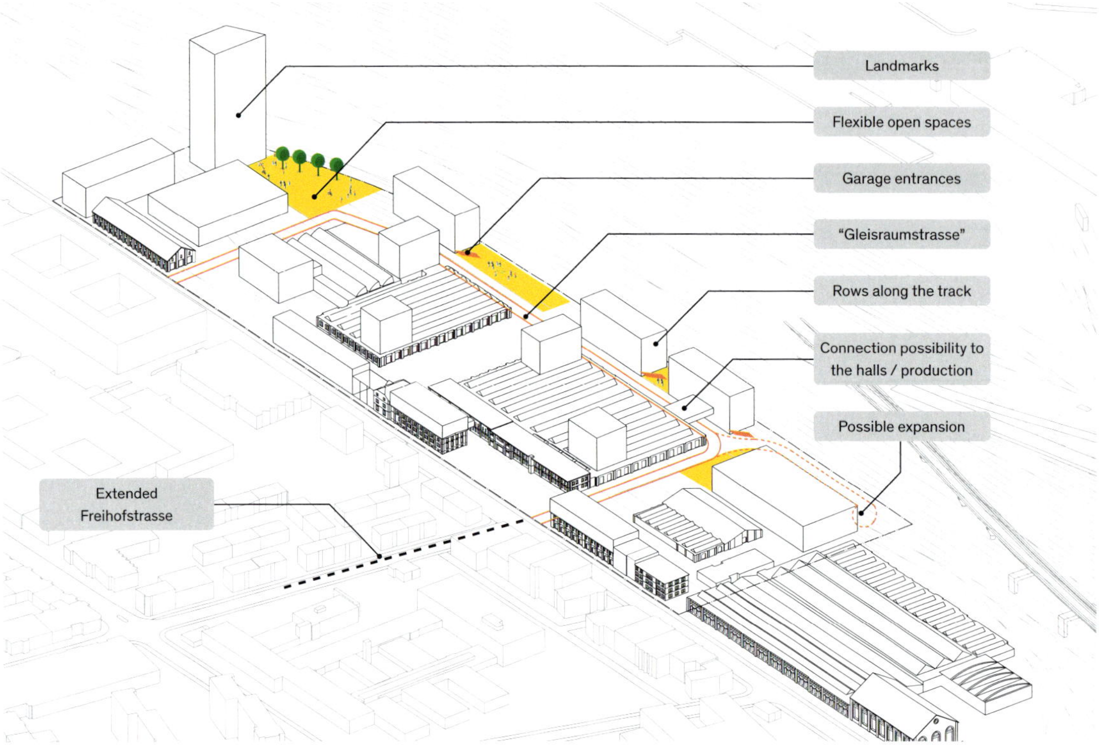

Concept Workshops West

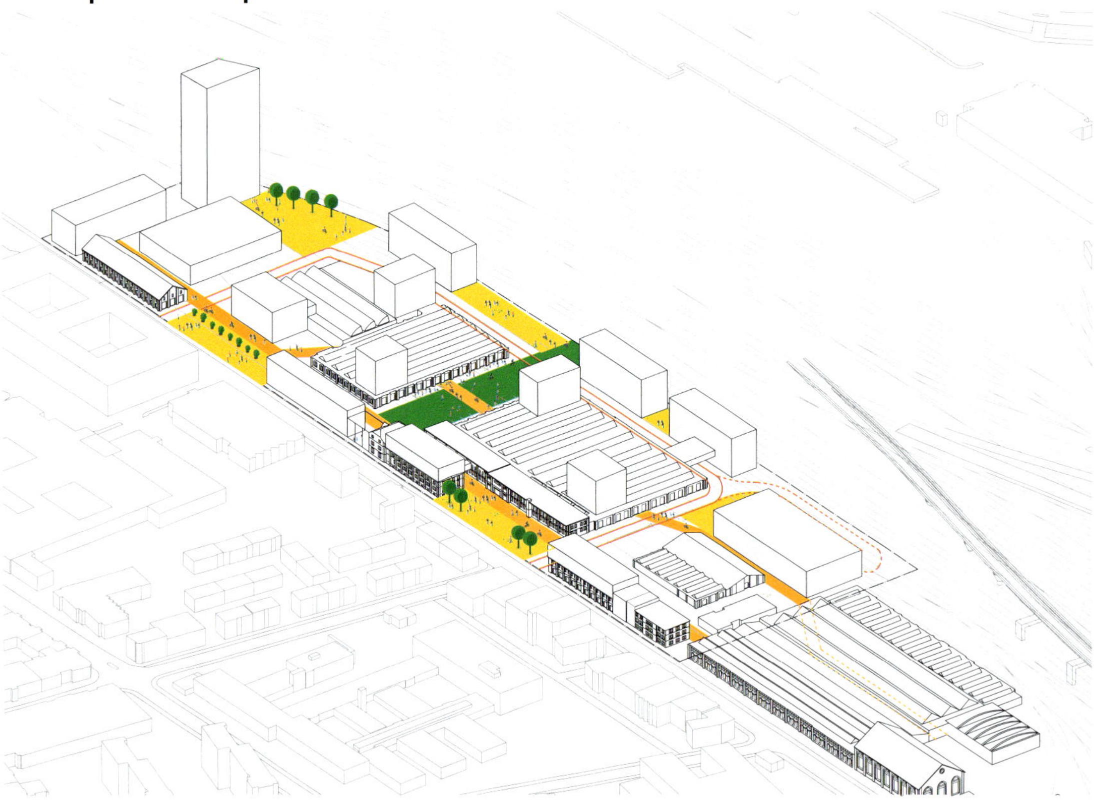

Concept 6: Open spaces with an identity
What was formerly the central shunting area is transformed with only minor changes into a public green space: the "Shunting Park." Flanked on both sides by the hall buildings, the park has a special identity-forming quality and can become a central meeting point and place to relax – situated in the middle of the future industrial park as an urban district. The "Shunting Park" docks directly onto Hohlstrasse and is thus easily accessible. On the other side, it opens up toward the tracks and creates a spatial openness and expanse that contrasts with the density of the district as a whole.

Concept 7: New addresses
In order to add further buildings along the tracks, a new road is to make the rear area accessible and create a new address for the buildings. The road links up with the intersection of Hohlstrasse/Freihofstrasse in the east, runs parallel to the tracks around the halls and back to Hohlstrasse in the west. This would require the SBB to dismantle tracks that are no longer in use. The "Gleisraumstrasse," or track area road, can be extended in the eastern part of the site to the SBB's workshops there. Access to parking facilities can be provided from the "Gleisraumstrasse."

Concept 8: Landmarks
New buildings can be developed along the new "Gleisraumstrasse," either as rows parallel to the tracks, or as compact, large-volume structures or tall focal points at the ends of the area. These buildings are highly visible in the city landscape due to their location by the tracks and are also attractive for investors due to their central location. The rows face the halls. This makes it possible to connect halls and office buildings directly via bridges, so that different unit types can be made available within a single complex.

Concept 9: Open spaces
Along the track area, spaces of varying quality are formed between the row buildings. As flexible open spaces, these should fulfill different requirements with regard to logistics, parking, prestige (entrance area) and recreation areas, and be used accordingly.

The overlapping of these individual elements results in a diverse, workplace-oriented urban district with a strong identity, which can meet different needs and offers a wide range of building and unit types.

As an exemplary toolbox, the study can be applied as guidance for other inner-city production sites.

Spaces and uses

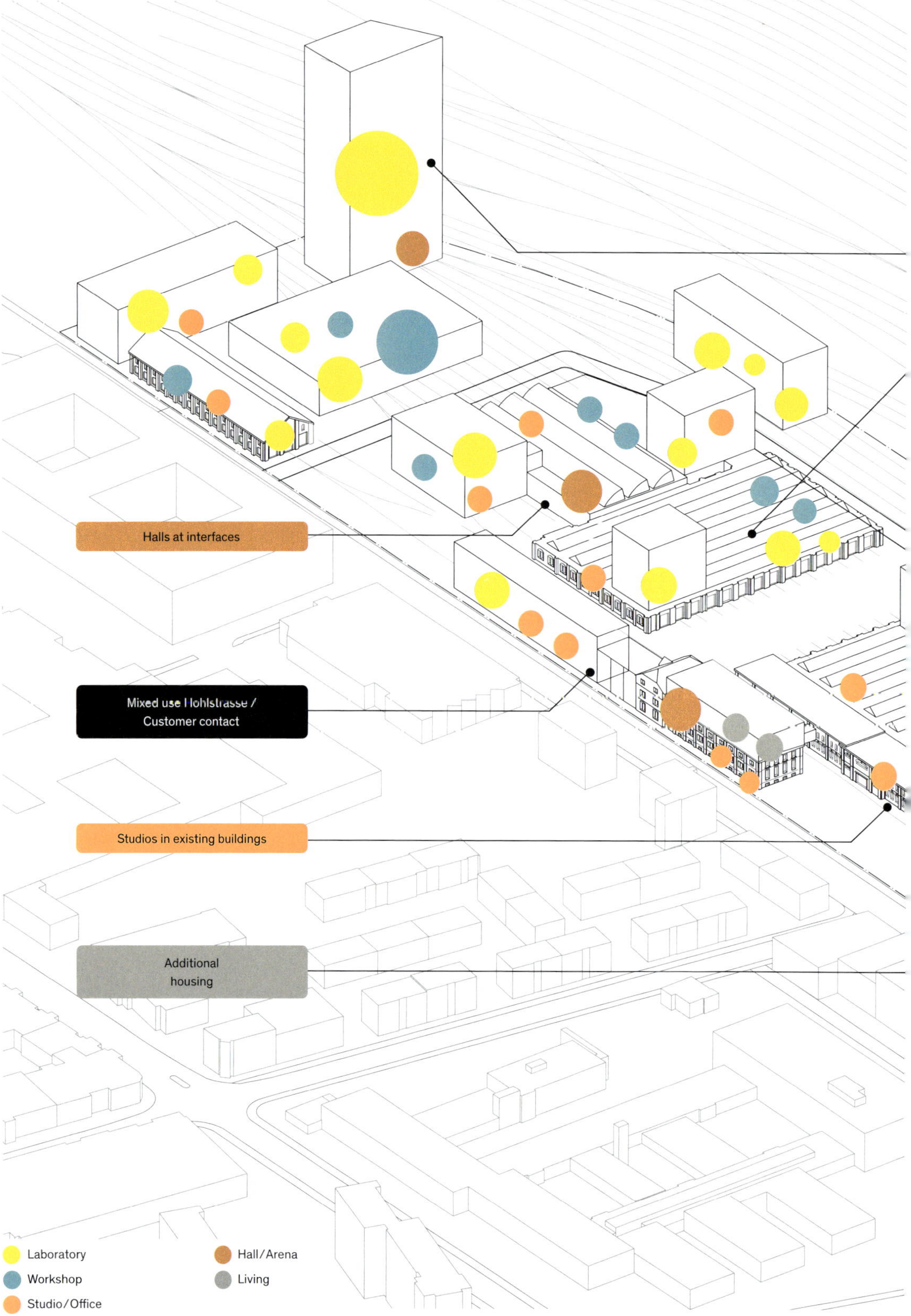

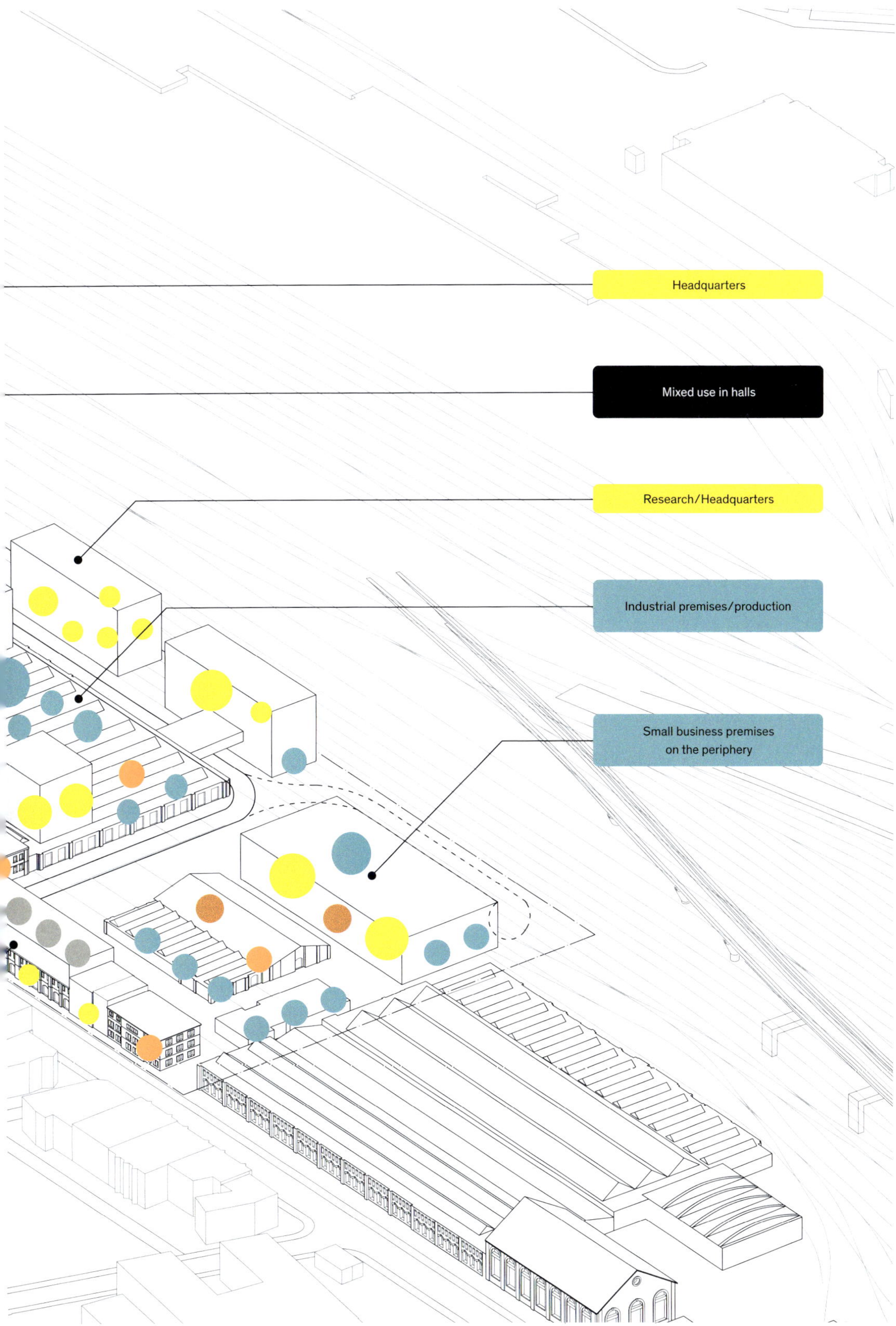
Headquarters
Mixed use in halls
Research/Headquarters
Industrial premises/production
Small business premises
on the periphery

Scenarios

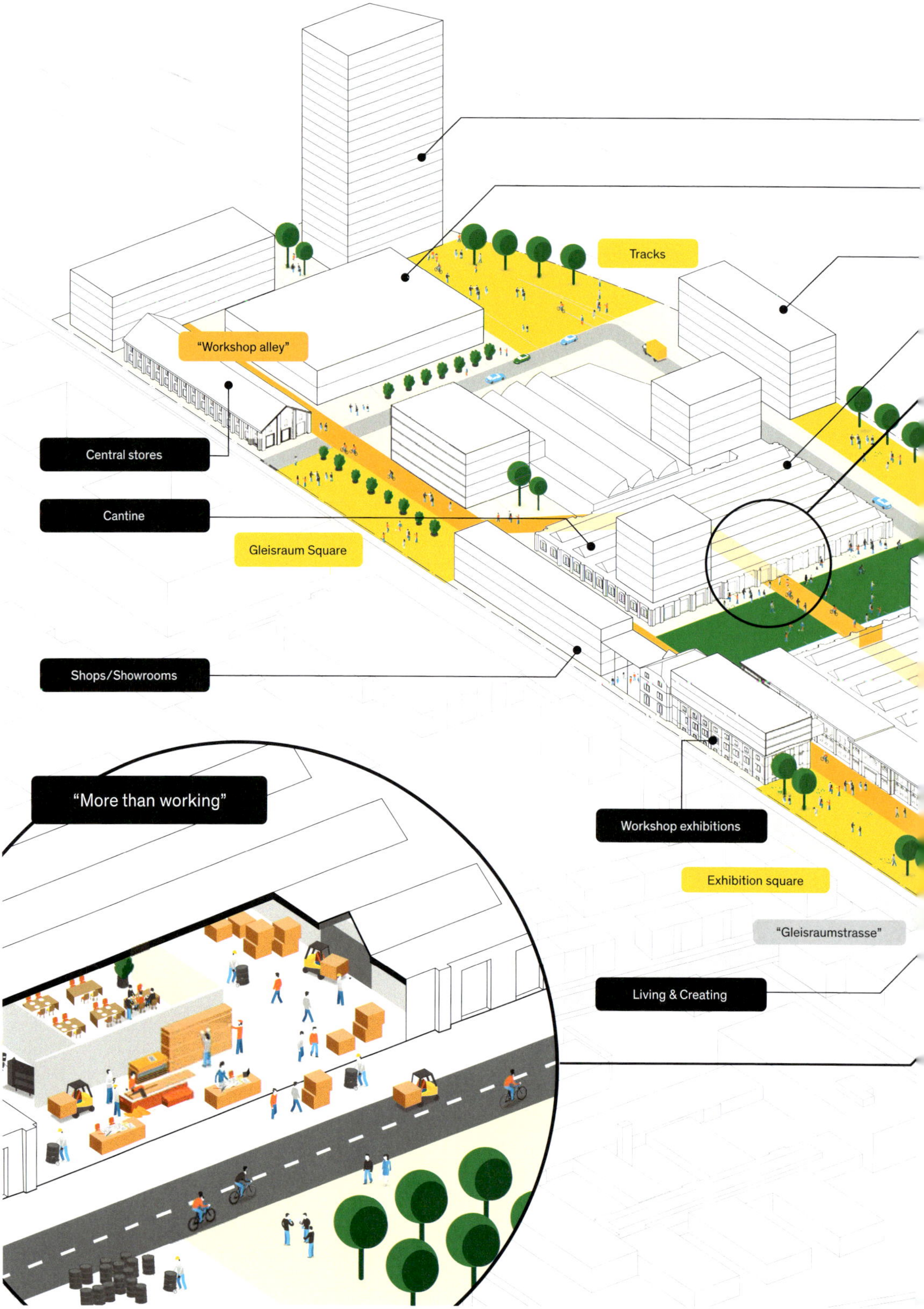
Tracks
"Workshop alley"
Central stores
Cantine
Gleisraum Square
Shops/Showrooms
"More than working"
Workshop exhibitions
Exhibition square
"Gleisraumstrasse"
Living & Creating

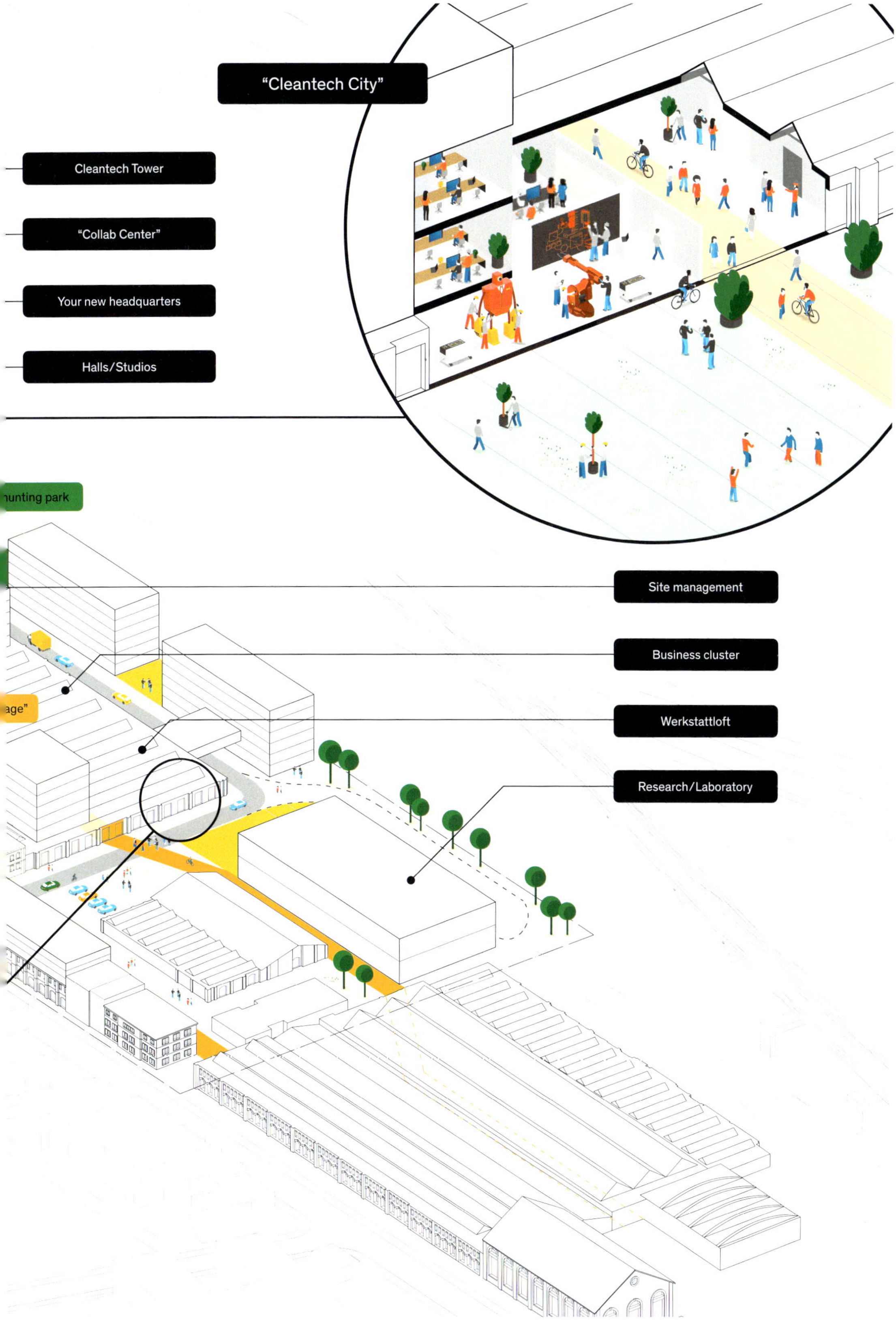
"Cleantech City"
Cleantech Tower
"Collab Center"
Your new headquarters
Halls/Studios
unting park
Site management
Business cluster
age"
Werkstattloft
Research/Laboratory

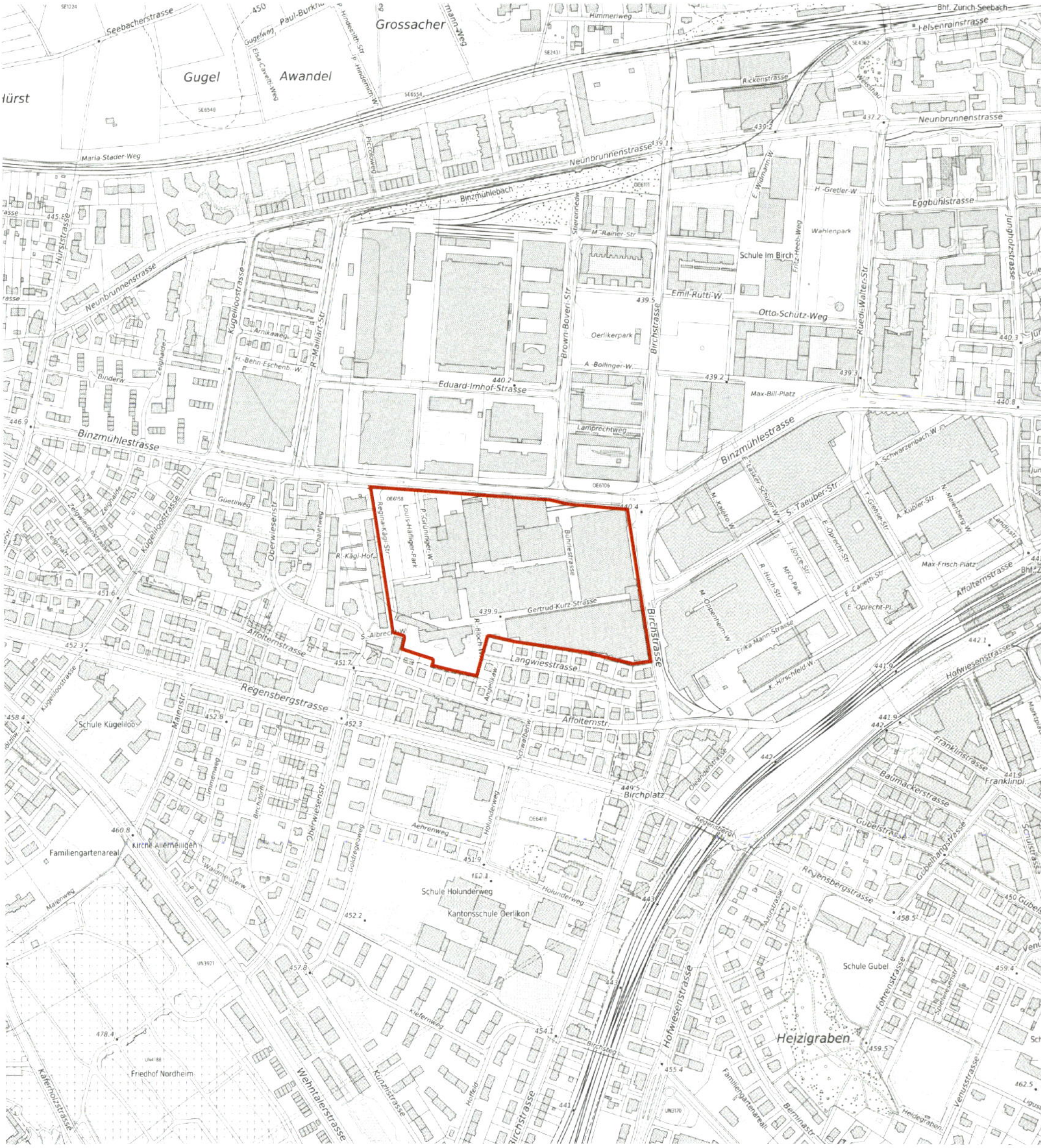

Site location on cadastre

0 50 100 200 m

RAD AREAL OERLIKON

Zurich

Post-Graduate Urban Design Studio
"The Industrious City: Rethinking Urban Industry in the Digital Age"
Taught by Hiromi Hosoya and Markus Schaefer
Harvard University Graduate School of Design
Spring semester 2018

The design studio proposes a series of projects for the redevelopment of the RAD industrial site located in Zurich-Oerlikon – one of the largest inner-city development zones in Switzerland. The aim of the scenario is to experiment with spaces, buildings, infrastructures, functions and narratives in order to envision a radical, mixed-use industrial urban area embedded within the context of the city. The 5.5-hectare site is a cradle of Swiss industrial history, and at the core of an ongoing political discussion on gentrification and renegotiating the presence of industries within the city limits. Today, the area is in the middle of a lively neighborhood, with playgrounds, meeting areas, various cooperatives, artisanal manufacturers and air defense industry.

The studio contributed to rethinking public and private development strategies for urban industry by providing project proposals for the stakeholders involved. The students made a field trip to Zurich, got acquainted with the site and met with prominent figures from fields as diverse as industrial production, digital industry, robotics, mobility start-ups, real estate, city administration, politics, urban farming, cooperative housing, creative industry, open-data activism and even science fiction. The following projects are both a record of the students' research and design thinking as well as a synthesis of this body of work into a set of legislative recommendations. Each student group was encouraged to develop a distinctive central hypothesis into which a more complex spatial, typological, social and economic project could be inserted. As such, the student projects as a whole can be read as a "How to Guide" for building a productive city for the RAD Areal, in which key ideas identified in the research segment of the semester have been used as starting points for the designs.

The following central topics form the basis for our How to Guide for Urban Industry in the RAD Areal, Oerlikon: industry as a civic attraction; cooperative thinking as a planning tool; the implementation of circular economies; new building typologies, new civic spaces; a finer-grain land use; and the idea of companies sharing facilities and services.

Maschinenfabrik Oerlikon (MFO) above, Schweizerische Werkzeugmaschinenfabrik Oerlikon (SWO, today RAD) below, around 1950

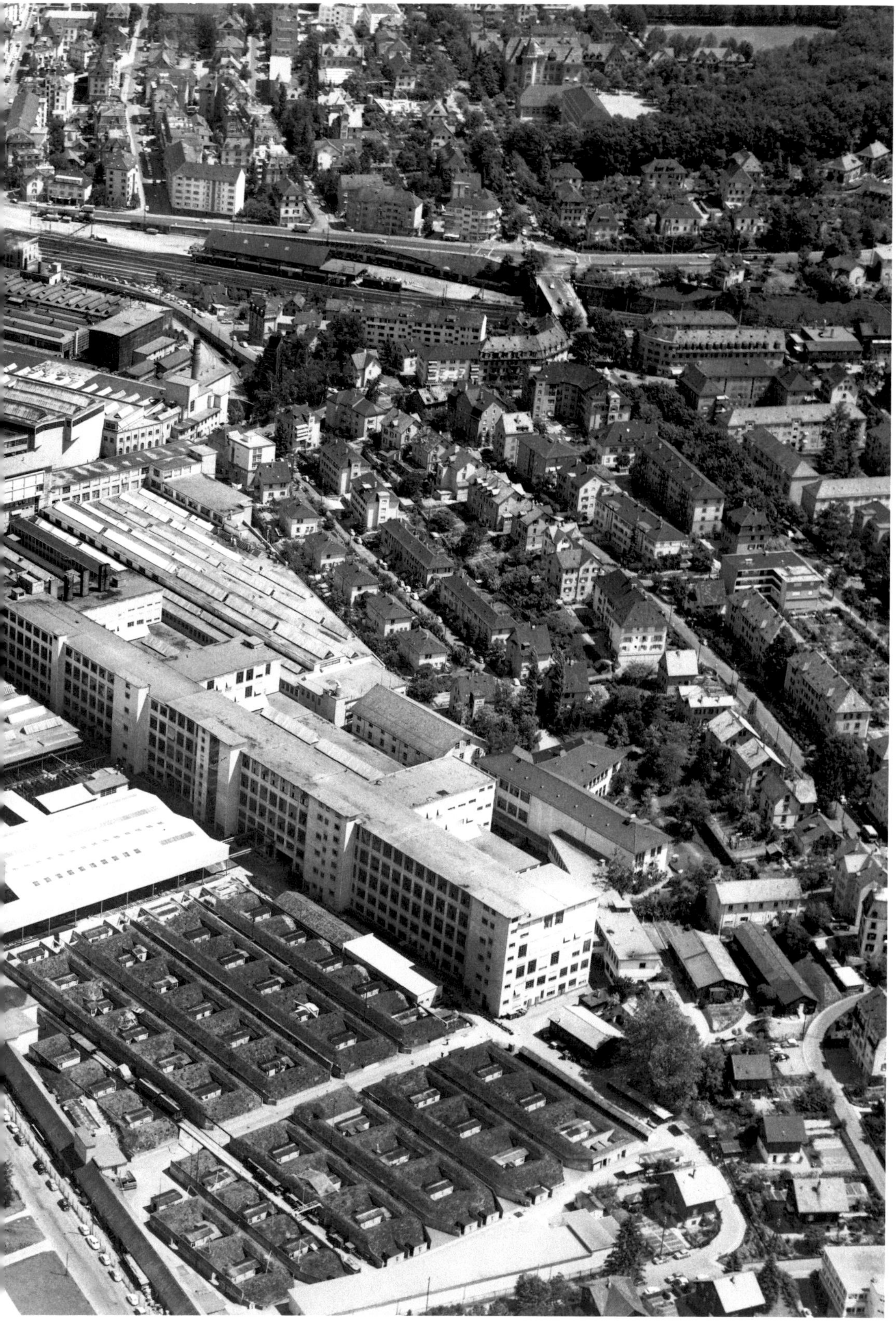

Early manufacturing facilities in Oerlikon with the Schweizerische Werkzeugmaschinenfabrik Oerlikon on the left

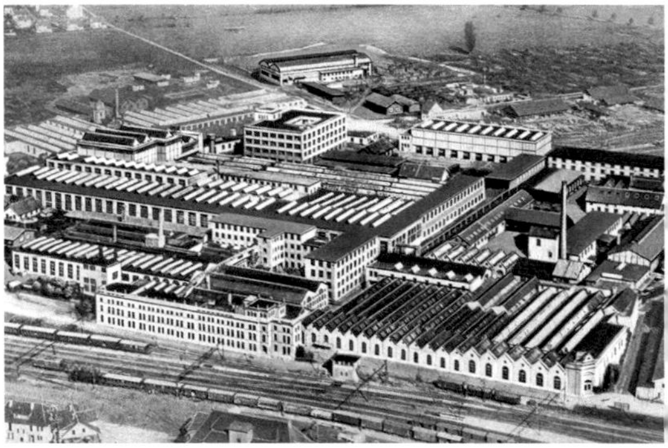

Early manufacturing facilities in Oerlikon

Ammunition labs, ca. 1950

Welfare building, ca. 1950

History

Since the 1870s, Oerlikon, then just outside the city of Zurich, has been an industrial cluster. Huber & Cie. developed into the Machine Factory Oerlikon (Maschinenfabrik Oerlikon, MFO) until it was merged with Brown Boveri, which in turn merged with ASEA to form ABB. In 1906, the Swiss Tool Manufacturing Factory (Schweizerische Werkzeugmaschinenfabrik Oerlikon, SWO) was founded on the RAD site and renamed Oerlikon Bührle, then Oerlikon Contraves, until it was purchased by Rheinmetall in 1999 and became Rheinmetall Air Defence (RAD) in 2009.

In the twentieth century, Oerlikon saw the production of machinery, locomotives, weapons and equipment for the space industry. Today it is still the seat of RAD, but also an increasing number of start-ups such as Climeworks.

Calculator assembly, ca. 1950

Tool production, ca. 1950

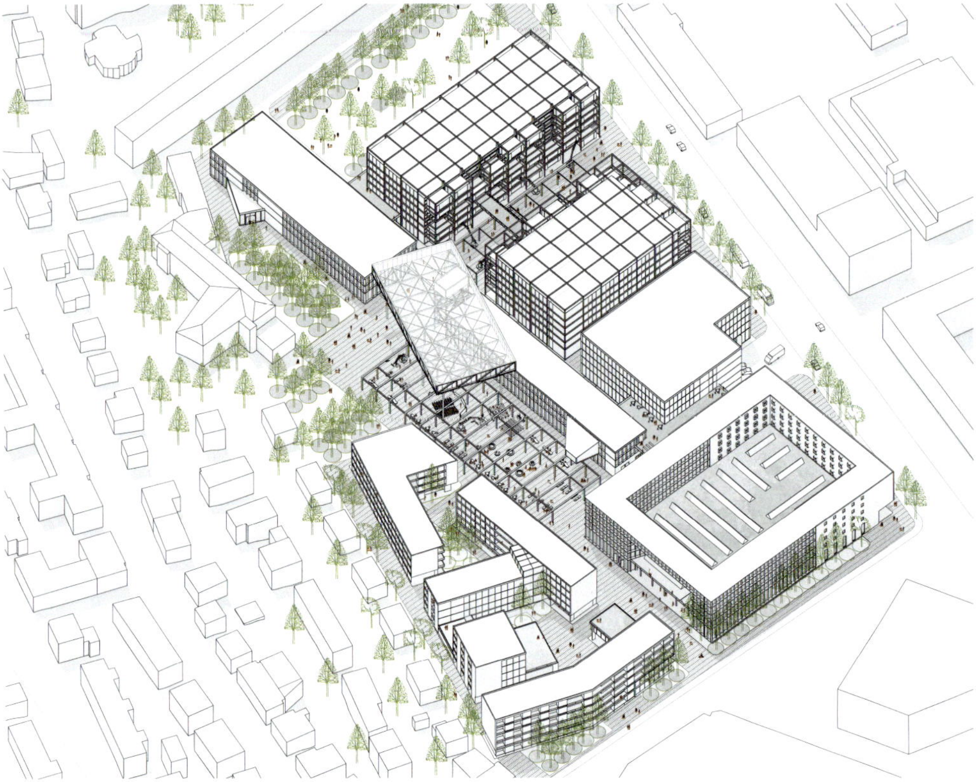

Industry as an Urban Attraction

What if...
Industry could be an attraction? Traditional industry, retail and entertainment are suffering from digital disruption. On the other hand, people crave authentic experiences. Could then the physical reality of production, concentrated, stacked and made accessible, become a new form of urban experience, an Experience Industry?

This project is about the culture of industry in the city. It celebrates our industrial heritage, its remaining industrial icons, as well as the culture of congestion that is the hallmark of urbanity. It accepts the fact that cities turn nature into culture, where culture is ultimately a product of our (collective) human imagination.

The project fosters the co-living and co-working character of the campus by providing mixed-use and public space sequences comprising innovative labs/workshops, light manufacturing factories, merchandise space and housing. The project introduces a central, L-shaped interior corridor leading from the Binzmühlestrasse to the Birchstrasse. This corridor is spatially intensified with a sky gallery over the marketplace, kinetic facades on the manufacturing buildings, and the juxtaposed entrances of a learning center and housing. It provides new relationships bringing together all the various ways that people gather. Therefore, the project satisfies the need for flexible industrial spaces but also establishes an interactive and dynamic urban infrastructure/platform for creative culture and domestic life.

Ya-shin Tzeng, Xin-yu Cao, Ping Zhang

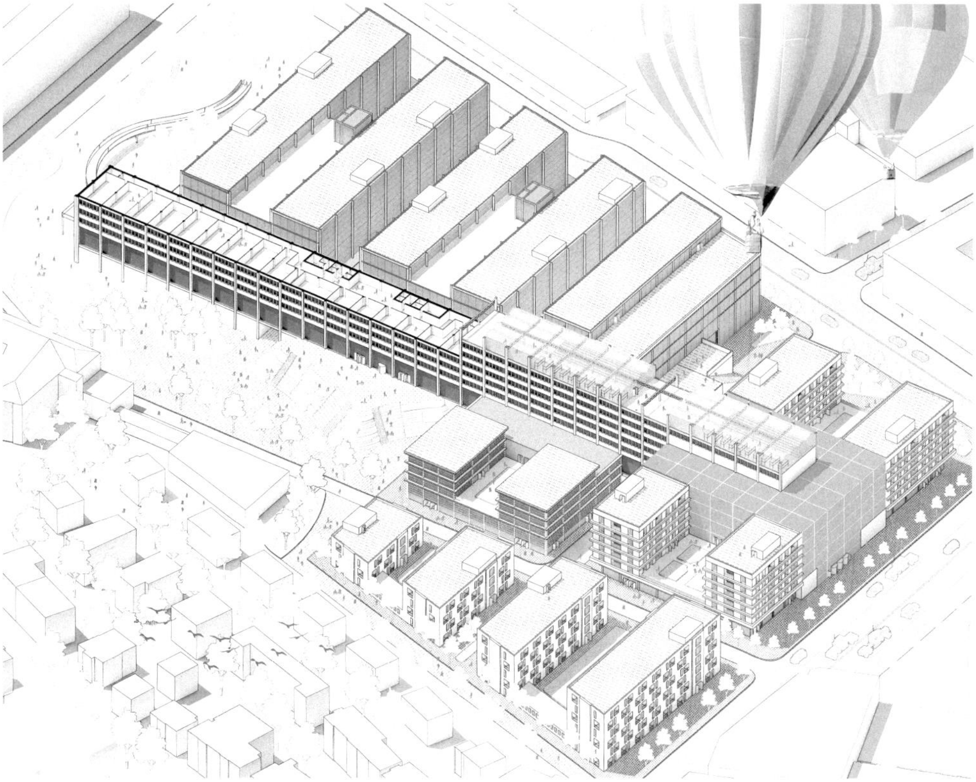

Cooperative Thinking as Planning Strategy

What if...
Urban production in combination with urban farming and new forms of communal living would allow for a concentration of value chains, increasingly self-sufficient but linked to the city and beyond, like a vertical village?

As we proceed into the twenty-first century, the sequestering of factories away from daily life is no longer necessary. It was this seclusion that prevented the urban environment from creating any sort of vitality or hybridity. We propose a new urban situation, one that is captivating for people to live in due to its dynamism, opportunities and exchanges between diverse populations. We did this by expanding upon the ideas of Charles Fourier and Jean-Baptiste André Godin. We re-explored the phalanstery and how such ideals of a self-contained community where people work and live together for their mutual benefit could be brought into the twenty-first century to create a productive, sustainable and lively environment. From this starting point we developed the "Vertical Village," a community that consists of many different flows: the industrial flow, residential flow, food-production flow and cultural flow. All of these flows are consolidated through the civic identity of the landscape and central market, thus giving visitors and residents access to them all. This arrangement generates a new urban metabolism, one in which materials are brought to the site, transformed and sold. Manufacturing and retail are both dying within cities. What happens when the two are combined and an interface for the public is established to interact with productive flows, both as a market and an experience? These new publicly accessible amenities combined with natural landscape elements could bring diversity and life to a site that has long been dominated by industrial uses.

Mike Hyungjoo Choi, Charles Smith, Zhengyu Qin

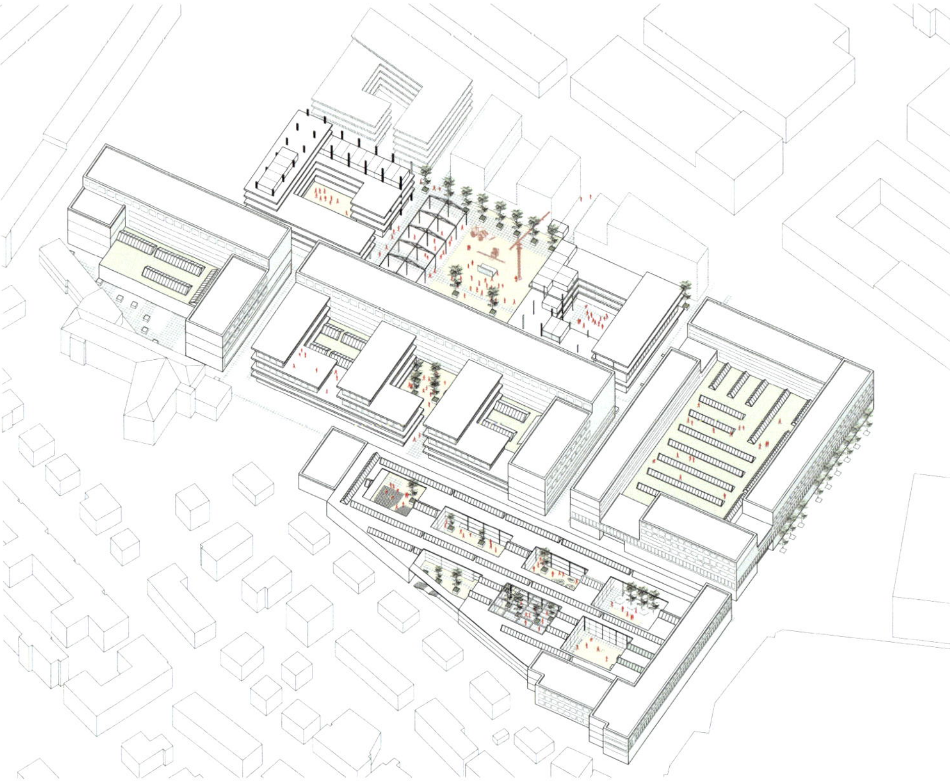

Implement Circular Economies

What if...
Urban production included the transformation and reinvention of the site itself, a gradual and participatory process modeled on ideas of a circular economy, forever changing, never ending, thinking forward to the future?

In addition to the three dimensions of space, our project adds the dimensions of materiality and time. Time is where processes unfold – from production to transformation – and where concepts of a circular economy can be introduced. Materiality, on the other hand, is the dimension that allows us to experience the flow of time through rebuilding, aging, developing patina, dismantling and recycling, when the cycle starts again.

Our project Forward to the Future provides a framework that enables spatial and material transformation in time and accommodates production through its flexible stages. The existing built framework will change and through time develop into the urban fabric, with spaces allocated for production, people and greenery. An important tool of the transformation and its implementation is the courtyard typology as well as modular units. The courtyard typology contextualizes the project in the context of Neu-Oerlikon and serves as a stable framework that allows transformation to occur and tangible relationships between human and green space to be generated. The flexible floor plates within the courtyard allow for modular units to be inserted. The design, building and installation of the modules occur on-site. Materials are reused after the demolition of existing buildings. In addition, new materials such as timber are introduced to the site.

The greenery is also flexible, such that it provides the opportunity for the people who inhabit the space to make it their own. For example, moveable pavers are used instead of concrete, to respect the temporality of space and its transformation. Trees and plants are placed in planters with wheels, which allows for flexibility, change and the ability of locals to design the space to suit their needs. In short, the industries, the materials and resources they use, and the waste they produce, understood as metabolic processes, allow the site to sustain itself through time, creating a self-sufficient, small neighborhood.

Ting Liang, Abbey Wallace

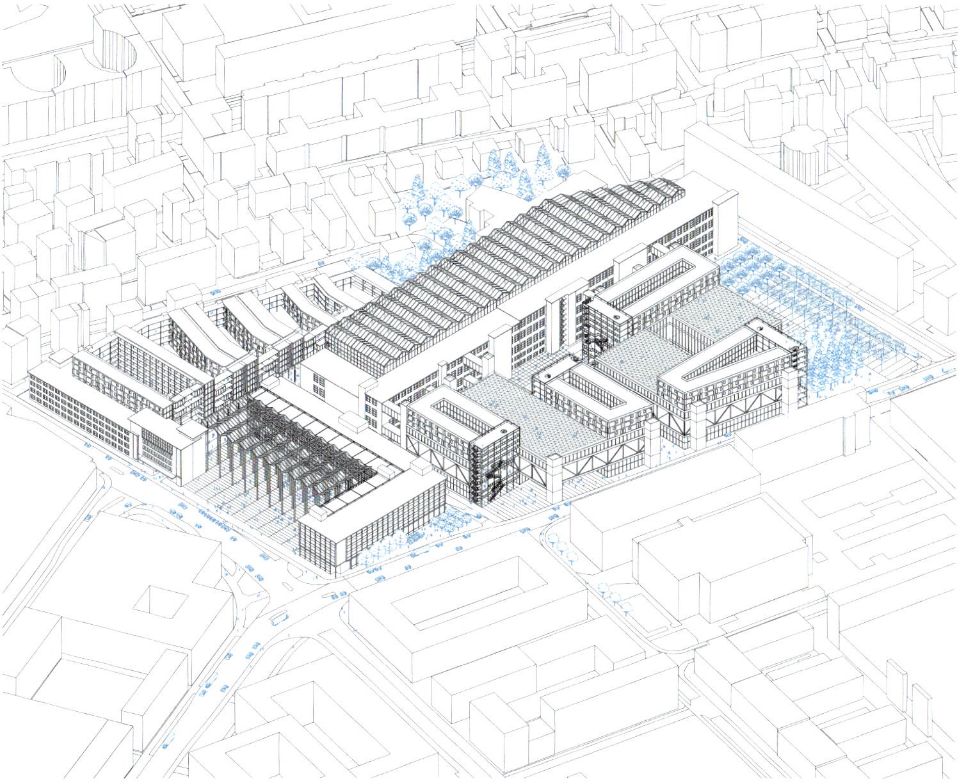

New Building Typologies, New Civic Space

What if…
Urban production would lead to the invention of new forms of urbanism and building typologies, dense, vertically stacked, and yet accessible, transparent, and exuberant, in the form of a Layered Fab-City?

This project focuses on the vertical integration of industrial production into urban life. It looks at specific strategies that will generate a social-industrial symbiosis, understanding that we already experience the vertical growth of industrial production. Traditional forms of industry – polluting, environmentally hazardous and involving heavy truck traffic – are now evolving toward greener, cleaner and more technology-oriented forms of production.
The above reality calls for the development of new zoning regulations and a departure from the modernist notions of clustering industries, monofunctional districts and the clear separation of uses in plan. Urban production today is dense, transparent and "glocal." Most importantly, it is based on coexistence and direct interaction with civic uses, allowing industrial activities to participate in a changing culture and economy. In this context, the project proposes the programmatic augmentation of the site in Zurich-Oerlikon, by inserting layers of a civic nature into the industrial complex. Through the combination of working, living, making, learning and recreation facilities, the city is remixed to the maximum and the district enjoys economic diversity as well as urban friction. In order to achieve this urban-industrial symbiosis, the strategies put into place expand from the architectural to the urban scale. At the building scale, diverse programs are stacked in section, providing versatile, multi-story urban production suites. In support of this mix, two approaches to vertical circulation are introduced: strategically positioned circulation cores and bridges address the growing importance of elevators in the age of vertical factories, and the thickening of the building facades celebrates vertical circulation while offering an interstitial space between the hybrid building and the public realm. At the urban scale, the project deals with the effects of vertical production on the circulation of people and goods. The active surface of the city is therefore multiplied, accommodating facilities for workers, residents and visitors alike. Goods occupy parts of the underground level of the district, along with key, upper levels of urban production. This allows for people to reclaim the level of the city. Ultimately, in the age of the city rejecting its traditional shop fronts, the proposal develops a new face of product and customer interaction at the street level.

Konstantina Tzemou, Xiyao Wang

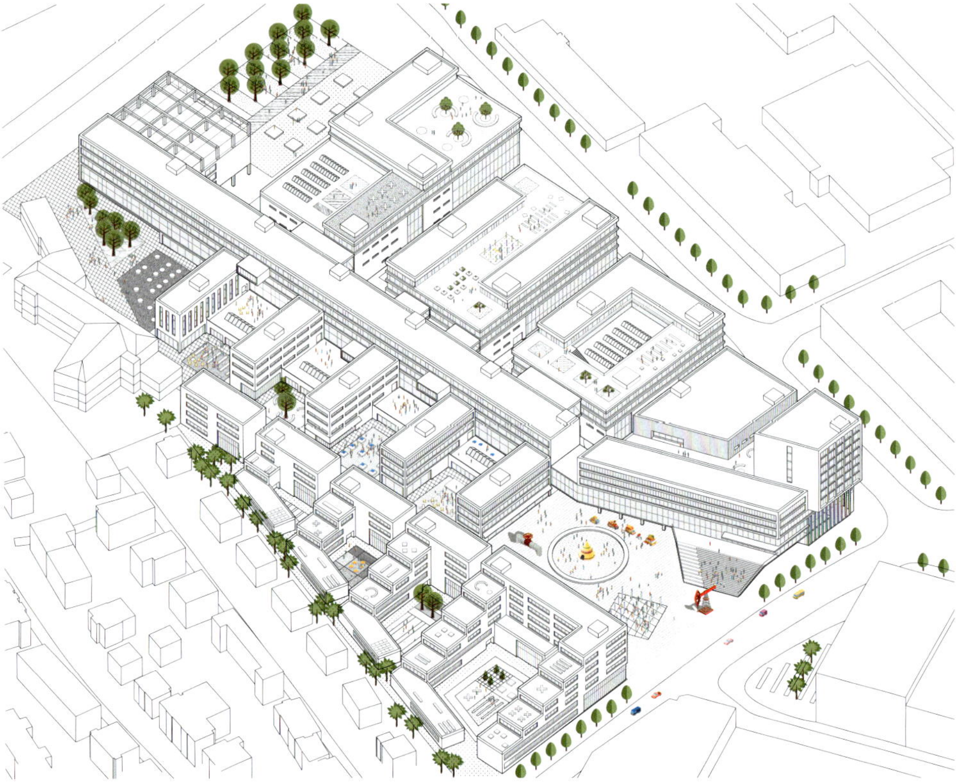

Finer-Grain Land Use

What if…
The site could be thought of as a cluster, accommodating all sizes of firms from large to small based on an agile business case, with those firms renting or purpose-building and profiting from a central interface linking all members and providing flexible space – a plug-in city?

Our proposal for the RAD site at Oerlikon intends to maintain its identity as a productive cluster and integrate it with residential life to create a new urban synergy. We utilize the existing spine structure as an interactive space to conceive small-, medium- and large-scale industries ranging from individual ateliers to light manufacturing as well as digital fabrication. In essence the physical appearance of industry, residence and open spaces, as well as public amenities, engenders a coexistence of production and social interaction within the urban context of Oerlikon.

From our perspective production should be embraced in the city as a part of the urban fabric, allowed to be seen, connected in proximity to shared daily life. Industry is evolving into two separate scales: the massive perimeter with large-scale factories, emissions and heavy logistical requirements still placed far from urban settlements, and urban industry, consisting of clusters of large, medium and small production places with access to skilled labor, urban innovation networks and urban consumers. In order to adapt appropriate manufacturing and industries, we modularize central industrial types that could be plugged into the central spine where productive and social transaction and exchange happens.

Through new proposed "plug-in" prototypes, industrial space becomes a flexible typology that could be customized and dedicated to various entrepreneurs and corporations. Such an industrial complex could be inserted and integrated in the motherboard that collectively hosts ground industrial circulation, a double-height spine above and adjustable offices in pent level. The cultural complex serves as a showcase for industry to expand its spectacle quality and transition into urban life. In addition, a semi-courtyard terrace typology is utilized for residential development not only to fit in between the two very different sides of the context of the site, but also to accommodate various types of housing typologies and enrich and mix the living experience.

Shenting Wang, Pojiang Nie

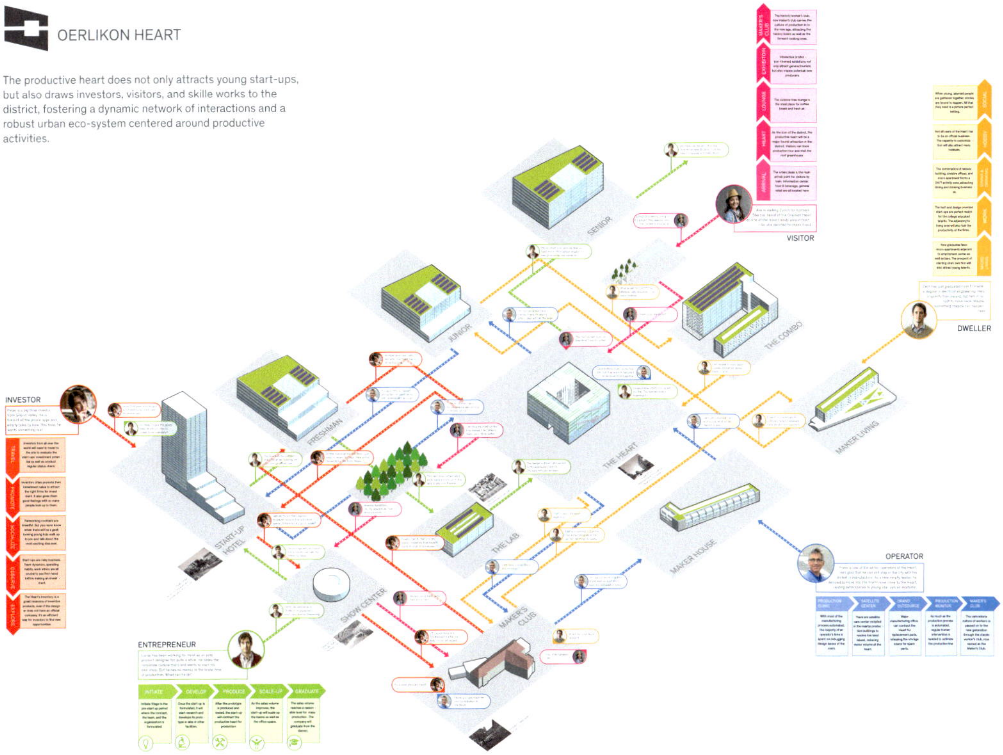

Companies Will Share

What if...
Production technologies were so advanced that production facilities for a campus of companies could be concentrated in an all-purpose, highly automated, vertical factory, supporting producers with a new industrial commons with a productive heart?

This project is based on the vision of a high-tech industrial commons that is physically manifested by the productive heart. This centrally located building is a flexible, on-site contract-manufacturing facility that can produce batches of customized goods at a reasonable price, higher than mass production but lower than customization. Micro-companies that lack the capital or the manufacturing know-how will share the facility and produce physical goods. By lowering both financial and technological barriers to entry for physical production, the productive heart will enable more producers, more creative products, and hence a more competitive economy.

In a compact form the facility integrates material supply, manufacturing, assembly, post-production and distribution all on one site, reducing costs for all. The productive heart is organized three-dimensionally with a robust vertical conveyor system lining the central courtyard where material flows in and out, reducing unnecessary wait times and improving the facility's efficiency. On the opposite side of the production center, a series of programs will engage the productive heart with the local production communities, including production clinics, intellectual property consulting, an open source library, a gift shop and pick-up location, and a fabrication hall. The basement will be used for fully automated temporary storage, and the rooftop, connected through the public stairs, will be open to the public and feature an urban farm.

The compact form of the productive heart allows for seamless integration between production space and urban space. It also activates an ecosystem of micro-companies and production start-ups surrounding the facility. As the development gradually replaces the existing buildings formerly used by RAD, the site will have designated spaces for start-ups in all stages. The concentration of creative, tech-savvy, and energetic entrepreneurs will attract retail, restaurants and cultural events. In the end the productive heart will bring production closer to people, producers next to each other and the productive soul back to the city.

Celine Zhou

Modular development in steps
There is no single concept that can fill the site in its entirety, since companies with very different requirements, sizes and business models, and even academic institutions, will be interested in joining the project. Large established firms have very specific requirements and need maximum flexibility. As they will probably invest in their customized solutions, they will certainly be interested in long-term leasing or even ownership. Medium-size companies, on the other hand, can operate in more generic spaces adapted to their specific needs. They might be interested in sharing facilities, equipment or even staff. Finally, there is a need for small units for companies involved in crafts, arts or start-ups that have shorter planning horizons. The site therefore should offer diverse solutions for a diverse clientele. The different models will also require different development strategies and timeframes. This means that the site inevitably will transform in a heterogeneous manner, from newly built to refurbished and temporary use, or even keep some empty lots. Inversely, this means that any tabula rasa approach with a planned top-down and fixed solution would not be feasible.

Robust strategy, flexible implementation
A robust, long- and short-term strategy that will offer reliability is necessary to attract tenants with very different time horizons. Only when potential tenants recognize the context they are operating in as stable are they willing to commit long-term. At the same time, a flexible implementation is needed for companies with very specific needs. A planning document that requires a high degree of definition, such as a *Gestaltungsplan*, will not be useful in this regard. This dual requirement begets an understanding between the owners, developers and city administration to both allow for flexibility and ensure quality.

The strategy needs to convey why the site is a good "place to work." It needs to provide convenience, stability and cost-effectiveness for firms. It also needs to offer synergies with other firms in sharing facilities, logistics and access to a talent pool. It must describe why the site is an attractive "place to be" and why it is worthwhile for employees and visitors to spend more time there.

Existing building stock as an asset
The existing building stock is already very dominant and structures the site in distinctive ways. Due to the flexible implementation, it will take a long time to define a new character for the site. The existing buildings have a scale, generosity and patina that would be difficult to achieve with new buildings. They can provide identity and visibility when well used. On the other hand, they need to be refurbished efficiently to comply with the demands of the new tenants and meet regulatory requirements.

Nevertheless, the site needs to be opened and better connected to the city. Focal points should be created by simple and effective interventions. While many buildings will remain, the urban network, the path system, accessibility and even the signage need to be adapted.

Temporary programs for activation
A curation of temporary programs should be carried out in order to activate the site and prime it for functions and uses that can become permanent at a later stage. Commercial programs will create a network of interested parties, cultural programs will put the site on the city map and an educational function, such as a temporary location for an academic institution, will generate liveliness. Temporary programs can also become fertile ground for tenants who would like to remain on-site permanently.

New buildings profit from industrial scale
New buildings can take advantage of the industrial context in that they are not primarily geared toward form but offer new typological solutions. They could match the unexpected generosity of the industrial scale, perhaps by combining housing and manufacturing or mixing other uses. Civic qualities and open spaces are opportunities for experimentation. Ground floors that have been dimensioned for industry (e.g., with 6m floor height) also provide flexibility for other uses.

On the other hand, without programmatic activation, large footprints and repetitive facades represent a downside of industrial typologies. The entrances of the NŒRD building, for example, have been minimized and placed equally on all four ground floor facades, resulting in unclear addresses and making companies hard to find. The buildings therefore need to be transformed and reprogrammed or reinvented in terms of their accessibility and transparency to become as flexible as possible.

Fine-grain spatiality
The new urban economy requires a fine spatial grain. A network of companies, from small to large, can generate economic diversity on the site and in the city. The site, with its different user groups, could connect thinkers and makers in a collaborative neighborhood. Manufacturing, product development and research can

be concentrated on one site, and according to current zoning regulations, the southern portion of the site can accommodate housing. New facilities and other urban functions, from gastronomy to events, can be added. A mixed-use quarter can be developed with places of high urbanity and interaction and others dedicated to logistics. In their respective ways, all these projects exhibit a mix of diverse functions.

Cooperation, co-working, sharing

Urbanity means exchange. On the site, this can be celebrated and employed for providing the central, urban location with specific infrastructure for cooperation. Shared facilities for leisure (e.g., the rooftop restaurant at the NŒRD) or production can be implemented. In the exchange between the different scales of companies and the different functions, new forms of cooperation are imaginable. Features of a circular economy could be set up. For the planning process this means that some forms of participation of future tenants need to be implemented. Cooperation needs to start before the companies come to the site.

Experience

With a diverse mix of buildings, spaces, users and firms, from small to large and young to well-established, the site could generate a unique urban experience for tenants and visitors alike. Urban industry could also become an attraction for visitors and even tourists.

Areal 2013
(Used by V-ZUG, blue)

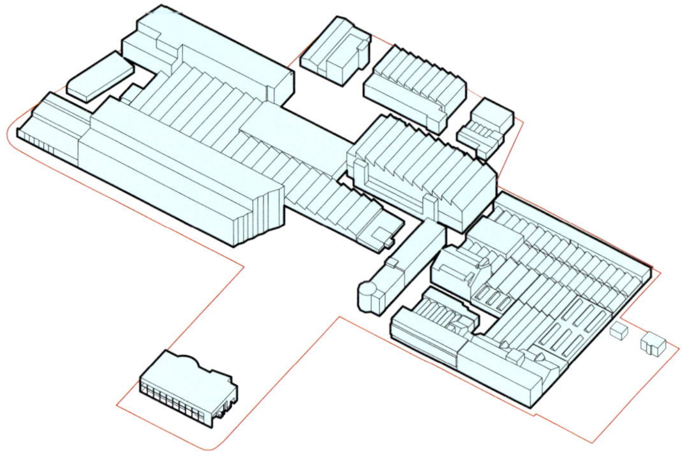

Consolidation
V-ZUG

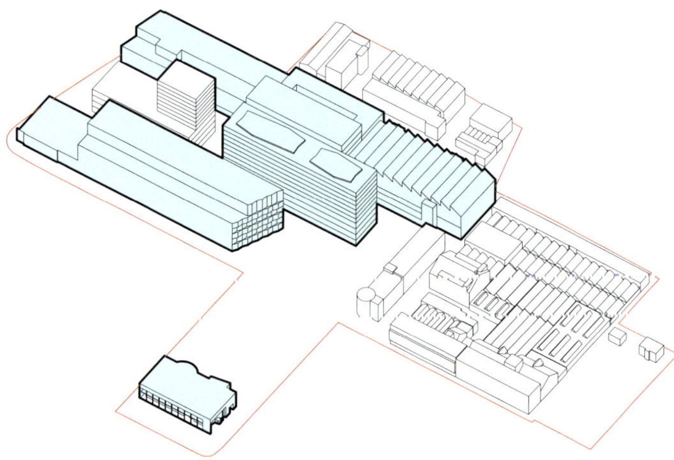

Tech Cluster Zug

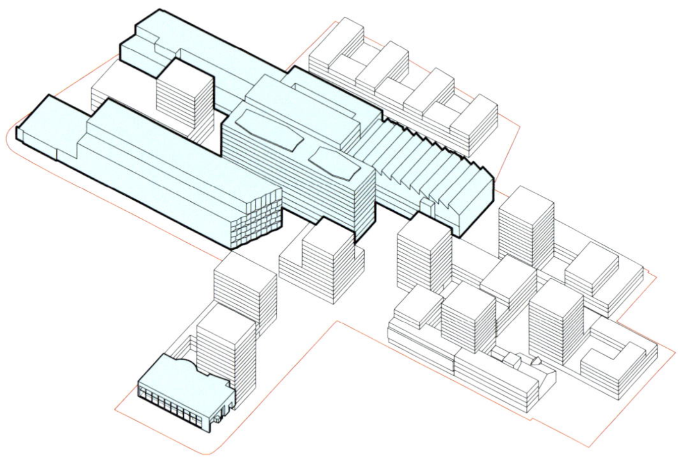

TECH CLUSTER ZUG

Zug, 2013–ca. 2045

In 2013, V-ZUG, in collaboration with the town of Zug, invited several offices for an international competition, the aim of which was to increase the density of its core area in the north of the town, halfway to the next town of Baar, to facilitate new industrial uses and to enhance them with urban functions. What began as a study is now a transformation project at various levels and scales, influencing corporate structure, industrial planning with automation and verticalization, real estate development, mobility, energy, digitalization, urban development, location strategy and much more. The broadest range of industrial partners, planners, architects, experts, entrepreneurs, company founders, neighbors, civil servants and politicians are all collaborating on a common idea.

Verzinkerei Zug – a galvanizing plant – was once situated at the gates to the town of Zug. In 1976, the plant merged with the Zug Metallwarenfabrik, a metal goods factory that was the market leader in cooking stoves and ovens at that time. Production was consolidated on the present site, while the Metallwarenfabrik premises next to Zug railway station were converted into the Metalli shopping, office and residential district. In 1981, Verzinkerei Zug AG became V-ZUG. Almost forty years later, the next step is being taken in the transformation process to form the Tech Cluster Zug (TCZ). The reasons behind this are a commitment to the location, to the workforce and to securing them in the region, as well as the will to develop the district in a long-term and sustainable manner. This site, where V-ZUG has been manufacturing alone and in enclosed premises until now, will in future be the publicly accessible home to an industrial cluster of companies, enhanced by urban services such as housing, shopping facilities, bars, restaurants and daycare centers, and will become increasingly connected to the town.

The Tech Cluster is a site for industry and urban production. It is also a part of the town where industrial processes, but also products and services for daily life play a natural part and can therefore be shown, tested and improved. The TCZ will be a laboratory on view to the public. For V-ZUG, the development of the site means not only a portfolio of real estate, but also a network of relationships, ideas and learning opportunities that can sustainably be built up and maintained over time. V-ZUG will become part of a cluster in which other companies can contribute their expertise. Production will continue to take place on the site without interruption. Conversions and interim uses are possible and areas can be developed in small stages. This will allow the realization of a mosaic of urban building blocks. V-ZUG is to concentrate its operations in the north of the site, where production is to be vertically stacked and highly automated. Their motto is: twice the production on half of the area. In the north, west and east, areas will become vacant for new businesses to settle and have their own addresses, while in the south, production, working, living and communal services can be arranged in groups of different building types along a dense network of alleys, squares and intimate courtyards. Existing buildings can be conveniently used for temporary purposes, and start-ups can be included. On neighboring sites, the largest wooden high-rise in Switzerland is being built, as well as a building with production in the base and cooperative housing above it. In the TCZ, which is directly connected with the new city bypass, the area logistics will be facilitated by internal alleys, while tree-lined entrance areas and green courtyards in the southern part will allow for small urban oases, thus translating the high density of the site into urban and spatial diversity. As a stepping-stone between the towns of Zug and Baar, the V-ZUG-Platz (V-ZUG square) closes the gap between Baarerstrasse and Industriestrasse and becomes the new center of the area.

To develop an area takes time. It takes even longer, however, to establish value chains, networks and an urban atmosphere in one place and to allow them to evolve. At the moment, only V-ZUG produces on the site – in the future, operations will be consolidated on approximately a third of the area, and V-ZUG will then be just one player among several within the newly emerging cluster. Step by step, the area will be expanded, initially for temporary use as incubators in the existing building stock, and later for new buildings.

In the first phase, the alley and spatial structure of the future complex is etched into the existing halls. Start-up companies will find their first low-cost spaces here; the existing halls can gradually be replaced by new groups of buildings. V-ZUG Immobilien, the real estate subsidiary, acts as developer, curator and director, to ensure that relationships, synergies and potential are not lost in the transformation. The site thus becomes a mosaic of different possibilities and space types.

With each completed stage, the technology cluster becomes more and more interwoven with its urban environment. The area becomes more open and permeable. New employees and residents bring life to the district, have lunch in the Tech Café, have their laundry done or take their children to the daycare center. Other small service providers may subsequently settle in the area. The TCZ serves as a model for production in an urban environment. The added value in the neighborhood increases.

The logistics of urban industry often put a strain on the environment. Two internal parallel alleys, with turning areas on the inner squares, will handle truck traffic efficiently, so that sensitive urban uses are not affected. On the north side at the edge of the site there is a central entrance and exit.

The area has two different types of open space: adjacent to the surrounding roads there are small urban squares with groups of trees that serve as interfaces to the town. This is where public services are situated, along with the addresses of the resident companies. Inside the area there are open spaces that are not directly visible from the outside, which can be used flexibly and informally and are also available to urban industry.

The site is to be operated CO_2-free. It will be supplied by the Multi Energy Hub, an energy network fed by two groundwater wells, a lake-water channel, its own photovoltaic plant, CO_2-free electricity and some biogas, which can be supplemented by Power2Gas. The energy network thus provides heat, cooling, electricity and gas available throughout the area and even to the surrounding neighborhood. Due to the mixed use, synergy effects can be exploited by cascading energy flows. On the other hand, V-ZUG anticipates possible CO_2 levies and is preparing for a future that is as climate-neutral as possible. The control of the energy supply from the grid is in the hands of the site operator, which makes it possible to contribute to the stability of the system beyond the site and also to profit financially from it.

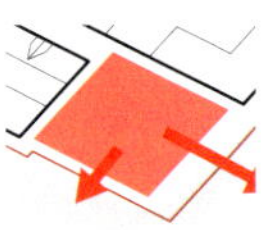

Urban squares
(Urban interface)

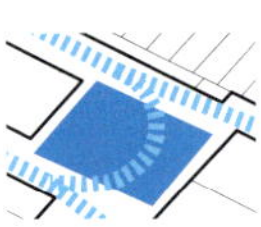

Workplaces and
logistics loop

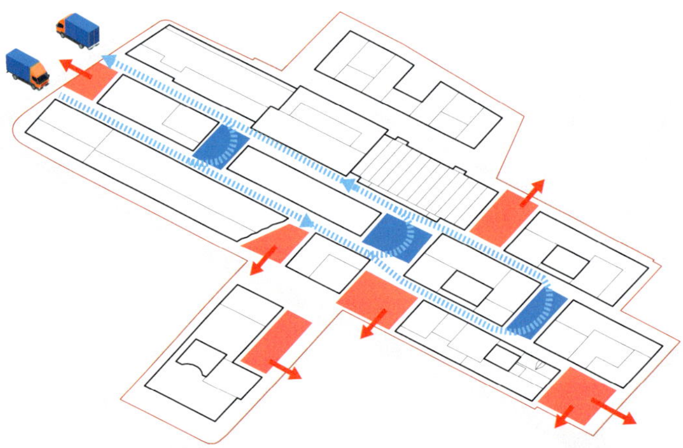

Structure of open space: Squares and logistics loop

V-ZUG Aerial View, 1949

Sheet metal production

V-ZUG Areal, 1975

Construction department

Assembly line, 1980

< Washing boiler manufacturing, 1930

Control and measuring equipment

< Pulling presses, 1957

Status of the planning 2018–ca. 2045

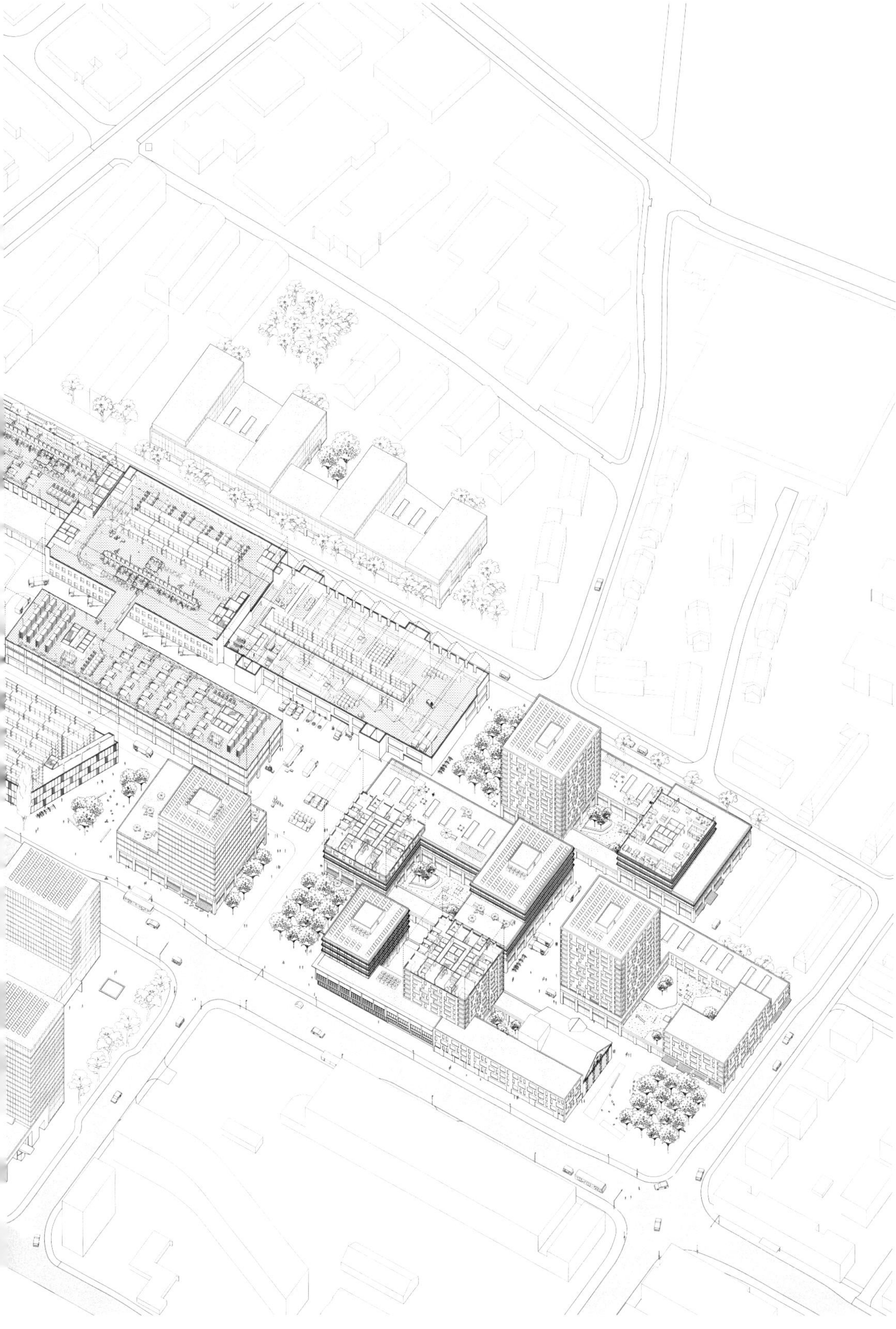

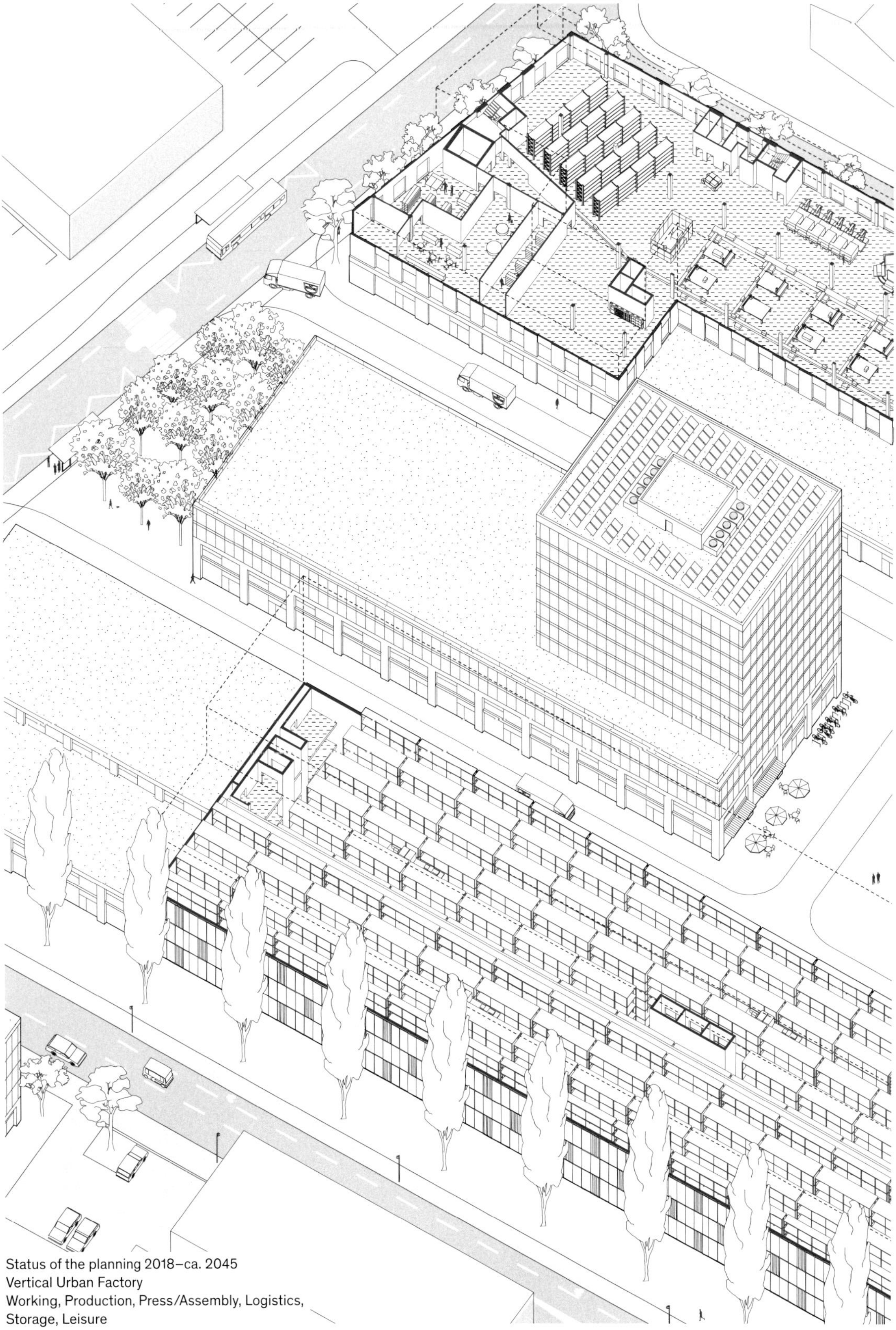

Status of the planning 2018–ca. 2045
Vertical Urban Factory
Working, Production, Press/Assembly, Logistics, Storage, Leisure

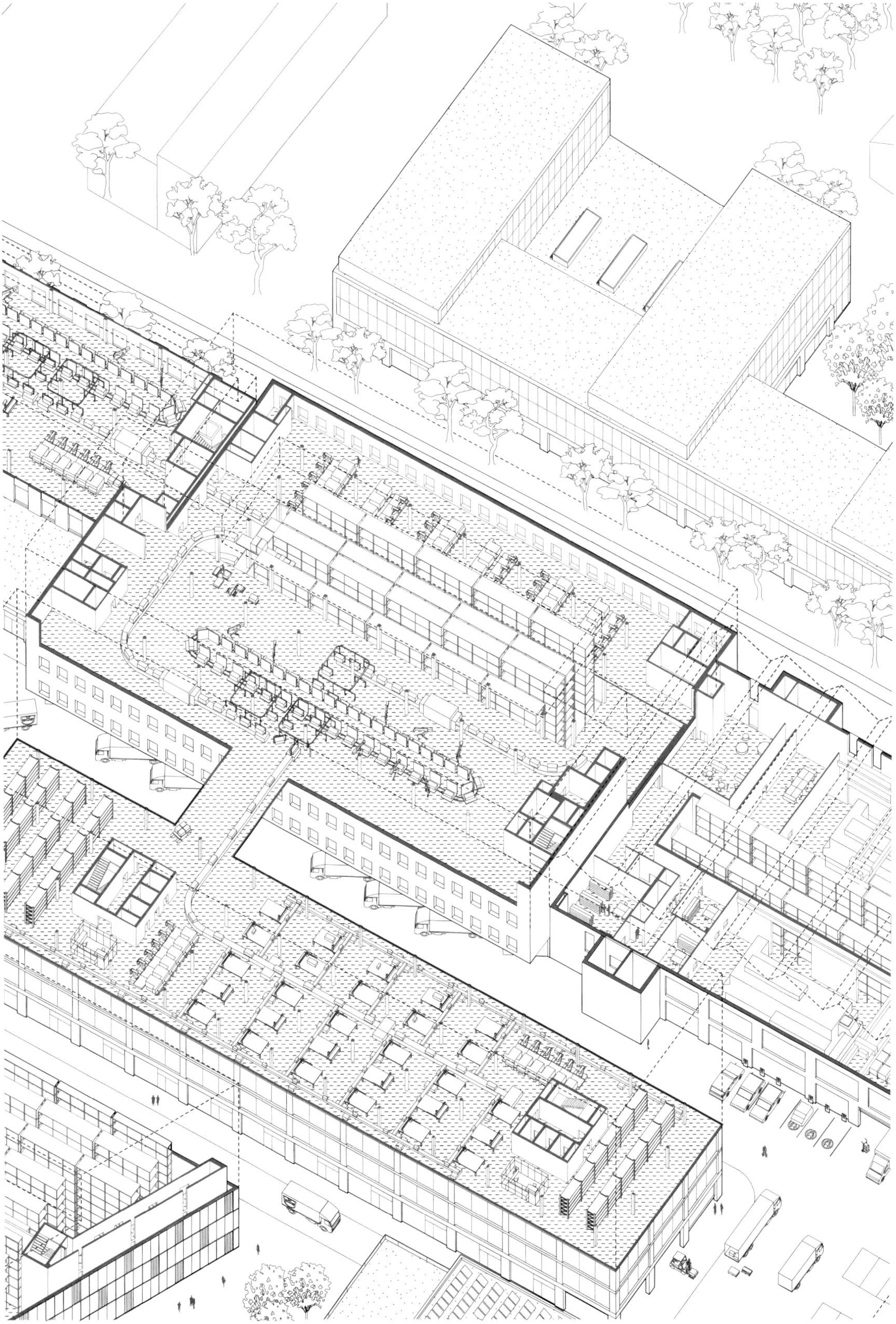

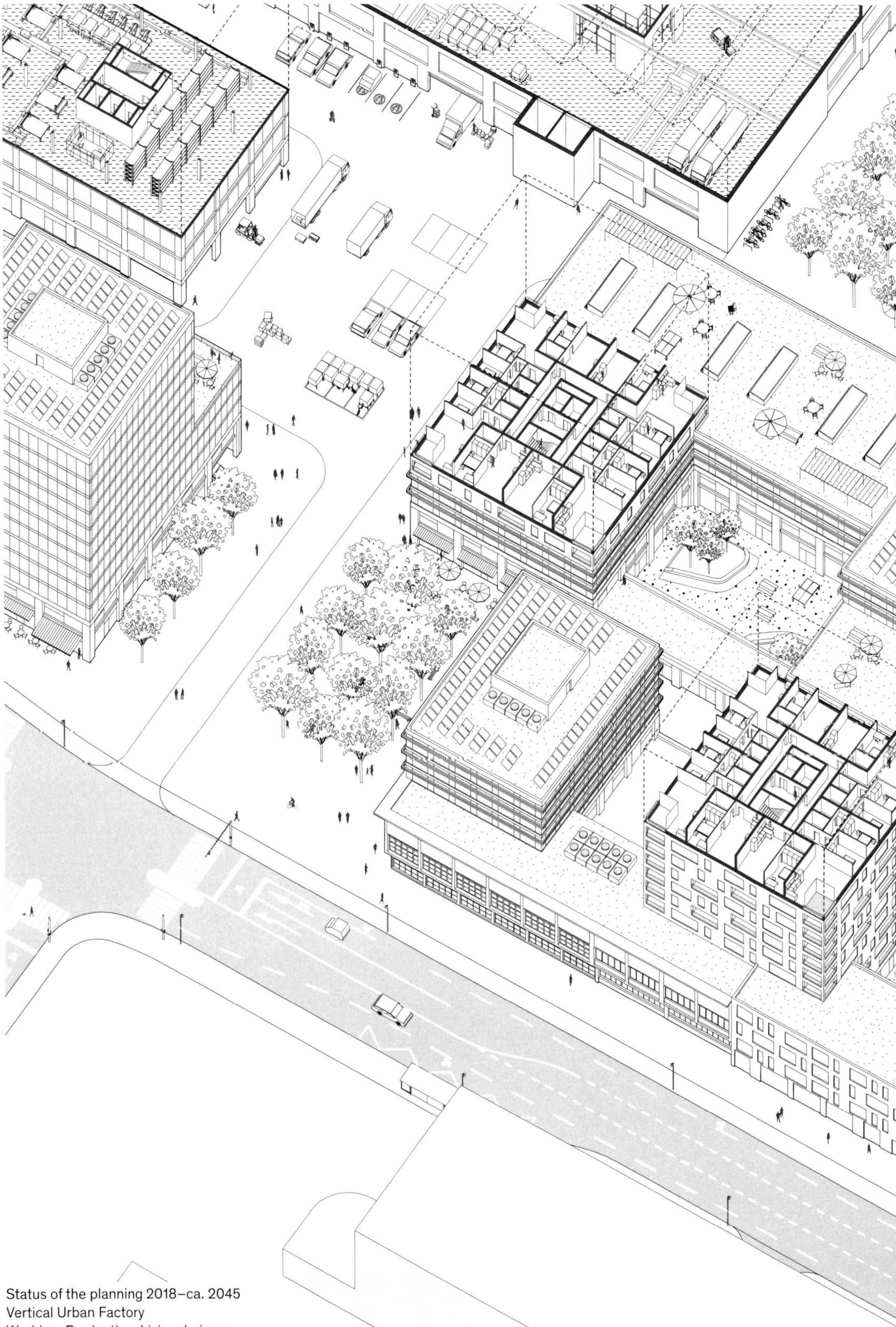

Status of the planning 2018–ca. 2045
Vertical Urban Factory
Working, Production, Living, Leisure

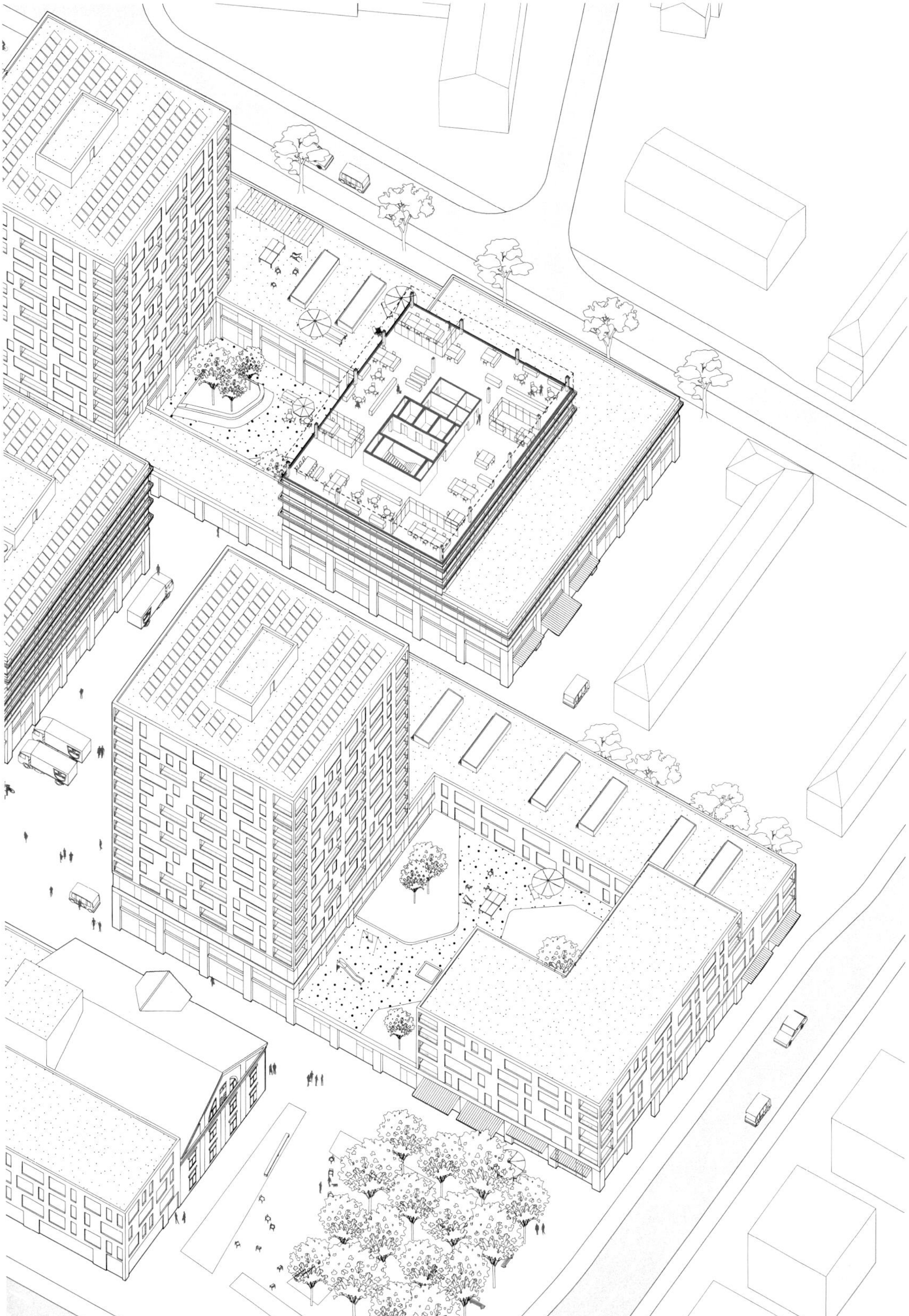

Status of the planning 2018–ca. 2045
Vertical Urban Factory
Working, Production, Living, Leisure

DELIVERY

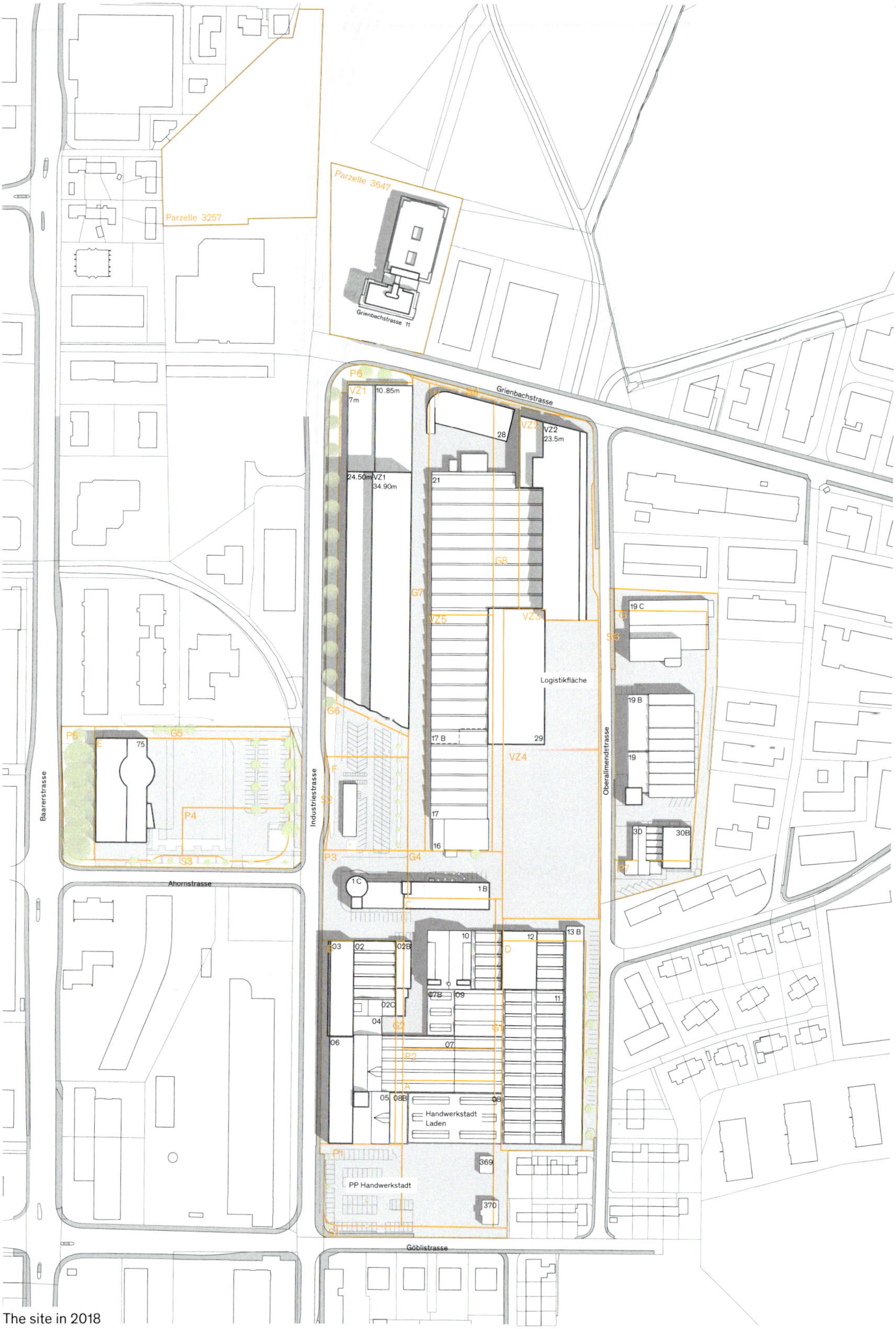

The site in 2018

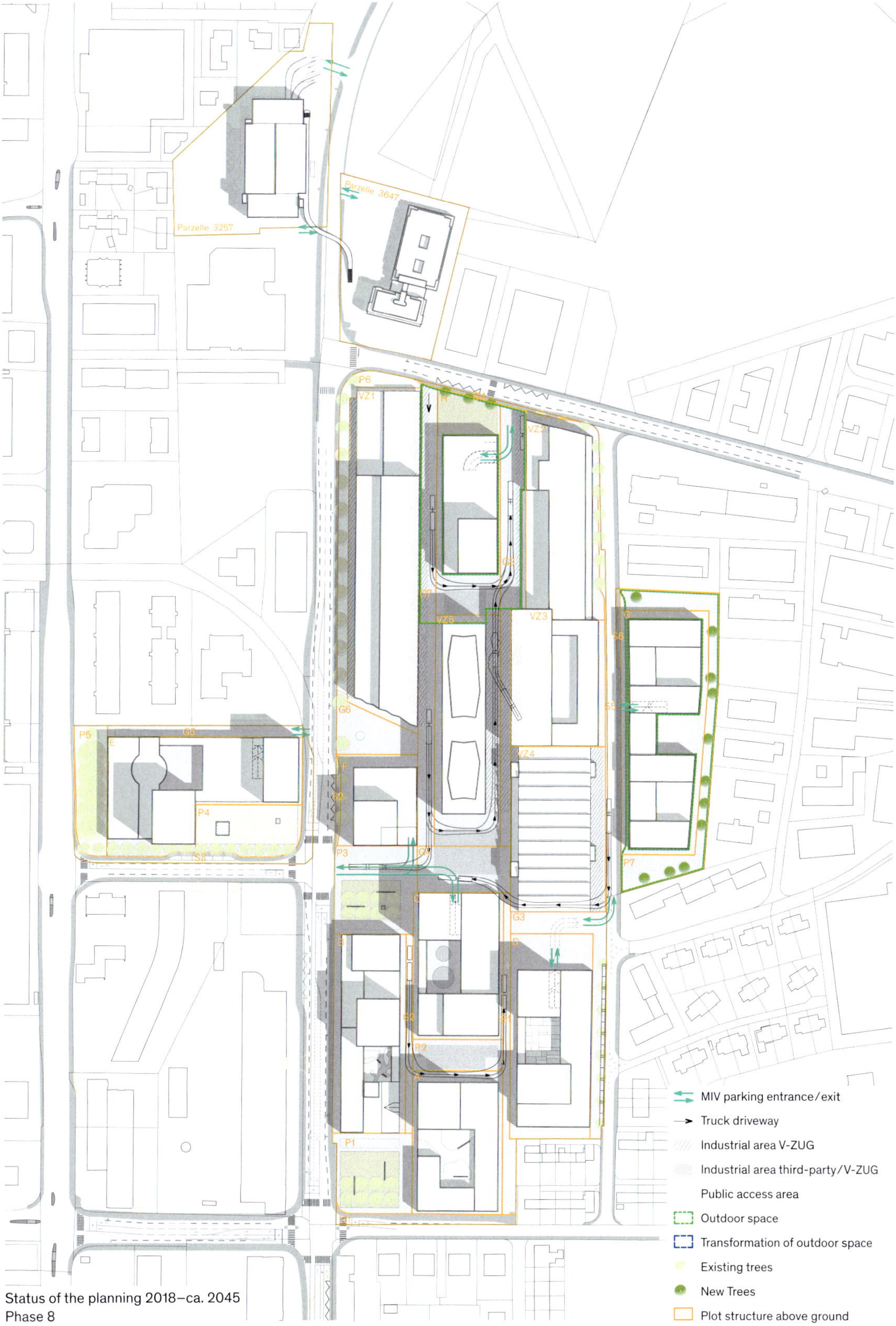

Status of the planning 2018–ca. 2045
Phase 8

Phase 1: Consolidation V-ZUG

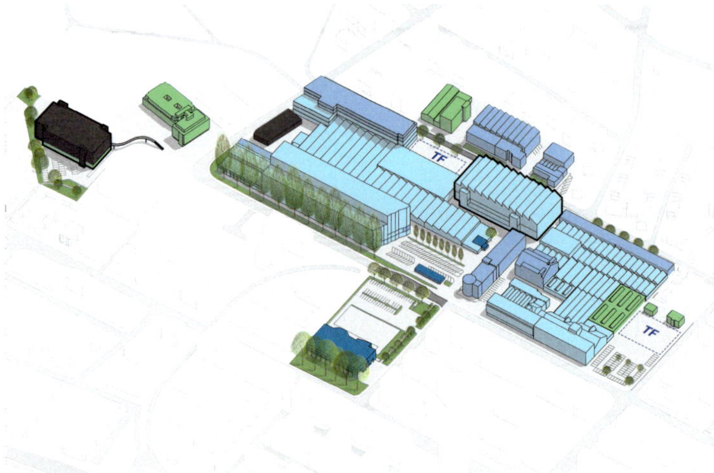

Phase 3: South Gate

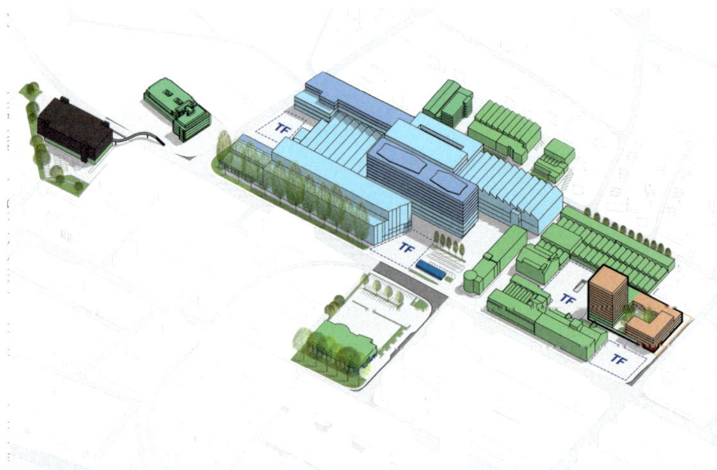

Phase 5: Kern and ADORA building sites

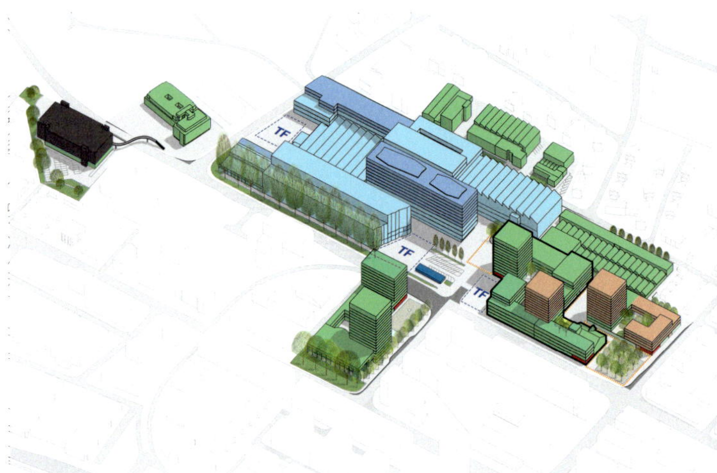

- Newly built
- Office, laboratory, commercial area V-ZUG
- Industrial area V-ZUG
- Special use area V-ZUG
- Office, laboratory, commercial area, third-party
- Industrial area, third-party
- Special use area, third-party
- Parking
- Residential
- Urban use
- Outdoor space transformation (TF)

Phase 2: Zephyr Central East and Zephyr Central West

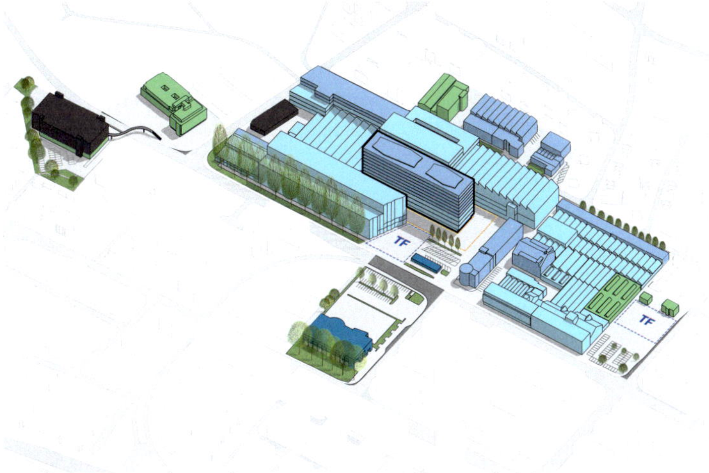

Phase 4: Temporary uses and establishment of the alley network

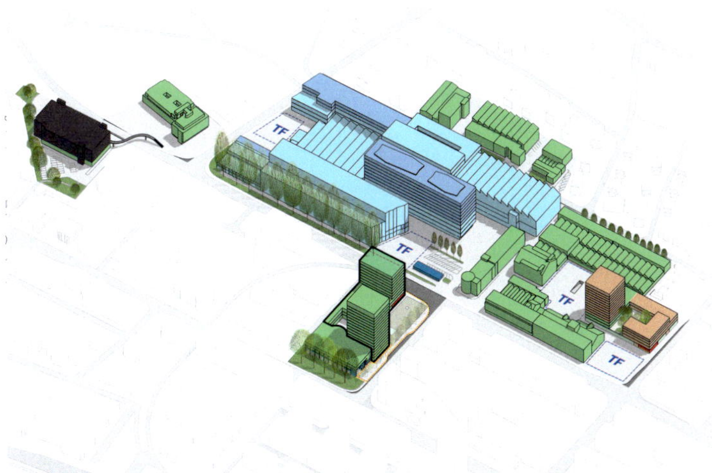

Phase 6: Moving in of new companies

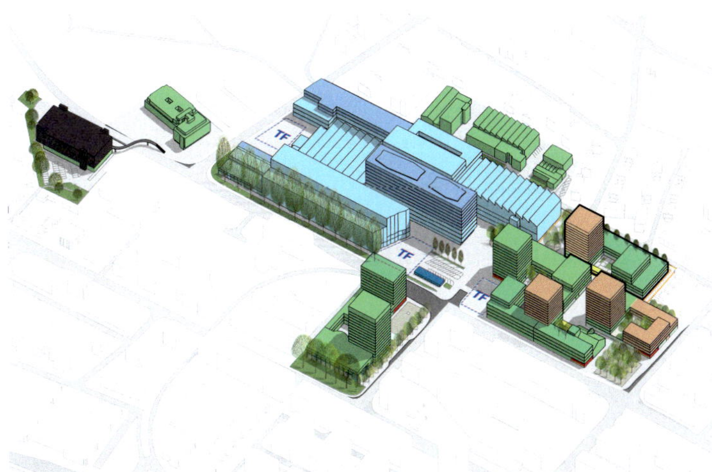

This diagram outlines the development of the Tech Cluster Zug. The new buildings for V-ZUG AG (blue) are under construction or will be built in the coming years. Projects will follow in the very south and west of the site. In later phases, the building plots in the central part of the site will be constructed. The development will be completed with the building plots to the east and north. The numbering refers to the development stages.

8. North Gate
In a later phase of the realization of the Tech Cluster Zug, the construction site North Gate with direct access from Grienbachstrasse will be developed. The existing halls on the field will be demolished.

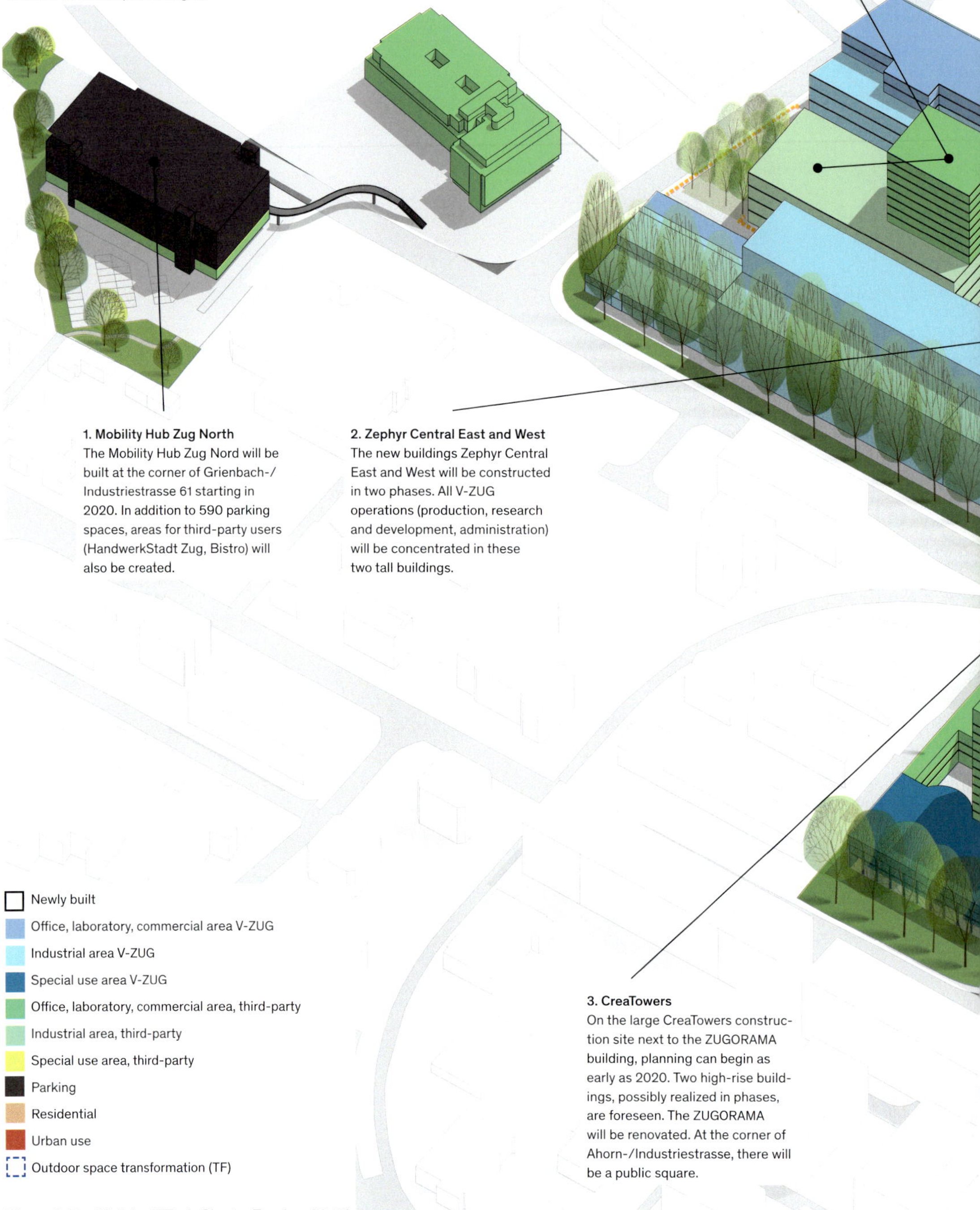

1. Mobility Hub Zug North
The Mobility Hub Zug Nord will be built at the corner of Grienbach-/Industriestrasse 61 starting in 2020. In addition to 590 parking spaces, areas for third-party users (HandwerkStadt Zug, Bistro) will also be created.

2. Zephyr Central East and West
The new buildings Zephyr Central East and West will be constructed in two phases. All V-ZUG operations (production, research and development, administration) will be concentrated in these two tall buildings.

3. CreaTowers
On the large CreaTowers construction site next to the ZUGORAMA building, planning can begin as early as 2020. Two high-rise buildings, possibly realized in phases, are foreseen. The ZUGORAMA will be renovated. At the corner of Ahorn-/Industriestrasse, there will be a public square.

- Newly built
- Office, laboratory, commercial area V-ZUG
- Industrial area V-ZUG
- Special use area V-ZUG
- Office, laboratory, commercial area, third-party
- Industrial area, third-party
- Special use area, third-party
- Parking
- Residential
- Urban use
- Outdoor space transformation (TF)

Phase 8: The “finished” Tech Cluster Zug (ca. 2045)

9. UNIMATIC
In a later phase of the realization of the Tech Cluster Zug, the UNIMATIC construction site east of Oberallmendstrasse will be developed. The existing building stock on this field will be demolished.

0. Zephyr Hangar
The Zephyr Hangar construction is the core of the new vertical production of V-ZUG. The new servo-press-line from Schuler was already brought in. The building will be operational by the end of 2020.

6. Urban Industries
On the Urban Industries site a mixed use is planned. The development of this site will complete the transformation of the southern area.

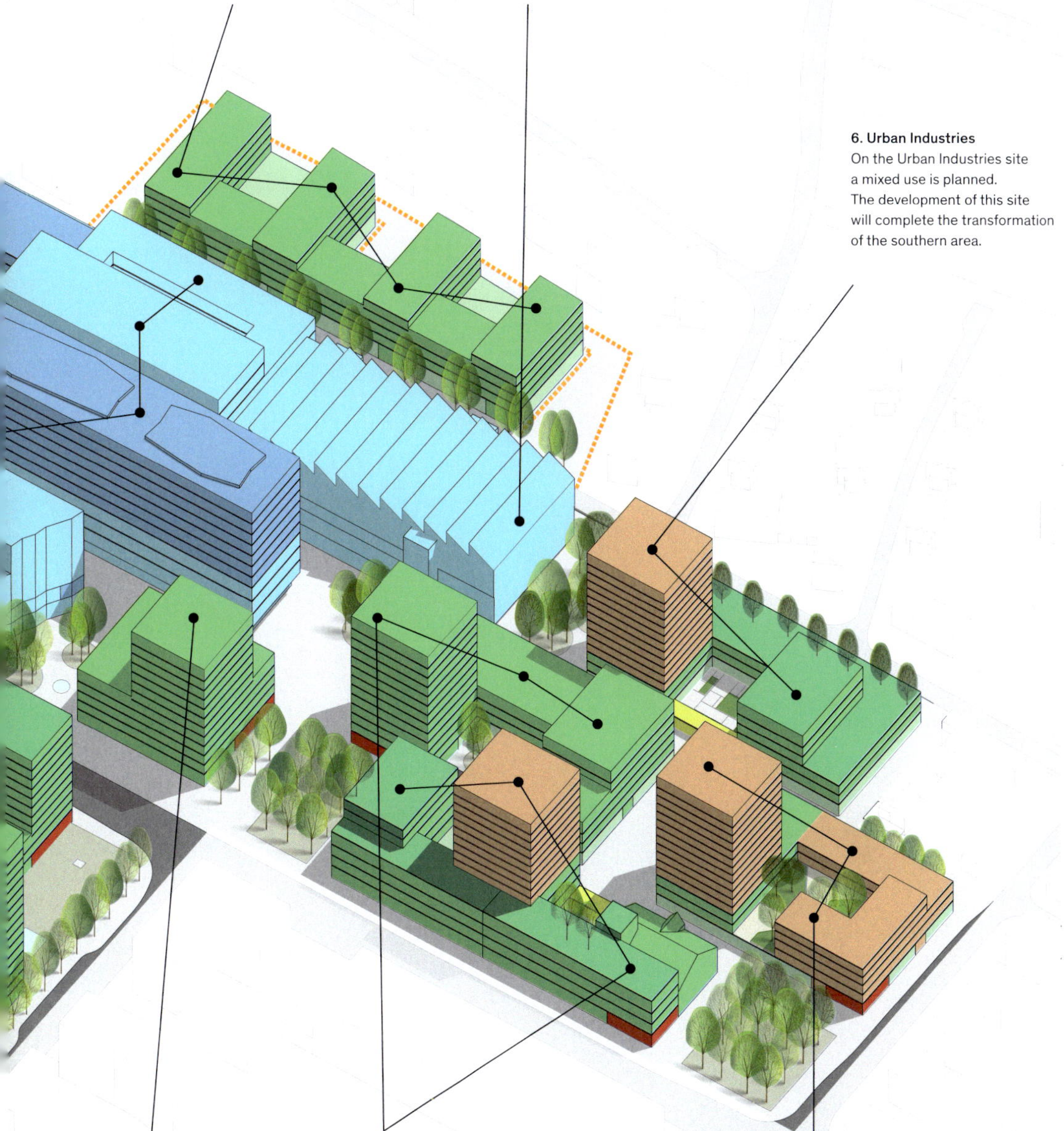

7. Campanile
After completion of the buildings in the southern area, the central Campanile building site can be developed. The open spaces around the Campanile, ADORA and Kern sites form a central square in the Tech Cluster Zug.

5. Kern and ADORA
The Kern and ADORA building sites can be developed simultaneously. The few protected existing buildings or building sections will be integrated into the new buildings.

4. South Gate
The first temporary user of the South Gate site moved in already in 2018. From 2021 this construction site can be completely redeveloped. Among other things, it is also possible to use it as a school.

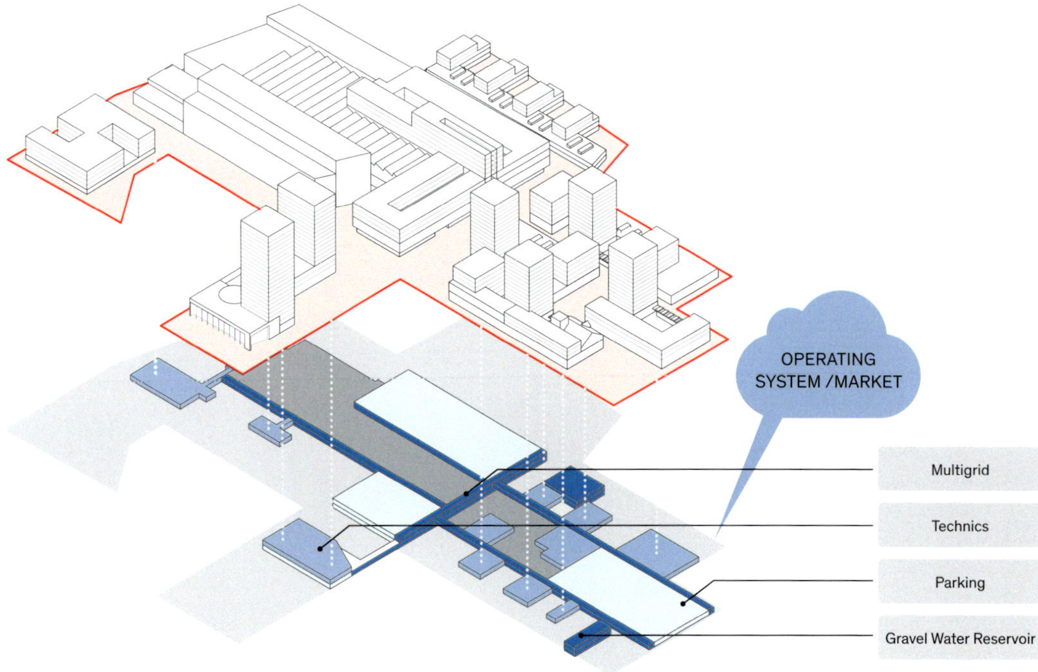

"Motherboard" with area infrastructure
from competition 2013

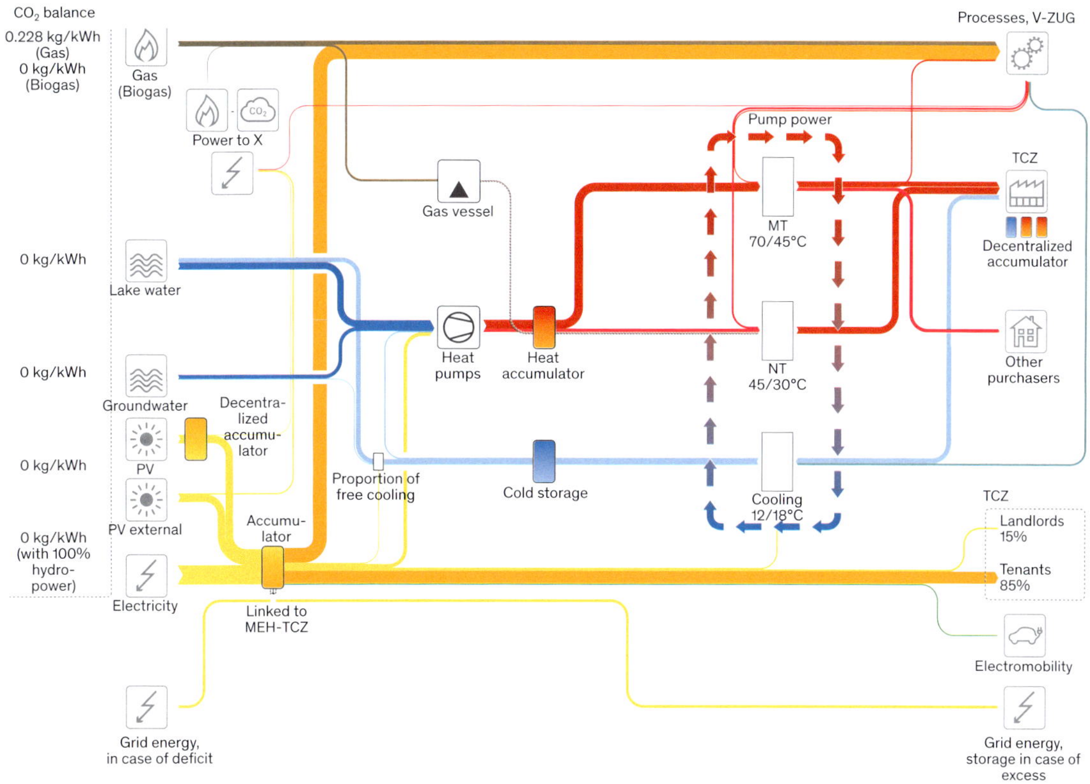

Multi Energy Hub
Planning status 2020

- Natural gas (MWh/a)
- Heating (MWh/a)
- Heating/BWW (MWh/a)
- Cooling (MWh/a)
- Electricity (MWh/a)

Mobility Hub Zug Nord, 2020–ca. 2022

HandwerkStadt
P

Sustainable mobility for the district

The Tech Cluster Zug is also a pioneer of sustainable mobility. Private vehicles arriving at the site's perimeter are directed to the Mobility Hub Zug Nord, and from there the area can be easily accessed on foot. In addition, there is a driverless electric minibus (currently in the test phase with drivers), which connects the neighborhood directly to Zug railway station.

The Mobility Hub has a store and a bistro on the ground floor. The upper floors are free of supporting columns and arranged as a continuous ramp, with a pick-up station for a fleet of electric vehicles that in the future will be able to park autonomously, and with potential to be substantially expanded. A pedestrian bridge leads from the pick-up station directly to the Tech Cluster Zug and into the town. Bicycles, electric scooters, mopeds and public transport services complete the mobility chain, and the connection to the Multi Energy Hub guarantees a local supply of energy.

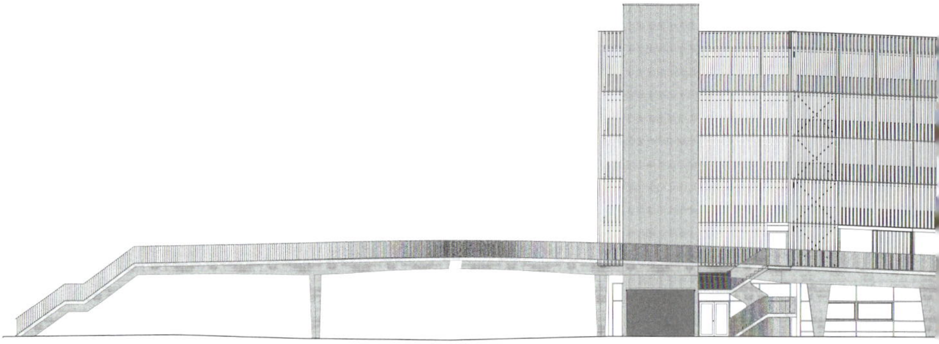

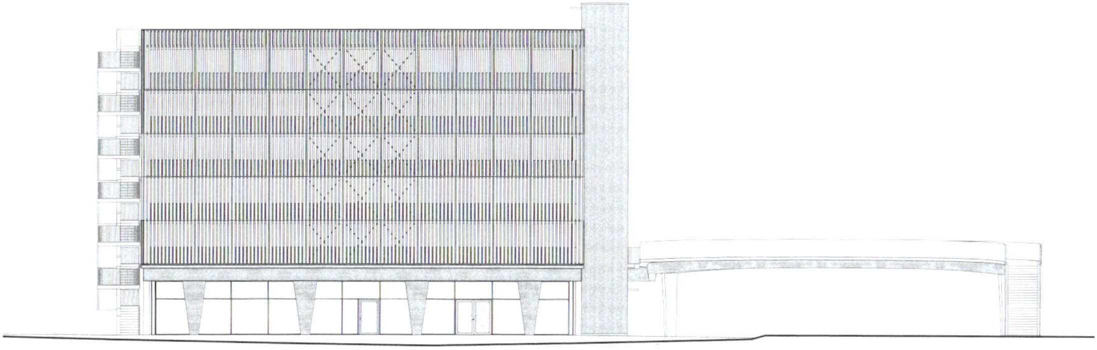

Visualization "Im Werk," Competition 2013

Competition 2013

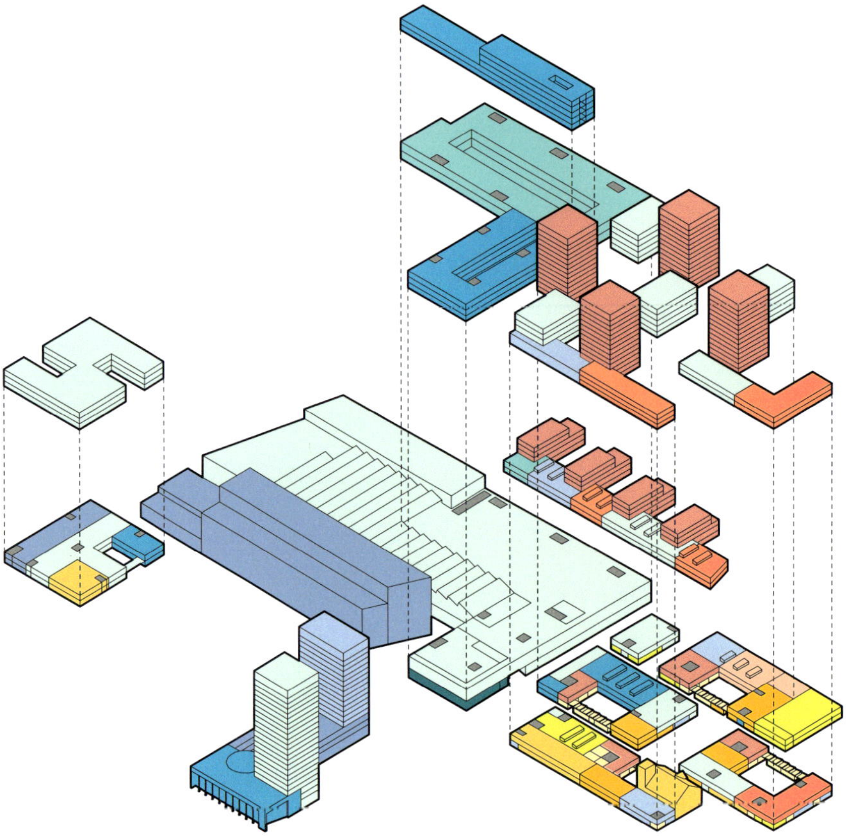

Use mix

A dense urban quarter / GFZ = 3.0

- Production
- Gym, FabLab, etc.
- Showroom/Sales
- Laboratories/Offices
- Residential
- Production
- Daycare Center
- Cultural Center
- Neighborhood Library
- Residential
- Canteen
- SoHo studio apartments

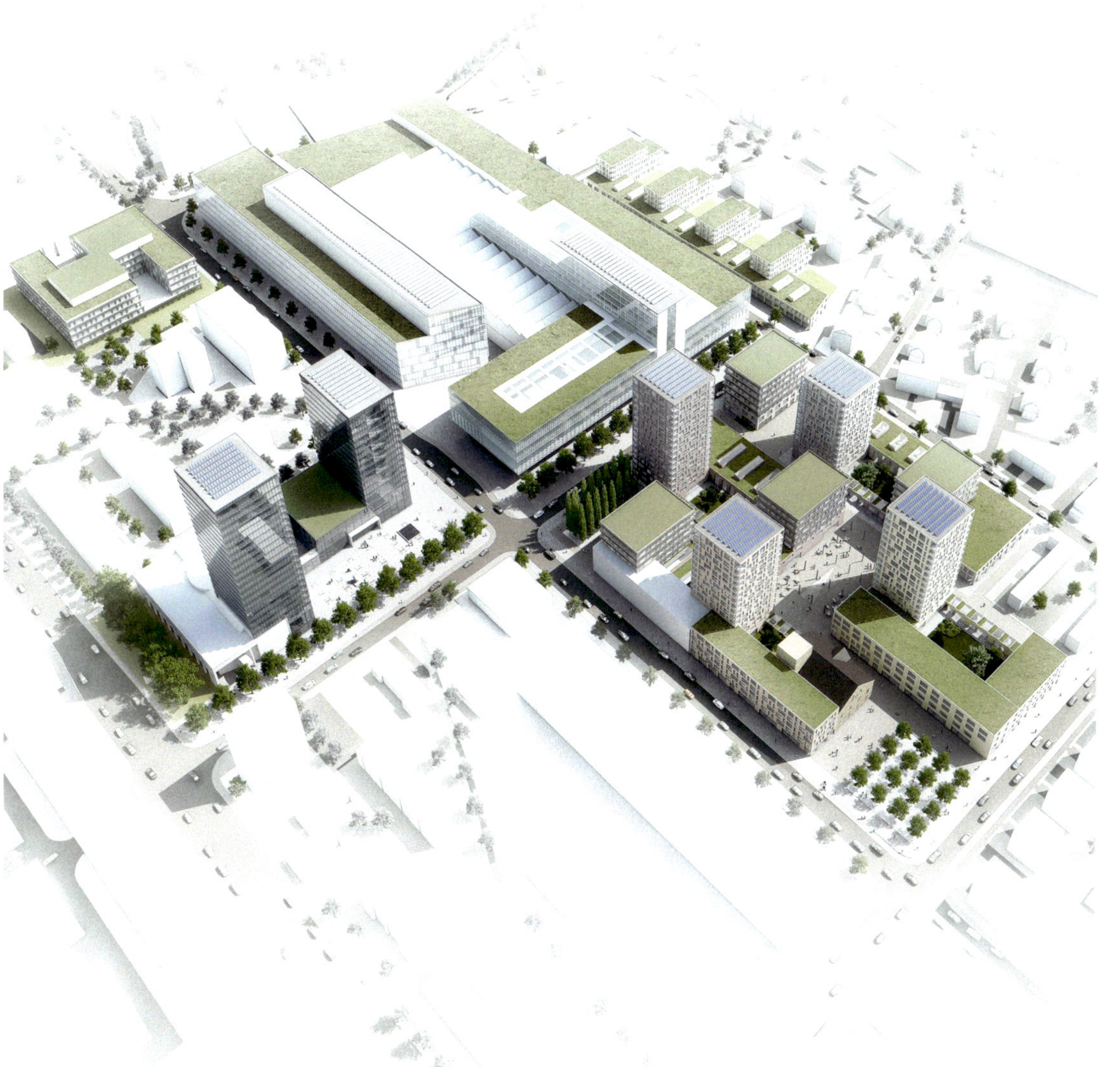

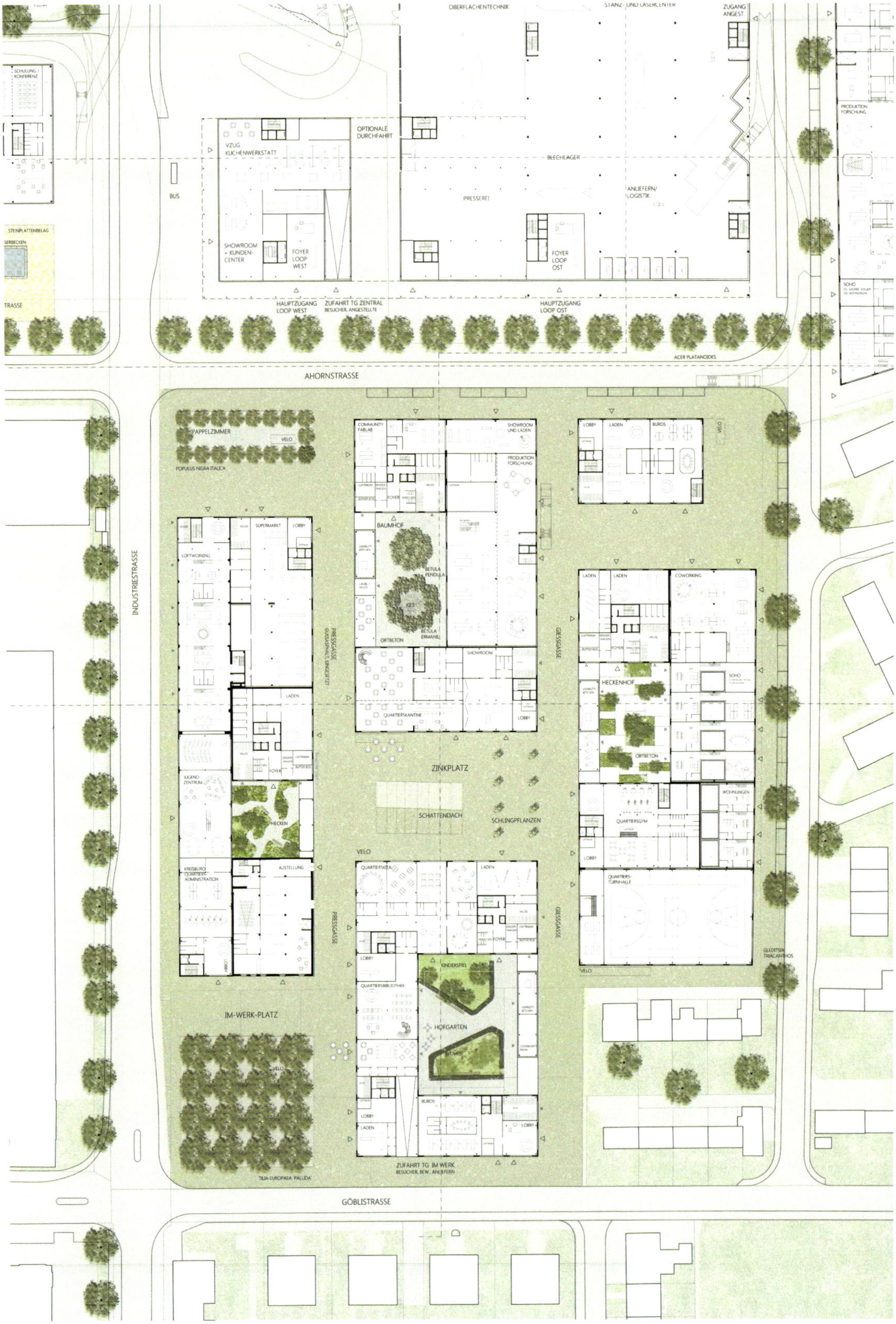
OBERFLÄCHENTECHNIK
STANZ- UND LASERCENTER
ZUGANG ANGEST.
OPTIONALE DURCHFAHRT
VZUG KÜCHENWERKSTATT
BLECHLAGER
PRESSEREI
ANLIEFERN/ LOGISTIK
BUS
SHOWROOM + KUNDEN-CENTER
FOYER LOOP WEST
FOYER LOOP OST
HAUPTZUGANG LOOP WEST
ZUFAHRT TG ZENTRAL
HAUPTZUGANG LOOP OST
ACER PLATANOIDES
AHORNSTRASSE
PAPPELZIMMER
POPULUS NIGRA ITALICA
INDUSTRIESTRASSE
BAUMHOF
BETULA PENDULA
ZINKPLATZ
SCHATTENDACH
SCHLINGPFLANZEN
HECKENHOF
PRESSGASSE
GIESSGASSE
HOFGARTEN
IM-WERK-PLATZ
TILIA EUROPAEA PALLIDA
ZUFAHRT TG IM WERK
GÖBLISTRASSE

Four scenarios “Im Werk,” Competition 2013

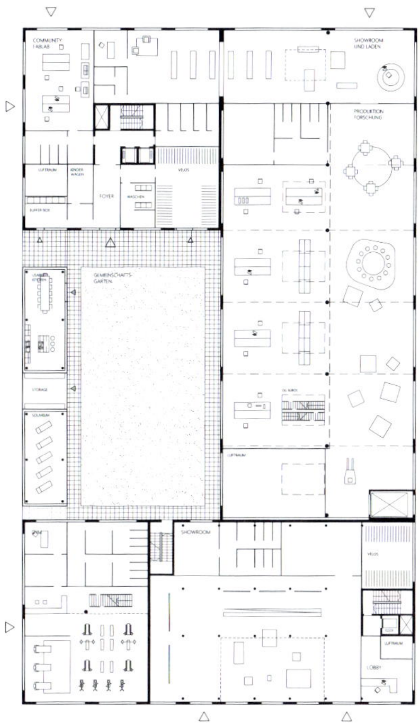

Focus on production

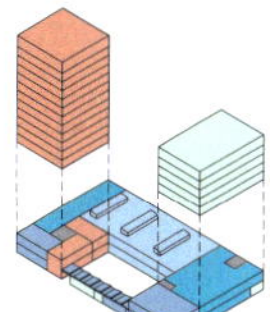

- Production
- Offices
- Showroom/Sales
- Gym, Fablab etc.

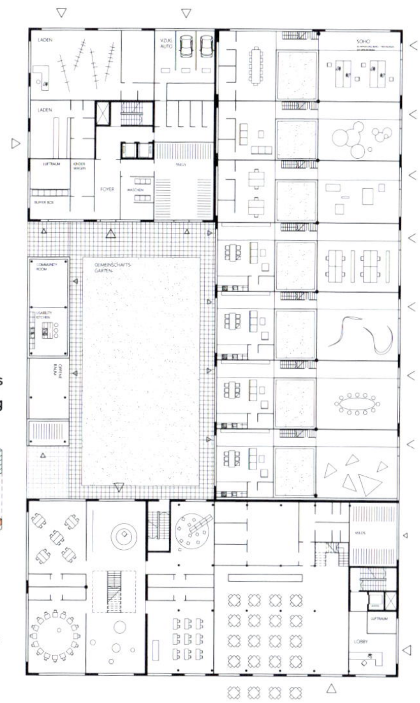

Focus on living

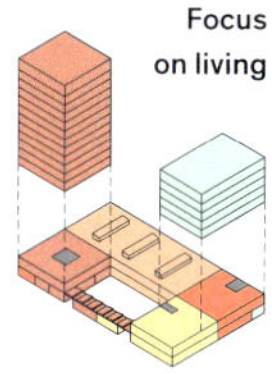

- Residences
- Canteen
- Loft living/offices
- Daycare Center

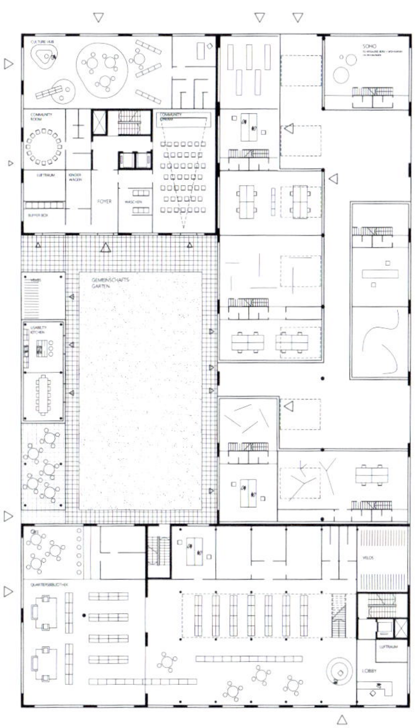

Focus on culture

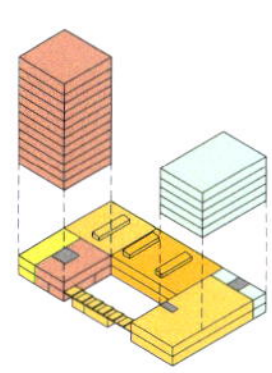

- SoHo studio apartments
- Cultural Center
- Neighborhood Library

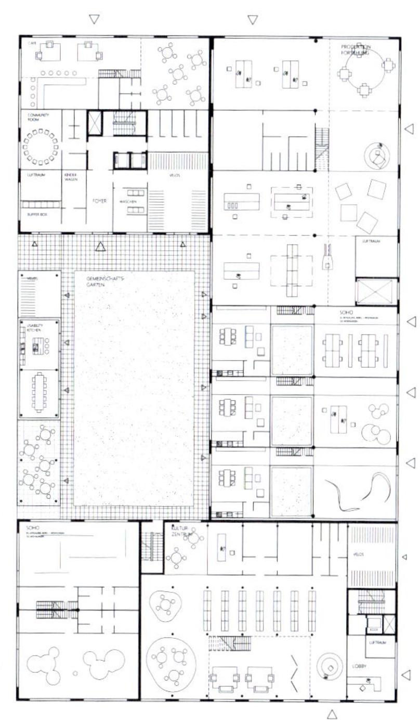

Mixed scenario

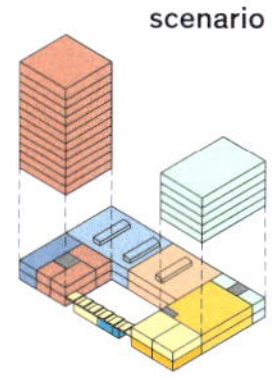

V-ZUG Areal, around 2010

Panasonic

SWISS MADE
FRONT

GERSAG
10 t
SWF

Connectedness
Deep Solidarity
Ministry for the Future
New Political Economy
Post-Capitalism
Proleptic Realism
Radically Unknowable
Science Fiction
Single World System
Singularity
Subsidiarity
The Near Future
The Old Normal

Interview by Markus Schaefer
April 15, 2020
Zurich and Davis, CA

EVENT HORIZON

Kim Stanley Robinson

Kim Stanley Robinson is an American science fiction writer. He is the author of about twenty books, including the internationally bestselling *Mars Trilogy,* and more recently *New York 2140,* or *Red Moon*. His latest novel, *The Ministry for the Future,* is set in Zurich, Switzerland. He was sent to the Antarctic by the US National Science Foundation's Ant-arctic Artists and Writers' Program in 1995, and returned in their Antarctic media program in 2016. In 2008, he was named a "Hero of the Environment" by *Time* magazine. He works with the Sierra Nevada Research Institute, the Clarion Science Fiction Writers' Workshop, and UC San Diego's Arthur C. Clarke Center for Human Imagination. His work has been translated into twenty-five languages, and won a dozen awards in five countries, including the Hugo, Nebula, Locus, and World Fantasy awards. In 2016, asteroid 72432 was named "Kimrobinson."

Dear Markus, I've been meaning to write you for a while to respond to your previous letter, but it's been a crazy year so far. In January I had to finish my novel. In February I made a long trip to the East Coast – I'm glad I got that one off before this big change in protocol. Same for March, as I went with a UC Davis graduate group in the natural sciences down the Grand Canyon for a week. I was gone March 11–19, and when we hiked up out of the canyon we came into a different world. Since then I've been catching up, or trying to.

I like your foreword to the book, and the vision it outlines. I think that along with the changes you are describing in infrastructures and systems, one of the crucial shifts will necessarily be to some kind of post-capitalism economic system. Mondragon's system of nested co-ops is one already-existing system working well that could serve as a model to plug in here, and I hear that a lot of European pre-capitalist commons and communes are still residual at the local level in some places in Northern Italy, often in or just under the Alps. The inventiveness of your utopian vision should extend to this crucial area, too.

Dear Stan, here in Zurich we are in lockdown. Public life is at a standstill. The economy is contracting. And yet, the Easter weekend was radiant, warm and teeming with life. Over China and Northern Italy, the skies are clearing up. For the first time in living memory, the canals in Venice are transparent rather than a murky gray – nature returning. We are in the largest collective experiment thinkable, induced by a tiny speck of RNA in an envelope of proteins that seems particularly adept at propagating through a highly interconnected global society – pure information, materially reproduced and passed on by each of its unwitting hosts. It is an experiment questioning the very connectedness that drives our economy, society, culture. Do you think it will have a lasting effect?

Yes, I think this event will have lasting effects, but having said that, I don't know which particular effects. It's an event that will be marked in world history and remembered in the way we remember the Spanish flu of 1918–1920. Maybe it will stand out even more than that pandemic, because it won't be confused with memories of World War One, and it's happening in an age of total Internet saturation; everyone knows everything. And so we see the amazing protocols of social distancing and sheltering in place being adhered to by a huge portion of the world population, while the people whose work is absolutely necessary for society to function are continuing to go to their jobs and work them, no matter the consequences. This is a case of mass social action, suggesting a deep solidarity or "everyone agrees"; no policing could force us to cooperate in this fashion. It's an agreement by everyone that this is worth doing, to save lives. Everyone feels endangered and that's surely part of it – anyone could get this disease. So, for now we see solidarity, and what comes down to a nearly universal belief in science and in government, at least in most countries. Surely these are positive things. But there is also enormous pressure to go back to the old normal. Economies depend on that old normal, and many people's livelihoods, and profit depends on the old normal coming back. These are enormous, stupendous pressures. But if we give into them, we may get a second wave of the pandemic, and also, we will return to the bad aspects of the old normal, the things that were destroying the biosphere we depend on, and so are sure to bring on events as bad as this pandemic, or worse, in that there won't be solutions. Some of the old normal was bad and should not be returned to.

So the good response would be to analyze this event, to find in it what we can put to use. For me, this means mainly a new political economy in which we pay ourselves to care for the biosphere, and dispense with the definition of profit we've been working with, which is so extractive and destructive, and leads to inequality as well as biosphere destruction. In short: I think we need to invent a global post-capitalist political economy, partly based on what we are learning now about what really matters.

You write science fiction. But of course, you always write about us. I am fascinated by science fiction, as for me it is a form of scenario planning. A set of "what ifs" in the face of systemic change and in your case the science is always sound. Human nature and the constraints of our material and ecological environment stay the same, and yet being put by the narrator at a new confluence of technology, economy and human history, past or future, where new narratives unfold. Do you think the Industrious City could be a stage for such a narrative? Is it believable and consistent?

Yes, I think it is a believable and consistent narrative. And I like your definition of science fiction – it is a form of scenario building, and then a narrative that tests the assumptions of the scenario, in a kind of thought experiment which is the plot, and the changed mentalities of the characters, and so on.

So, from my point of view as a novelist, one thing that can happen in this situation is that the novel gets mistaken for the entire world, and then gets criticized for not including every aspect of the world. This isn't right; a novel (and also a scenario) is a story, not a world, and it has to engage in what Fredric Jameson once called "world reduction" to get to a coherent single narrative. So things get left out that are implied by the scenario but not explicitly discussed.

I bring this up because your title, *Industrious City,* makes it very clear what your proposal, your design fiction, your science fiction scenario, is about: it's about the city as a built infrastructure and also a social system, and it has a focus on making things that we need, and how we could do that in a less fragile, brittle, globalized-for-profit way. That's a great topic for a scenario, it's focused and thinkable, and the fact that the not-city – meaning farms, oceans, the backcountry, wilderness, space, etc. – is not emphasized in your project is okay. There are implications that extend out from this scenario to the rest of the world and biosphere, but they don't have to be enumerated and spelled out and discussed in full here; that's for another project. For your project, the focus is good – it allows for some concrete plans and proposals, and reconsiderations.

You explored interstellar travel, the terraforming of Mars, Manhattan as a new Venice after the rise of the sea level, the colonization of the Moon and and now Zurich as a place from where the future is being planned. It seems that you come from the future and approach the present, your narrative a magnifying glass moving along the axis of time, approaching the now. What do you think are the biggest challenges of the near future and where will they lead us?

Since science fiction is basically stories set in the future, it has a very big temporal stretch. Far future science fiction is a form of fantasy, because in millions of years almost anything might be conceivable. Then the near future is a very different aspect of the genre, being a kind of "proleptic realism" that tries to catch the current moment on the fly, so to speak, by portraying its trajectory just a few years beyond the now.

In between those two zones of time, or sub-genres of science fiction, is a middle zone I sometimes call "future history" that tries to imagine scenarios about a century or even two centuries from now. That is quite an extreme mental exercise given the current pace of changes, and the fact that we could in the next century create either a mass extinction event or a prosperous permaculture, given where we are right now. So, this less populated zone of science fiction is where most of my writing has been set. But now, the pace of change and the impacts of what we do now are so accelerated that my fiction has been moving closer and closer to the present, to that zone of "proleptic realism."

Here we are all the same kind of science fiction writers, making the future together, and we all see the same challenges, I think. Climate change, decarbonization and the reduction of inequality between humans are the big challenges facing us now. Right now, in fact. So, asking where they will lead us is impossible to answer – it depends on what we do now. The various scenarios of near-future science fiction are only that – scenarios, made to explore consequences of our current actions. Given the status of the current moment, the near future (like 30 years from now) is *radically unknowable*. But we can still think about it, and try to plan a good one.

Can we dwell for a moment on this idea of the radically unknowable? Early science fiction, Jules Verne for example, was based on the idea that the future can be extrapolated from trends in science and technology. General Motors' Futurama at the New York World Fair in 1939 showed the world of the 60s and was not so far off. In Switzerland, many cities are now planning for 2040, also twenty years into the future. But of course, we all still extrapolate trends. How can we plan for the unknowable? In my mind science fiction is the better method as it anticipates radical change and suggests scenarios rather than set solutions.

What I've been thinking that makes me talk about radically unknowable is we are in effect standing at a crossroads, or in alpine terms, on a ridge that drops away sharply in two directions, left and right – good and bad; and this ridge is coming to an end, and we will trend one way or another. So the old idea that history has a trajectory that can be estimated, as by Jules Verne say, is no longer quite the case.

What can be said for sure is mostly about physical systems. The world will heat up because of CO_2 in the atmosphere. But how much? This depends on what we do now. And much, much else depends on what we do now.

So, if we do the right things now, we dodge the mass extinction event, we extend our understanding and our powers, we begin to establish a civilization in balance with the biosphere. That's the good future.

The bad one: We could cross over certain tipping points and run out of water, food, coastlines and so on – so many catastrophes that we might not cope with them well. That's the bad future. And it's bearing down on us. The momentum right now is toward the bad future.

The good that could come from this coronavirus pandemic is a general realization that the bad options are very bad, and we will be stimulated to change fast to avoid the even worse futures bearing down. That could happen.

The last thing to say is that there is no room really for a "halfway" future in between these two options. If we do things right, it will get quite good. If we do things wrong, it will go bad. If we don't do anything, that's doing things wrong, and it will go bad. So we are confronted with a big choice – now.

In the Venice Biennale Salons you were part of, organized by Hiromi and me in 2014, Didier Sornette from the ETH was discussing his concept of a "singularity," for him a mathematical consequence of super-exponential growth, a moment when immanent to its dynamics a system has to radically change as it cannot sustain its own growth. Based on his formulas and

looking at the world economy and world population, he places that moment of change at 2050 +/– 20 years. And of course, this would not be a single event but rather a perfect storm of individual impasses, each one individually completely controllable. So, the problem might not be one of the next state, but rather of the transition to that state. The systems ecologist C.S. Holling wrote that nature is "lumpy" and "episodic," meaning that both in space and time things are not equally distributed but clustered. When things change, they change together and fast.

This science fiction story is another way of describing the destruction of the natural world by the over-extraction of resources (including people's lives) in the unconstrained pursuit of profit. We do need to change, and change is coming, so yes, to that extent this story is right: change is coming. But predicting the when and how and what of the future is always a matter of guessing. Proposing mathematical formulas to do it just makes it quantified guessing. Hedge fund managers do this all the time. But there are too many factors involved, and human agency is one of them. No formula predicted the Paris Agreement. You can't quantify human agency in this process; we decide to do things or not do things, and we agree about them or we fight. So this kind of quantification is perhaps an aid to thinking for some people, but it's never definitive.

"The singularity" began as a science fiction idea in a Vernor Vinge story called *True Names* published in 1981. It postulates a take-over by our own intelligent machines. But there will be no moment of the future when humans won't be in control of history. Technology is the result of human political decisions, science and the physical laws of nature. At all times, history is the result of an actor network in which humans decide, in a group process, what to try for.

Our book has two very different mentalities weaving through each other: the factual world of academic essays, reference projects and case studies, and the world of experience, discourse and narrative, however imperfect and incomplete. While the factual portion of the book is in one layout, the narrative one is in another, allowing the reader to pivot back and forth between fact and fiction. Currently, you and I are in the fictional portion, gently floating sideways. As you know in space there is no right side up. But as Alfonso Cuarón has shown in his breathtaking movie *Gravity,* we are still Earth-bound creatures. Sandra Bullock as Dr. Ryan Stone had to fall back to Earth like Icarus and had to be reborn to appreciate this. How do you navigate the world, between daily life at Davis, CA, and flights of fancy at Echus Overlook on Mars? How can we be people with two legs – Antaeus and Icarus at once?

I very much like this idea of the two mentalities, but you won't be surprised when I say this: all the pages that are about the future should be marked as fictional, whether they pretend to be factual or are purely narrative. Well, that's not entirely true: if you print the time of sunrise and sunset, that should be a fact. If you print the human population in the year 2050, it should be fiction. Same with the amount of CO_2 in the air. Those trends that include human decisions and then subsequent actions have no inevitable trajectories. They depend to a very great degree on political decisions we make now. This is why I talk about radical unknowability. We are at an inflection point, and as in complexity theory, it's a strong case of sensitive dependence on initial conditions. Those initial conditions are being changed by us day by day. Now, in April 2020, it's more than ever clear that world history can change on a dime. So, we'll see what happens, but it's best to do good things right now.

Your most recent book is called *The Ministry for the Future.* Large parts of it play out in Switzerland, as the eponymous Ministry is located in Zurich. What is this institution and why did you place it in Zurich?

In my novel, the Ministry for the Future is a new subsidiary body of the Paris Agreement on climate change, established to try to strengthen compliance with the Agreement's goals by dedicating a permanent agency to the defense of the people and animals who will exist in times to come. The efforts of this agency from approximately 2028 to 2058 form the plot of the book.

I set it in Zurich because Switzerland has often been the headquarters for international aid agencies of various kinds, going back to the Red Cross. Also, because the novel is very global in its plot and settings, I wanted an anchor in terms of place, somewhere that the book would keep setting out from and going back to. In Shakespeare's phrase, "to give it a local habitation and a name."

Most importantly, I set it in Zurich because my wife and I lived in Zurich in 1986 and 1987, and my memories of that time and place were so strong and affectionate that I wanted to get them into a book somehow. I felt they would strengthen any book I put them in, and I think that happened here.

Switzerland is of course an interesting choice. The country was able to keep a strong sense of the local. On the other hand, it is entirely dependent on connectedness, on globalization even. Prior to industrialization, international trade and the export of goods, it was a country that exported settlers and soldiers, unable to feed even its own population. Some form of globalization will need to remain in the future. Otherwise, we would be entirely unable to keep our current prosperity and, more importantly and modestly, the stability, safety and livelihood it allows for. Do you think there is space and time for rethinking the balance of global and local?

Yes, I think this rethinking is very important for everyone, especially perhaps now that we have experienced this Covid-19 as a global experience.

Global and local are terms for a human and even economic discussion, and this is crucial. We see now that after globalization we are in a single world economy, a late capitalism that made profit its one metric for success, which led to overly-fragile supply chains but more importantly, a great deal of harm to people and environments, as the drive to maximize profit extracted too much from them. It was not sustainable and now it is crashing the system. We need to devise and institute new metrics for success that are more inclusive and more sustainable.

So we need to rethink our plans and reemphasize the local, but it remains true that the global is a real thing that won't go away. We are a single world system, but a system includes subsidiary systems with their own semi-autonomy.

It's always good to shift these terms to the ecological to find solutions to the problems created by thinking in terms of the economic. The global is the planet, our one and only home, a single biosphere with known inputs and processes and energy webs of all kinds. The local is then maybe the watershed or the biome, the particular places that are home to a particular network of creatures who evolved to prosper there.

Integrating these two ways of seeing and understanding our situation is, I think, part of what you are doing with your project. The city is at the scale of the biome, and it exists in a watershed. It has its own climate and geography and energy flows, and the humans in it have to match these natural and physical energy flows. If there is a discrepancy between the human and the planetary, it can't last for long; we are the ones who have to get that into a balance. It's the project for our time.

PRODUCTIVE CITIES

Iwan Baan

p. 371
SelgasCano, Second Home, Los Angeles, USA, 2019

372–373
Marktown Park, East Chicago, IL, USA, 2015

374 above
SelgasCano, Second Home, Los Angeles, USA, 2019

374 below
Mexico City, Mexico, 2018

375 above
Tokyo, Japan, 2011

375 below
Ekaterinburg, Russia, 2015

376–378
Alberto Kalach, Biblioteca Vasconcelos Library, Mexico City, Mexico, 2017

379
Mexico City, Mexico, 2018

380
New York, USA, 2014

381
Diller Scofi dio + Renfro, High Line, New York, USA 2014

382
BIG, Superkilen, Copenhagen, Denmark, 2012

383
BIG + JDS, MTN – Mountain Dwellings, Copenhagen, Denmark, 2014

384–387
Zabaleen, Cairo, Egypt, 2013

388–389
Torre David, Caracas, Venezuela, 2011

390–391
SelgasCano, Second Home, Lisbon, Portugal, 2017

392
SelgasCano, Second Home, Los Angeles, USA, 2019

393
SelgasCano, Second Home, Lisbon, Portugal, 2017

394–395
SelgasCano, Second Home, London, Holland Park, UK, 2017

396–397
SANAA, Vitra, Weil am Rhein, Germany, 2013

398–399
BIG, Superkilen, Copenhagen, Denmark, 2012

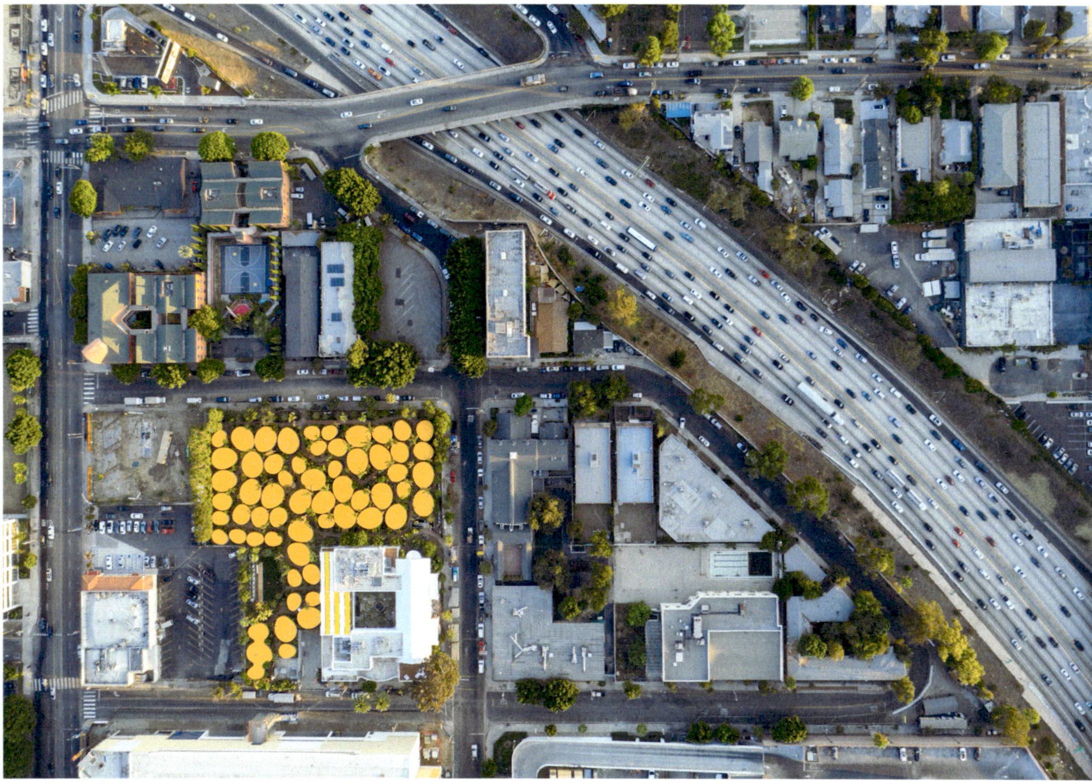

CO
CO
CO
CO
650
640
640
640
370
370
370
360
330
330
330
330
250
240
230
420
410
410

CO
CO
CO
CO
CO
640
630
630
630
630
360
360
350
350
340
330
330
330
330
330
200
220
220
210
230
400
410
400

JOHN W. WILLIAMS INC.
Weichsel Beef

CITRIVEGA

The New York Times

CW
CV
CU
CT

EPILOGUE

Transformation

Every present wrestles with its past while witnessing the emergence of its future. If that future is seen as an extrapolation of ongoing growth, we call it progress. But how do we talk about transformation, the transition to a new way of living and working – truly more sustainable, circular, inclusive and resilient? How do we envision change beyond progress and growth?

We still see sustainability as a continuation of our existing way of life, albeit with less consumption, waste or emissions. And resilience is something we want to understand as "robustness," a kind of "hardening" of infrastructures and buildings, of flows and processes in the service of the status quo. Resilience, as ecologists understand it, however, allows an ecosystem under stress to adjust its performance radically while its structure and function are kept intact – the once verdant summer landscape for example hibernating under layers of snow during winter, or a forest constantly regrowing after recurring bush fires.

Giving up industry altogether, returning to an economy based on manufacturing or craft, is not an option. Our contemporary lives would be unthinkable and our urban infrastructures dysfunctional without industry. We are surrounded by industrial products which even for a post-industrial society have to be produced somewhere. The digital cloud would not feed us, and the capital markets not clothe us. No value is created without some form of material production somewhere. There is no easy way out of our technological dependencies.

Equally, there is no alternative to urbanity. The countryside is not antithetical to the urban, it is simply less of it and more peripheral in location. Cities and the countryside are linked by manifold relationships. No system exists in isolation.

The necessity of change is obvious; the path of transformation, however, is not.

The Industrious City is a vision for Switzerland. It is also a case study for beyond. It suggests directions for achieving resilience in an urban and industrial culture – by maintaining diversity and redundancy, balancing connectedness and embeddedness, managing data and matter, encouraging learning and participation, promoting subsidiarity in governance and management, and by increasing our understanding of complex adaptive systems and their dynamics.

Of greater importance is the simple and basic pleasure of living and working in a green and inclusive, performant and productive, tangible and exciting urban landscape, rich in experiences and opportunities, connected and open to the world and yet with sensible boundaries and autonomies. That is the Industrious City.

ACKNOWLEDGEMENTS

We are very thankful to all those who contributed to this book, including our colleagues and friends from our office, Damjan Kokalevski, Oliver Franz, Thorben Westerhuys, Alexander Kneer, Mélanie Christine Rose Jeannet, Christian Calle Figueroa and Toru Shimizu.

Our special appreciation goes to Iwan Baan, Joël Tettamanti, Jos Schmid and Géraldine Recker for their striking photo essays of cities, infrastructure, people and factories. We are grateful to Jos for the substantial amount of time he invested in photographing the interview series together with us. We also want to thank Iwan for his friendship and contribution of his remarkable photos.

We are indebted to Felix Lehner, the founder of Stiftung Sitterwerk, and his assistant Catherine Heeb for their kindness and also for allowing us to publish the exceptional artworks of Paul McCarthy and Alex Hanimann produced at the Kunstgiesserei St. Gallen.

There are many others who contributed to *The Industrious City* whom we would very much like to recognize.

We are especially thankful to Mohsen Mostafavi and Diane Davis for giving us the opportunity to teach a design studio titled "The Industrious City" at the Harvard University Graduate School of Design (GSD) in the spring semester of 2018. We also thank the students who took part in the studio for their creative design work: Xin-yu Cao, Mike Hyungjoo Choi, Ting Liang, Pojiang Nie, Zhengyu Qin, Charles Smith, Konstantina Tzemou, Ya-shin Tzeng, Abbey Wallace, Shenting Wang, Xiyao Wang, Ping Zhang and Celine Zhou. Thanks to Radu-Remus Macovei and the staff at GSD for their assistance in coordination and communications.

We are grateful to Kim Stanley Robinson, Anna Schindler, Barbara Zeleny, Fabio Gramazio, Matthias Kohler, Mike Guyer, Momoyo Kaijima, Alex Krieger, Yasushi Ikeda, Hiroto Kobayashi, Yasushi Sakai and Nina Rappaport for their friendship, insight and intellectual support. We would also like to thank Yukiko Franz for her intuition and help in curating the photographs in the book and Thomas Held for his support in last minute edits. We are grateful to Ryohei Kaneda, Izumi Soeda and Minami Osada, who are very talented young designers, architects and students respectively, for contributing to the production of this book from a remote location in Tokyo.

Our special and sincere thanks also go to Iurii Goncharenko for his remarkable illustrations, Anna Page for her valuable time in starting this book and Sarah Asseel for her essential work and research.

Finally, our deepest appreciation goes to Lars Müller, Maya Rüegg, Audrey Solomon and Esther Butterworth from Lars Müller Publishers for their patience, professionalism and commitment to this book. Thank you, Lars, for the fun, relaxed and tolerant attitude whose importance you reminded us of throughout the process.

We worked on this book from January 2018 to June 2020. We thank our son, Juri Alexander Hosoya, for being most compassionate and positive, even though we were always busy. Looking ahead to a bright future, we would like to dedicate this book to him and his generation's future endeavors.

Hiromi Hosoya, Markus Schaefer

Biographies

Editors, Concept

Hiromi Hosoya is a founding partner of Hosoya Schaefer Architects. She has bachelor degrees in English Literature, Fine Arts and Architecture, as well as a Master in Architecture from Harvard University Graduate School of Design. For five years she worked at Toyo Ito & Associates in Tokyo until she became independent in 2003. She has taught interdisciplinary design studios at Cornell University in 2005 and 2006 and was a professor at the Academy of Fine Arts Vienna, Austria from 2007 to 2012. In addition, she taught an advanced architecture design studio and an urban design studio at Harvard GSD in 2011 and 2018.

Markus Schaefer is a founding partner of Hosoya Schaefer Architects. He has a Master in Architecture from the Harvard University Graduate School of Design and a Master in Neurobiology from the University of Zurich. He worked for OMA / Rem Koolhaas in Rotterdam for five years and was a director and co-founder of AMO (1999–2003). He was a studio critic at the Berlage Institute (2005–2007), a professor at the Academy of Fine Arts in Vienna (2007–2012) and a main tutor at the Moscow Graduate School of Urbanism at the National Research University Higher School of Economics in collaboration with the Strelka Institute, teaching Advanced Urban Design (2017–2018). In addition, he taught an advanced urban design studio at Harvard GSD in 2018.

Hosoya Schaefer Architects is a Zurich-based office for architecture, urban design and research, and was founded by Markus Schaefer and Hiromi Hosoya in 2003. With innovation as a core competence, the office is involved in building design and realization, urban design and media installations. The office has won numerous international awards and is working on a wide spectrum of projects such as the new urban quarters HafenCity Elbbrücken and Wilhelmsburg Elbinsel in Hamburg, Germany. In Switzerland, the office won first prizes for the Engadin Airport near St. Moritz, the railroad station area and station square project of Herisau, the conversion of the MEWA-Areal in Wädenswil, the Tech Cluster Zug and the Christoph-Merian primary school in Basel. By combining academia, practice and research, Hosoya Schaefer Architects bring solid perspectives on urbanism, systemic thinking and innovative solutions to their projects, working toward a common, urban future.

Editorial Assistance

Damjan Kokalevski is an architect and curator based in Zurich and educated in Skopje, Vienna and Tokyo. He completed his doctoral dissertation titled *Performing the Archive: Skopje. From the Ruins of the City of the Future* at ETH Zurich, supervised by Professor Dr. Philip Ursprung and Professor Dr. Felicity Scott, GSAPP Columbia University New York. He contributed to the exhibition *Metabolism: The City of the Future* at the Mori Art Museum, Tokyo (2012) and curated the exhibition *Performative Archive: Skopje, Discussing Urban Reconstruction* with gta Exhibitions, Zurich (2014). He is the author of the book titled *Skopje Walkie Talkie* published by Spector Books in 2019. Along with his academic career, Kokalevski has gained substantial experience as a practicing architect and urban researcher.

Photography

Iwan Baan is a Dutch photographer with a focus on images that show how individuals, communities and societies create, and interact within their built environment. The inaugural recipient of the Julius Shulman award for photography has collaborated with many of the world's most prominent architects and his works have won numerous awards, including the Golden Lion for Best Installation at the 2012 Venice Architecture Biennale.

Géraldine Recker is a Swiss architect and photographer. She received her master's degree in architecture at ETH Zurich in 2019, defending her thesis on water infrastructure as an architecture of the commons. During her exchange semester at Harvard University GSD in 2016, she developed a deep fascination with the concept of the sublime which she continues to explore with her camera and integrates in her architectural works. She currently lives in London and works with the architecture photographer Hélène Binet.

Jos Schmid grew up in Arosa, Switzerland. After the Matura in Chur, he studied Photography in California, USA. From 1998 to 2001 he was first assistant / studio manager at Richard Avedon in NYC. Since 2002 he has had a studio in Zurich. He photographs frequently for publications like *Die Zeit, The Guardian* and *Der Spiegel.* In 2019 he photographed portraits for the UEK Report "Administrative Versorgungen" for the Swiss Government. He is married to the theater director Barbara-David Brüesch.

Joël Tettamanti was born in Cameroun and grew up in Lesotho and Switzerland. From 1997 to 2001, Joël studied visual communication and photography at Ecole Cantonale d'Art de Lausanne (ECAL). His early works focus on the Swiss landscape, its mountains and the plateau region (*UrbanScape Switzerland,* 2005). His interest in places of passage and borders takes him from Switzerland to France, Greenland and Mexico, China and Spain. Tettamanti's work is often commissioned for magazines, with which he collaborates regularly. His works have entered prestigious public and private art collections. Since his first book titled *Local Studies* (etc. publications, 2006), he has published several monographs combining traditional means of printing with contemporary techniques.

Essays

Philipp Aerni is Director of the Center for Corporate Responsibility and Sustainability (CCRS). He is an interdisciplinary social scientist with a master's degree in Geography and a PhD in Agricultural Economics. During his postdoctoral research in public policy, he focused on the role of science, technology and innovation for sustainable development with a particular interest in institutional framework conditions that enable effective public-private partnerships to become drivers of sustainable change. Prior to his position at CCRS, Dr. Aerni worked at Harvard University, ETH Zurich, the University of Bern, as well as at the Food and Agriculture Organization of the United Nations (FAO). As CCRS Director, he closely collaborates with the CCRS advisory board as well as the CCRS team in the design and implementation of the Center's research, teaching and outreach activities.

Alex Krieger has combined a career of teaching and practice, dedicating himself in both to understanding how to improve the quality of place and life in our major urban areas. He is a professor at the Harvard Graduate School of Design, where he has taught since 1977. He has been Chairman of the Department of Urban Planning and Design (1998–2004, 2009–2010 2019–2020) and Director of the Urban Design Program (1990–2001). In 2017, *The Harvard Crimson* named him one of "15 Professors of the Year." In 2016, he received the Boston Society of Architects Award of Honor, for "outstanding contributions to architecture and to the profession" which is the BSA's lifetime achievement award. In 2013, he was appointed by President Obama to sit on the US Fine Arts Commission and is currently on his second four-year term on the commission. He has written extensively on American urbanization for various publications. Mr. Krieger is also a principal at NBBJ, a global design practice.

Nina Rappaport is an architectural historian, curator, educator, writer and consultant in urban manufacturing. She is the author of *Vertical Urban Factory* (Actar, 2015, paperback edition, 2020) and co-editor of *The Design of Urban Manufacturing* (Routledge 2020). She curated the traveling exhibition *Vertical Urban Factory,* which opened in 2011 in New York and continues to travel. She is Publications Director at the Yale School of Architecture where she edits *Constructs,* a book series, and exhibition catalogs. She is co-editor of the book *Ezra Stoller: Photographer* (Yale University Press, 2012) and author of the book *Support and Resist: Structural Engineers and*

Design Innovation (The Monacelli Press, 2008). She was a Visiting Professor at Politecnico di Turin (2019) and Sapienza Universita di Roma (2018). She is a lecturer at the Michael Graves College of Public Architecture at Kean University, writes for numerous journals, and lectures internationally.

Anna Schindler, born in 1968, has been the director of the Office for Urban Development of the City of Zurich since November 2011. The office is part of the Presidential Department and consists of five agencies: City and Neighborhood Development, Economic Development, Migration and Integration, Foreign Affairs and Smart City Zurich. Anna Schindler studied geography at the University of Bern, where she specialized in urban development issues. She worked as a culture and architecture editor for different German and English publications and as a communication consultant. In addition, she was a lecturer at the University of Zurich and the Zurich University of Applied Sciences (ZHAW), where she taught media science, cultural communication and management. Anna Schindler lives in Zurich with her family.

Daniel Wiener is a member of the Board of Directors and Chief Financial Officer of the Swiss logistics infrastructure company Cargo sous terrain (CST). He is the founder and president of the Global Infrastructure Basel Foundation (GIB), which has been promoting sustainable and resilient infrastructure finance since 2009. GIB is the issuer of the globally recognized, independent SuRe® Standard for Sustainable and Resilient Infrastructure. Daniel was the co-founder and – until the spring of 2020 – the long-term Chairman of ecos, the leading Switzerland-based international consulting firm for sustainable development, located in Basel. Since 1987, ecos has supported businesses, public institutions, associations, NGOs, municipalities and national governments in designing and implementing sustainable development strategies, financial solutions, innovations and projects. He is an economist, who holds a post-graduate degree in Arts Management from the University of Basel.

Barbara Zeleny has been working for SBB Immobilien since 2015. She is the project lead for development projects by the SBB. A graduate in architecture from Harvard University, Barbara Zeleny brings with her many years of professional experience in project development and building construction in an international environment. She is interested in new approaches to development processes and always strives for a holistic understanding of urbanity.

Gesa Ziemer (Prof. Dr. phil.) is professor for cultural theory and director of the CityScienceLab, a cooperation with MIT Media Lab (research group City Science) in Cambridge, USA. Her research focuses on the digitalization of cities, new forms of collaboration and the interface between artistic practice and society. She is a member of the Scientific Council of Germany and holds a guest professorship at Lucerne University of Applied Science and Arts. Currently she is setting up a technology and innovation lab for the United Nations (UNTIL Hamburg). Some of her published books are: *New Stakeholders of Urban Change: A Question of Culture and Attitude?* (edited with Hilke Marit Berger, jovis, 2017) and *Complicity. New Perspectives on Collectivity* (transcript, 2016).